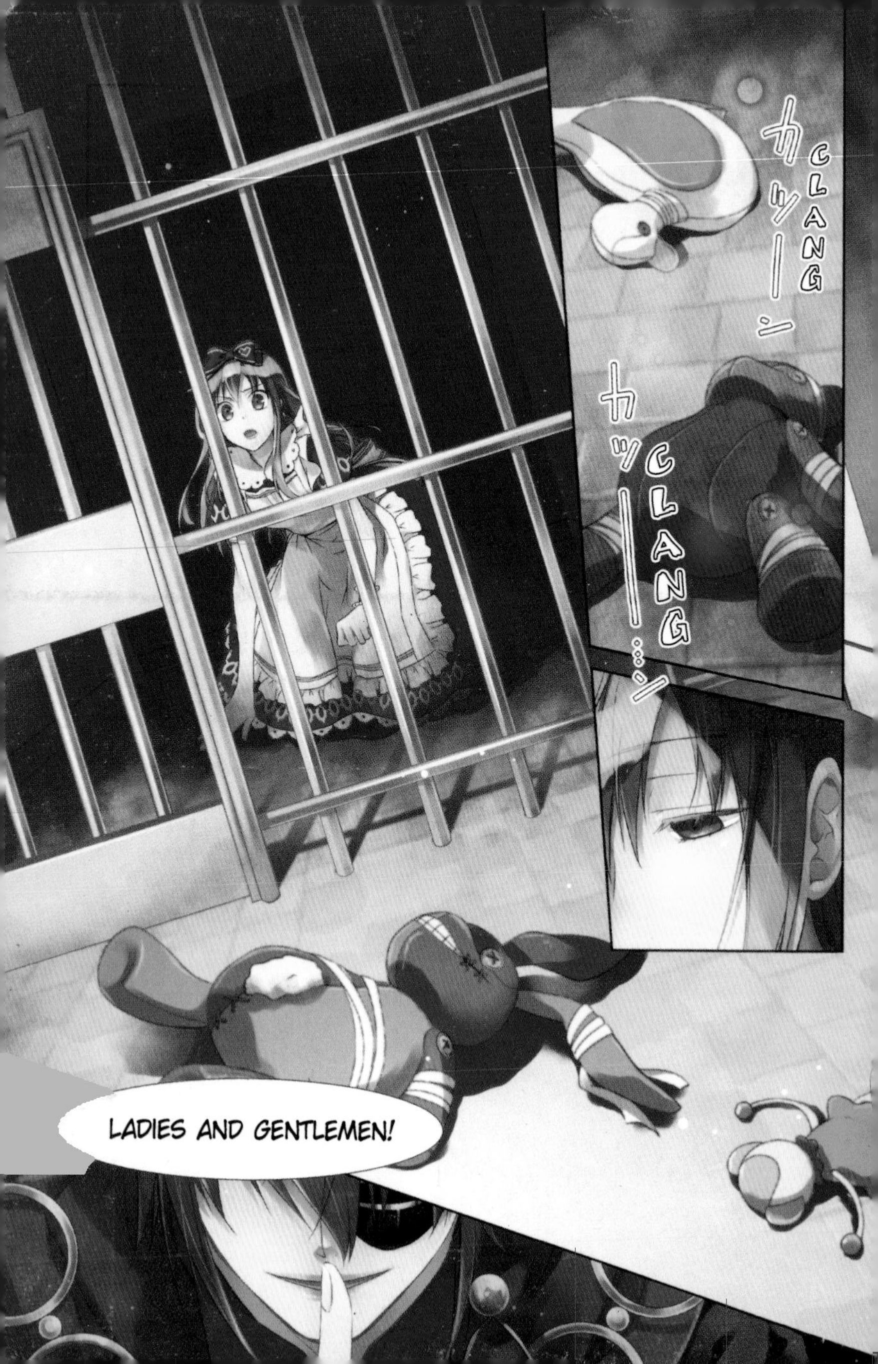
カッーン
CLANG
カッー…ン
CLANG
LADIES AND GENTLEMEN!

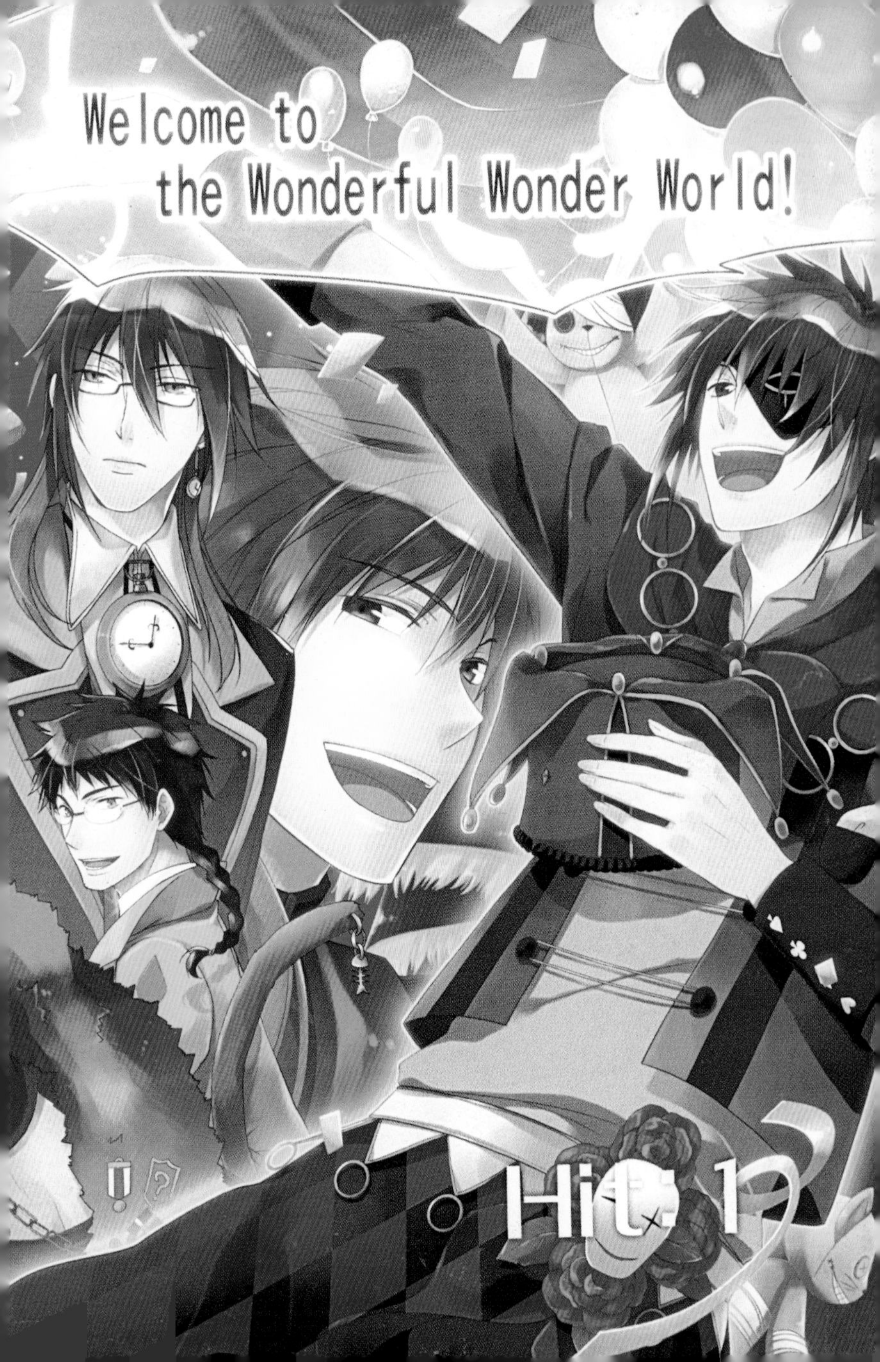
Welcome to
the Wonderful Wonder World!
Hit: 1

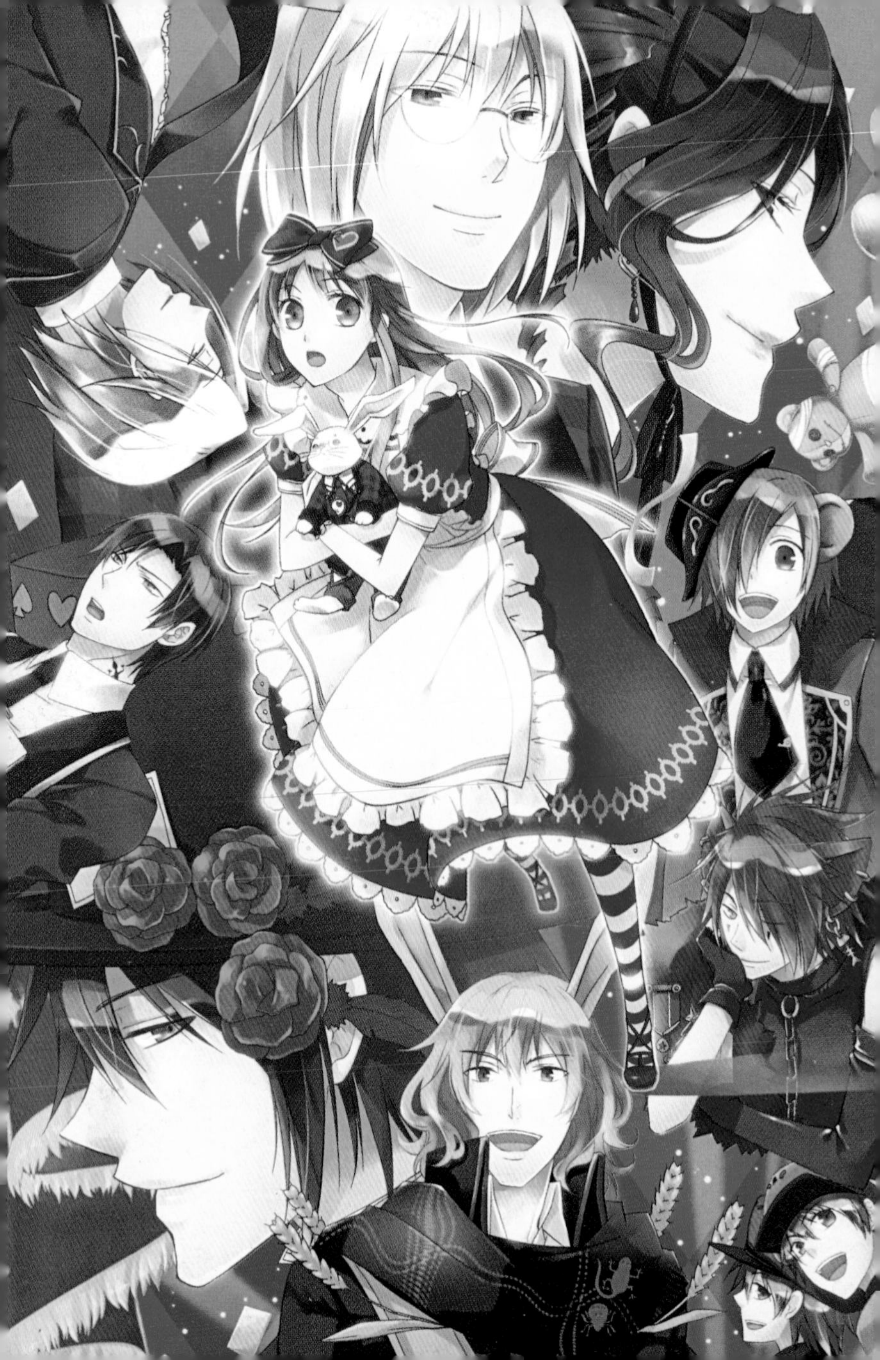

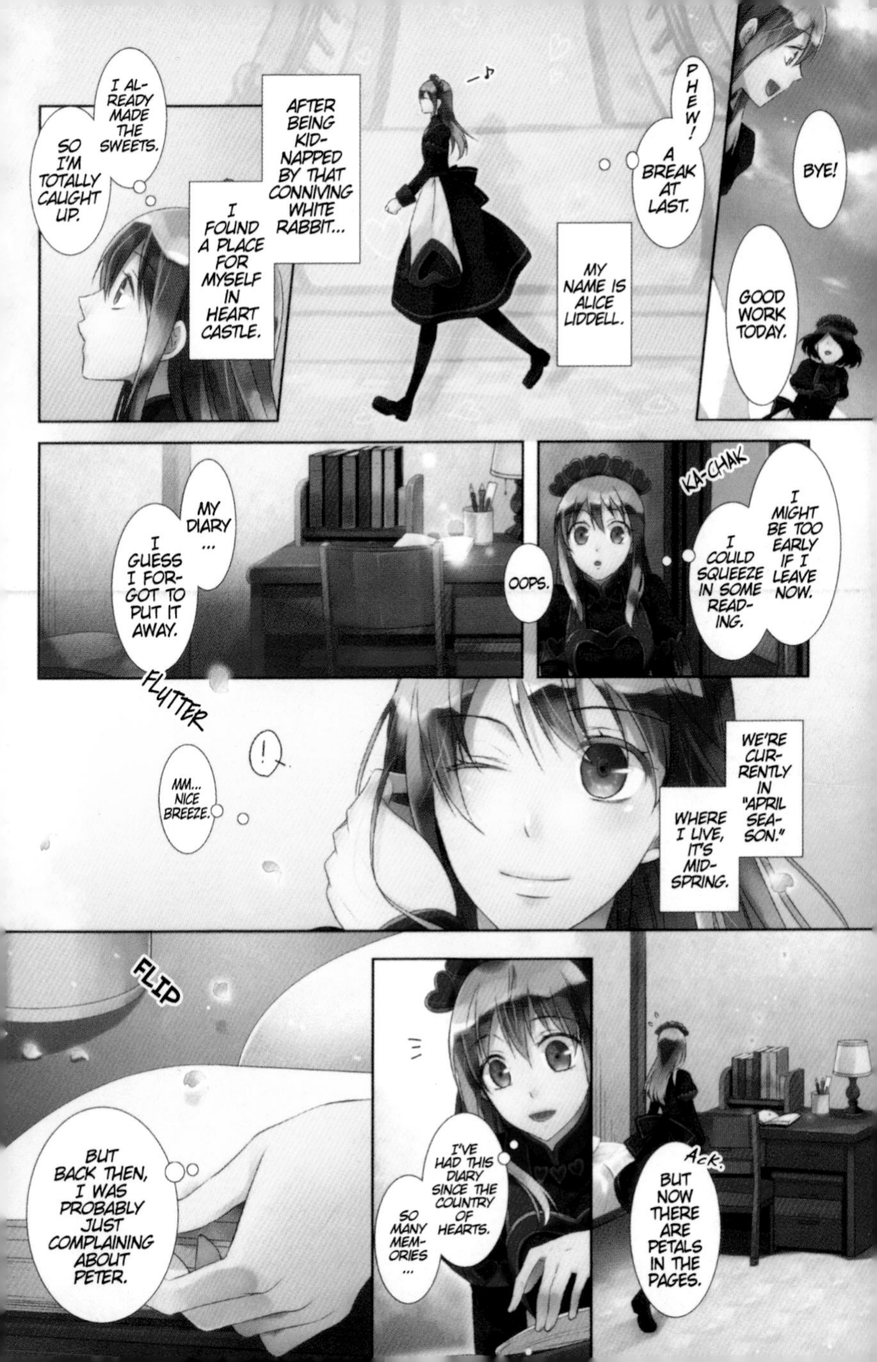
BYE!
GOOD WORK TODAY.
PHEW! A BREAK AT LAST.
MY NAME IS ALICE LIDDELL.
AFTER BEING KIDNAPPED BY THAT CONNIVING WHITE RABBIT...
I FOUND A PLACE FOR MYSELF IN HEART CASTLE.
I ALREADY MADE THE SWEETS.
SO I'M TOTALLY CAUGHT UP.
KA-CHAK
I MIGHT BE TOO EARLY IF I LEAVE NOW.
I COULD SQUEEZE IN SOME READING.
OOPS.
MY DIARY...
I GUESS I FORGOT TO PUT IT AWAY.
WE'RE CURRENTLY IN "APRIL SEASON."
WHERE I LIVE, IT'S MIDSPRING.
!
MM... NICE BREEZE.
FLUTTER
ACK.
BUT NOW THERE ARE PETALS IN THE PAGES.
I'VE HAD THIS DIARY SINCE THE COUNTRY OF HEARTS.
SO MANY MEMORIES...
FLIP
BUT BACK THEN, I WAS PROBABLY JUST COMPLAINING ABOUT PETER.

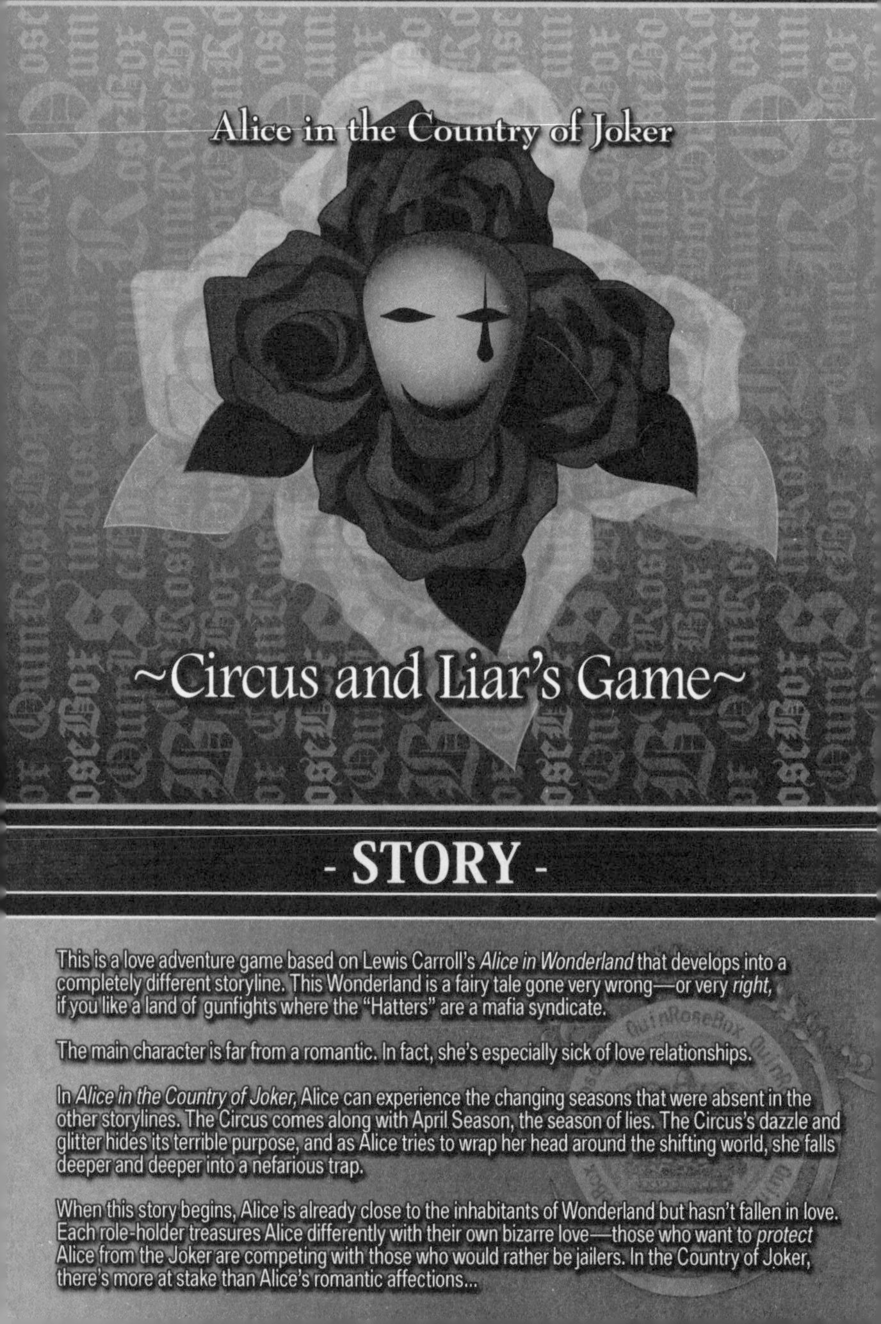
Alice in the Country of Joker
~Circus and Liar's Game~

- STORY -

This is a love adventure game based on Lewis Carroll's *Alice in Wonderland* that develops into a completely different storyline. This Wonderland is a fairy tale gone very wrong—or very *right*, if you like a land of gunfights where the "Hatters" are a mafia syndicate.

The main character is far from a romantic. In fact, she's especially sick of love relationships.

In *Alice in the Country of Joker,* Alice can experience the changing seasons that were absent in the other storylines. The Circus comes along with April Season, the season of lies. The Circus's dazzle and glitter hides its terrible purpose, and as Alice tries to wrap her head around the shifting world, she falls deeper and deeper into a nefarious trap.

When this story begins, Alice is already close to the inhabitants of Wonderland but hasn't fallen in love. Each role-holder treasures Alice differently with their own bizarre love—those who want to *protect* Alice from the Joker are competing with those who would rather be jailers. In the Country of Joker, there's more at stake than Alice's romantic affections...

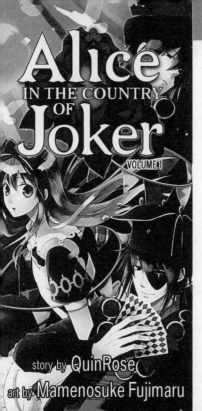

Alice
IN THE COUNTRY OF
Joker

VOLUME 1

story by **QuinRose**

art by **Mamenosuke Fujimaru**

STAFF CREDITS

translation	**Angela Liu**
adaptation	**Lianne Sentar**
lettering	**Laura Scoville**
cover design	**Michael David**
proofreader	**Shanti Whitesides**
assistant editor	**Bambi Eloriaga-Amago**
editor	**Adam Arnold**
publisher	**Jason DeAngelis**
	Seven Seas Entertainment

ALICE IN THE COUNTRY OF JOKER: CIRCUS AND LIAR'S GAME VOL. 1
Copyright © Mamenosuke Fujimaru / QuinRose 2011
First published in Japan in 2011 by ICHIJINSHA Inc., Tokyo.
English translation rights arranged with ICHIJINSHA Inc., Tokyo, Japan.

ISBN: 978-1-937867-15-7

Printed in Canada

First Printing: December 2012

10 9 8 7 6 5 4 3 2

FOLLOW US ONLINE: www.gomanga.com

READING DIRECTIONS

This book reads from *right to left*, Japanese style.
If this is your first time reading manga, you start
reading from the top right panel on each page and
take it from there. If you get lost, just follow the
numbered diagram here. It may seem backwards
at first, but you'll get the hang of it! Have fun!!

Character

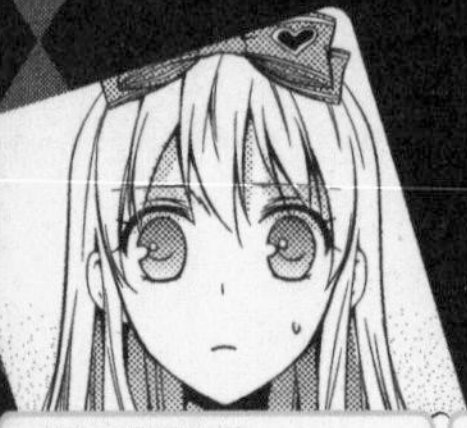

Alice Liddell

An average teenage girl...with a heavy complex. After being dragged to Wonderland by the White Rabbit, she's managed to adapt and even enjoy her bizarre surroundings.

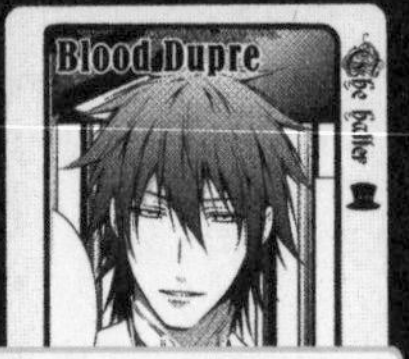
Blood Dupre

The dangerous, shadowy leader of the mafia group known as the Hatter Family. He's incredibly smart, but due to his temperamental moods and his desire to keep things "interesting," he often digs his own grave—and the graves of many others.

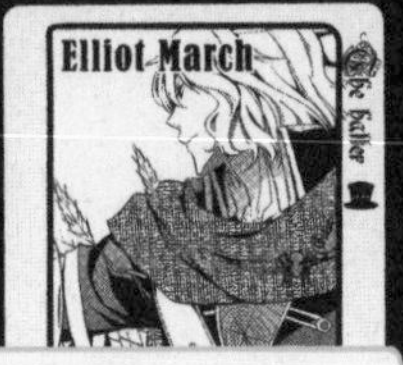
Elliot March

The No. 2 of the Hatter Family and Blood's right-hand man, Elliot is an ex-criminal and an escaped convict. After partnering with Blood, he improved his violent nature and thinks for several seconds before shooting. In his mind, this is a vast improvement.

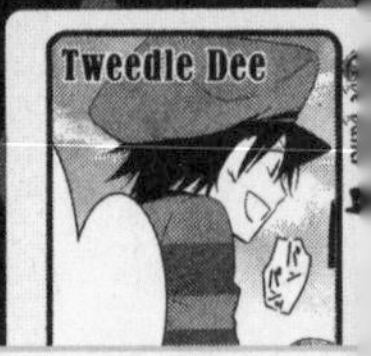
Tweedle Dee

Gatekeeper of the Hatter territory, Dee loves days off. He and his brother can be innocent at times, but their (frequent) malice and unsavory activities earned them the nickname "Bloody Twins." He can shifts his body between a child and an adult version of itself.

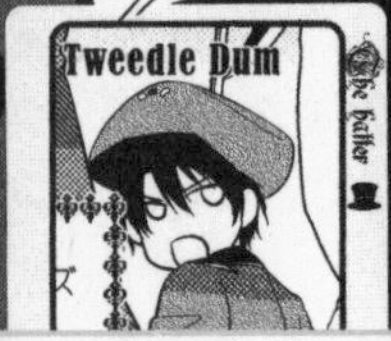
Tweedle Dum

The other Bloody Twin, Dum loves money. He can also become an adult when he feels like it.

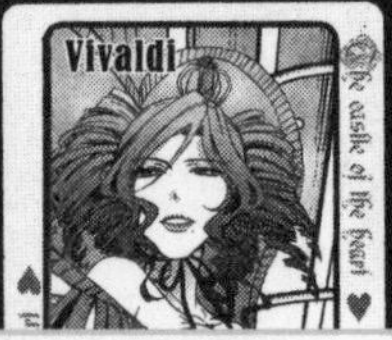
Vivaldi

Ruthless and cruel, Vivaldi is an arrogant beauty with a wild temper. She takes her fury out on everyone around her, including her poor subordinates. Although a picture-perfect Mad Queen, she cares for Alice as if Alice were her little sister... or a very interesting plaything.

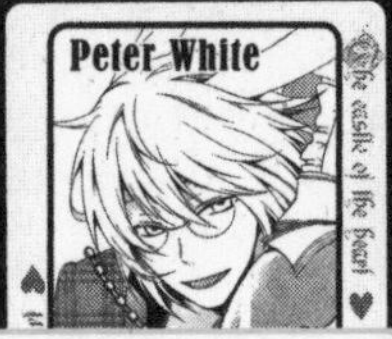
Peter White

Prime Minister of Heart Castle who has rabbit ears growing out of his head. He loves Alice and hates everything else. His cruel, irrational actions are disturbing, but he acts like a completely different person—er, rabbit?—when in the throes of his love for Alice.

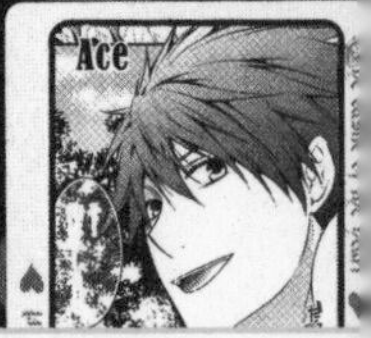
Ace

The Knight of Hearts and subordinate of Vivaldi. He's a very unlucky (yet strangely positive) man...who tends to plow forward and only worsen his situation. Ace is one of the Clockmaker's few friends and visits Julius frequently—usually getting lost on the way.

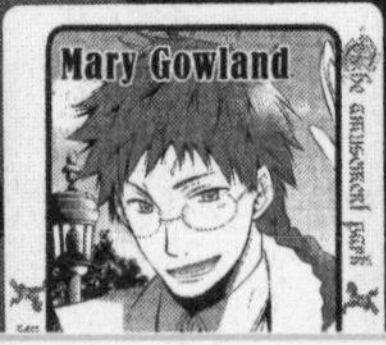
Mary Gowland

The owner of the Amusement Park. He hides his hated first name, Mary, but pretty much everyone already knows it. His full name is a play on words that sounds like "Merry Go Round" when said quickly. He's a terrible, terrible musician.

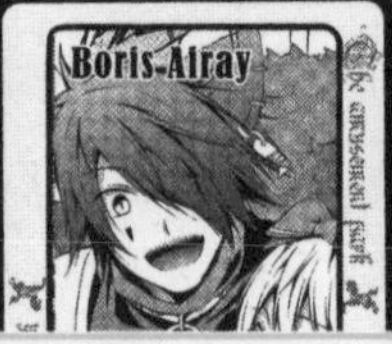
Boris Airay

A riddle-loving cat with a signature smirk, he has a tendency to pose questions and never answer them. Since seeing the Sleepy Mouse whets his appetite, he carries a fork and knife at all times.

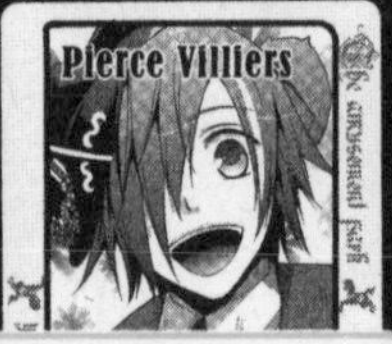
Pierce Villiers

An insomniac mouse who drinks too much coffee. He's terrified of Boris but loves Nightmare, who brings precious sleep. He used to be a part of the Hatter family, but after relentless bullying from the cat and twins, he's become a runaway.

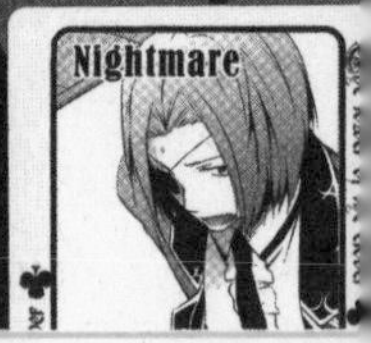
Nightmare

A sickly nightmare who often coughs up blood. He has the power to read people's thoughts and enter dreams. He technically holds a high position and has many subordinates, but since he can't even take care of his own health, he leaves most things to Gray.

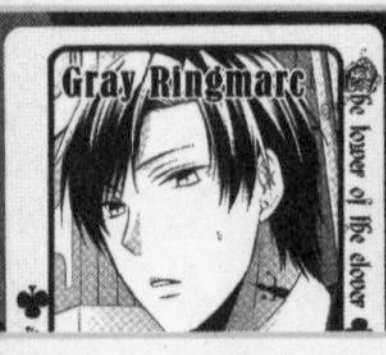
Gray Ringmarc

Nightmare's subordinate. This sound thinker with a strong work ethic is surprisingly good with a blade. Elliot considers Gray a comrade, since they share a strong dedication to their bosses...which annoys Gray.

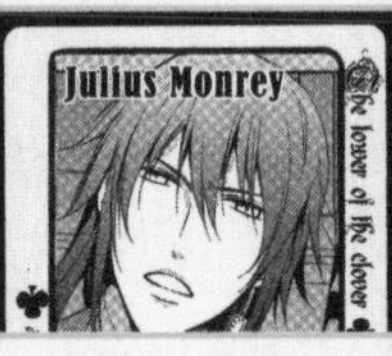
Julius Monrey

This gloomy Clockmaker is also known as the Undertaker. Despite being a sarcastic workaholic, he gets along with Ace. He had some part in the imprisonment of Elliot, the March Hare, and is thus the target for hatred.

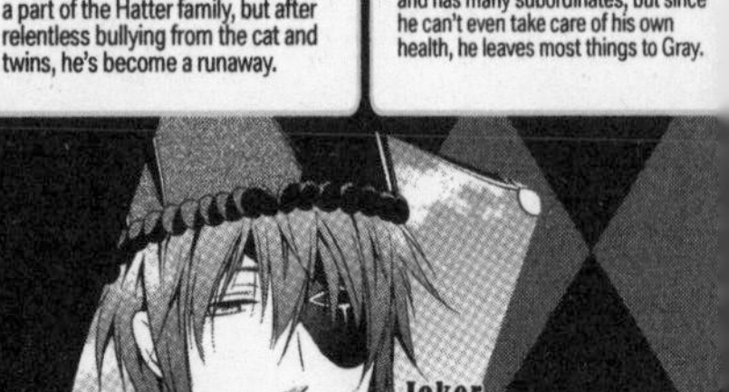

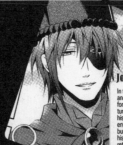

Joker

In the Circus, Joker is the leader... and the warden. He exists in two forms: White and Black, which take turns controlling either his body or his mask. This poor card loves to entertain his uninterested peers, but can't seem tounderstand why his friendly affections are rarely returned.

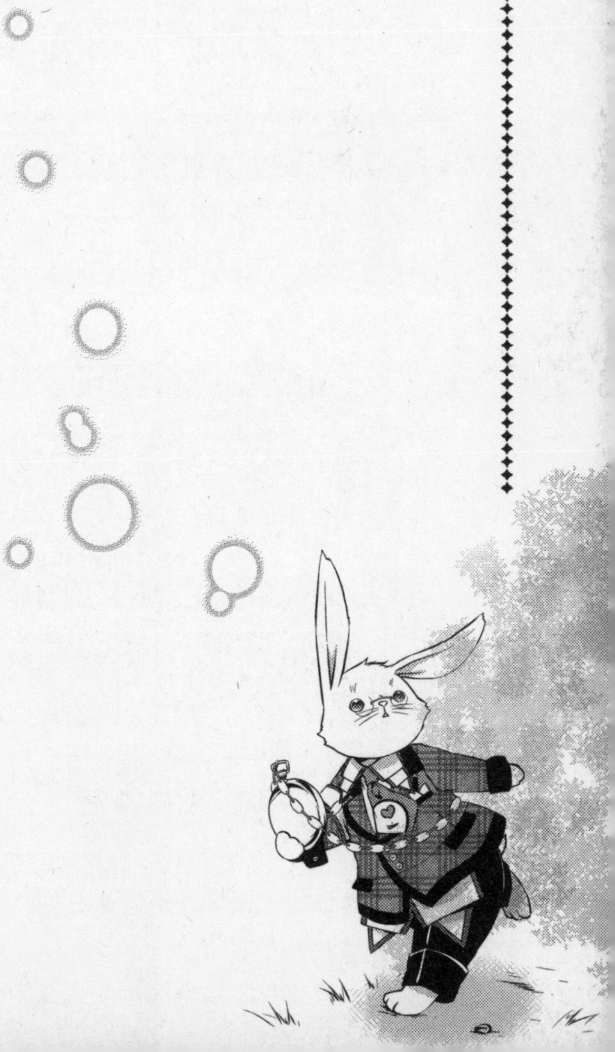

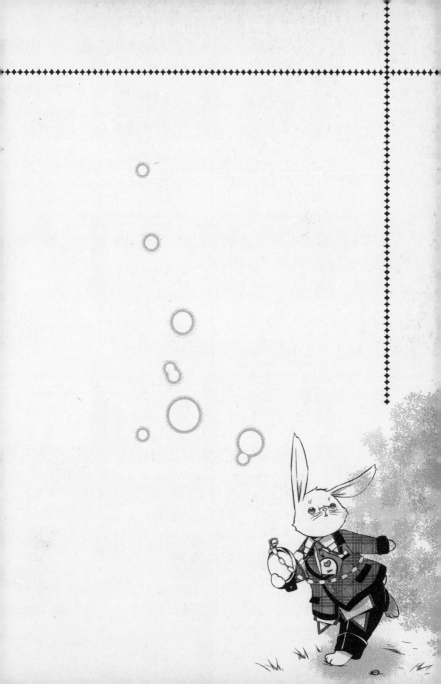

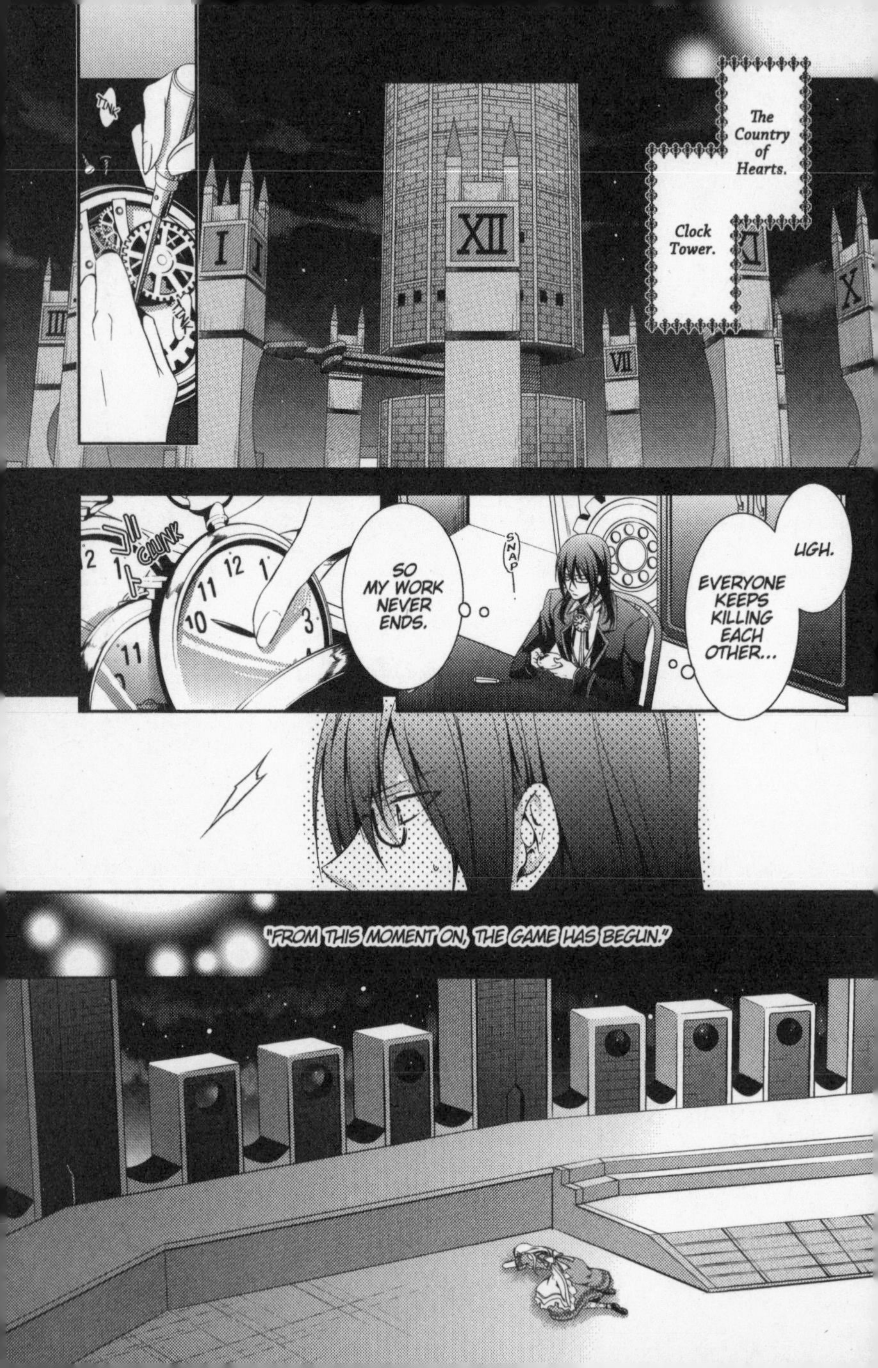
The Country of Hearts.
Clock Tower.
TINK
TINK
UGH.
EVERYONE KEEPS KILLING EACH OTHER...
SNAP
SO MY WORK NEVER ENDS.
CLINK
"FROM THIS MOMENT ON, THE GAME HAS BEGUN."

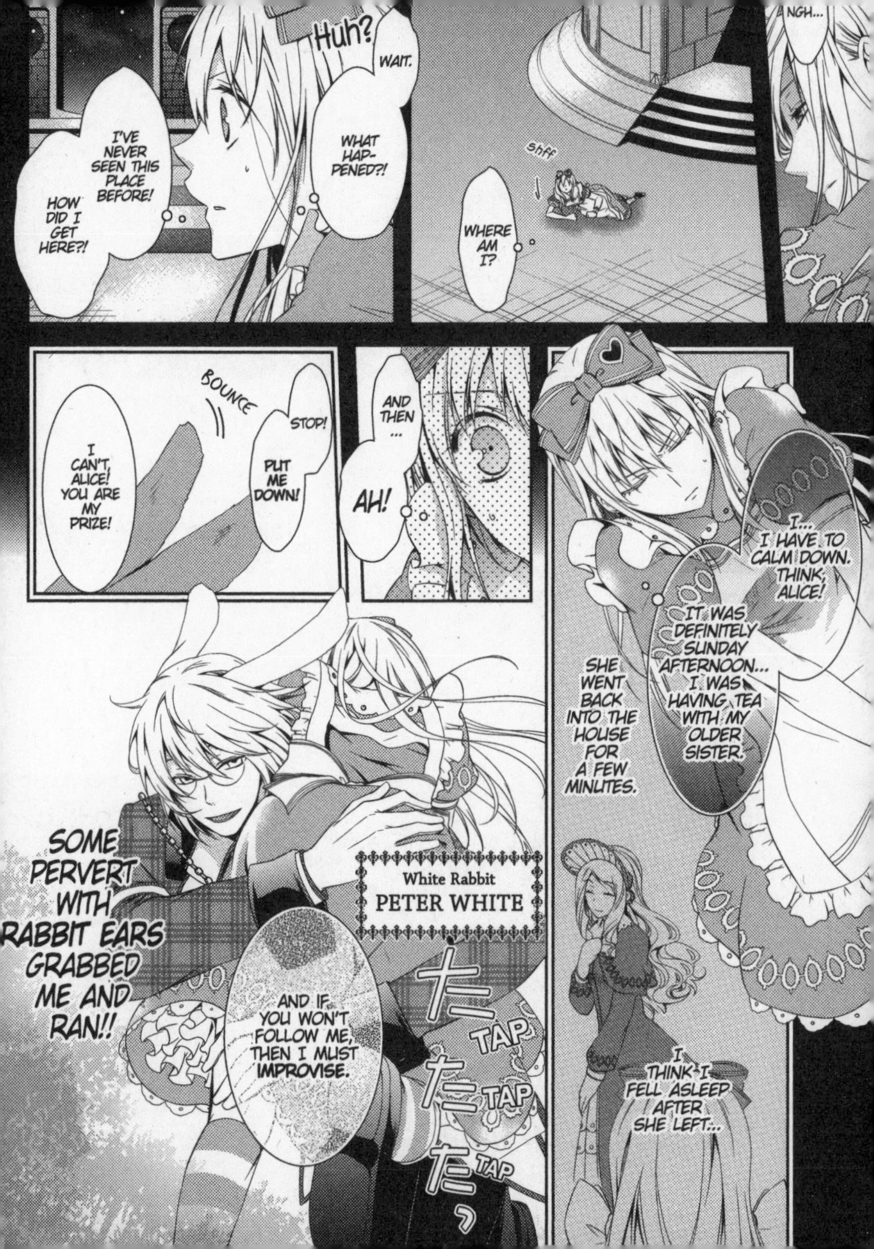
NGH...
sniff
!
WHERE AM I?
Huh?
WAIT.
WHAT HAP-PENED?!
I'VE NEVER SEEN THIS PLACE BEFORE!
HOW DID I GET HERE?!
I... I HAVE TO CALM DOWN. THINK, ALICE!
IT WAS DEFINITELY SUNDAY AFTERNOON... I WAS HAVING TEA WITH MY OLDER SISTER.
SHE WENT BACK INTO THE HOUSE FOR A FEW MINUTES.
I THINK I FELL ASLEEP AFTER SHE LEFT...
AND THEN...
AH!
STOP!
PUT ME DOWN!
BOUNCE
I CAN'T, ALICE! YOU ARE MY PRIZE!
White Rabbit
PETER WHITE
TAP
TAP
TAP
AND IF YOU WON'T FOLLOW ME, THEN I MUST IMPROVISE.
SOME PERVERT WITH RABBIT EARS GRABBED ME AND RAN!!

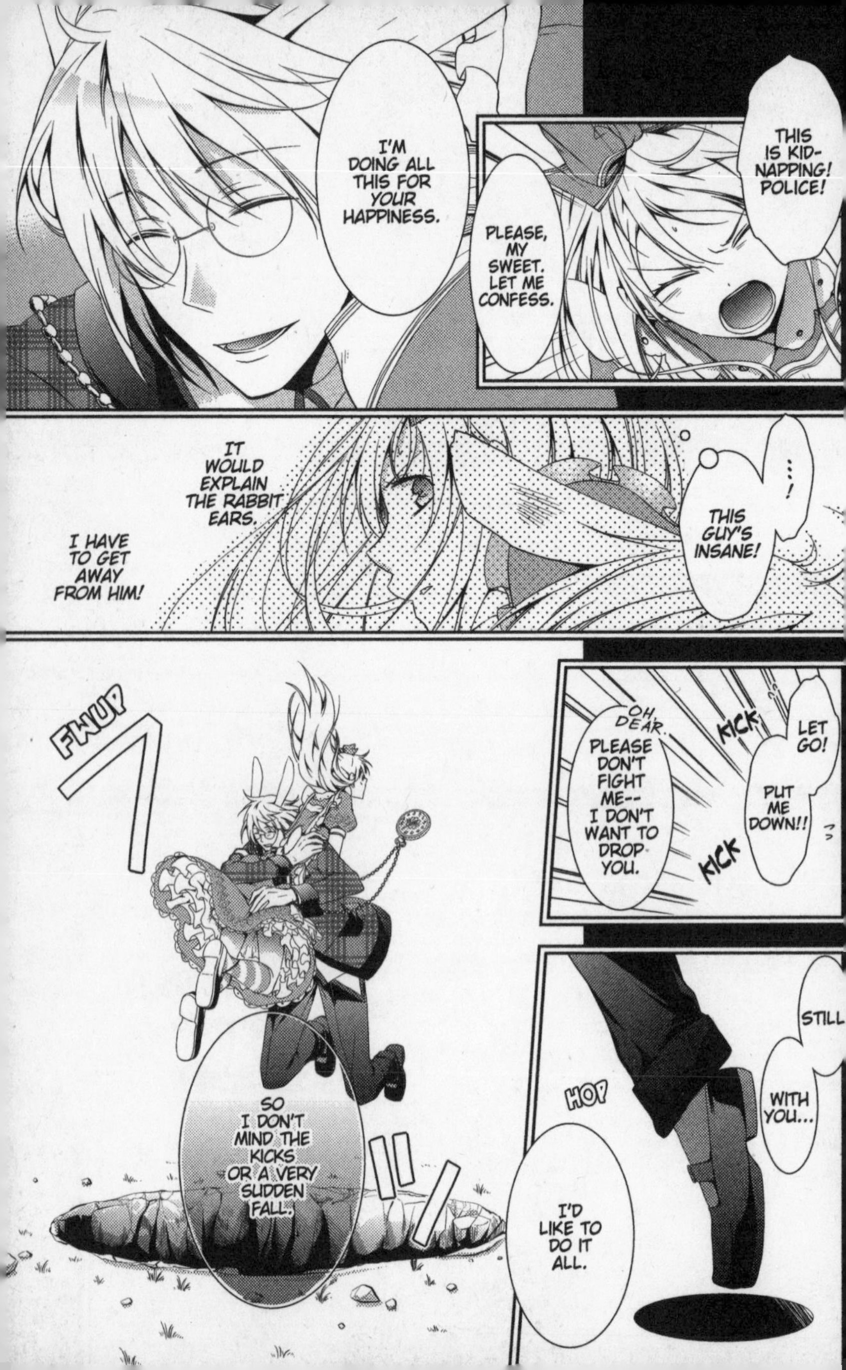
THIS IS KID-NAPPING! POLICE!
PLEASE, MY SWEET. LET ME CONFESS.
I'M DOING ALL THIS FOR YOUR HAPPINESS.
...!
THIS GUY'S INSANE!
IT WOULD EXPLAIN THE RABBIT EARS.
I HAVE TO GET AWAY FROM HIM!
LET GO!
PUT ME DOWN!!
KICK
KICK
OH, DEAR.
PLEASE DON'T FIGHT ME-- I DON'T WANT TO DROP YOU.
STILL
WITH YOU...
HOP
I'D LIKE TO DO IT ALL.
FWUP
SO I DON'T MIND THE KICKS OR A VERY SUDDEN FALL.

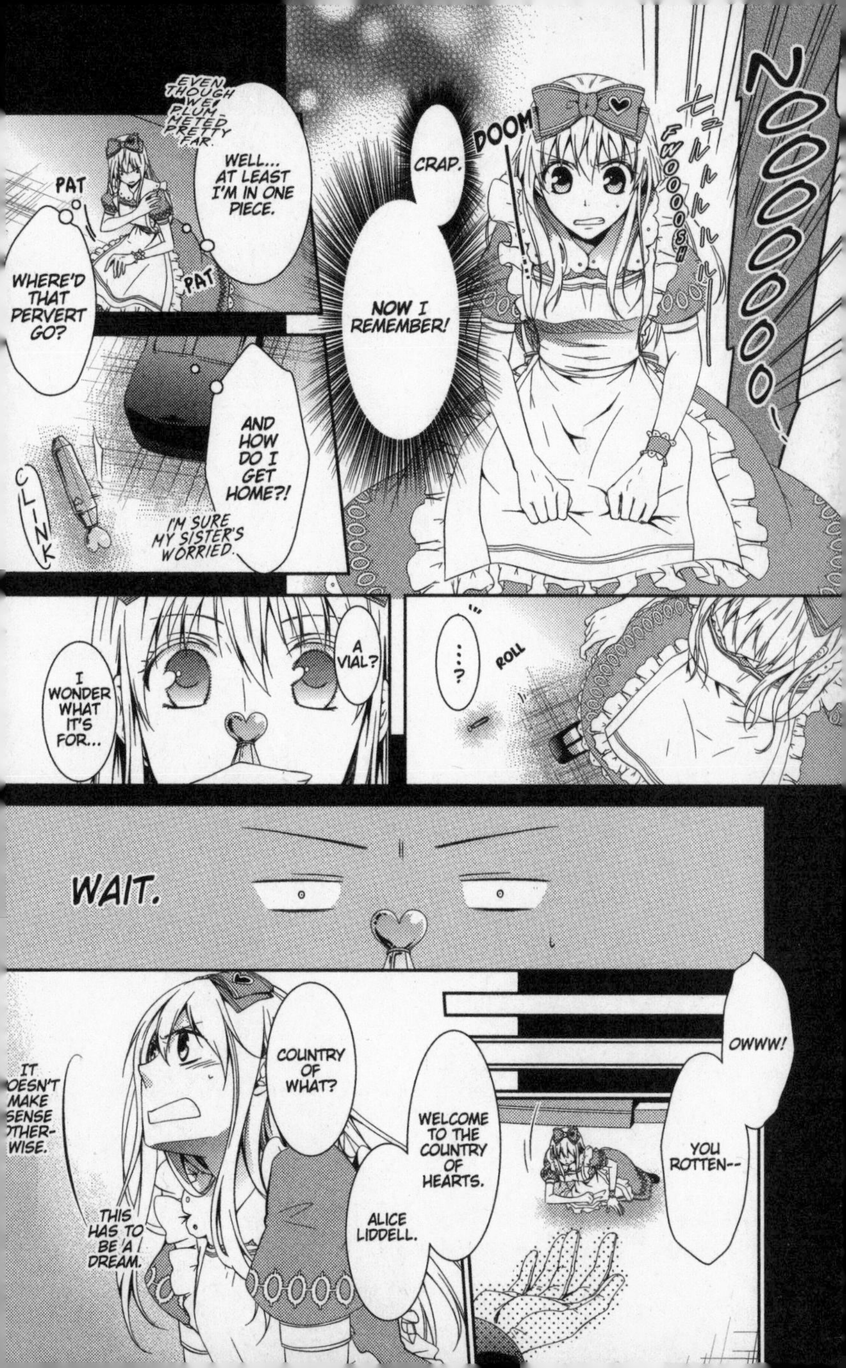
ZOOOOOOOO...
FWOOOOSH
DOOM
CRAP.
NOW I REMEMBER!
EVEN THOUGH WE PLUMMETED PRETTY FAR.
WELL... AT LEAST I'M IN ONE PIECE.
PAT
PAT
WHERE'D THAT PERVERT GO?
AND HOW DO I GET HOME?!
I'M SURE MY SISTER'S WORRIED.
CLINK
...?
ROLL
A VIAL?
I WONDER WHAT IT'S FOR...
WAIT.
OWWW!
YOU ROTTEN--
WELCOME TO THE COUNTRY OF HEARTS.
ALICE LIDDELL.
COUNTRY OF WHAT?
IT OESN'T MAKE ENSE OTHER-WISE.
THIS HAS TO BE A DREAM.

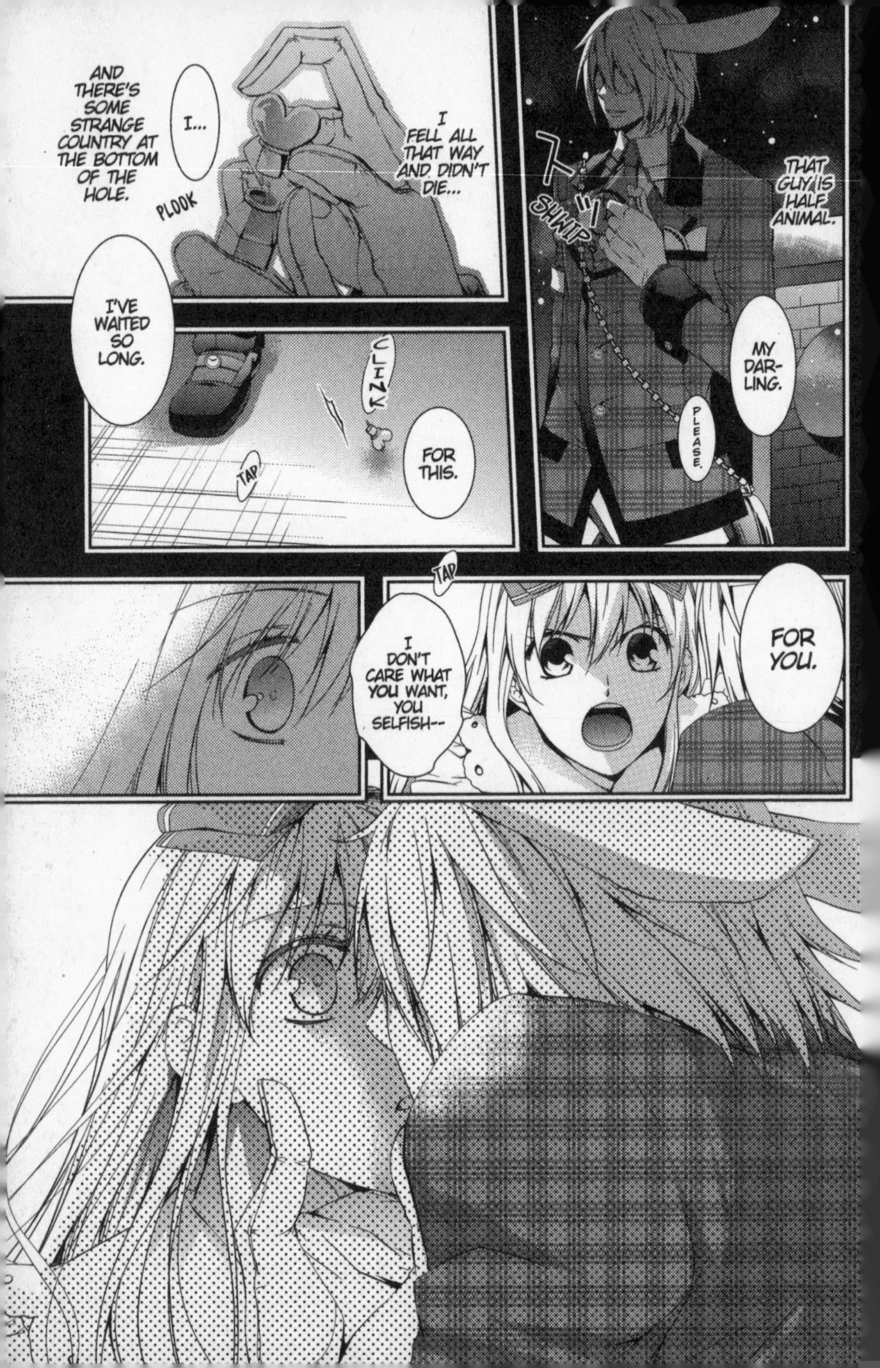
THAT GUY IS HALF ANIMAL.
SHWIP
MY DARLING.
PLEASE.
I FELL ALL THAT WAY AND DIDN'T DIE...
I...
AND THERE'S SOME STRANGE COUNTRY AT THE BOTTOM OF THE HOLE.
PLOOK
CLINK
FOR THIS.
TAP
I'VE WAITED SO LONG.
FOR YOU.
TAP
I DON'T CARE WHAT YOU WANT, YOU SELFISH--

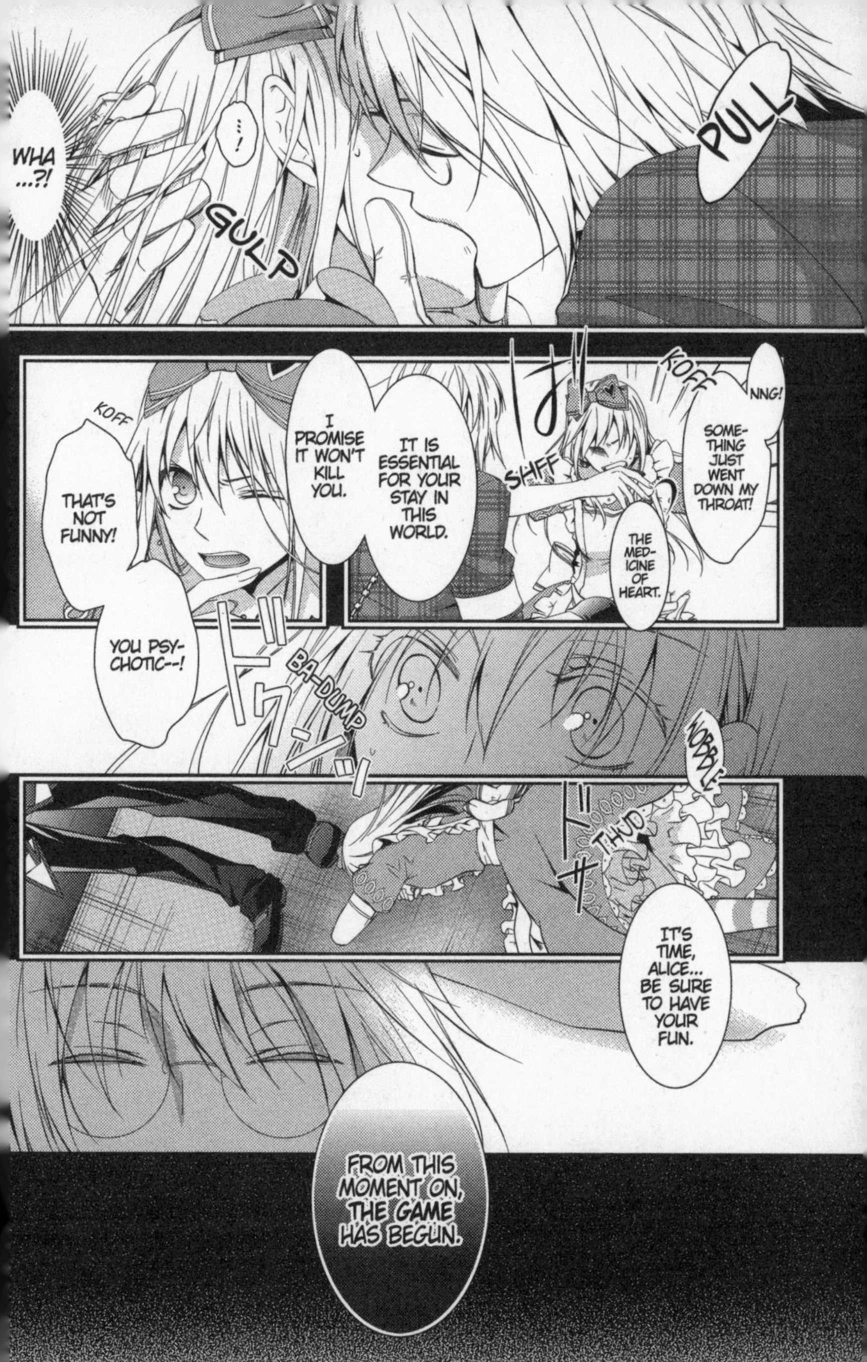
PULL
...!
GULP
WHA ...?!
KOFF
NNG!
SOME-THING JUST WENT DOWN MY THROAT!
SHFF
THE MED-ICINE OF HEART.
IT IS ESSENTIAL FOR YOUR STAY IN THIS WORLD.
I PROMISE IT WON'T KILL YOU.
KOFF
THAT'S NOT FUNNY!
YOU PSY-CHOTIC--!
BA-DUMP
WOBBLE
THUD
IT'S TIME, ALICE... BE SURE TO HAVE YOUR FUN.
FROM THIS MOMENT ON, THE GAME HAS BEGUN.

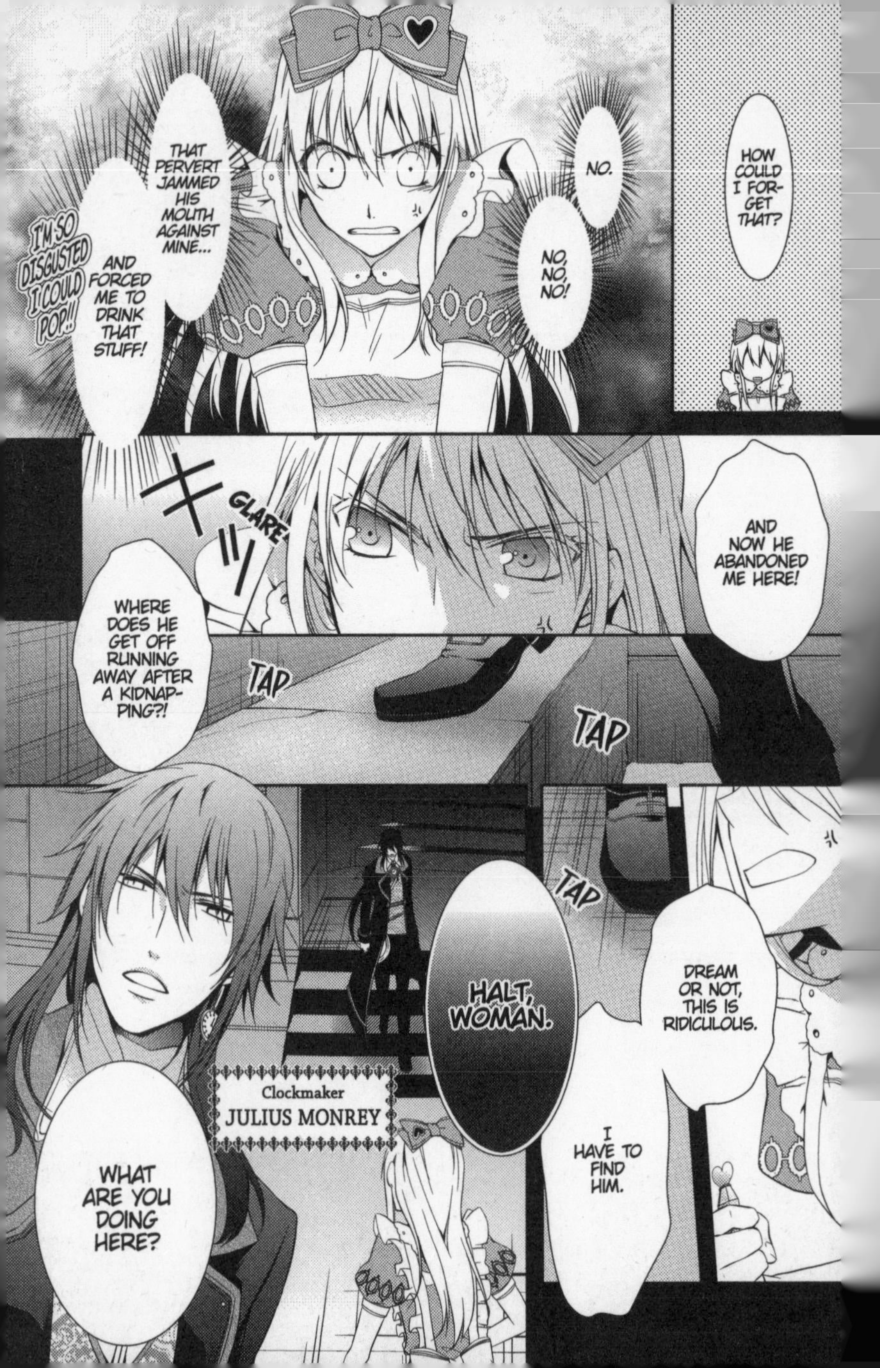
HOW COULD I FOR-GET THAT?
NO.
NO, NO, NO!
THAT PERVERT JAMMED HIS MOUTH AGAINST MINE...
AND FORCED ME TO DRINK THAT STUFF!
I'M SO DISGUSTED I COULD POP!!
AND NOW HE ABANDONED ME HERE!
GLARE
WHERE DOES HE GET OFF RUNNING AWAY AFTER A KIDNAP-PING?!
TAP
TAP
DREAM OR NOT, THIS IS RIDICULOUS.
I HAVE TO FIND HIM.
TAP
HALT, WOMAN.
Clockmaker
JULIUS MONREY
WHAT ARE YOU DOING HERE?

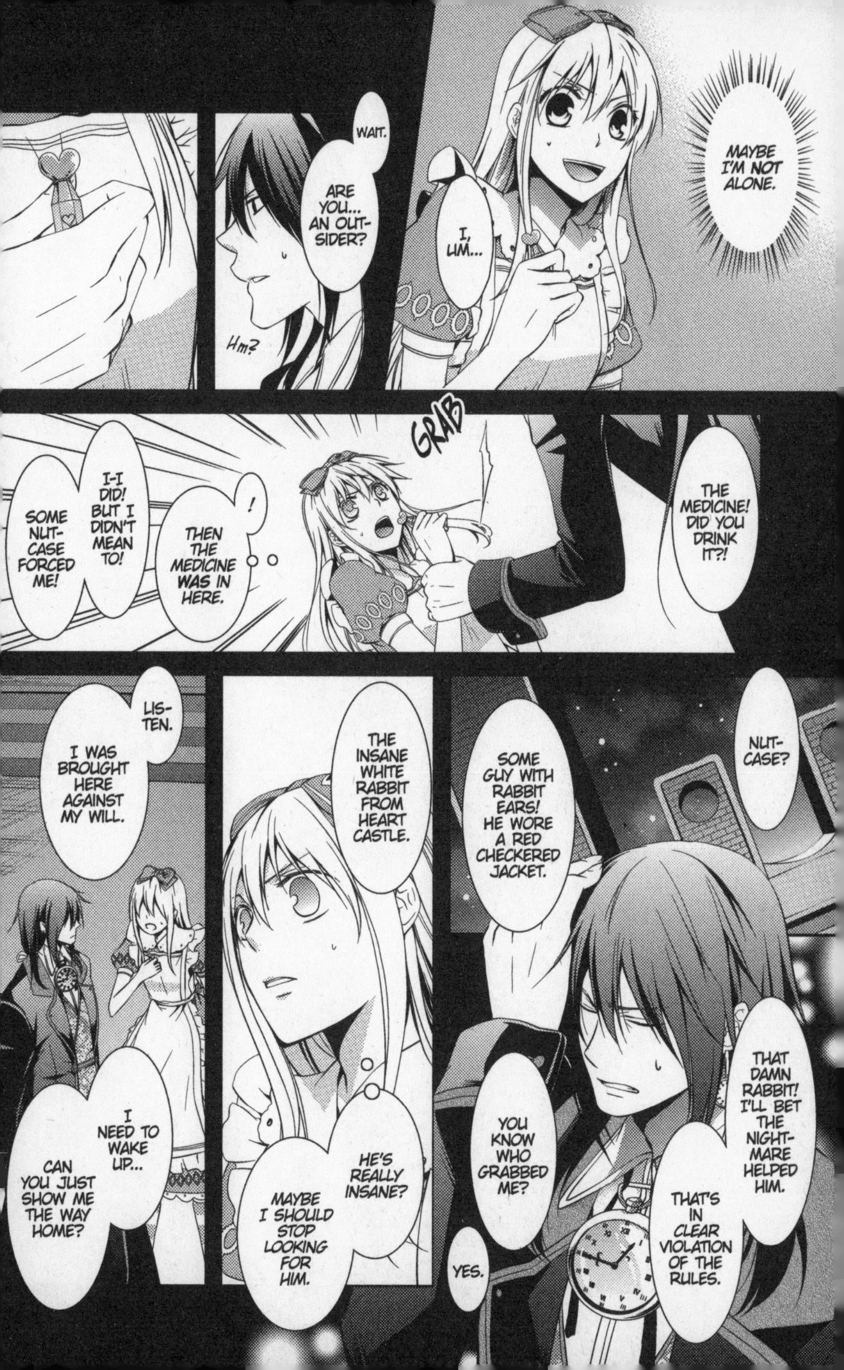
MAYBE I'M NOT ALONE.
I, UM...
WAIT.
ARE YOU... AN OUT-SIDER?
Hm?
THE MEDICINE! DID YOU DRINK IT?!
GRAB
!
THEN THE MEDICINE WAS IN HERE.
I-I DID! BUT I DIDN'T MEAN TO!
SOME NUT-CASE FORCED ME!
NUT-CASE?
SOME GUY WITH RABBIT EARS! HE WORE A RED CHECKERED JACKET.
THAT DAMN RABBIT! I'LL BET THE NIGHT-MARE HELPED HIM.
THAT'S IN CLEAR VIOLATION OF THE RULES.
YOU KNOW WHO GRABBED ME?
YES.
THE INSANE WHITE RABBIT FROM HEART CASTLE.
HE'S REALLY INSANE?
MAYBE I SHOULD STOP LOOKING FOR HIM.
LIS-TEN.
I WAS BROUGHT HERE AGAINST MY WILL.
I NEED TO WAKE UP...
CAN YOU JUST SHOW ME THE WAY HOME?

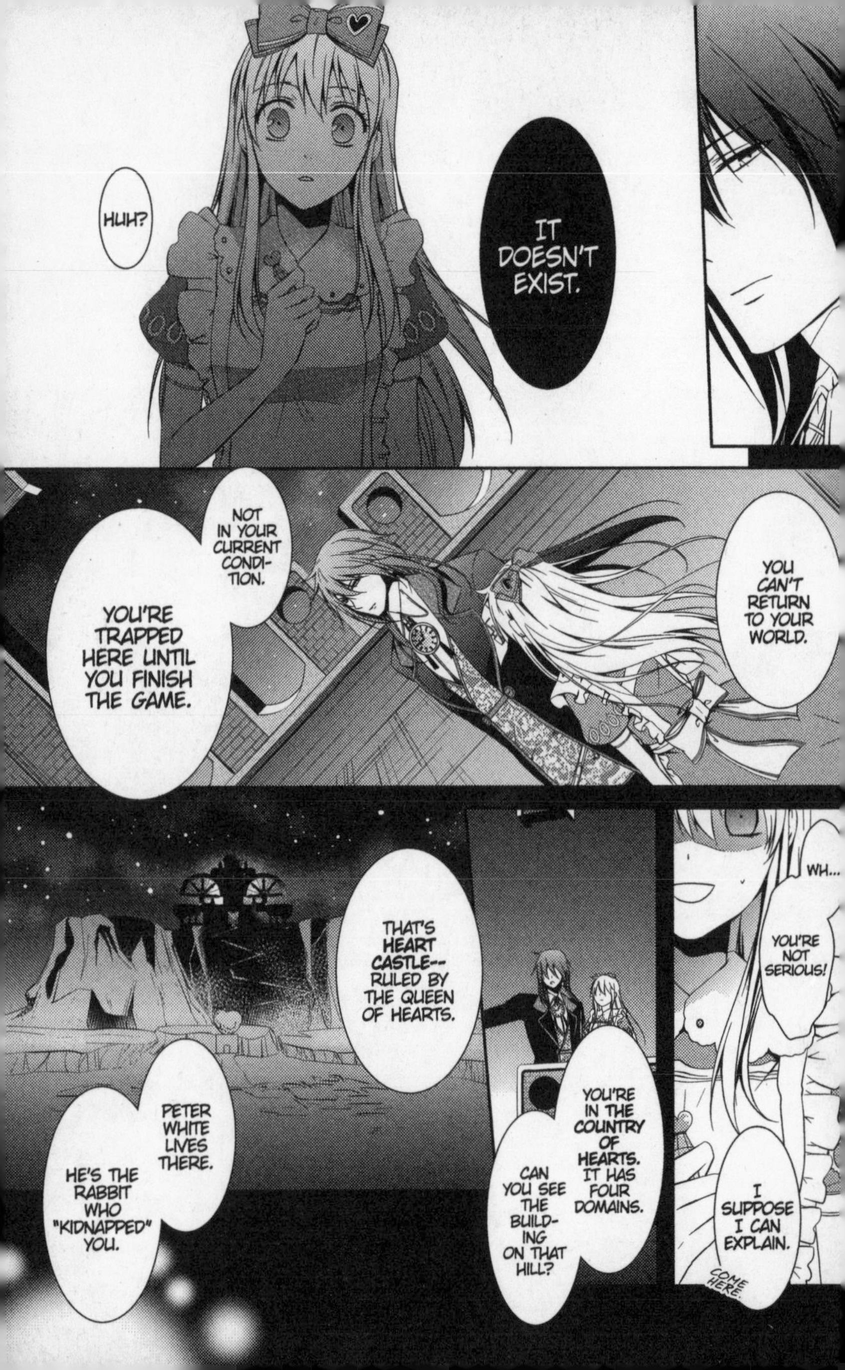
IT DOESN'T EXIST.
HUH?
YOU CAN'T RETURN TO YOUR WORLD.
NOT IN YOUR CURRENT CONDI-TION.
YOU'RE TRAPPED HERE UNTIL YOU FINISH THE GAME.
WH...
YOU'RE NOT SERIOUS!
I SUPPOSE I CAN EXPLAIN.
COME HERE.
YOU'RE IN THE COUNTRY OF HEARTS. IT HAS FOUR DOMAINS.
CAN YOU SEE THE BUILD-ING ON THAT HILL?
THAT'S **HEART CASTLE**-- RULED BY THE QUEEN OF HEARTS.
PETER WHITE LIVES THERE.
HE'S THE RABBIT WHO "KIDNAPPED" YOU.

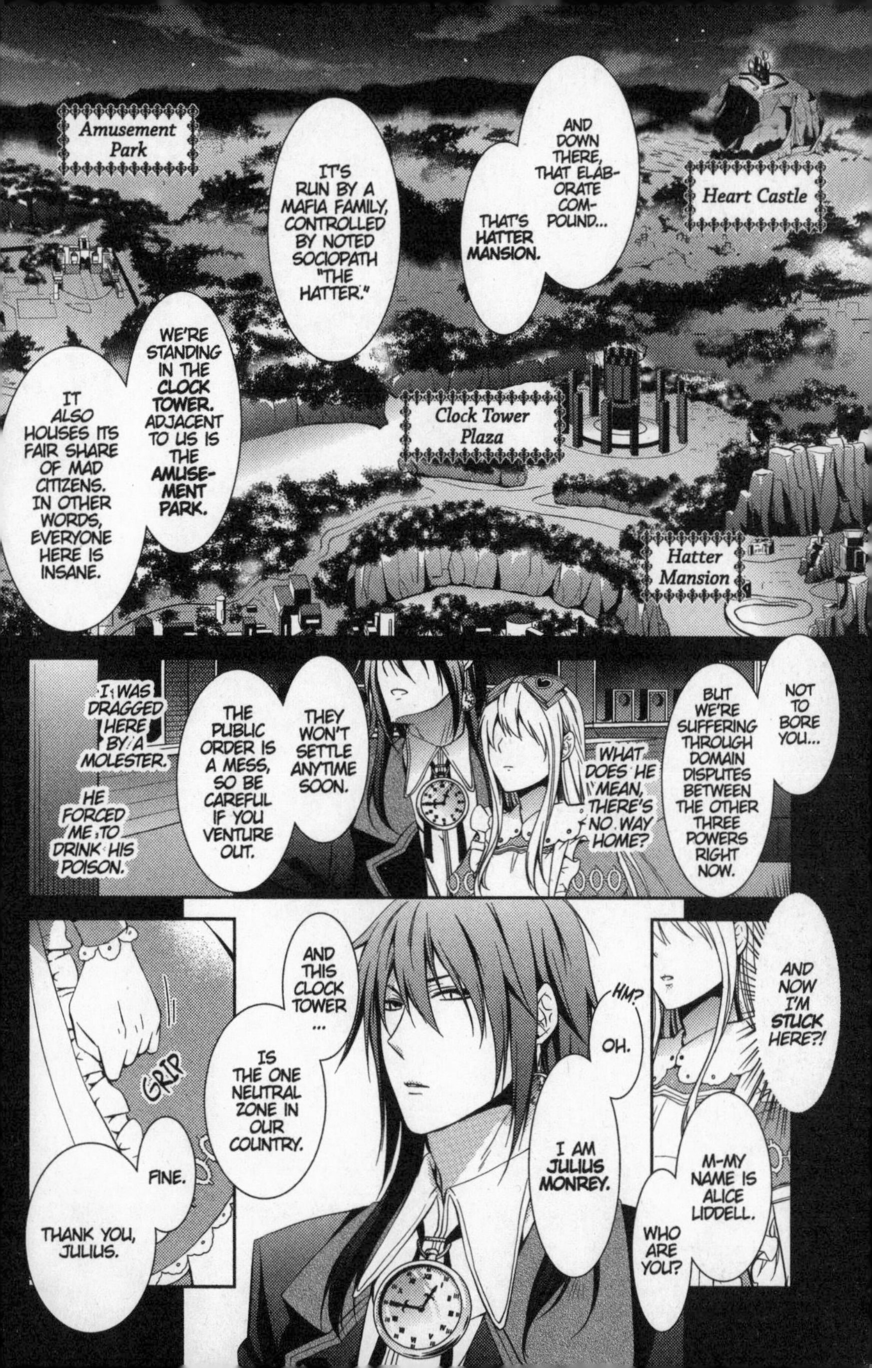

Heart Castle
AND DOWN THERE, THAT ELABORATE COMPOUND...
THAT'S HATTER MANSION.
IT'S RUN BY A MAFIA FAMILY, CONTROLLED BY NOTED SOCIOPATH "THE HATTER."
Amusement Park
Clock Tower Plaza
Hatter Mansion
WE'RE STANDING IN THE CLOCK TOWER. ADJACENT TO US IS THE AMUSEMENT PARK.
IT ALSO HOUSES ITS FAIR SHARE OF MAD CITIZENS. IN OTHER WORDS, EVERYONE HERE IS INSANE.
NOT TO BORE YOU...
BUT WE'RE SUFFERING THROUGH DOMAIN DISPUTES BETWEEN THE OTHER THREE POWERS RIGHT NOW.
WHAT DOES HE MEAN, THERE'S NO WAY HOME?
THEY WON'T SETTLE ANYTIME SOON.
THE PUBLIC ORDER IS A MESS, SO BE CAREFUL IF YOU VENTURE OUT.
I WAS DRAGGED HERE BY A MOLESTER.
HE FORCED ME TO DRINK HIS POISON.
AND NOW I'M STUCK HERE?!
M-MY NAME IS ALICE LIDDELL.
WHO ARE YOU?
HM?
OH.
I AM JULIUS MONREY.
AND THIS CLOCK TOWER...
IS THE ONE NEUTRAL ZONE IN OUR COUNTRY.
GRIP
FINE.
THANK YOU, JULIUS.

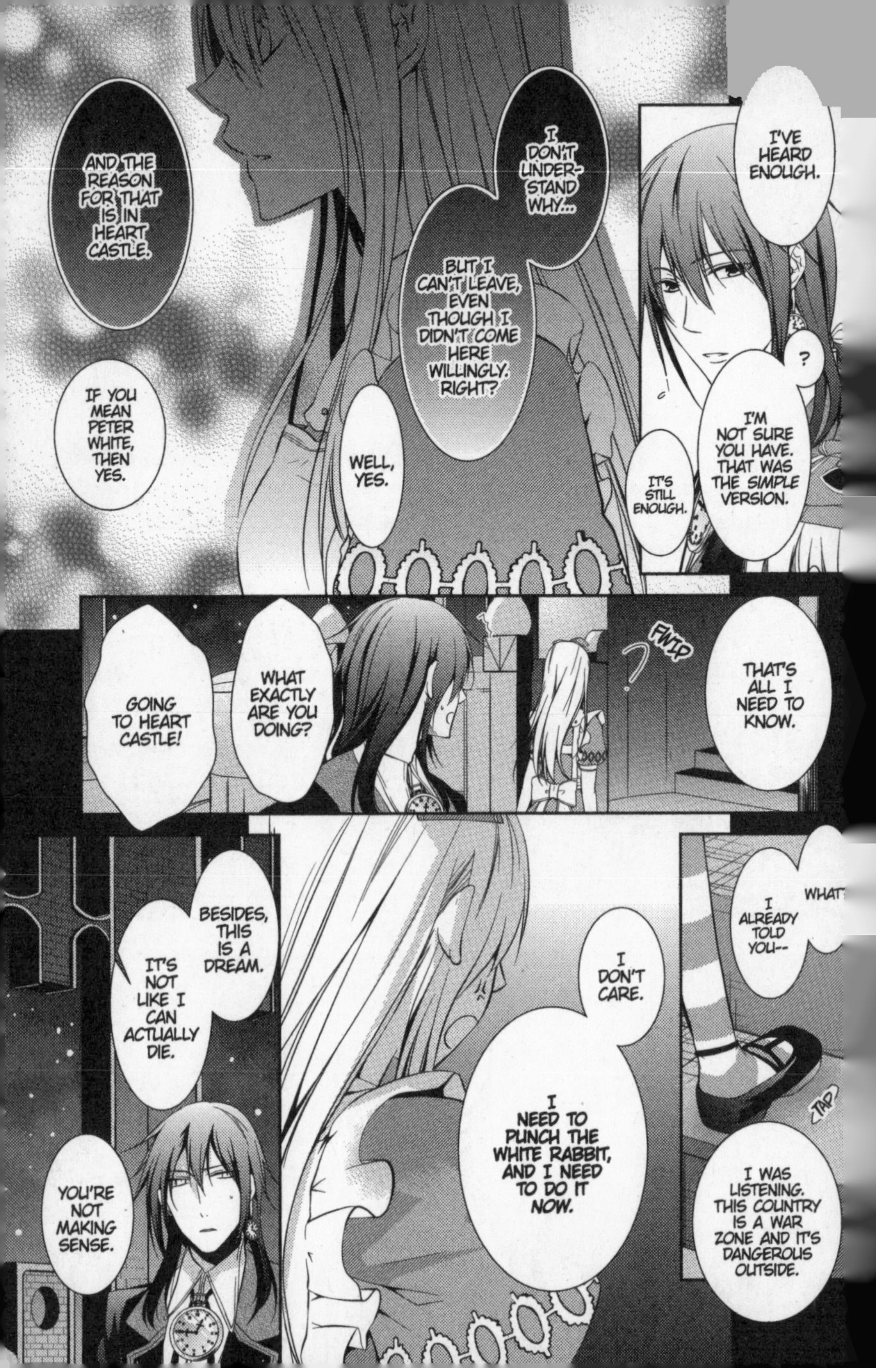
I DON'T UNDER-STAND WHY...
BUT I CAN'T LEAVE, EVEN THOUGH I DIDN'T COME HERE WILLINGLY. RIGHT?
WELL, YES.
AND THE REASON FOR THAT IS IN HEART CASTLE.
IF YOU MEAN PETER WHITE, THEN YES.
I'VE HEARD ENOUGH.
?
I'M NOT SURE YOU HAVE. THAT WAS THE SIMPLE VERSION.
IT'S STILL ENOUGH.
THAT'S ALL I NEED TO KNOW.
FWIP
?
WHAT EXACTLY ARE YOU DOING?
GOING TO HEART CASTLE!
WHAT?
I ALREADY TOLD YOU--
TAP
I WAS LISTENING. THIS COUNTRY IS A WAR ZONE AND IT'S DANGEROUS OUTSIDE.
I DON'T CARE.
I NEED TO PUNCH THE WHITE RABBIT, AND I NEED TO DO IT NOW.
BESIDES, THIS IS A DREAM.
IT'S NOT LIKE I CAN ACTUALLY DIE.
YOU'RE NOT MAKING SENSE.

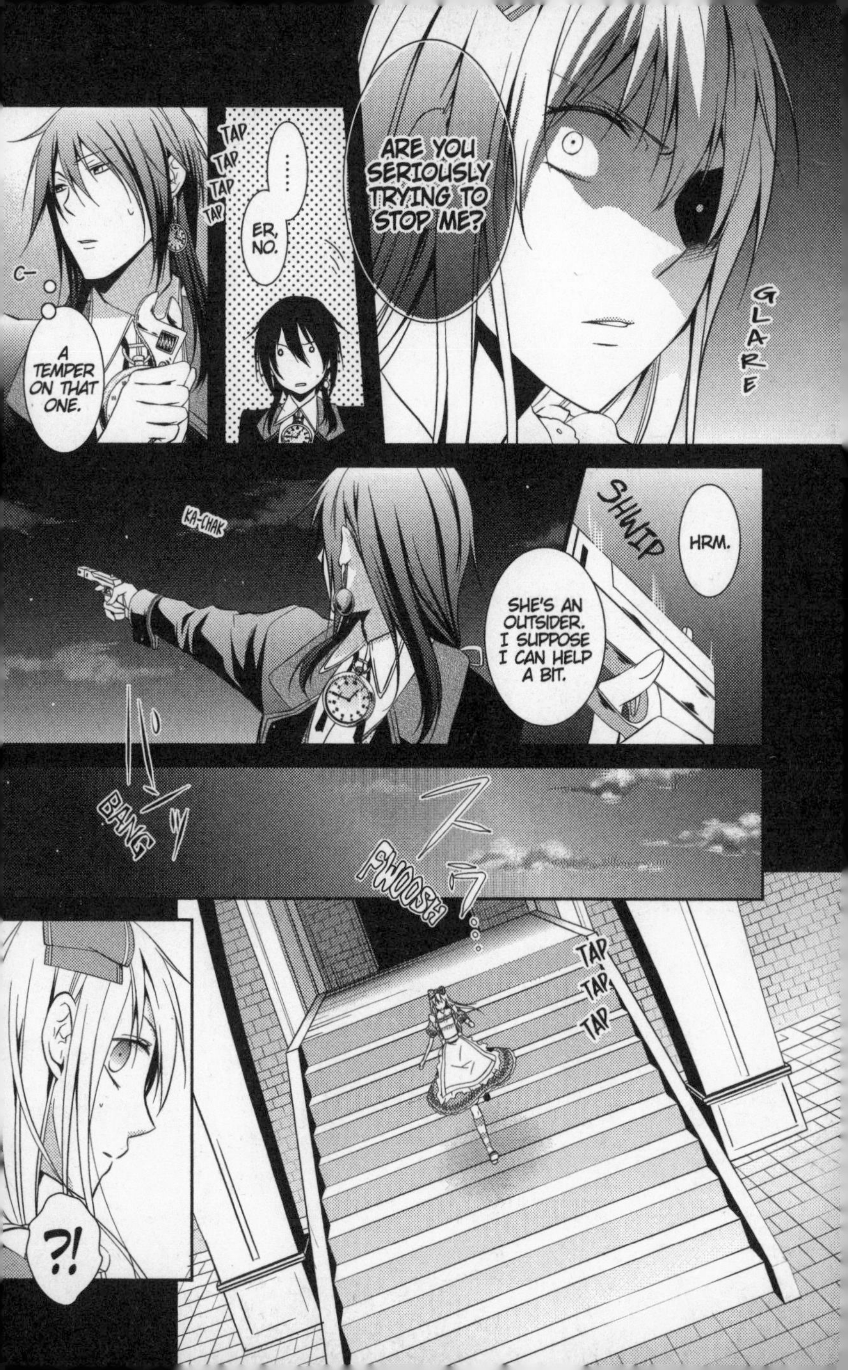

ARE YOU SERIOUSLY TRYING TO STOP ME?
GLARE
...
ER, NO.
TAP TAP TAP TAP
C—
A TEMPER ON THAT ONE.
HRM.
SHWIP
SHE'S AN OUTSIDER. I SUPPOSE I CAN HELP A BIT.
KA-CHAK
FWOOSH
BANG
TAP TAP TAP
?!

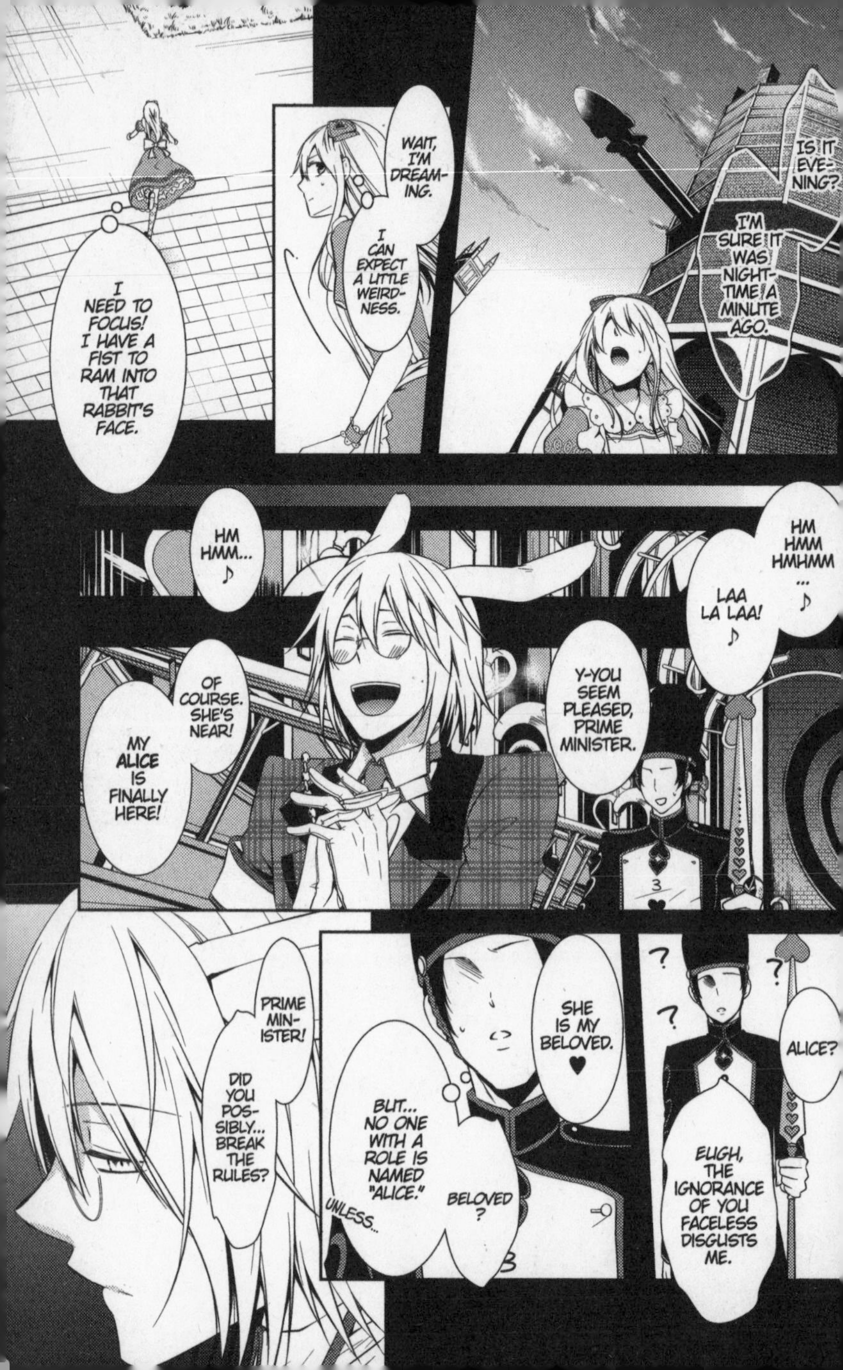
IS IT EVENING?
I'M SURE IT WAS NIGHTTIME A MINUTE AGO.
WAIT, I'M DREAMING.
I CAN EXPECT A LITTLE WEIRDNESS.
I NEED TO FOCUS! I HAVE A FIST TO RAM INTO THAT RABBIT'S FACE.
HM HMM HMHMM ... ♪
LAA LA LAA! ♪
HM HMM... ♪
Y-YOU SEEM PLEASED, PRIME MINISTER.
OF COURSE. SHE'S NEAR!
MY ALICE IS FINALLY HERE!
ALICE?
EUGH, THE IGNORANCE OF YOU FACELESS DISGUSTS ME.
SHE IS MY BELOVED. ♥
BELOVED?
BUT... NO ONE WITH A ROLE IS NAMED "ALICE."
UNLESS...
PRIME MINISTER!
DID YOU POSSIBLY... BREAK THE RULES?

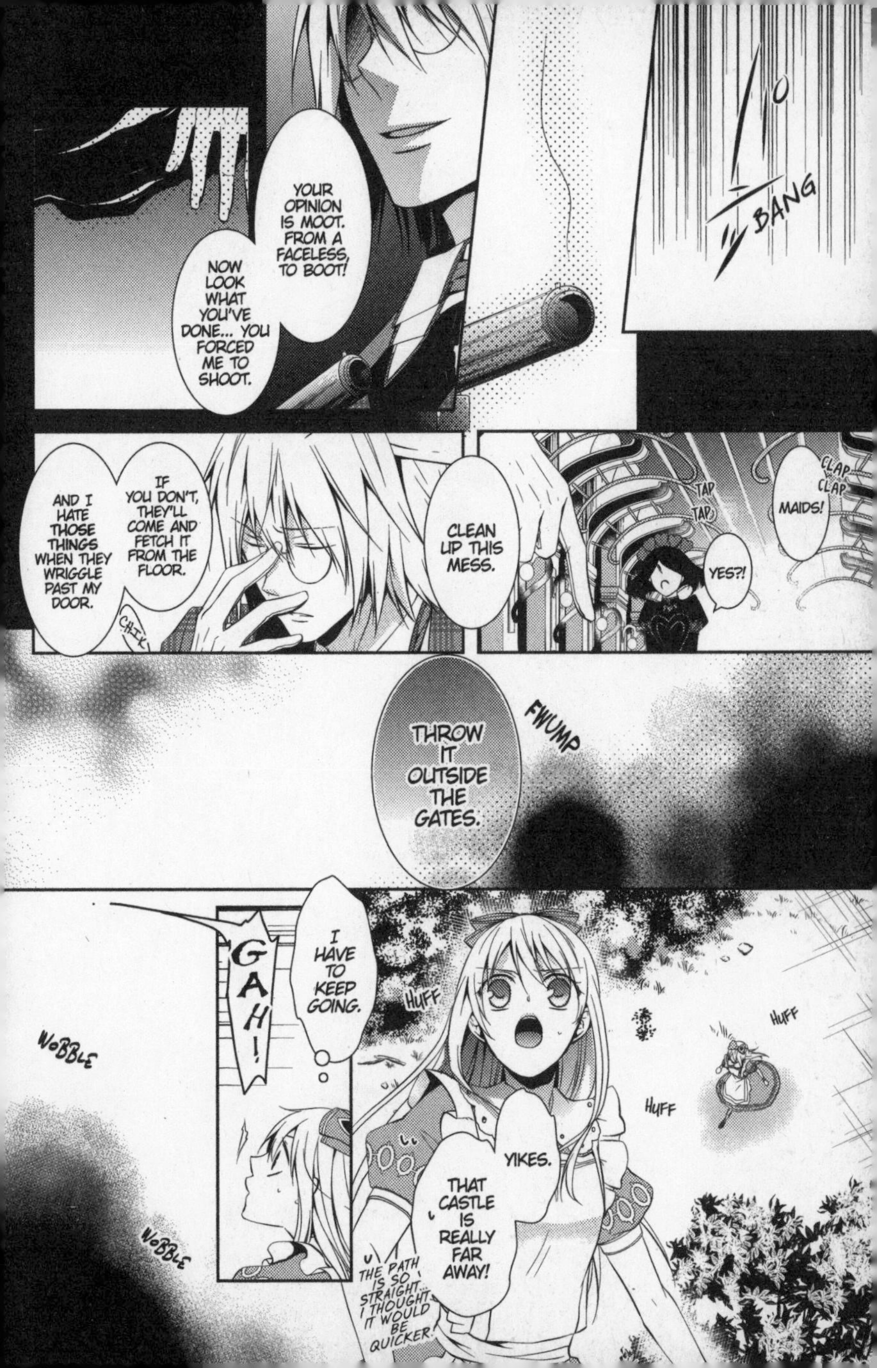
BANG
YOUR OPINION IS MOOT. FROM A FACELESS, TO BOOT!
NOW LOOK WHAT YOU'VE DONE... YOU FORCED ME TO SHOOT.
CLAP CLAP
MAIDS!
TAP TAP
YES?!
CLEAN UP THIS MESS.
IF YOU DON'T, THEY'LL COME AND FETCH IT FROM THE FLOOR.
AND I HATE THOSE THINGS WHEN THEY WRIGGLE PAST MY DOOR.
CHIK
FWUMP
THROW IT OUTSIDE THE GATES.
HUFF
HUFF
HUFF
I HAVE TO KEEP GOING.
GAH!
YIKES.
THAT CASTLE IS REALLY FAR AWAY!
THE PATH IS SO STRAIGHT... I THOUGHT IT WOULD BE QUICKER!
WOBBLE
WOBBLE

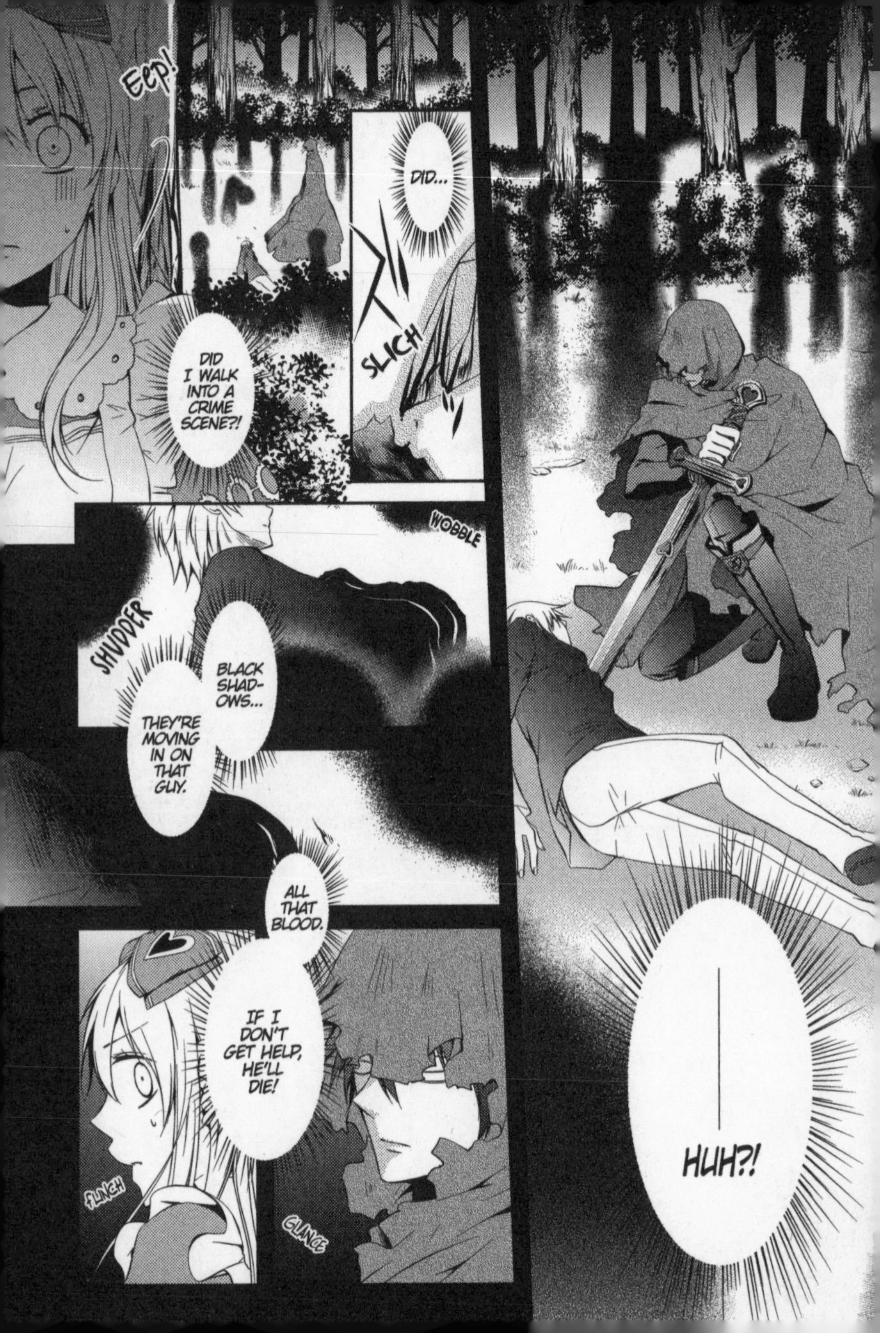HUH?!
SLICH
DID...
Eep!
DID I WALK INTO A CRIME SCENE?!
WOBBLE
SHUDDER
BLACK SHADOWS...
THEY'RE MOVING IN ON THAT GUY.
ALL THAT BLOOD.
GLANCE
IF I DON'T GET HELP, HE'LL DIE!
FLINCH

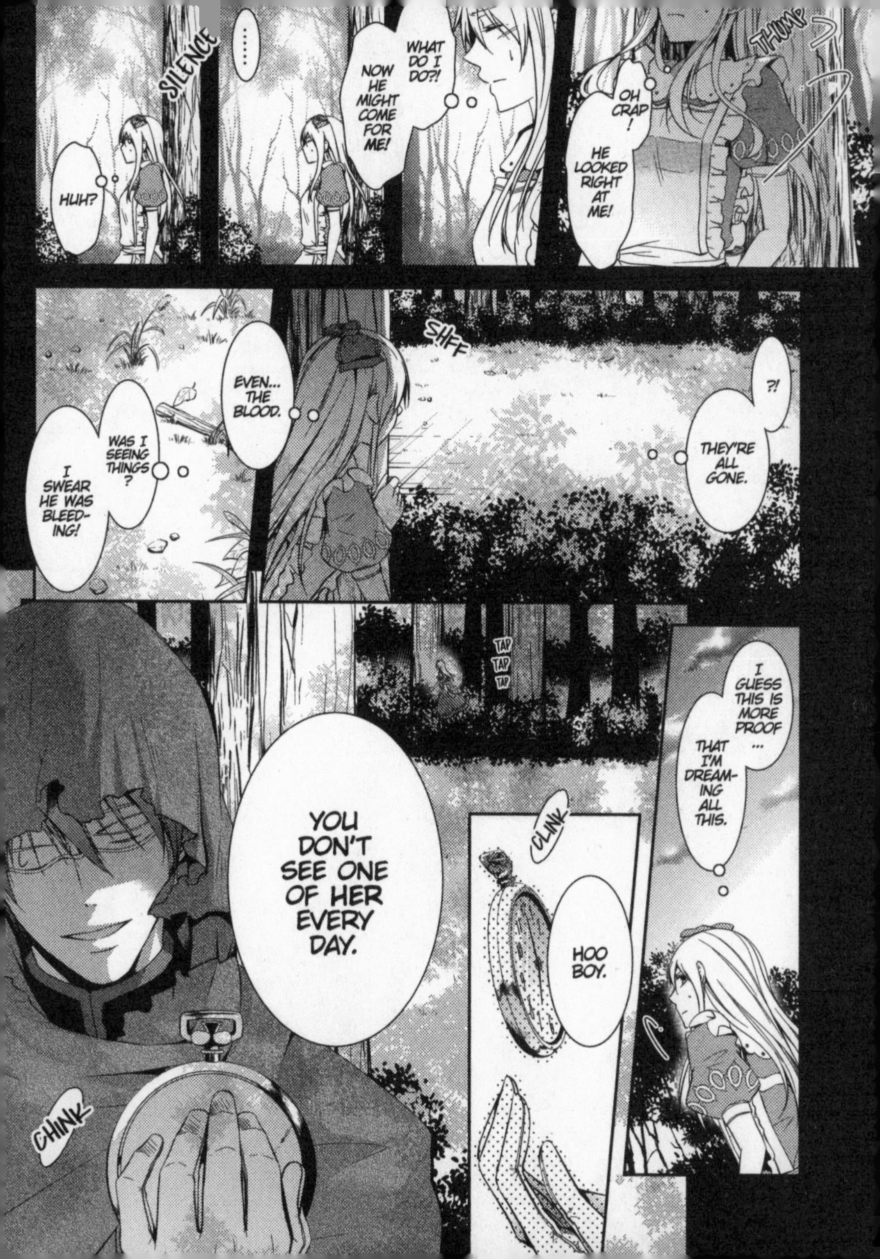
THUMP
OH CRAP! HE LOOKED RIGHT AT ME!
WHAT DO I DO?! NOW HE MIGHT COME FOR ME!
......
SILENCE
HUH?
SHFF
?!
THEY'RE ALL GONE.
EVEN... THE BLOOD.
WAS I SEEING THINGS?
I SWEAR HE WAS BLEEDING!
I GUESS THIS IS MORE PROOF...
THAT I'M DREAMING ALL THIS.
TAP TAP TAP
CLINK
HOO BOY.
YOU DON'T SEE ONE OF HER EVERY DAY.
CHINK

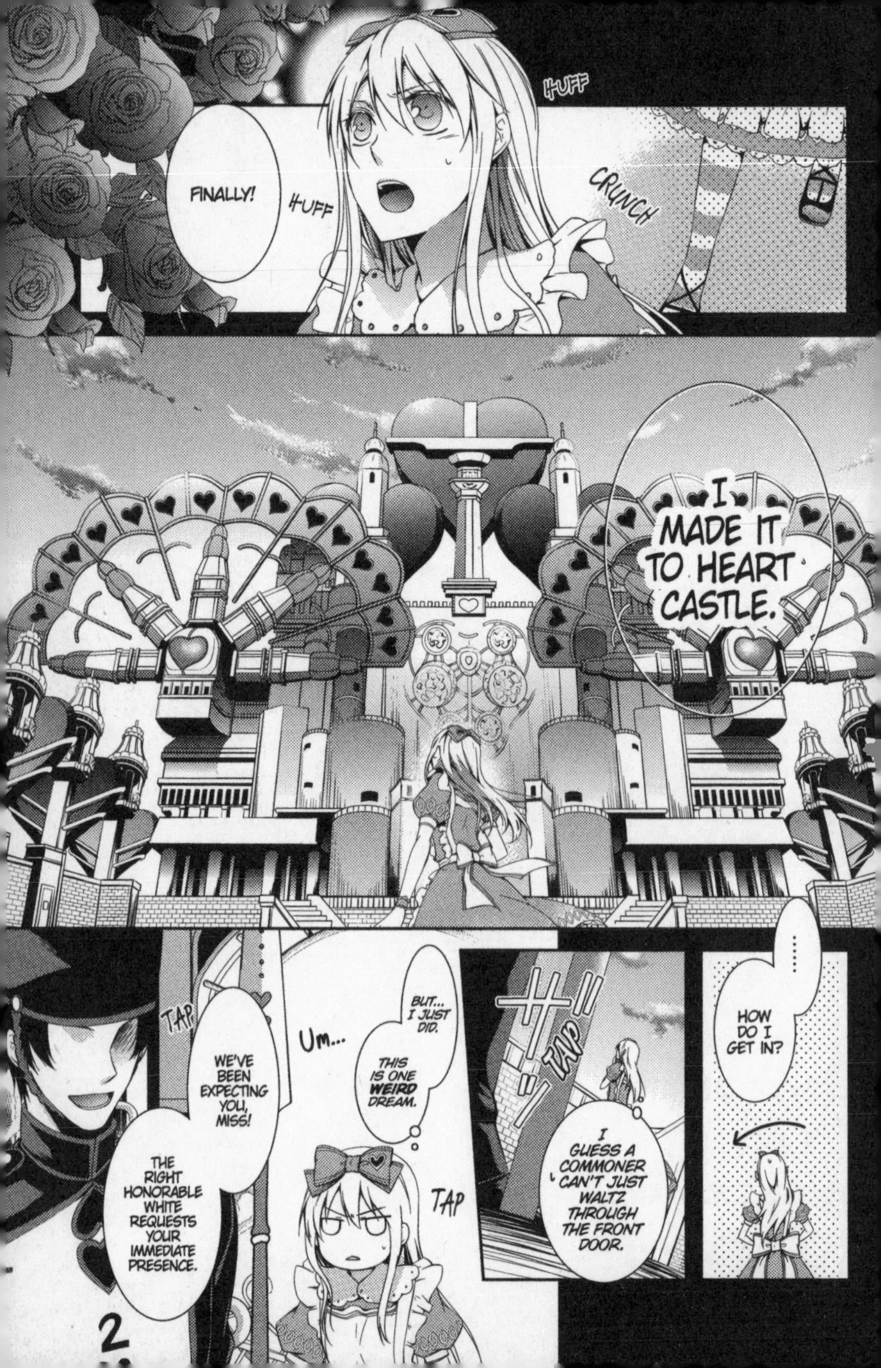
HUFF
CRUNCH
HUFF
FINALLY!
I MADE IT TO HEART CASTLE.
......
HOW DO I GET IN?
TAP
I GUESS A COMMONER CAN'T JUST WALTZ THROUGH THE FRONT DOOR.
BUT... I JUST DID.
THIS IS ONE WEIRD DREAM.
Um...
TAP
TAP
WE'VE BEEN EXPECTING YOU, MISS!
THE RIGHT HONORABLE WHITE REQUESTS YOUR IMMEDIATE PRESENCE.

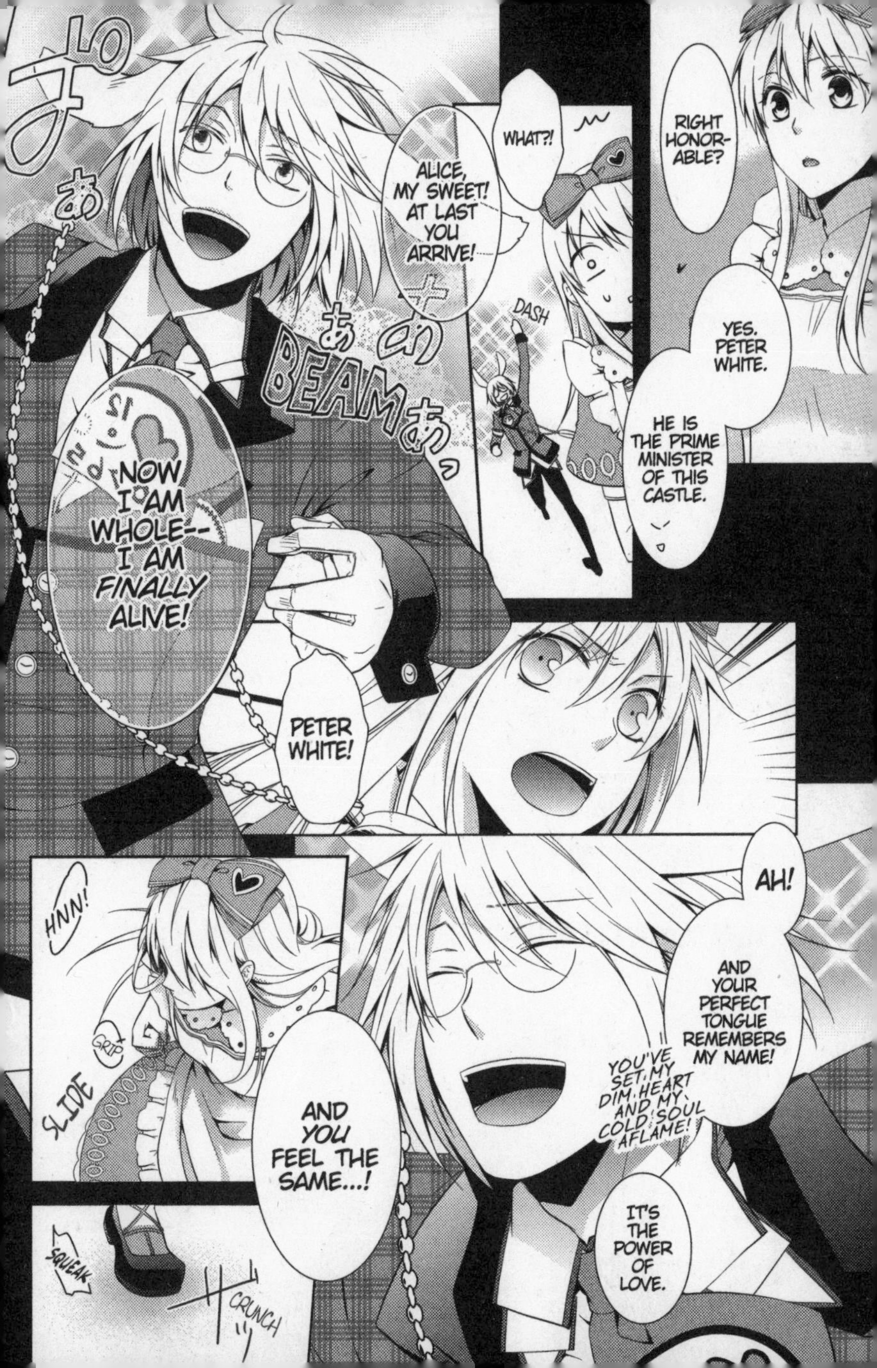
RIGHT HONORABLE?
YES. PETER WHITE.
HE IS THE PRIME MINISTER OF THIS CASTLE.
WHAT?!
ALICE, MY SWEET! AT LAST YOU ARRIVE!
DASH
BEAM
NOW I AM WHOLE-- I AM FINALLY ALIVE!
12
PETER WHITE!
AH!
AND YOUR PERFECT TONGUE REMEMBERS MY NAME!
YOU'VE SET MY DIM HEART AND MY COLD SOUL AFLAME!
AND YOU FEEL THE SAME...!
IT'S THE POWER OF LOVE.
HNN!
GRIP
SLIDE
SQUEAK
CRUNCH

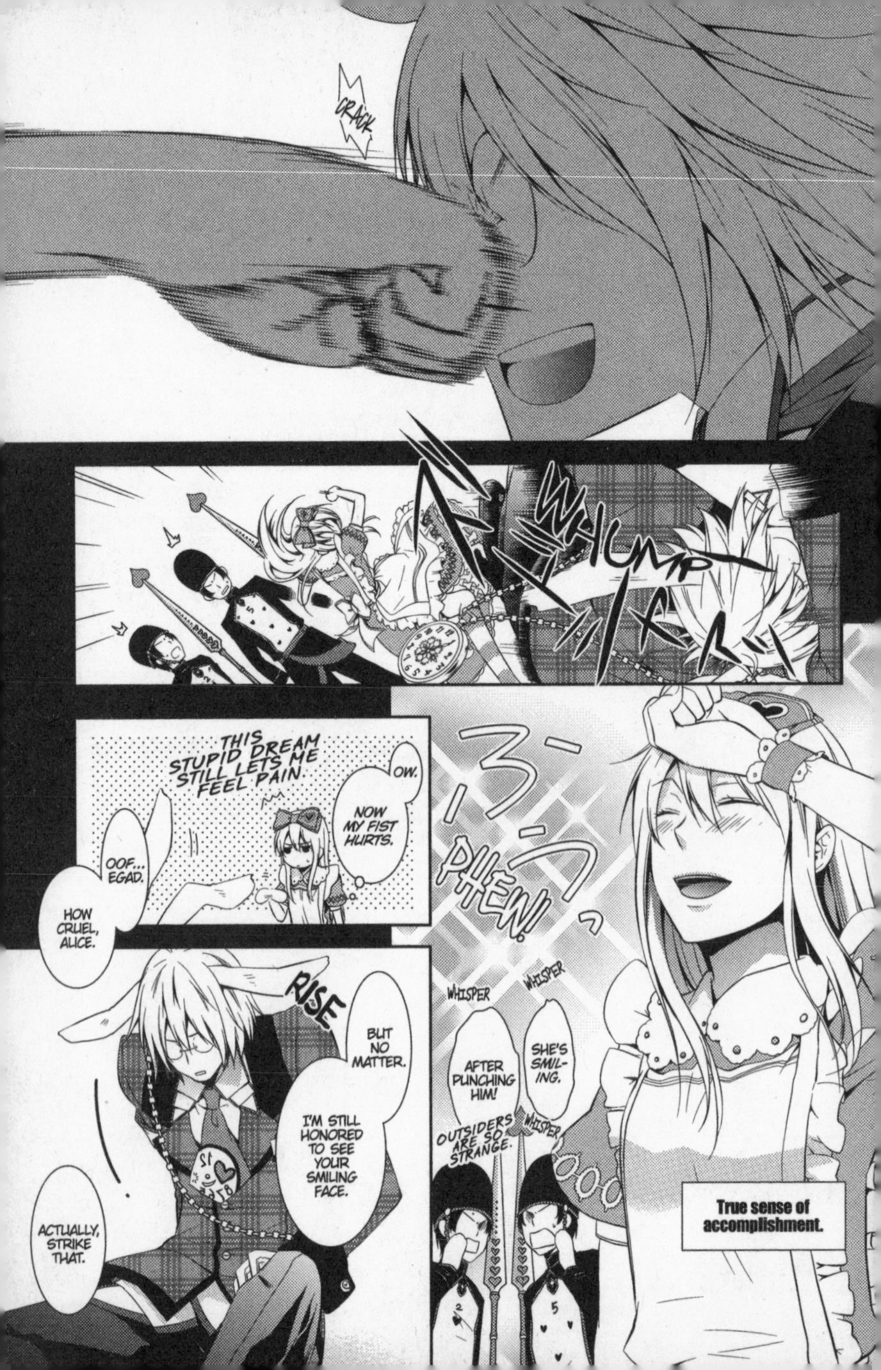
CRACK
WHUMP
PHEW!
WHISPER
SHE'S SMIL-ING.
WHISPER
AFTER PUNCHING HIM!
WHISPER
OUTSIDERS ARE SO STRANGE.
True sense of accomplishment.
OW.
NOW MY FIST HURTS.
THIS STUPID DREAM STILL LETS ME FEEL PAIN.
OOF... EGAD.
HOW CRUEL, ALICE.
RISE
BUT NO MATTER.
I'M STILL HONORED TO SEE YOUR SMILING FACE.
ACTUALLY, STRIKE THAT.

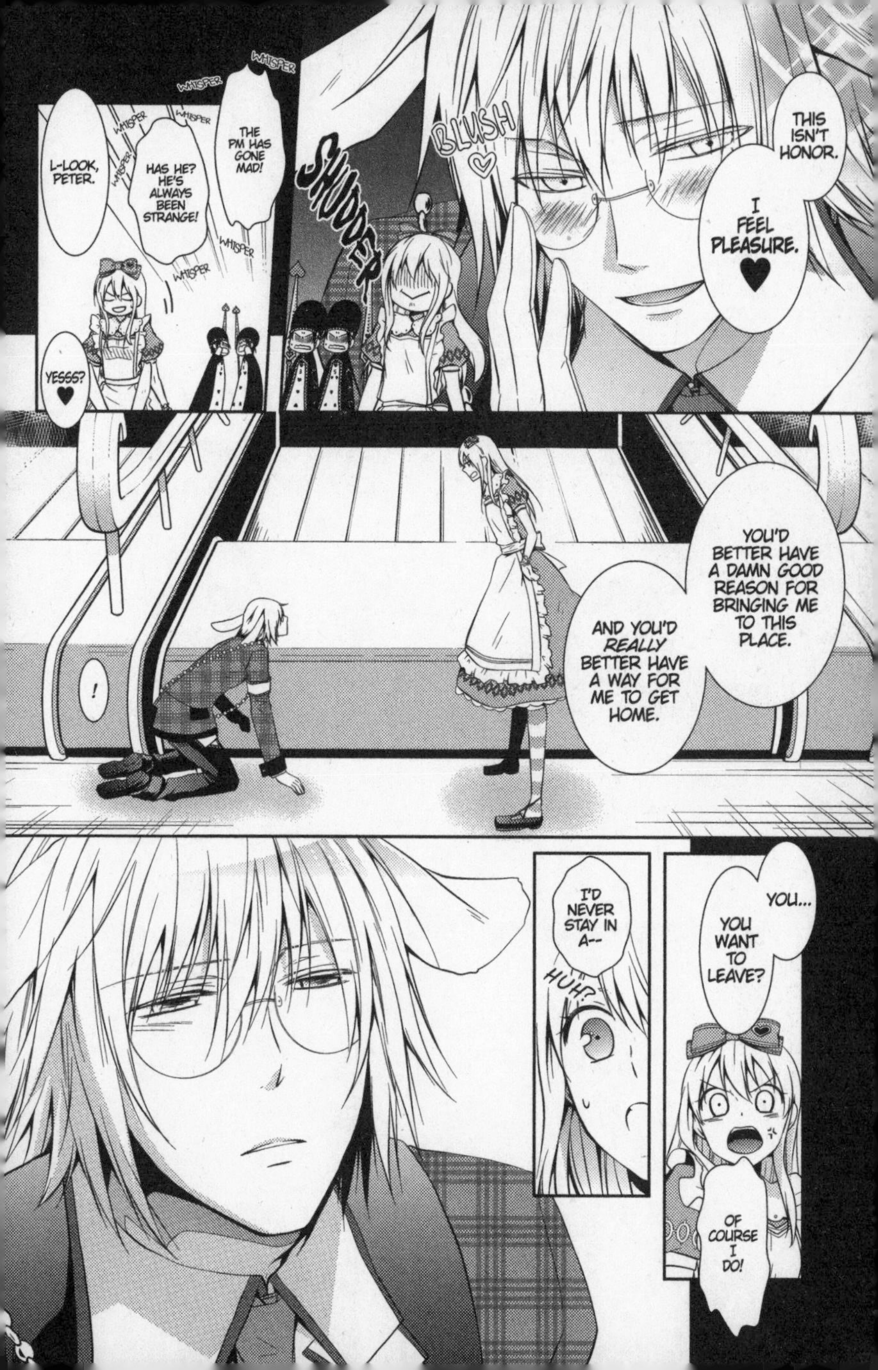
THIS ISN'T HONOR.
I FEEL PLEASURE. ♥
BLUSH ♥
SHUDDER
WHISPER
THE PM HAS GONE MAD!
WHISPER
WHISPER
HAS HE? HE'S ALWAYS BEEN STRANGE!
WHISPER
WHISPER
WHISPER
WHISPER
L-LOOK, PETER.
YESSS? ♥
YOU'D BETTER HAVE A DAMN GOOD REASON FOR BRINGING ME TO THIS PLACE.
AND YOU'D *REALLY* BETTER HAVE A WAY FOR ME TO GET HOME.
!
YOU...
YOU WANT TO LEAVE?
OF COURSE I DO!
I'D NEVER STAY IN A--
HUH?

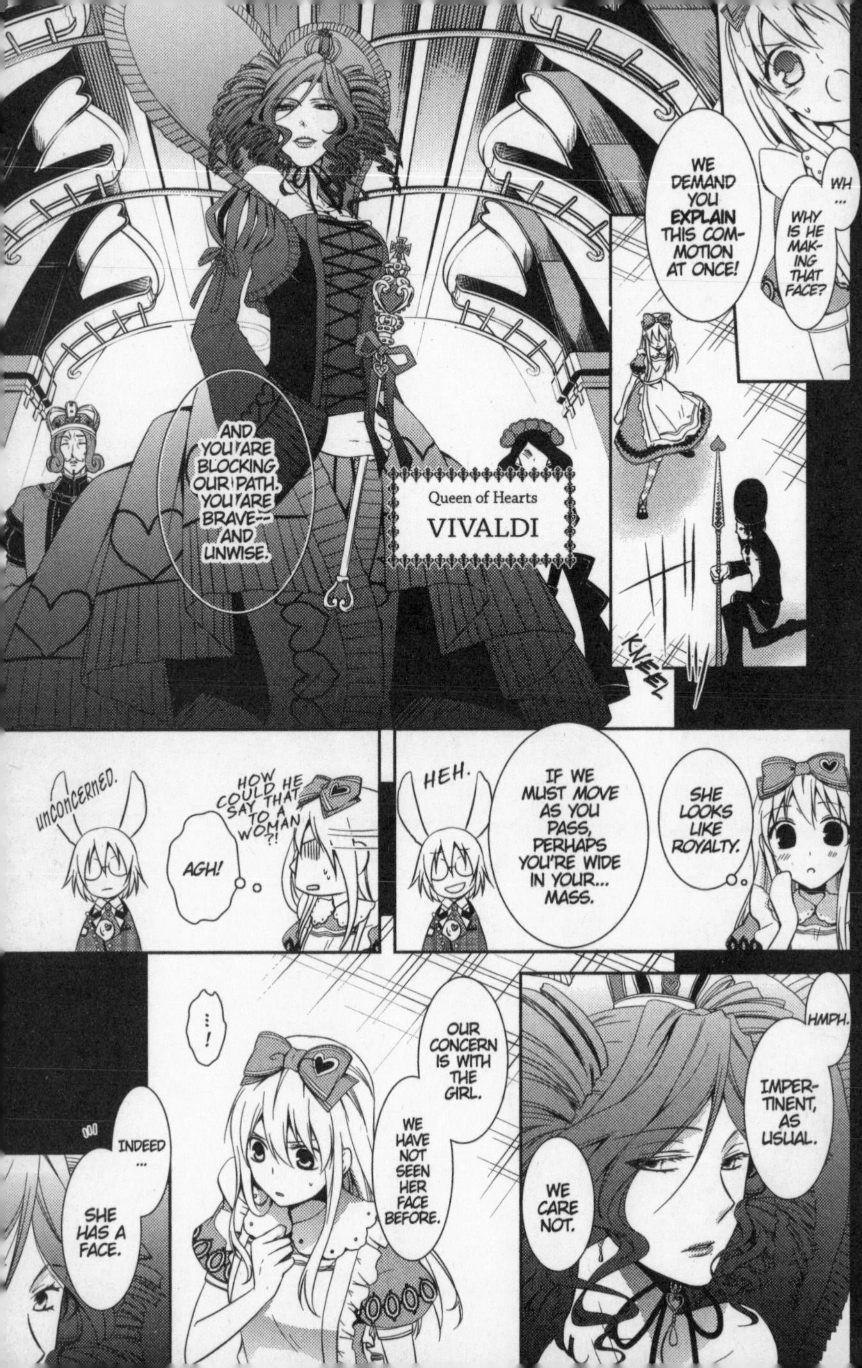
WH... WHY IS HE MAKING THAT FACE?
WE DEMAND YOU EXPLAIN THIS COMMOTION AT ONCE!
KNEEL
Queen of Hearts
VIVALDI
AND YOU ARE BLOCKING OUR PATH. YOU ARE BRAVE-- AND UNWISE.
SHE LOOKS LIKE ROYALTY.
IF WE MUST MOVE AS YOU PASS, PERHAPS YOU'RE WIDE IN YOUR... MASS.
HEH.
HOW COULD HE SAY THAT TO A WOMAN?!
AGH!
UNCONCERNED.
HMPH.
IMPERTINENT, AS USUAL.
WE CARE NOT.
OUR CONCERN IS WITH THE GIRL.
WE HAVE NOT SEEN HER FACE BEFORE.
...!
INDEED...
SHE HAS A FACE.

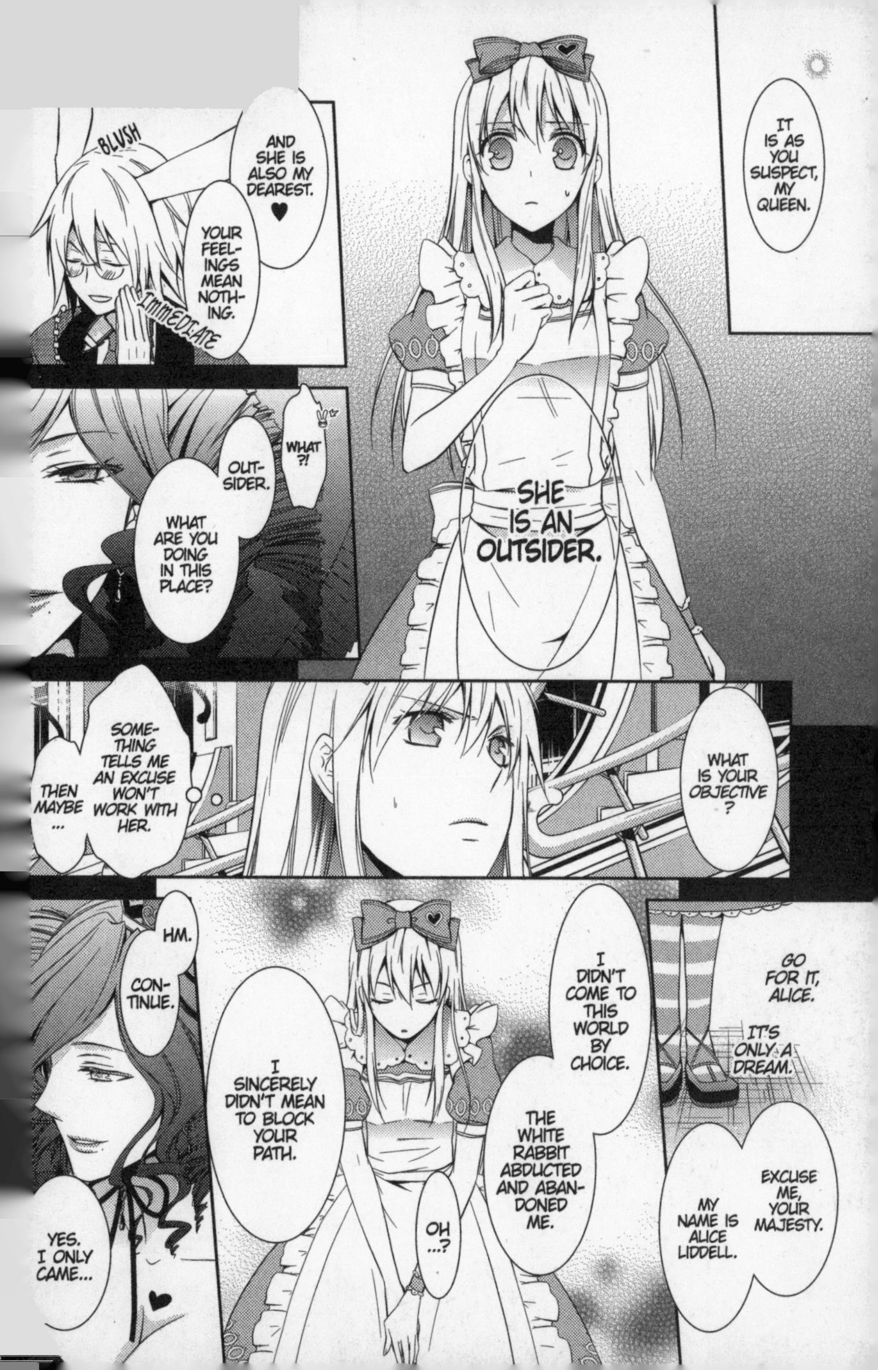
IT IS AS YOU SUSPECT, MY QUEEN.
SHE IS AN OUTSIDER.
AND SHE IS ALSO MY DEAREST.
BLUSH
YOUR FEEL-INGS MEAN NOTH-ING.
IMMEDIATE
WHAT ?!
OUT-SIDER.
WHAT ARE YOU DOING IN THIS PLACE?
WHAT IS YOUR OBJECTIVE ?
SOME-THING TELLS ME AN EXCUSE WON'T WORK WITH HER.
THEN MAYBE ...
GO FOR IT, ALICE.
IT'S ONLY A DREAM.
EXCUSE ME, YOUR MAJESTY.
MY NAME IS ALICE LIDDELL.
I DIDN'T COME TO THIS WORLD BY CHOICE.
THE WHITE RABBIT ABDUCTED AND ABAN-DONED ME.
OH ...?
I SINCERELY DIDN'T MEAN TO BLOCK YOUR PATH.
HM.
CON-TINUE.
YES. I ONLY CAME...

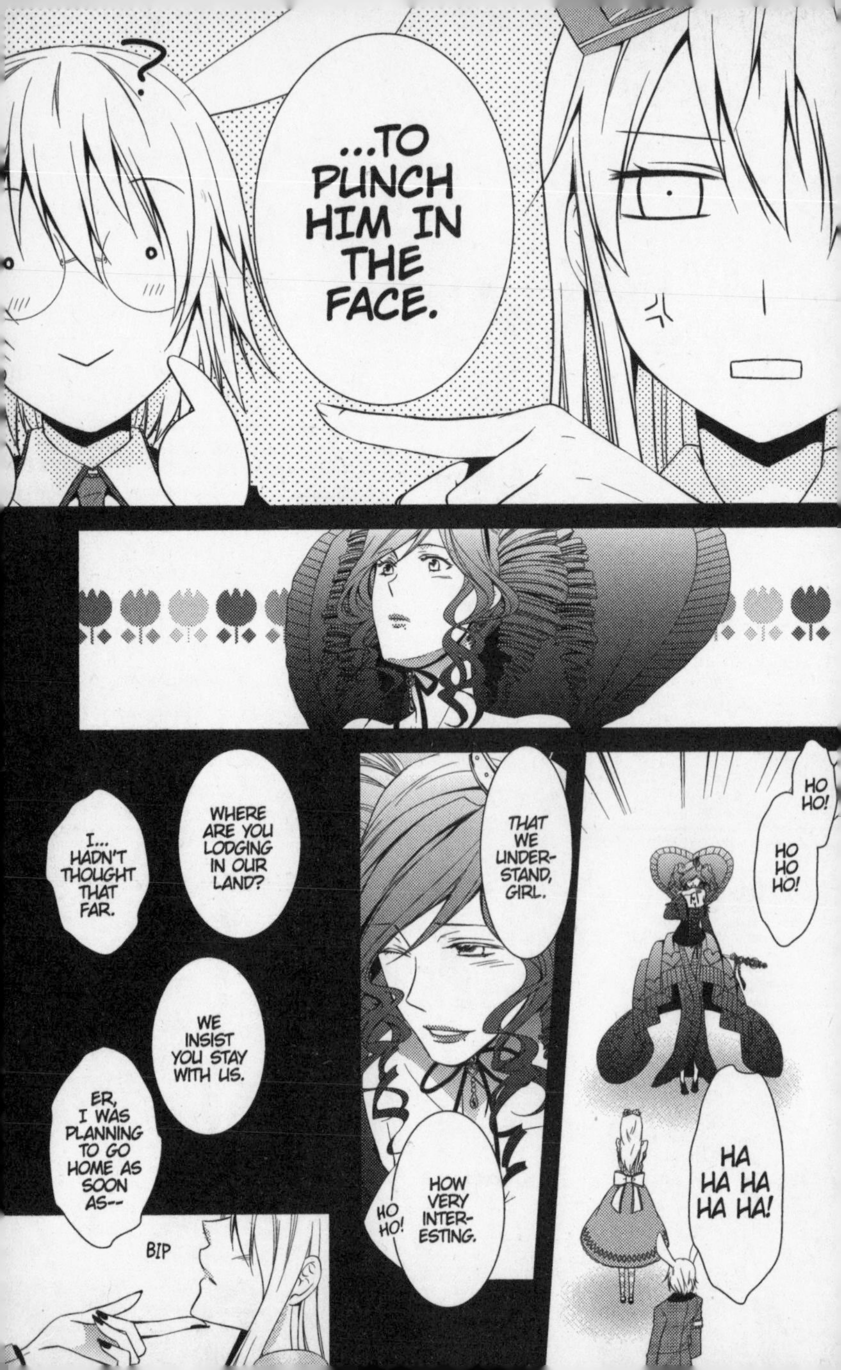
...TO PUNCH HIM IN THE FACE.
HO HO!
HO HO HO!
HA HA HA HA HA!
THAT WE UNDER-STAND, GIRL.
HOW VERY INTER-ESTING.
HO HO!
WHERE ARE YOU LODGING IN OUR LAND?
I... HADN'T THOUGHT THAT FAR.
WE INSIST YOU STAY WITH US.
ER, I WAS PLANNING TO GO HOME AS SOON AS--
BIP

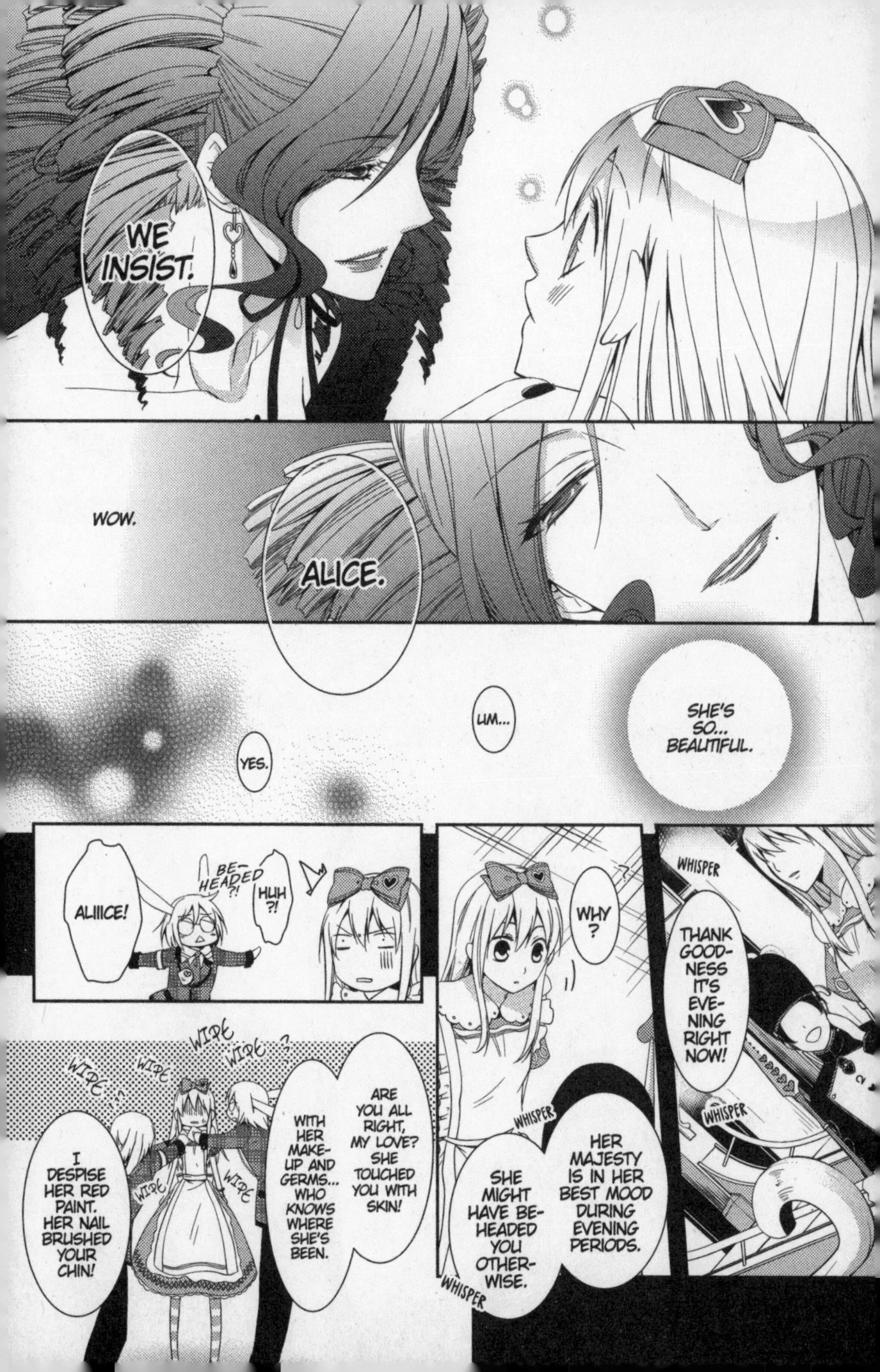
WE INSIST.
ALICE.
WOW.
SHE'S SO... BEAUTIFUL.
UM...
YES.
WHISPER
THANK GOODNESS IT'S EVENING RIGHT NOW!
WHISPER
HER MAJESTY IS IN HER BEST MOOD DURING EVENING PERIODS.
WHISPER
SHE MIGHT HAVE BE-HEADED YOU OTHER-WISE.
WHISPER
WHY?
HUH?!
BE-HEADED?!
ALIIICE!
WIPE
WIPE
ARE YOU ALL RIGHT, MY LOVE? SHE TOUCHED YOU WITH SKIN!
WITH HER MAKE-UP AND GERMS... WHO KNOWS WHERE SHE'S BEEN.
WIPE
WIPE
WIPE
WIPE
I DESPISE HER RED PAINT. HER NAIL BRUSHED YOUR CHIN!

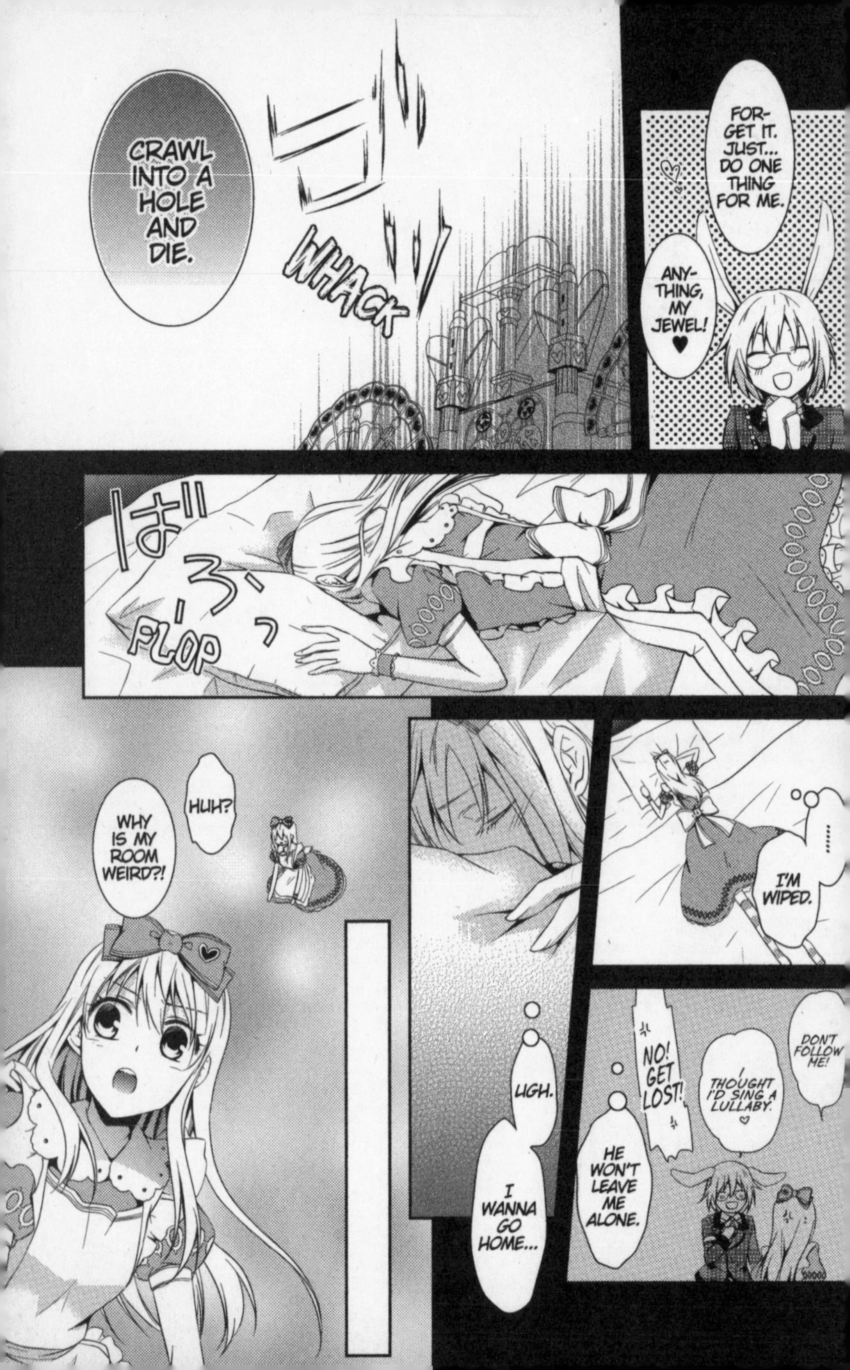
FOR-GET IT. JUST... DO ONE THING FOR ME.
ANY-THING, MY JEWEL! ♥
CRAWL INTO A HOLE AND DIE.
WHACK
FLOP
......
I'M WIPED.
DON'T FOLLOW ME!
I THOUGHT I'D SING A LULLABY. ♡
NO! GET LOST!
HE WON'T LEAVE ME ALONE.
UGH.
I WANNA GO HOME...
HUH?
WHY IS MY ROOM WEIRD?!

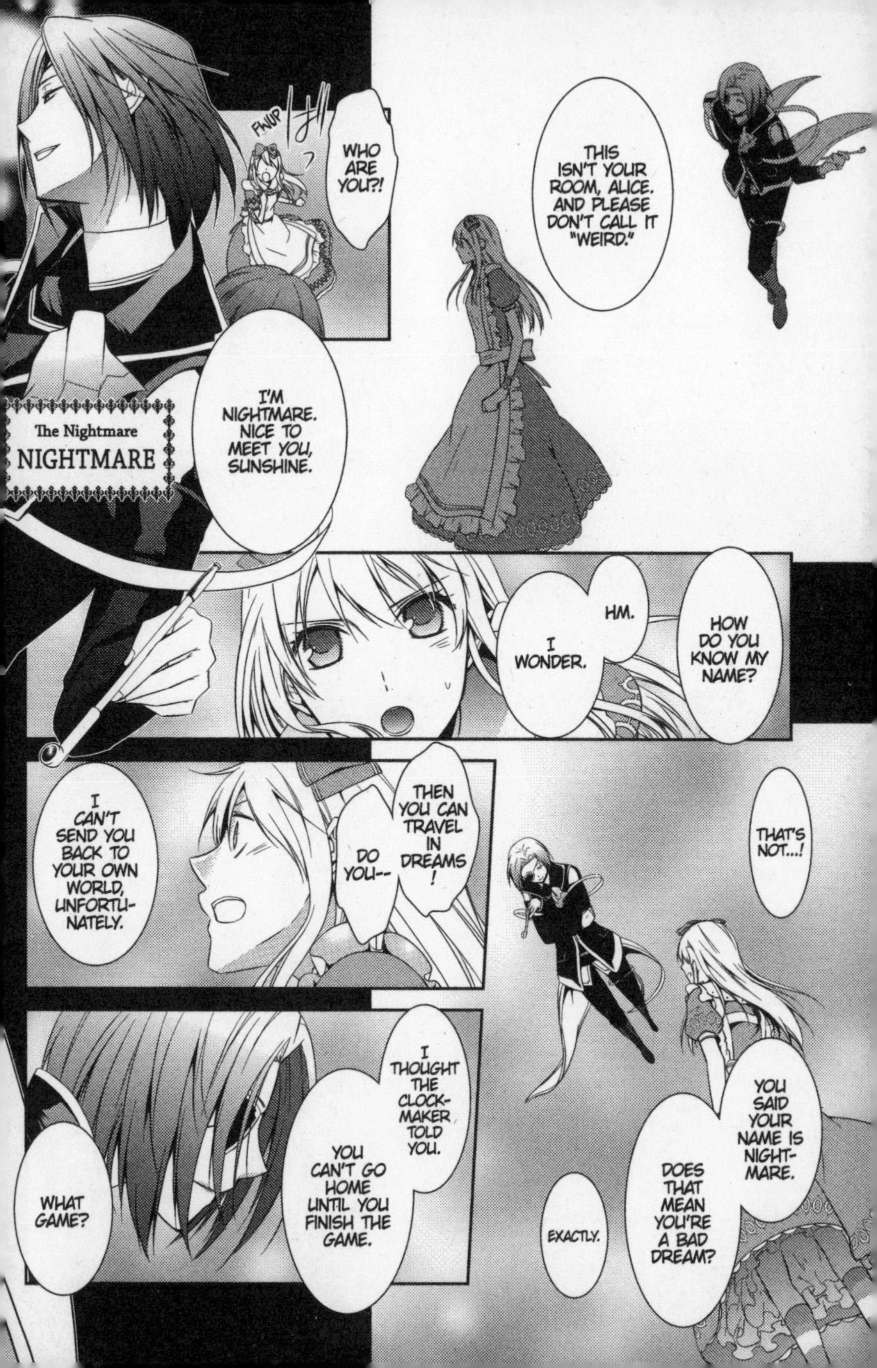
THIS ISN'T YOUR ROOM, ALICE. AND PLEASE DON'T CALL IT "WEIRD."
FWUP
WHO ARE YOU?!
The Nightmare
NIGHTMARE
I'M NIGHTMARE. NICE TO MEET YOU, SUNSHINE.
HOW DO YOU KNOW MY NAME?
HM.
I WONDER.
THAT'S NOT...!
YOU SAID YOUR NAME IS NIGHT-MARE.
DOES THAT MEAN YOU'RE A BAD DREAM?
EXACTLY.
THEN YOU CAN TRAVEL IN DREAMS!
DO YOU--
I CAN'T SEND YOU BACK TO YOUR OWN WORLD, UNFORTU-NATELY.
I THOUGHT THE CLOCK-MAKER TOLD YOU.
YOU CAN'T GO HOME UNTIL YOU FINISH THE GAME.
WHAT GAME?

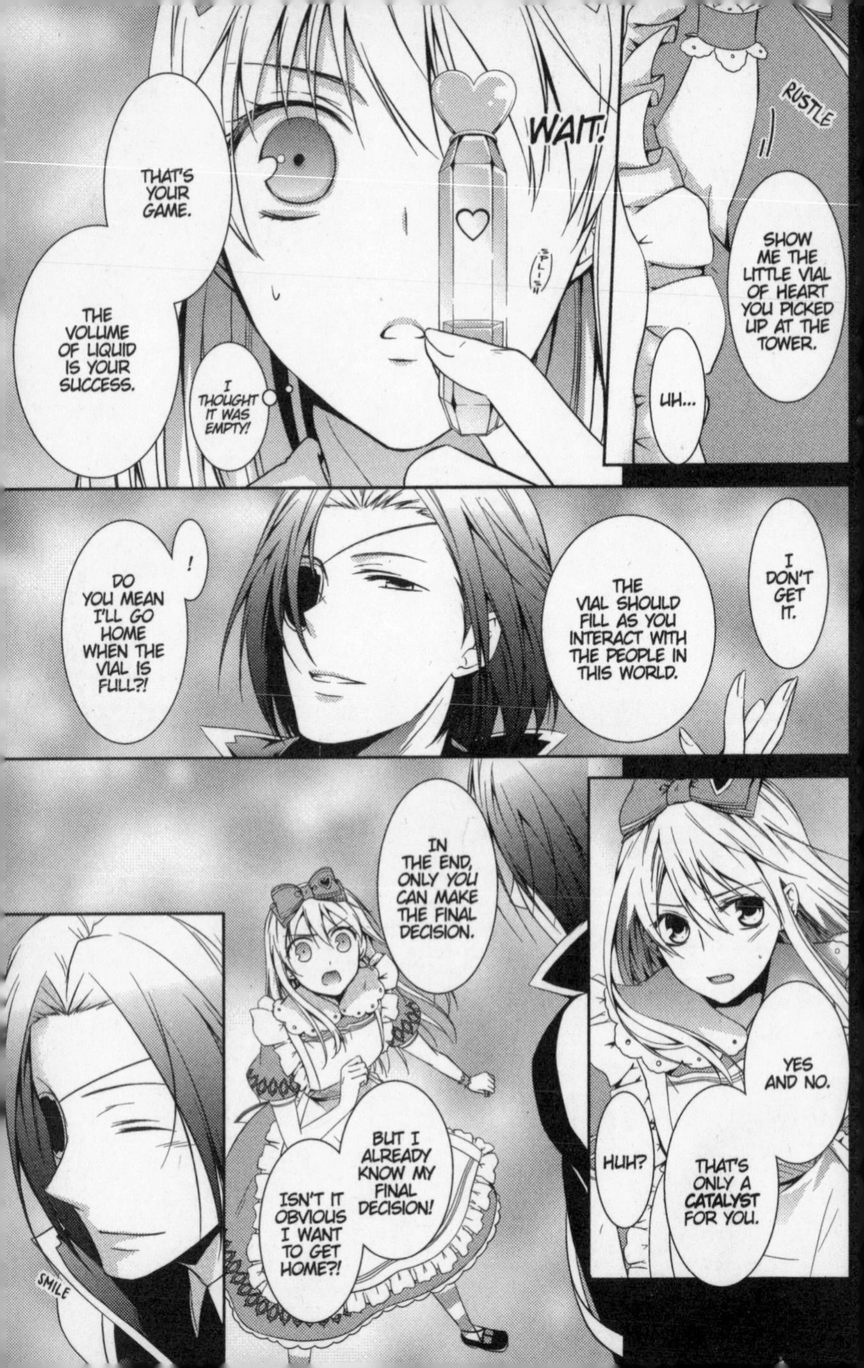
RUSTLE
SHOW ME THE LITTLE VIAL OF HEART YOU PICKED UP AT THE TOWER.
UH...
WAIT!
SPLISH
I THOUGHT IT WAS EMPTY!
THAT'S YOUR GAME.
THE VOLUME OF LIQUID IS YOUR SUCCESS.
I DON'T GET IT.
THE VIAL SHOULD FILL AS YOU INTERACT WITH THE PEOPLE IN THIS WORLD.
!
DO YOU MEAN I'LL GO HOME WHEN THE VIAL IS FULL?!
YES AND NO.
HUH?
THAT'S ONLY A CATALYST FOR YOU.
IN THE END, ONLY YOU CAN MAKE THE FINAL DECISION.
BUT I ALREADY KNOW MY FINAL DECISION!
ISN'T IT OBVIOUS I WANT TO GET HOME?!
SMILE

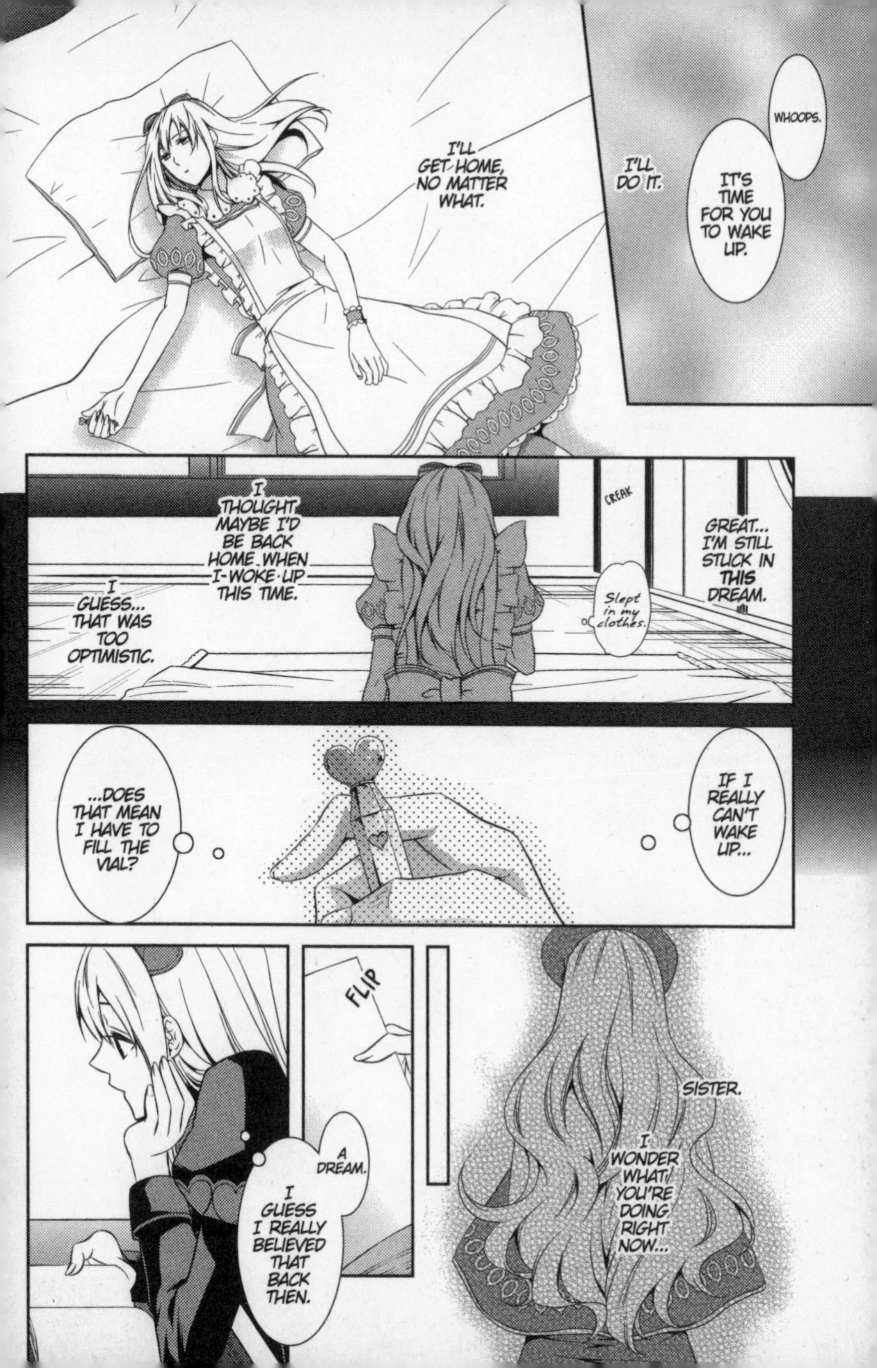
WHOOPS.
IT'S TIME FOR YOU TO WAKE UP.
I'LL DO IT.
I'LL GET HOME, NO MATTER WHAT.
CREAK
GREAT... I'M STILL STUCK IN THIS DREAM.
Slept in my clothes.
I THOUGHT MAYBE I'D BE BACK HOME WHEN I WOKE UP THIS TIME.
I GUESS... THAT WAS TOO OPTIMISTIC.
IF I REALLY CAN'T WAKE UP...
...DOES THAT MEAN I HAVE TO FILL THE VIAL?
SISTER.
I WONDER WHAT YOU'RE DOING RIGHT NOW...
FLIP
A DREAM.
I GUESS I REALLY BELIEVED THAT BACK THEN.

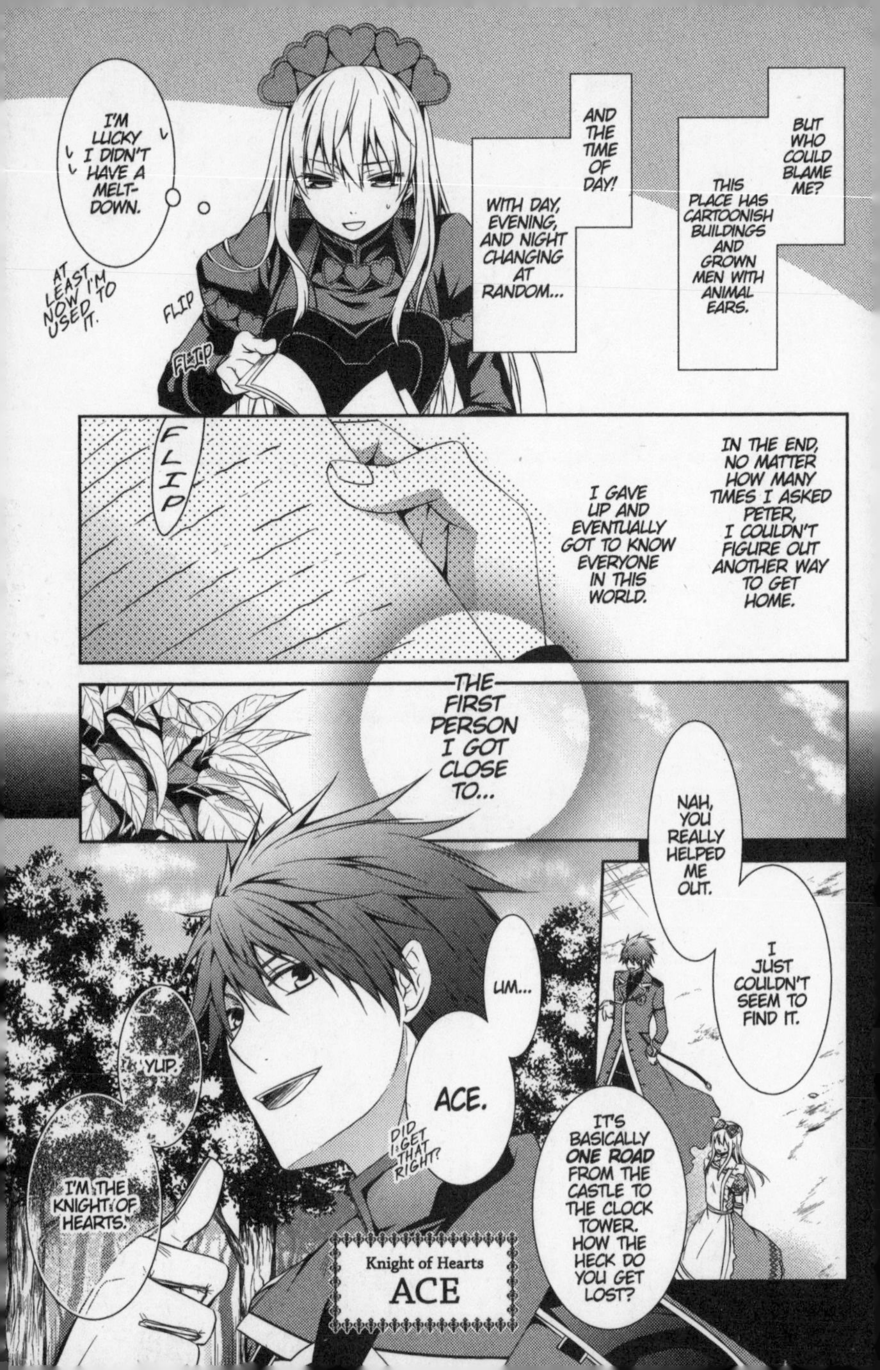
BUT WHO COULD BLAME ME?
THIS PLACE HAS CARTOONISH BUILDINGS AND GROWN MEN WITH ANIMAL EARS.
AND THE TIME OF DAY!
WITH DAY, EVENING, AND NIGHT CHANGING AT RANDOM...
I'M LUCKY I DIDN'T HAVE A MELT-DOWN.
AT LEAST NOW I'M USED TO IT.
FLIP
FLIP
IN THE END, NO MATTER HOW MANY TIMES I ASKED PETER, I COULDN'T FIGURE OUT ANOTHER WAY TO GET HOME.
I GAVE UP AND EVENTUALLY GOT TO KNOW EVERYONE IN THIS WORLD.
FLIP
THE FIRST PERSON I GOT CLOSE TO...
NAH, YOU REALLY HELPED ME OUT.
I JUST COULDN'T SEEM TO FIND IT.
IT'S BASICALLY ONE ROAD FROM THE CASTLE TO THE CLOCK TOWER. HOW THE HECK DO YOU GET LOST?
UM...
ACE.
DID I GET THAT RIGHT?
YUP.
I'M THE KNIGHT OF HEARTS.
Knight of Hearts
ACE

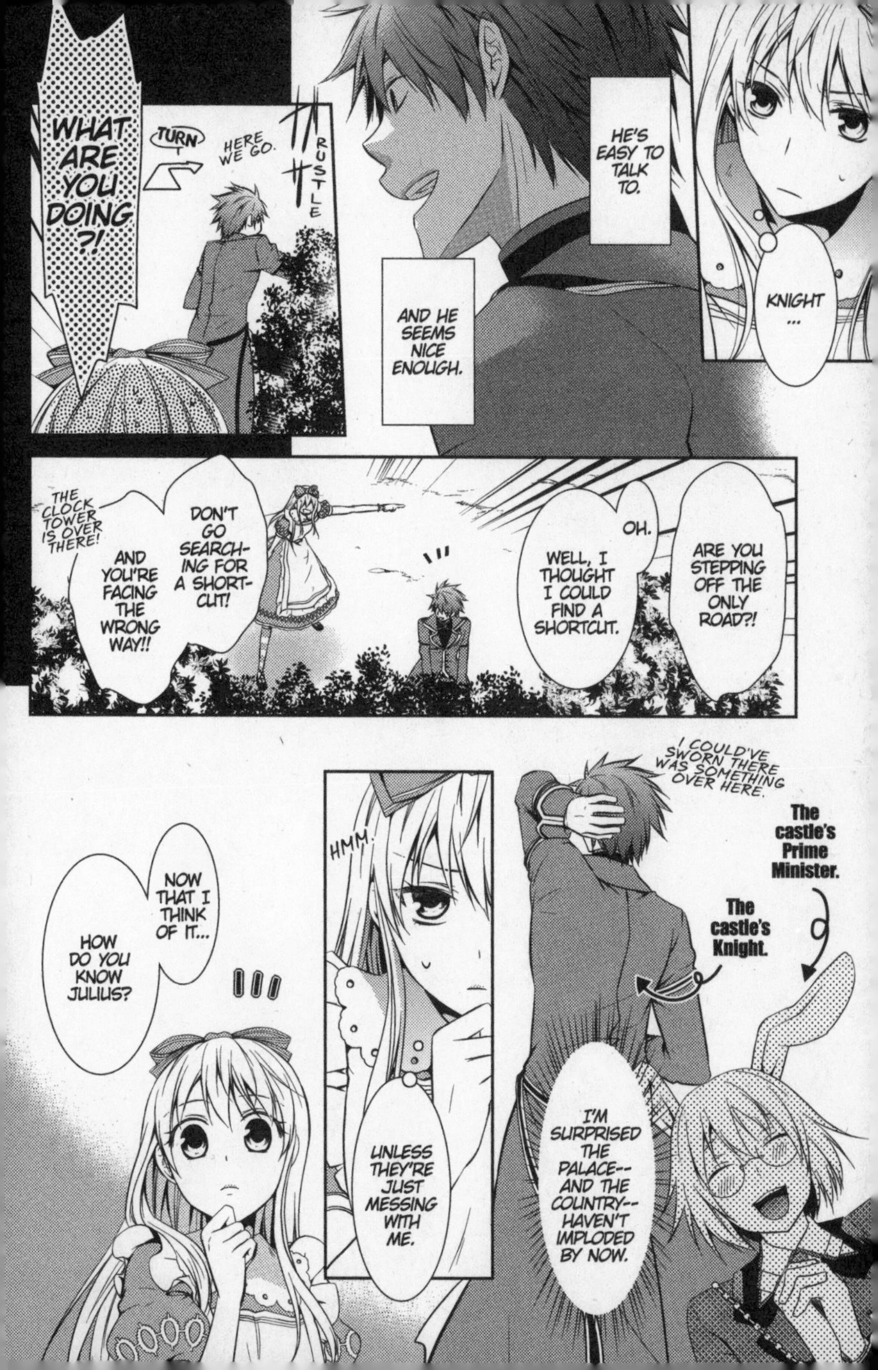
KNIGHT...
HE'S EASY TO TALK TO.
AND HE SEEMS NICE ENOUGH.
RUSTLE
HERE WE GO.
TURN
WHAT ARE YOU DOING?!
ARE YOU STEPPING OFF THE ONLY ROAD?!
OH.
WELL, I THOUGHT I COULD FIND A SHORTCUT.
DON'T GO SEARCHING FOR A SHORTCUT!
AND YOU'RE FACING THE WRONG WAY!!
THE CLOCK TOWER IS OVER THERE!
I COULD'VE SWORN THERE WAS SOMETHING OVER HERE.
The castle's Prime Minister.
The castle's Knight.
I'M SURPRISED THE PALACE-- AND THE COUNTRY-- HAVEN'T IMPLODED BY NOW.
HMM.
UNLESS THEY'RE JUST MESSING WITH ME.
NOW THAT I THINK OF IT...
HOW DO YOU KNOW JULIUS?

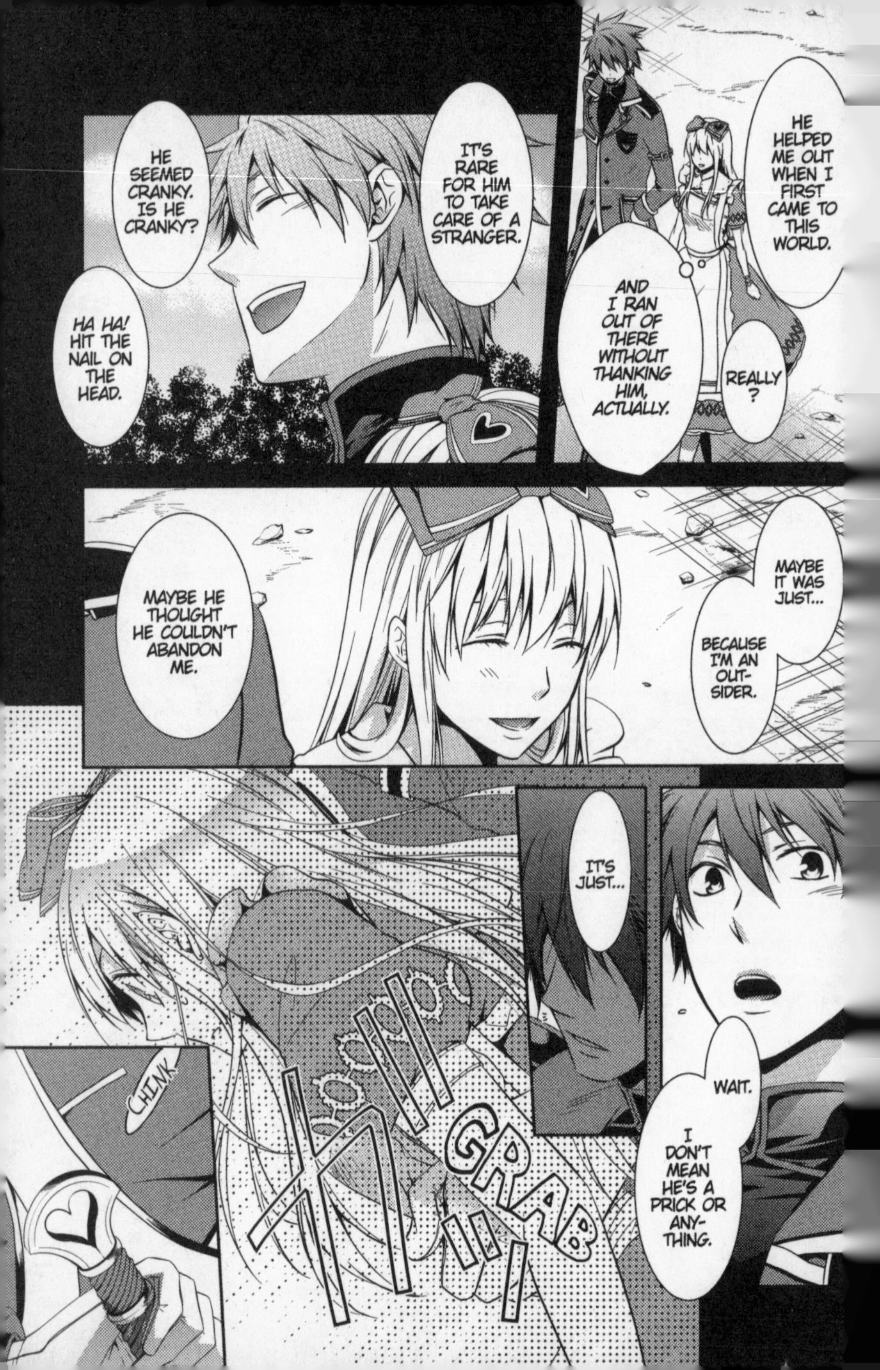
HE HELPED ME OUT WHEN I FIRST CAME TO THIS WORLD.
REALLY?
AND I RAN OUT OF THERE WITHOUT THANKING HIM, ACTUALLY.
IT'S RARE FOR HIM TO TAKE CARE OF A STRANGER.
HE SEEMED CRANKY. IS HE CRANKY?
HA HA! HIT THE NAIL ON THE HEAD.
MAYBE IT WAS JUST...
BECAUSE I'M AN OUT-SIDER.
MAYBE HE THOUGHT HE COULDN'T ABANDON ME.
I DON'T MEAN HE'S A PRICK OR ANY-THING.
IT'S JUST...
WAIT.
GRAB
CHINK

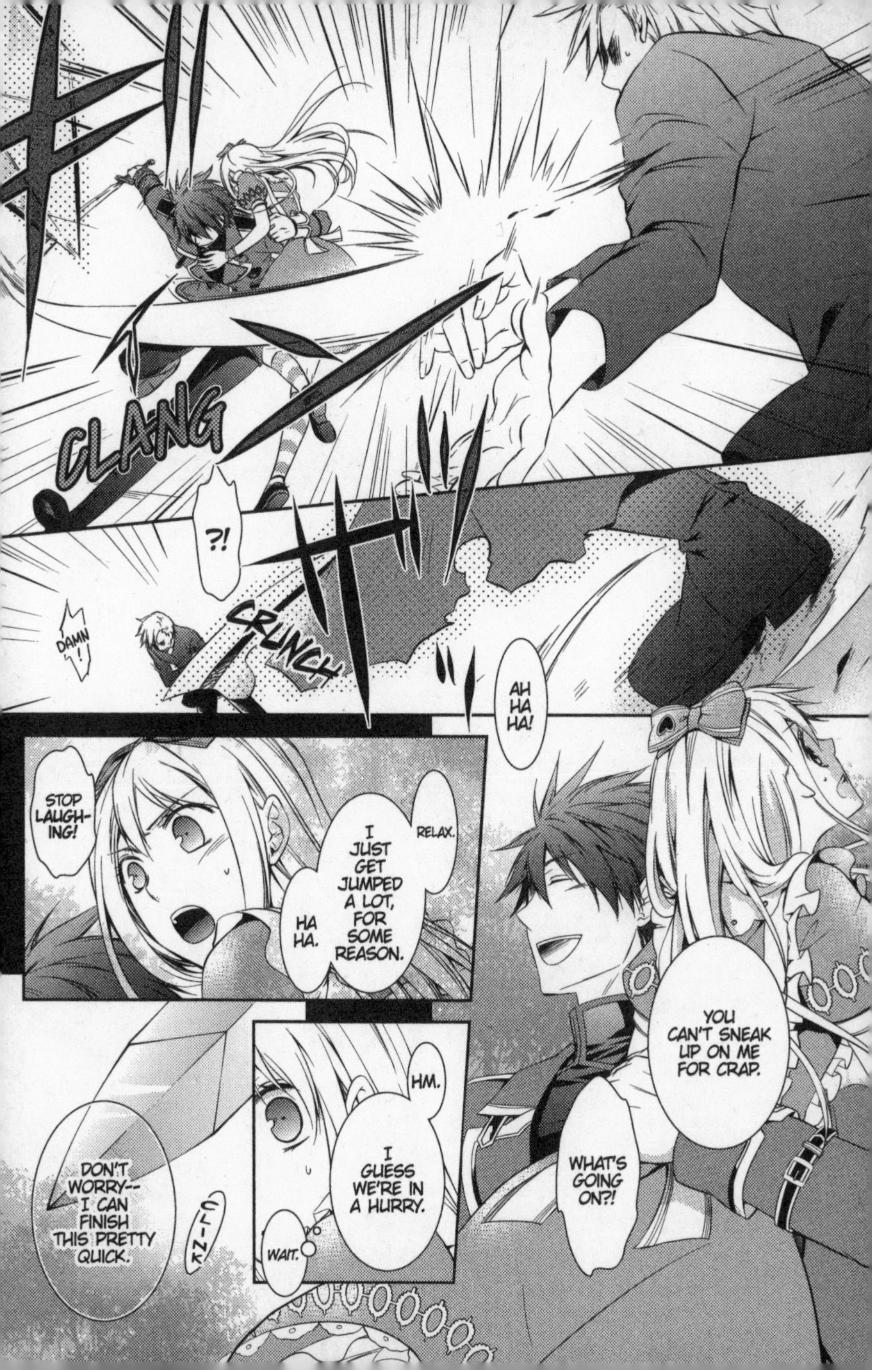
CLANG
?!
CRUNCH
DAMN!
AH HA HA!
YOU CAN'T SNEAK UP ON ME FOR CRAP.
WHAT'S GOING ON?!
STOP LAUGHING!
RELAX.
I JUST GET JUMPED A LOT, FOR SOME REASON.
HA HA.
HM.
I GUESS WE'RE IN A HURRY.
WAIT.
DON'T WORRY-- I CAN FINISH THIS PRETTY QUICK.
CLINK

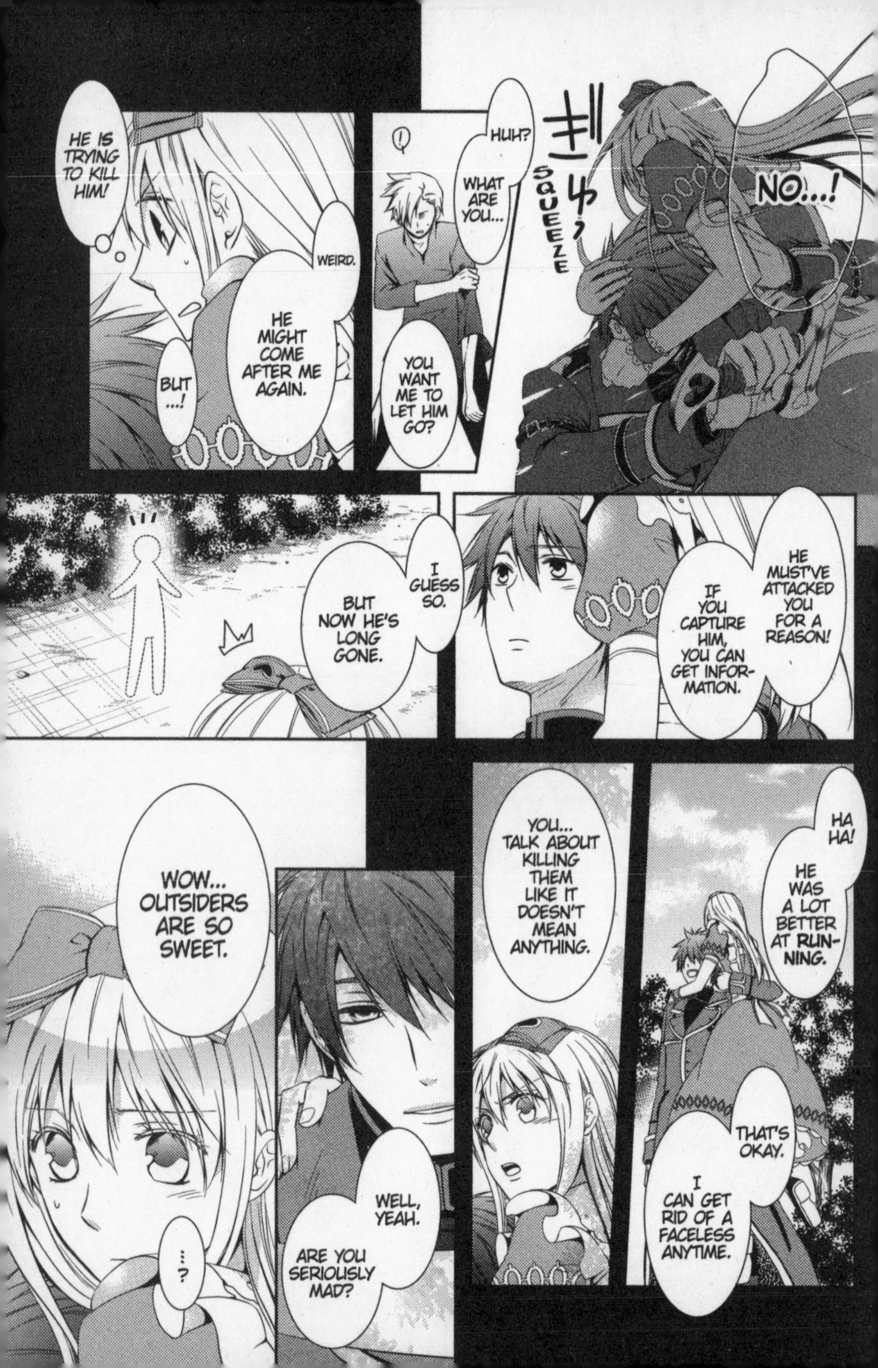
NO...!
SQUEEZE
HUH?
WHAT ARE YOU...
!
WEIRD.
HE MIGHT COME AFTER ME AGAIN.
YOU WANT ME TO LET HIM GO?
HE IS TRYING TO KILL HIM!
BUT ...!
HE MUST'VE ATTACKED YOU FOR A REASON!
IF YOU CAPTURE HIM, YOU CAN GET INFORMATION.
I GUESS SO.
BUT NOW HE'S LONG GONE.
HA HA! HE WAS A LOT BETTER AT RUNNING.
THAT'S OKAY.
I CAN GET RID OF A FACELESS ANYTIME.
YOU... TALK ABOUT KILLING THEM LIKE IT DOESN'T MEAN ANYTHING.
WELL, YEAH.
ARE YOU SERIOUSLY MAD?
WOW... OUTSIDERS ARE SO SWEET.
...?

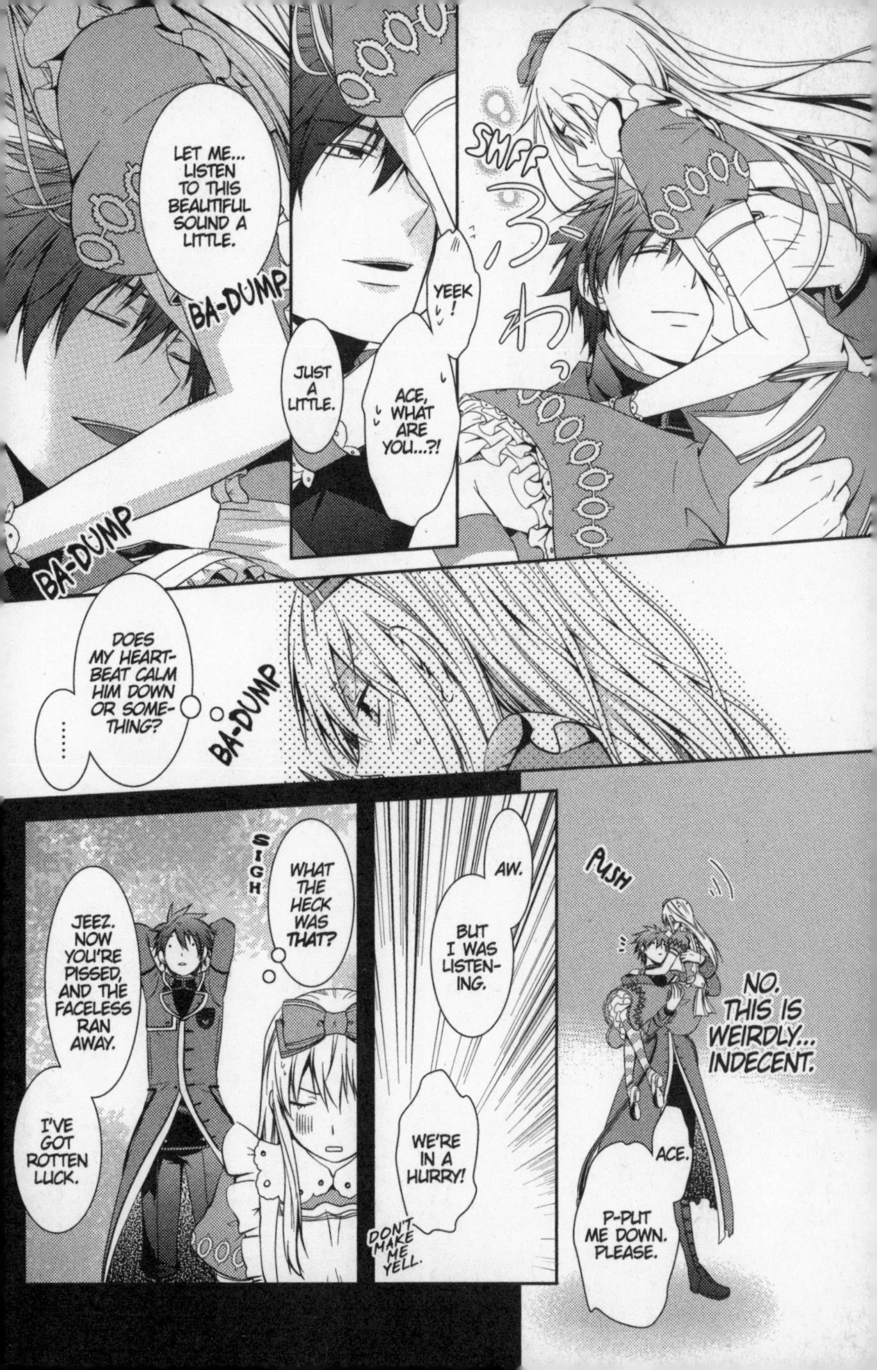
SHFF
ふわっ
YEEK!
ACE, WHAT ARE YOU...?!
JUST A LITTLE.
LET ME... LISTEN TO THIS BEAUTIFUL SOUND A LITTLE.
BA-DUMP
BA-DUMP
BA-DUMP
DOES MY HEART-BEAT CALM HIM DOWN OR SOME-THING?
......
PUSH
NO. THIS IS WEIRDLY... INDECENT.
ACE.
P-PUT ME DOWN. PLEASE.
AW.
BUT I WAS LISTEN-ING.
WE'RE IN A HURRY!
DON'T MAKE ME YELL.
SIGH
WHAT THE HECK WAS THAT?
JEEZ. NOW YOU'RE PISSED, AND THE FACELESS RAN AWAY.
I'VE GOT ROTTEN LUCK.

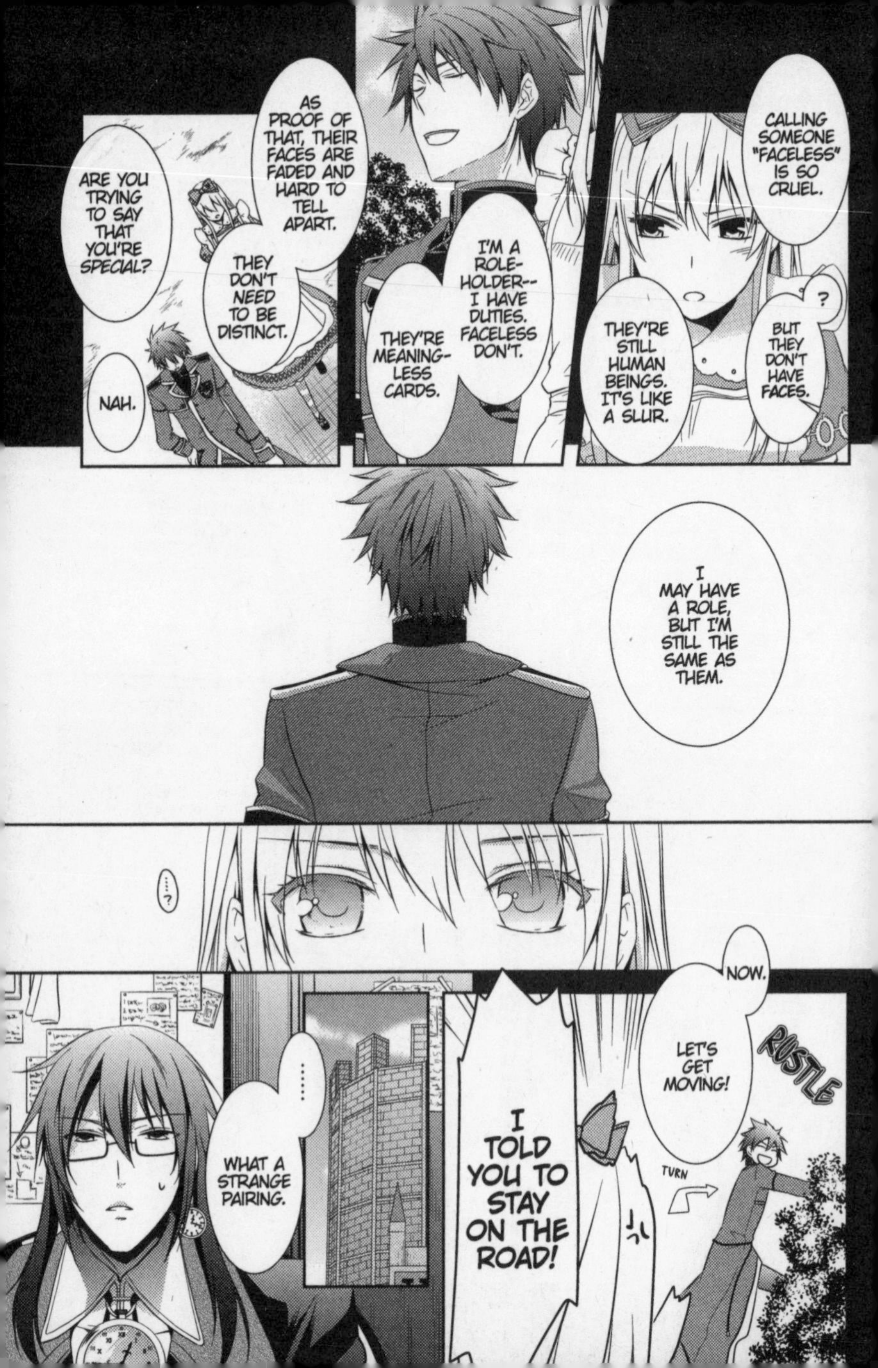
CALLING SOMEONE "FACELESS" IS SO CRUEL.
?
BUT THEY DON'T HAVE FACES.
THEY'RE STILL HUMAN BEINGS. IT'S LIKE A SLUR.
I'M A ROLE-HOLDER-- I HAVE DUTIES. FACELESS DON'T.
THEY'RE MEANING-LESS CARDS.
AS PROOF OF THAT, THEIR FACES ARE FADED AND HARD TO TELL APART.
ARE YOU TRYING TO SAY THAT YOU'RE SPECIAL?
THEY DON'T NEED TO BE DISTINCT.
NAH.
I MAY HAVE A ROLE, BUT I'M STILL THE SAME AS THEM.
...?
NOW.
LET'S GET MOVING!
RUSTLE
TURN
I TOLD YOU TO STAY ON THE ROAD!
......
WHAT A STRANGE PAIRING.

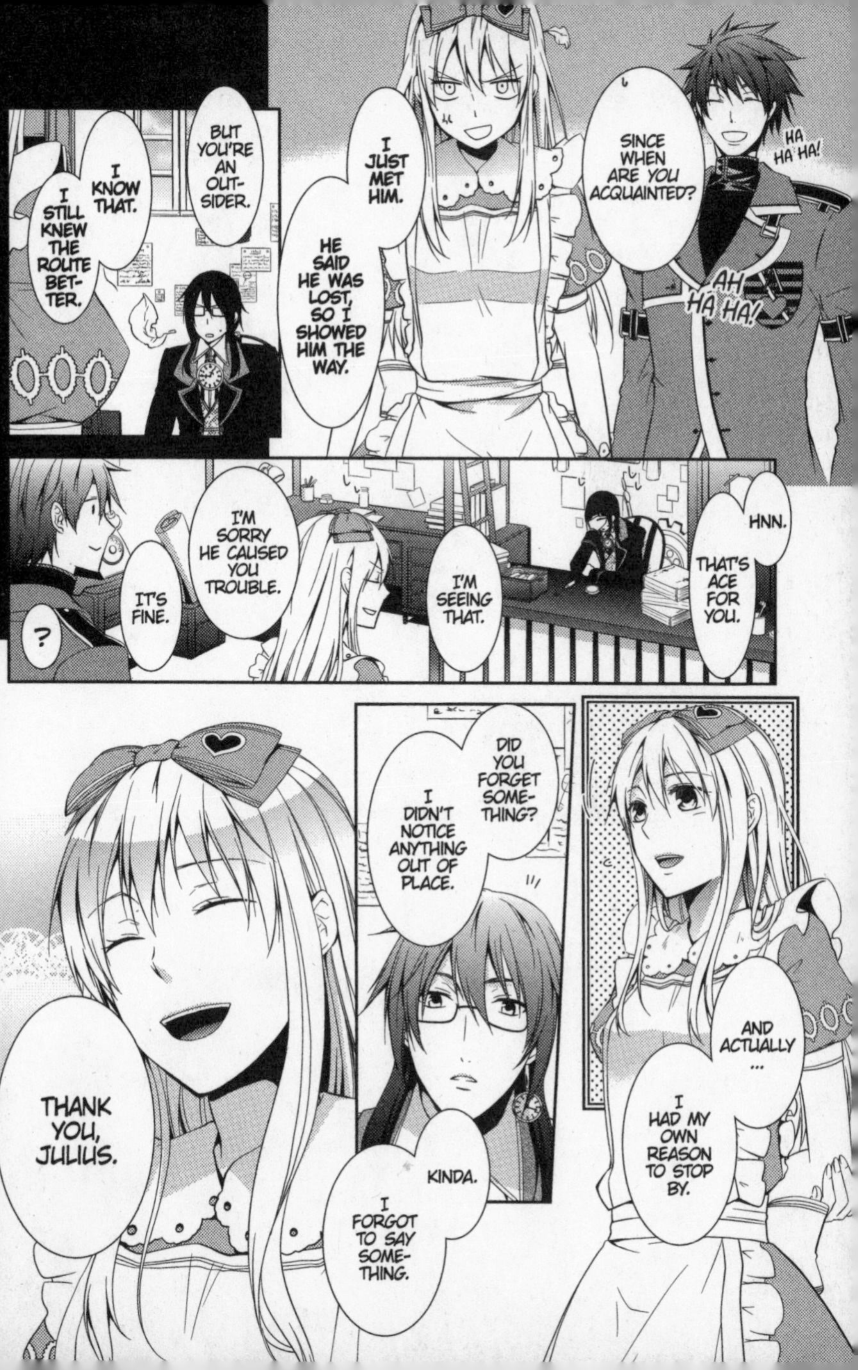
SINCE WHEN ARE YOU ACQUAINTED?
HA HA HA!
AH HA HA!
I JUST MET HIM.
HE SAID HE WAS LOST, SO I SHOWED HIM THE WAY.
BUT YOU'RE AN OUT-SIDER.
I KNOW THAT.
I STILL KNEW THE ROUTE BET-TER.
HNN.
THAT'S ACE FOR YOU.
I'M SEEING THAT.
I'M SORRY HE CAUSED YOU TROUBLE.
IT'S FINE.
?
AND ACTUALLY ...
I HAD MY OWN REASON TO STOP BY.
DID YOU FORGET SOME-THING?
I DIDN'T NOTICE ANYTHING OUT OF PLACE.
KINDA.
I FORGOT TO SAY SOME-THING.
THANK YOU, JULIUS.

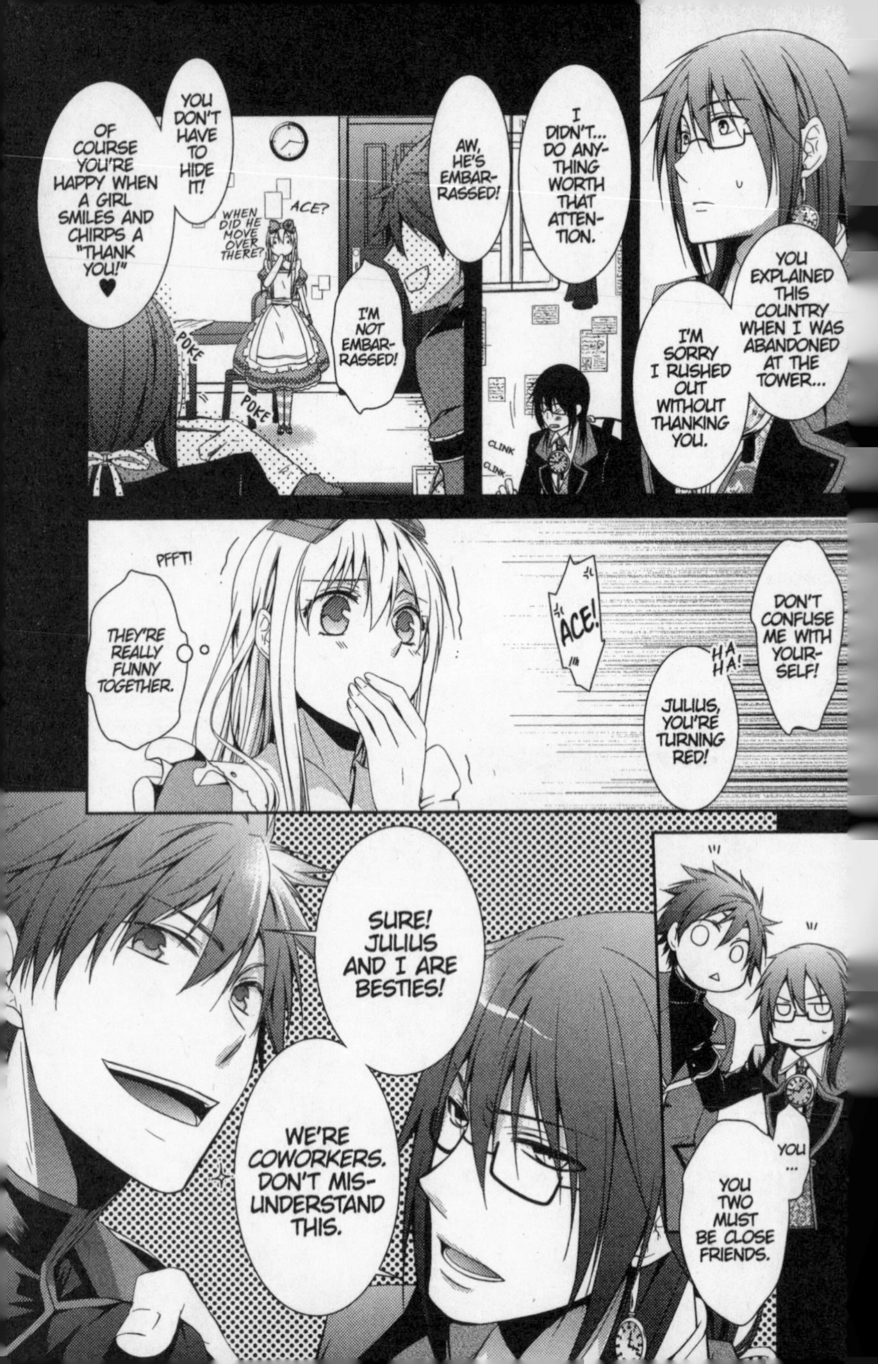
YOU EXPLAINED THIS COUNTRY WHEN I WAS ABANDONED AT THE TOWER...
I'M SORRY I RUSHED OUT WITHOUT THANKING YOU.
CLINK
CLINK
I DIDN'T... DO ANYTHING WORTH THAT ATTENTION.
AW, HE'S EMBARRASSED!
I'M NOT EMBARRASSED!
ACE?
WHEN DID HE MOVE OVER THERE?
YOU DON'T HAVE TO HIDE IT!
OF COURSE YOU'RE HAPPY WHEN A GIRL SMILES AND CHIRPS A "THANK YOU!" ♥
POKE
POKE
DON'T CONFUSE ME WITH YOURSELF!
HA HA!
JULIUS, YOU'RE TURNING RED!
ACE!
PFFT!
THEY'RE REALLY FUNNY TOGETHER.
YOU...
YOU TWO MUST BE CLOSE FRIENDS.
SURE! JULIUS AND I ARE BESTIES!
WE'RE COWORKERS. DON'T MISUNDERSTAND THIS.

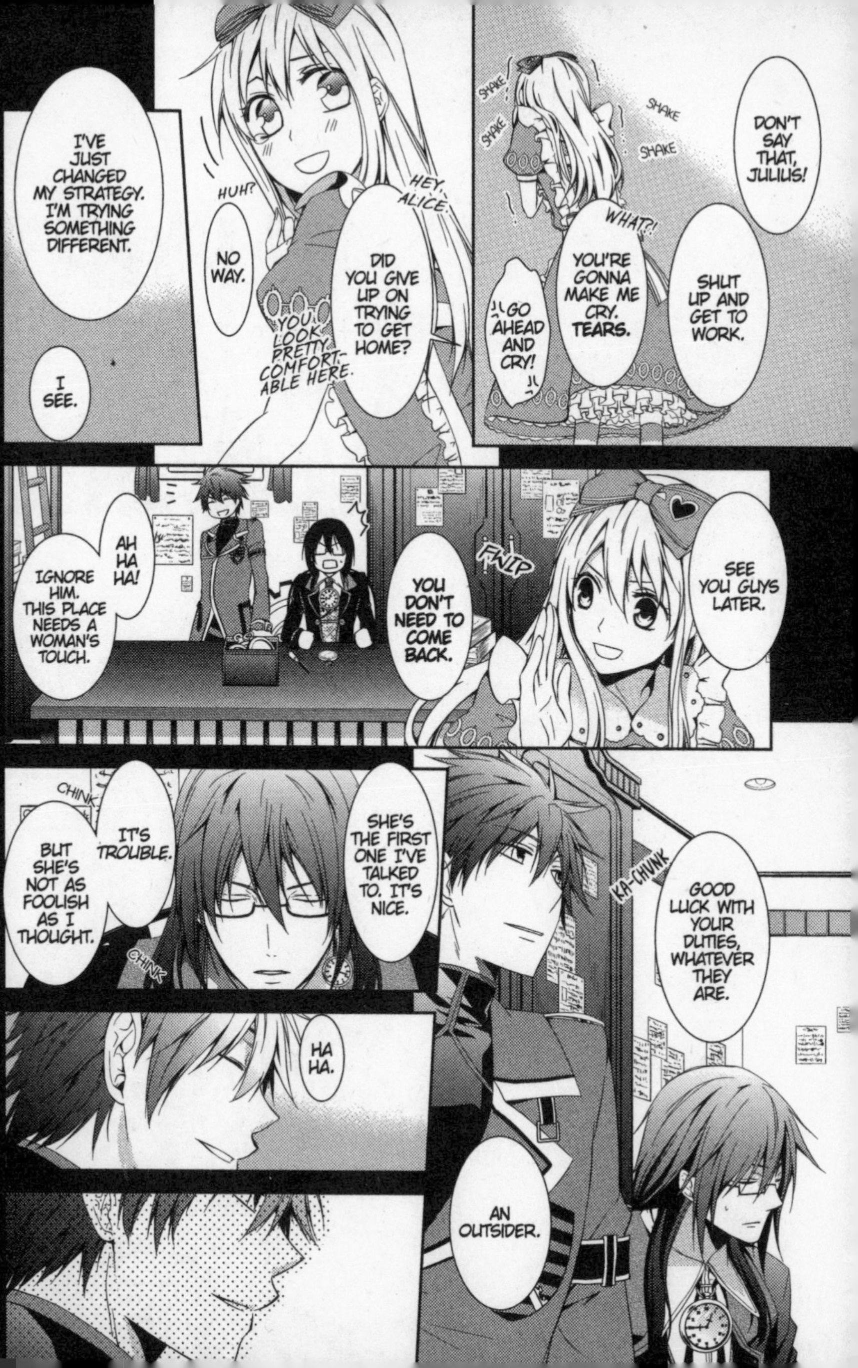
SHAKE
SHAKE
SHAKE
SHAKE
DON'T SAY THAT, JULIUS!
SHUT UP AND GET TO WORK.
WHAT?!
YOU'RE GONNA MAKE ME CRY. TEARS.
GO AHEAD AND CRY!
HEY, ALICE.
DID YOU GIVE UP ON TRYING TO GET HOME?
YOU LOOK PRETTY COMFORT-ABLE HERE.
HUH?
NO WAY.
I'VE JUST CHANGED MY STRATEGY. I'M TRYING SOMETHING DIFFERENT.
I SEE.
SEE YOU GUYS LATER.
FWIP
YOU DON'T NEED TO COME BACK.
AH HA HA!
IGNORE HIM. THIS PLACE NEEDS A WOMAN'S TOUCH.
GOOD LUCK WITH YOUR DUTIES, WHATEVER THEY ARE.
KA-CHUNK
AN OUTSIDER.
SHE'S THE FIRST ONE I'VE TALKED TO. IT'S NICE.
IT'S TROUBLE.
CHINK
BUT SHE'S NOT AS FOOLISH AS I THOUGHT.
CHINK
HA HA.

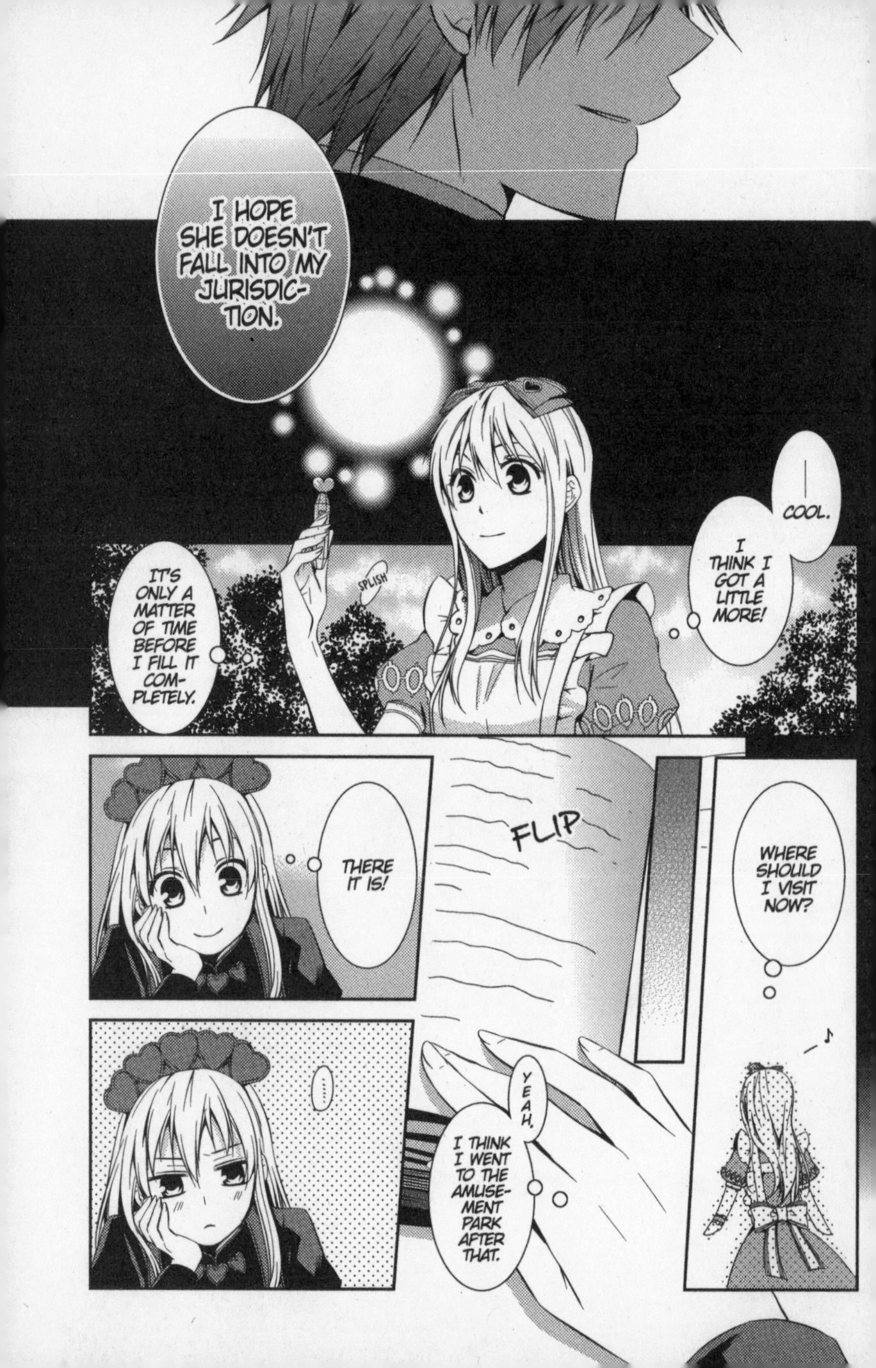

I HOPE SHE DOESN'T FALL INTO MY JURISDICTION.
—COOL.
I THINK I GOT A LITTLE MORE!
SPLISH
IT'S ONLY A MATTER OF TIME BEFORE I FILL IT COMPLETELY.
WHERE SHOULD I VISIT NOW?
—♪
FLIP
THERE IT IS!
YEAH, I THINK I WENT TO THE AMUSEMENT PARK AFTER THAT.
...

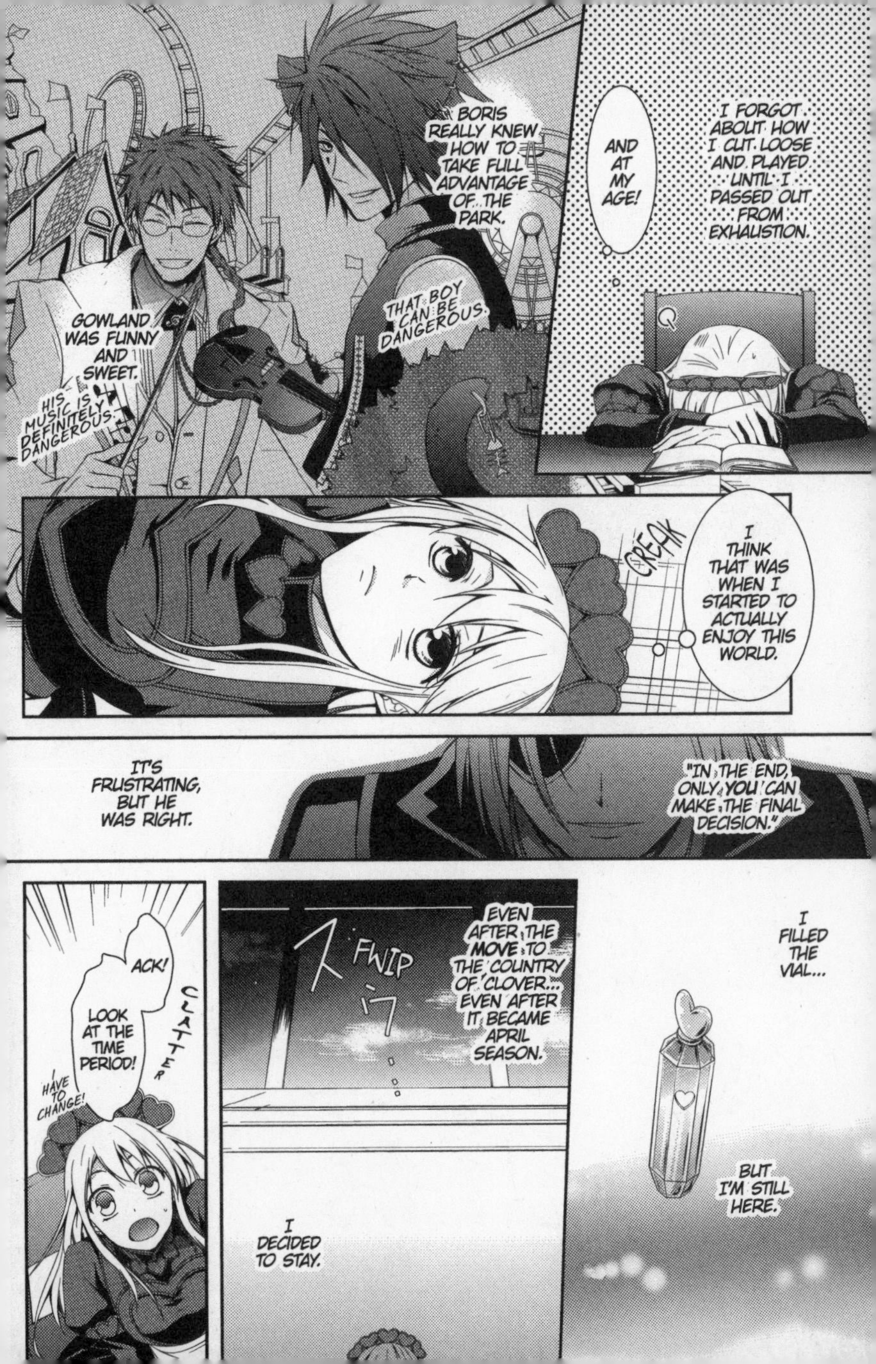
I FORGOT ABOUT HOW I CUT LOOSE AND PLAYED UNTIL I PASSED OUT FROM EXHAUSTION.
AND AT MY AGE!
BORIS REALLY KNEW HOW TO TAKE FULL ADVANTAGE OF THE PARK.
THAT BOY CAN BE DANGEROUS.
GOWLAND WAS FUNNY AND SWEET.
HIS MUSIC IS DEFINITELY DANGEROUS.
CREAK
I THINK THAT WAS WHEN I STARTED TO ACTUALLY ENJOY THIS WORLD.
"IN THE END, ONLY YOU CAN MAKE THE FINAL DECISION."
IT'S FRUSTRATING, BUT HE WAS RIGHT.
I FILLED THE VIAL...
BUT I'M STILL HERE.
EVEN AFTER THE MOVE TO THE COUNTRY OF CLOVER... EVEN AFTER IT BECAME APRIL SEASON.
FWIP
I DECIDED TO STAY.
ACK!
LOOK AT THE TIME PERIOD!
CLATTER
I HAVE TO CHANGE!

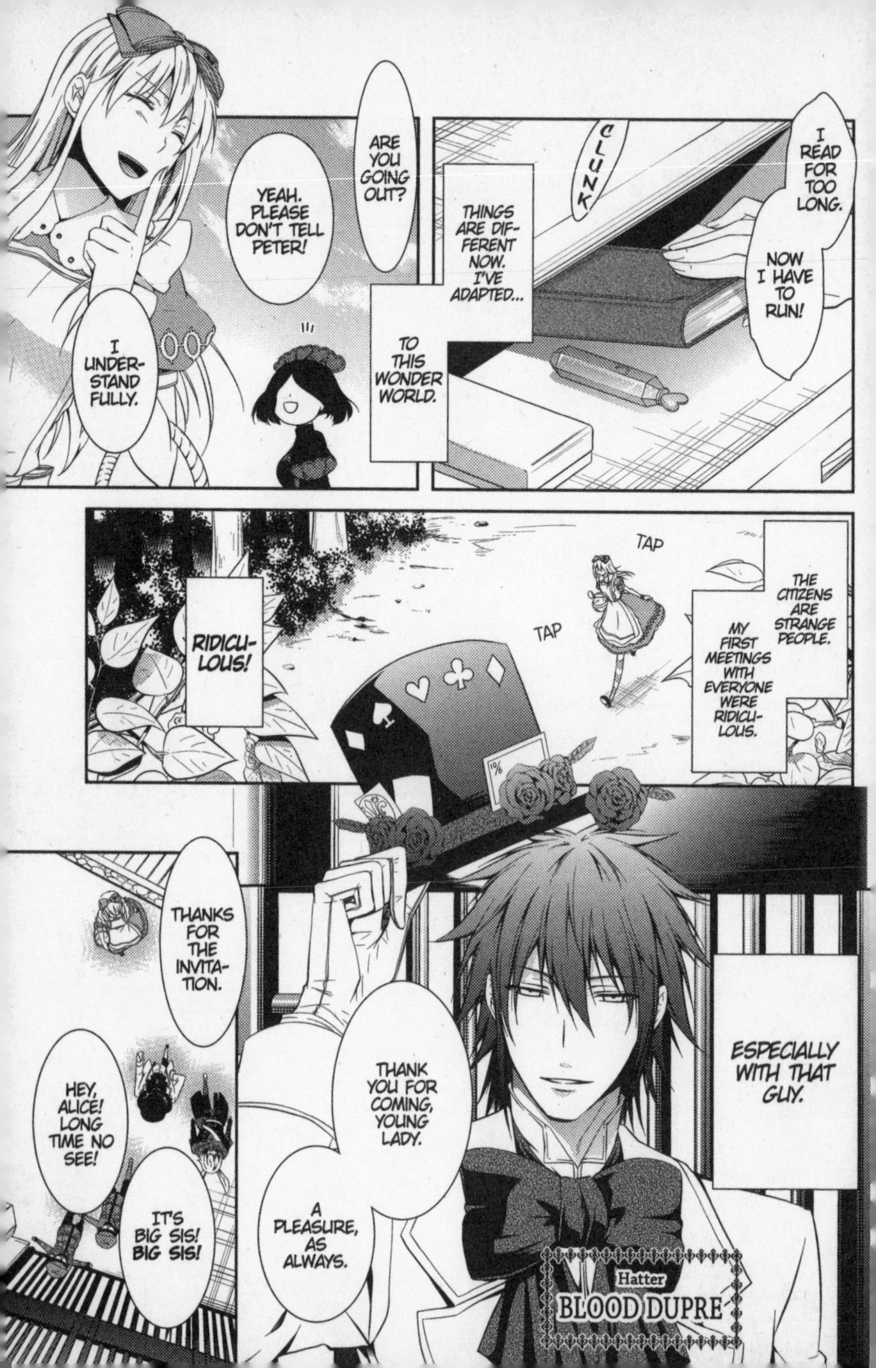
I READ FOR TOO LONG.
NOW I HAVE TO RUN!
CLUNK
THINGS ARE DIFFERENT NOW. I'VE ADAPTED...
TO THIS WONDER WORLD.
ARE YOU GOING OUT?
YEAH. PLEASE DON'T TELL PETER!
I UNDERSTAND FULLY.
THE CITIZENS ARE STRANGE PEOPLE.
MY FIRST MEETINGS WITH EVERYONE WERE RIDICULOUS.
TAP
TAP
RIDICULOUS!
ESPECIALLY WITH THAT GUY.
THANK YOU FOR COMING, YOUNG LADY.
A PLEASURE, AS ALWAYS.
Hatter
BLOOD DUPRE
THANKS FOR THE INVITATION.
HEY, ALICE! LONG TIME NO SEE!
IT'S BIG SIS! BIG SIS!

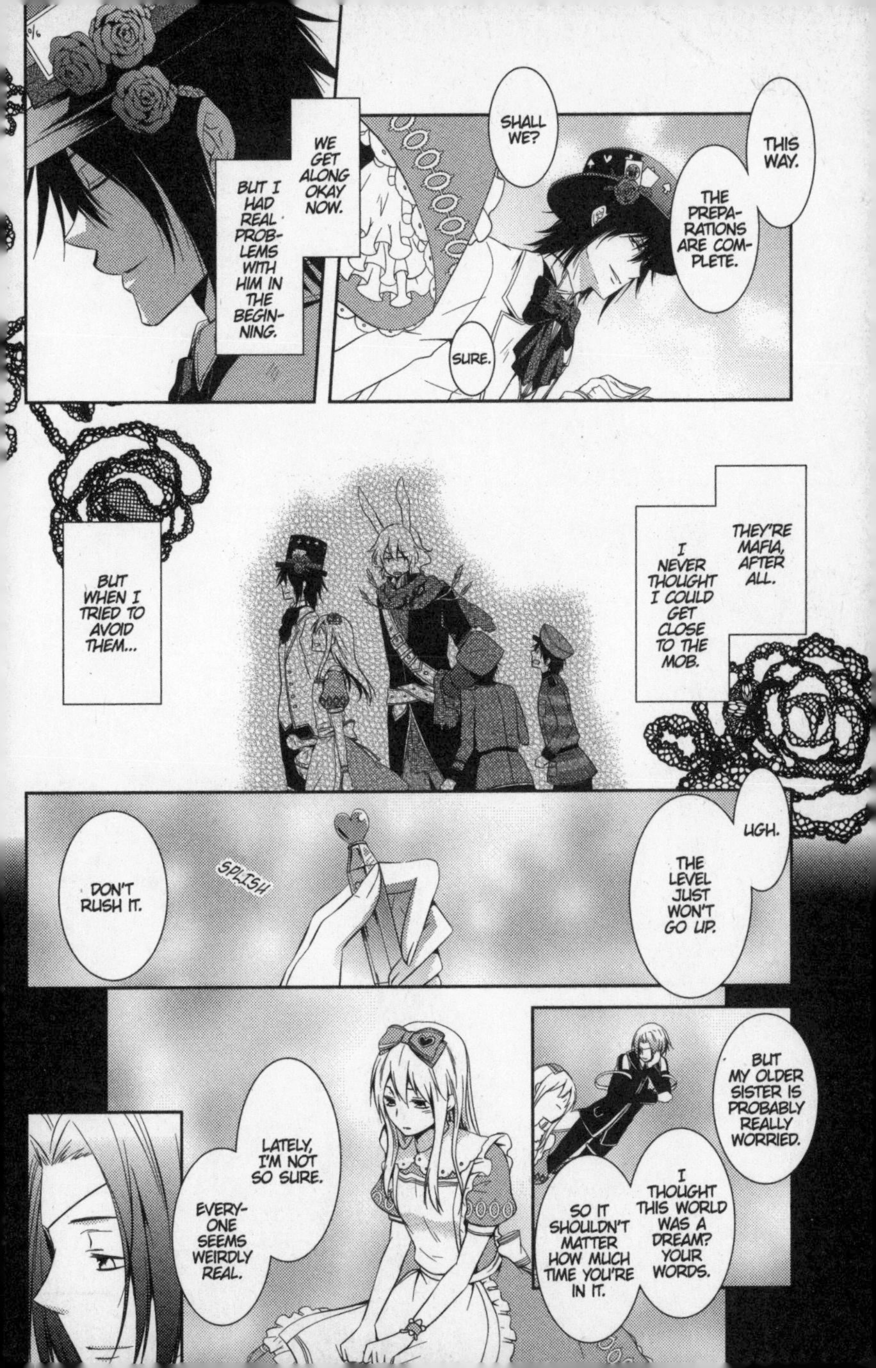
THIS WAY.
THE PREPARATIONS ARE COMPLETE.
SHALL WE?
SURE.
WE GET ALONG OKAY NOW.
BUT I HAD REAL PROBLEMS WITH HIM IN THE BEGINNING.
THEY'RE MAFIA, AFTER ALL.
I NEVER THOUGHT I COULD GET CLOSE TO THE MOB.
BUT WHEN I TRIED TO AVOID THEM...
UGH.
THE LEVEL JUST WON'T GO UP.
SPLISH
DON'T RUSH IT.
BUT MY OLDER SISTER IS PROBABLY REALLY WORRIED.
I THOUGHT THIS WORLD WAS A DREAM? YOUR WORDS.
SO IT SHOULDN'T MATTER HOW MUCH TIME YOU'RE IN IT.
LATELY, I'M NOT SO SURE.
EVERYONE SEEMS WEIRDLY REAL.

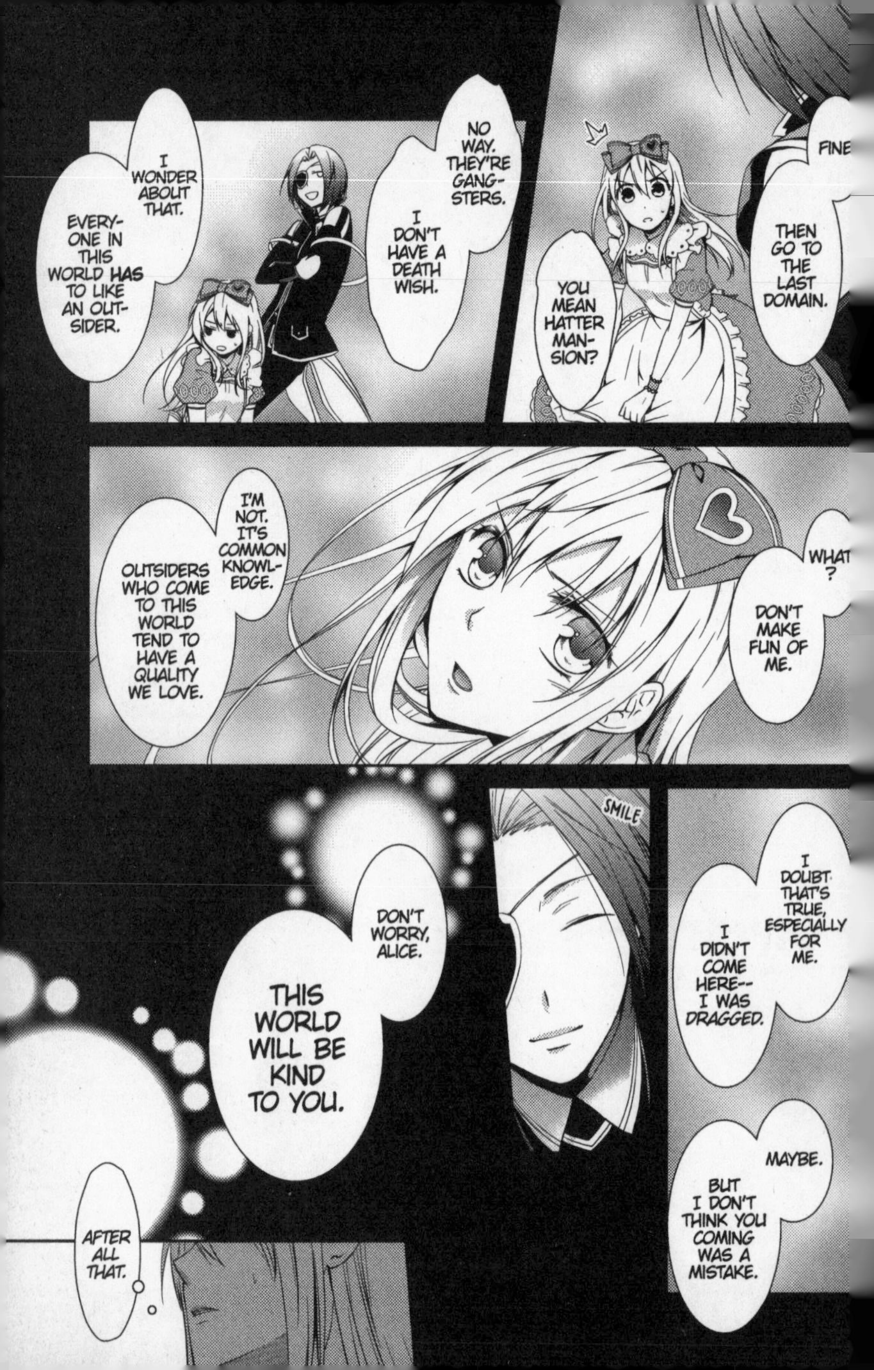
FINE
THEN GO TO THE LAST DOMAIN.
YOU MEAN HATTER MANSION?
NO WAY. THEY'RE GANGSTERS.
I DON'T HAVE A DEATH WISH.
I WONDER ABOUT THAT.
EVERYONE IN THIS WORLD HAS TO LIKE AN OUTSIDER.
WHAT?
DON'T MAKE FUN OF ME.
I'M NOT. IT'S COMMON KNOWLEDGE.
OUTSIDERS WHO COME TO THIS WORLD TEND TO HAVE A QUALITY WE LOVE.
I DOUBT THAT'S TRUE, ESPECIALLY FOR ME.
I DIDN'T COME HERE--I WAS DRAGGED.
SMILE
DON'T WORRY, ALICE.
THIS WORLD WILL BE KIND TO YOU.
MAYBE.
BUT I DON'T THINK YOU COMING WAS A MISTAKE.
AFTER ALL THAT.

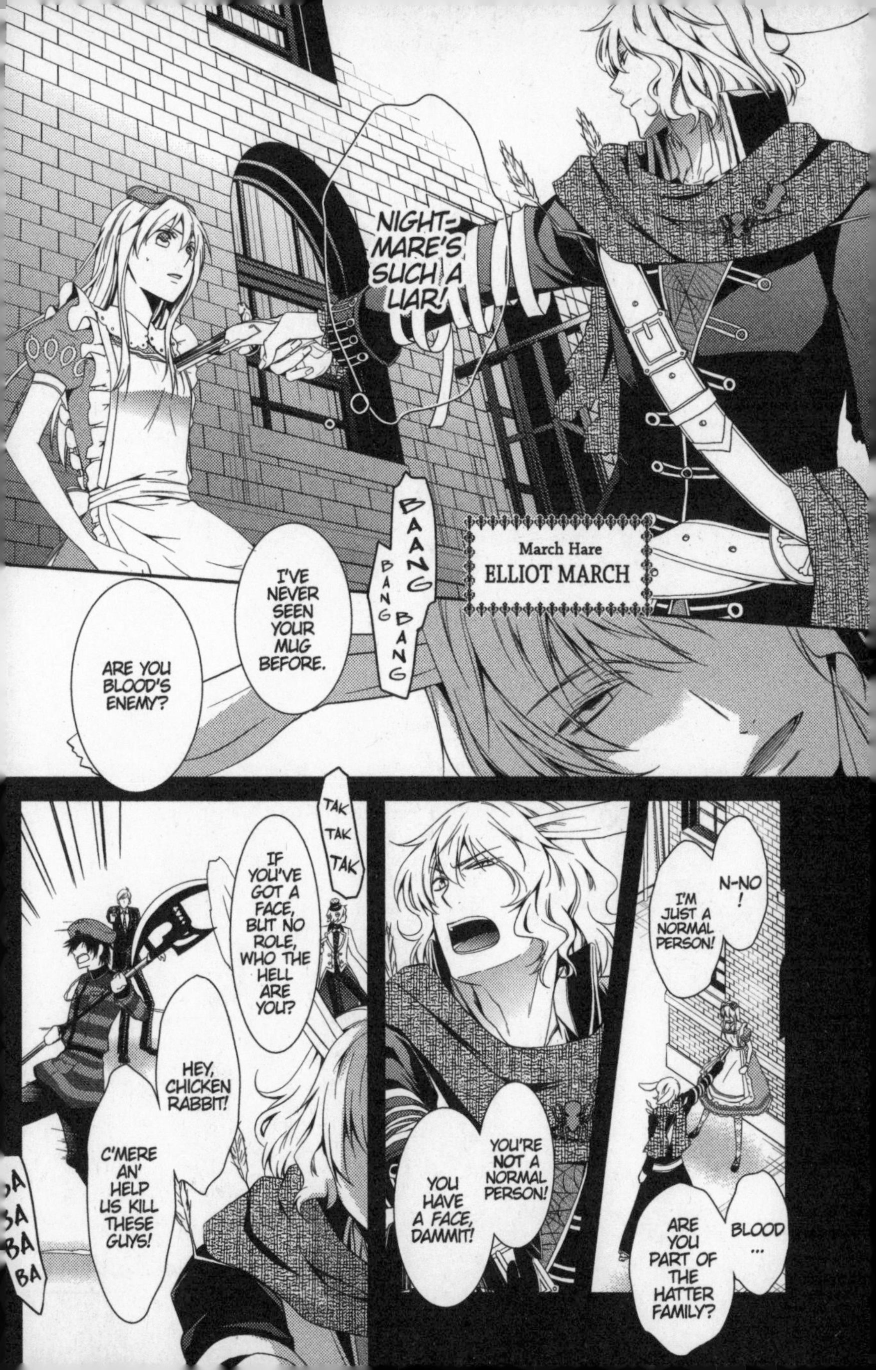
NIGHT-MARE'S SUCH A LIAR!
March Hare
ELLIOT MARCH
BAAANG
BANG BANG
I'VE NEVER SEEN YOUR MUG BEFORE.
ARE YOU BLOOD'S ENEMY?
N-NO!
I'M JUST A NORMAL PERSON!
BLOOD...
ARE YOU PART OF THE HATTER FAMILY?
YOU'RE NOT A NORMAL PERSON!
YOU HAVE A FACE, DAMMIT!
TAK TAK TAK
IF YOU'VE GOT A FACE, BUT NO ROLE, WHO THE HELL ARE YOU?
HEY, CHICKEN RABBIT!
C'MERE AN' HELP US KILL THESE GUYS!
BA BA BA BA

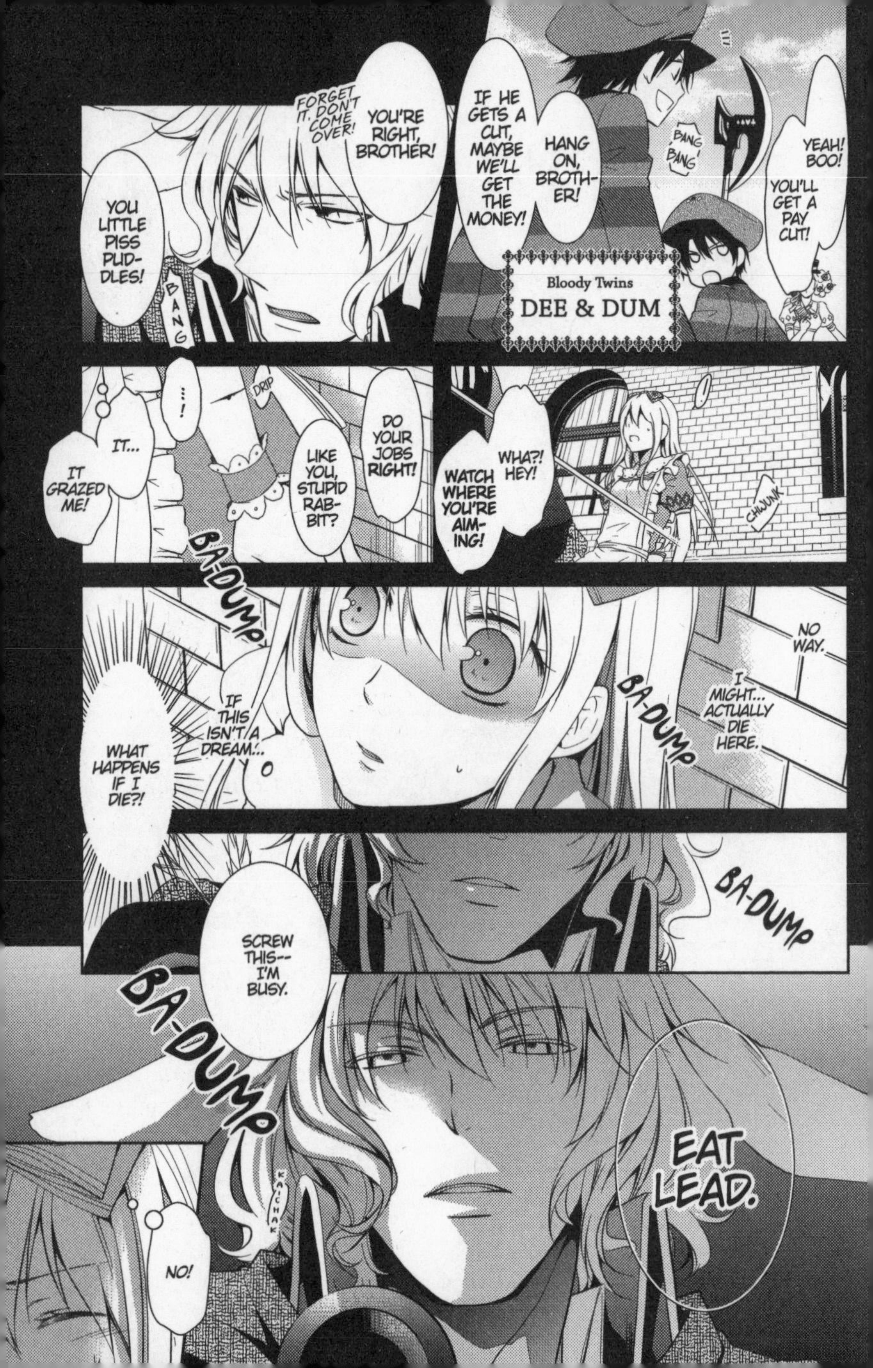
YEAH! BOO! YOU'LL GET A PAY CUT!
BANG BANG
HANG ON, BROTHER!
IF HE GETS A CUT, MAYBE WE'LL GET THE MONEY!
Bloody Twins
DEE & DUM
YOU'RE RIGHT, BROTHER!
FORGET IT. DON'T COME OVER!
YOU LITTLE PISS PUD-DLES!
BANG
!
WHA?! HEY!
WATCH WHERE YOU'RE AIM-ING!
CHWUNK
DO YOUR JOBS RIGHT!
LIKE YOU, STUPID RAB-BIT?
DRIP
...!
IT...
IT GRAZED ME!
NO WAY.
I MIGHT... ACTUALLY DIE HERE.
BA-DUMP
IF THIS ISN'T A DREAM...
WHAT HAPPENS IF I DIE?!
BA-DUMP
BA-DUMP
SCREW THIS-- I'M BUSY.
BA-DUMP
EAT LEAD.
KAICHAK
NO!

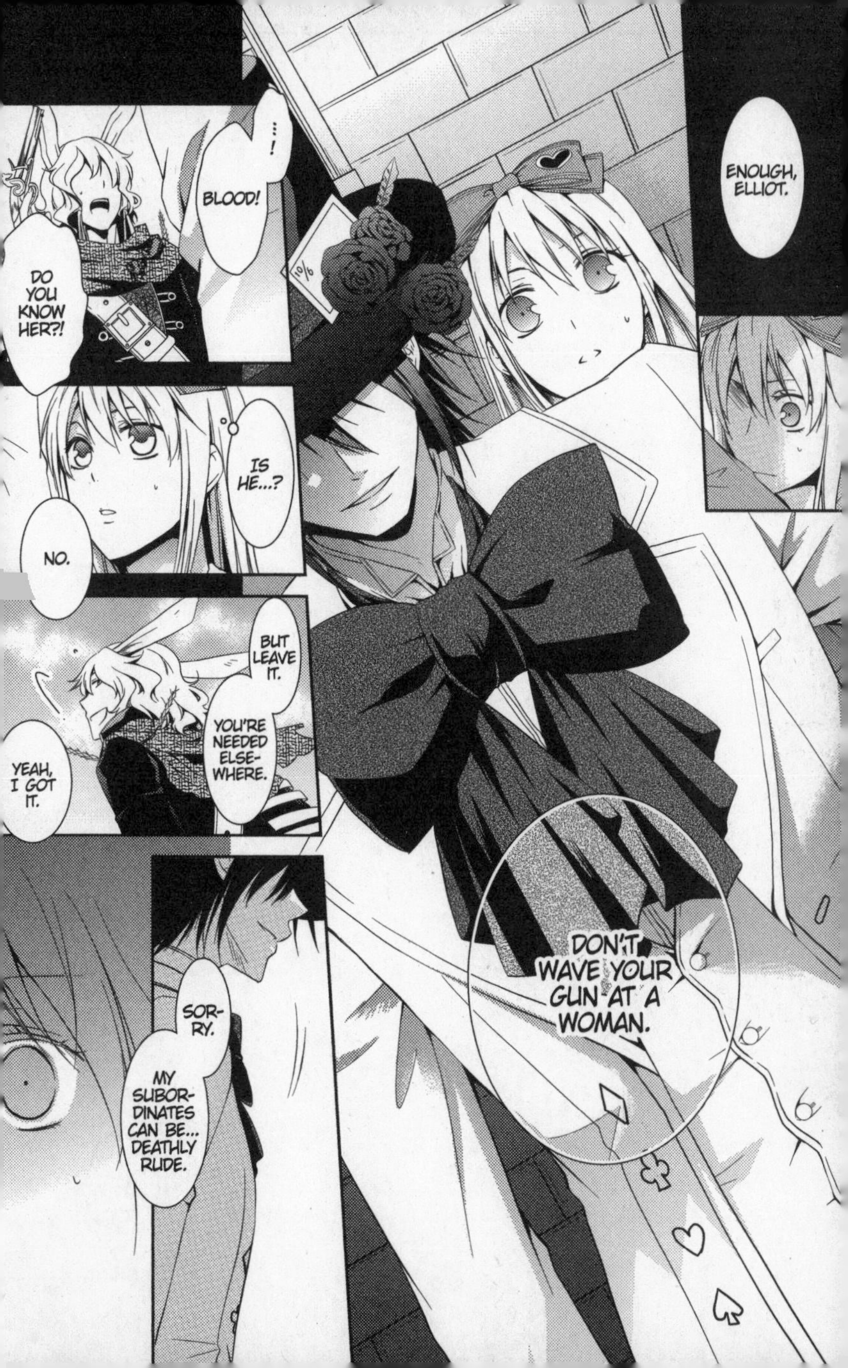
ENOUGH, ELLIOT.
DON'T WAVE YOUR GUN AT A WOMAN.
...!
BLOOD!
DO YOU KNOW HER?!
IS HE...?
NO.
BUT LEAVE IT.
YOU'RE NEEDED ELSE-WHERE.
YEAH, I GOT IT.
SOR-RY.
MY SUBOR-DINATES CAN BE... DEATHLY RUDE.

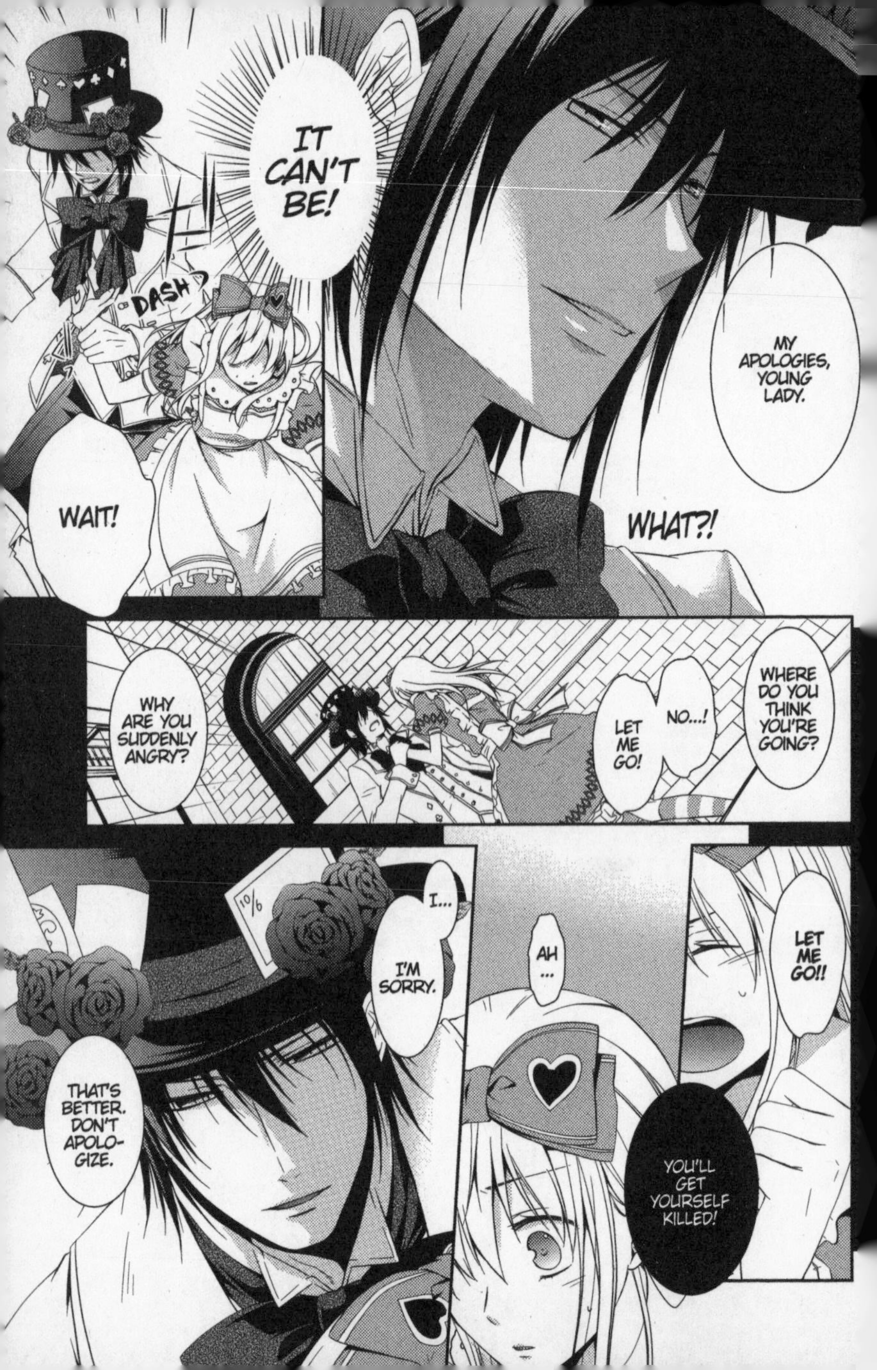
MY APOLOGIES, YOUNG LADY.
WHAT?!
IT CAN'T BE!
DASH
WAIT!
WHERE DO YOU THINK YOU'RE GOING?
NO...!
LET ME GO!
WHY ARE YOU SUDDENLY ANGRY?
LET ME GO!!
AH ...
YOU'LL GET YOURSELF KILLED!
I...
I'M SORRY.
THAT'S BETTER. DON'T APOLO-GIZE.

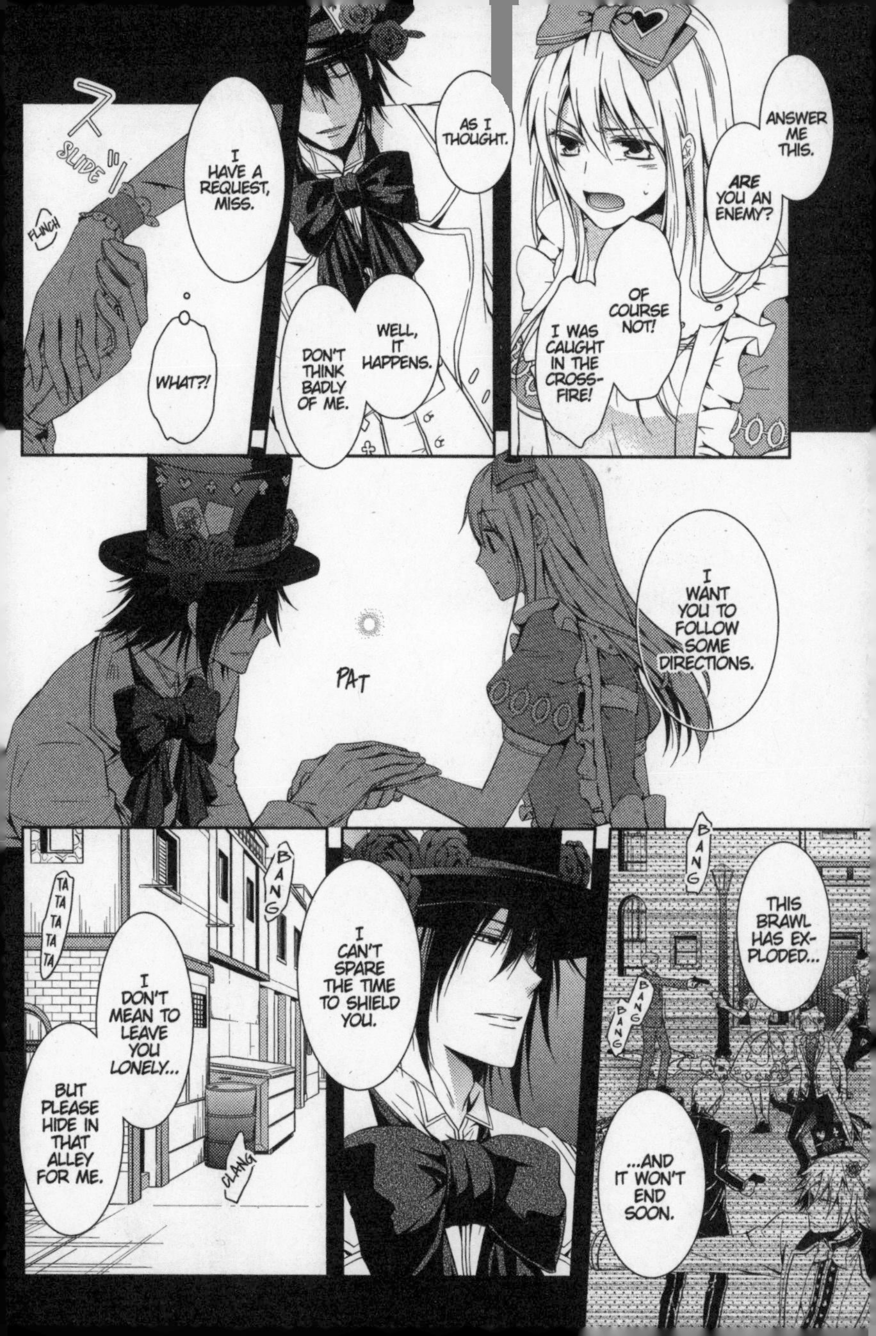
ANSWER ME THIS.
ARE YOU AN ENEMY?
OF COURSE NOT!
I WAS CAUGHT IN THE CROSS-FIRE!
AS I THOUGHT.
WELL, IT HAPPENS.
DON'T THINK BADLY OF ME.
I HAVE A REQUEST, MISS.
SLIDE
FLINCH
WHAT?!
I WANT YOU TO FOLLOW SOME DIRECTIONS.
PAT
BANG
THIS BRAWL HAS EX-PLODED...
BANG
BANG
...AND IT WON'T END SOON.
I CAN'T SPARE THE TIME TO SHIELD YOU.
BANG
TA TA TA TA TA TA
I DON'T MEAN TO LEAVE YOU LONELY...
BUT PLEASE HIDE IN THAT ALLEY FOR ME.
CLANG

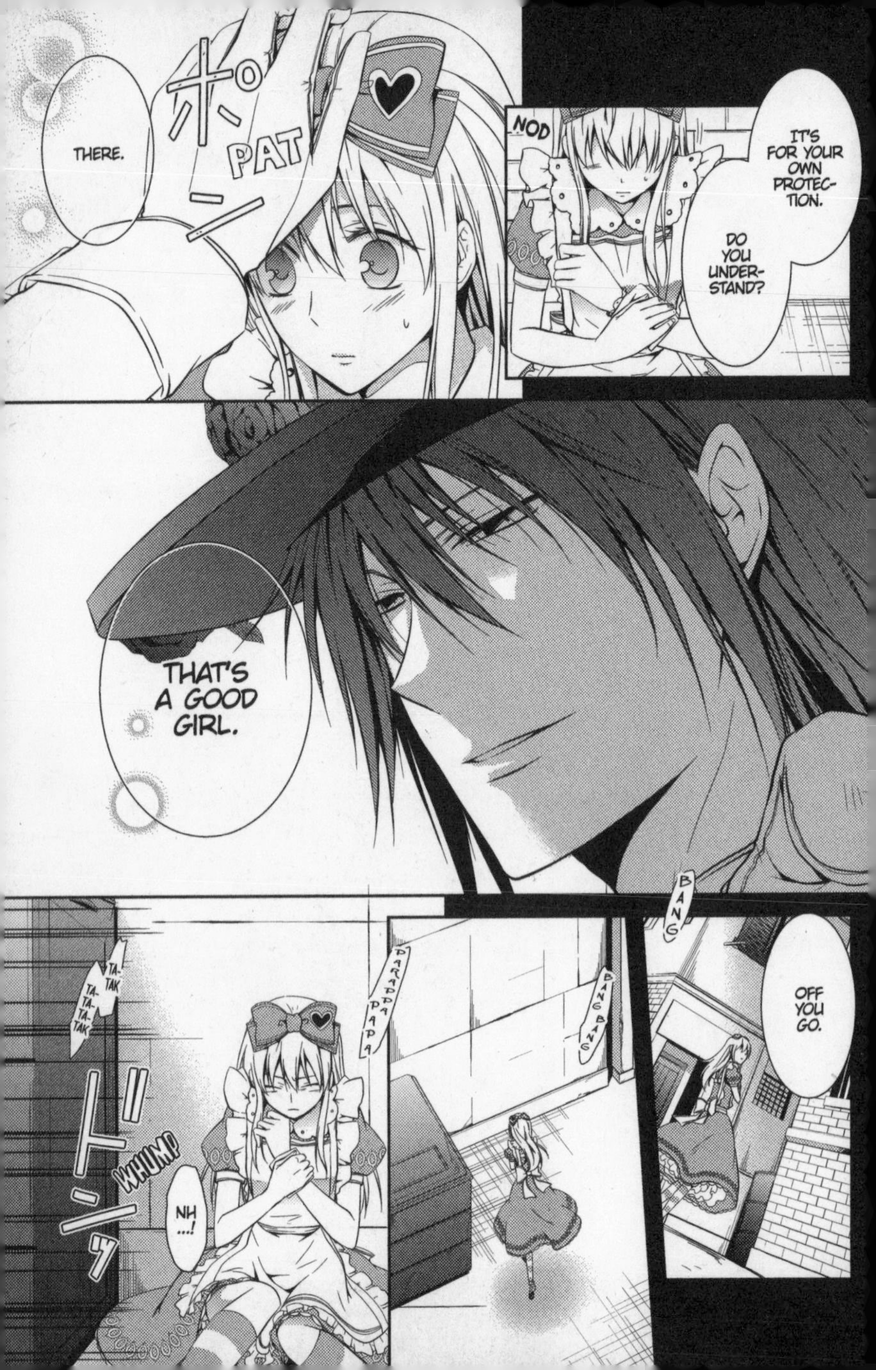
NOD
IT'S FOR YOUR OWN PROTECTION.
DO YOU UNDERSTAND?
PAT
THERE.
THAT'S A GOOD GIRL.
BANG
OFF YOU GO.
PARAPPA PAPA
BANG BANG
TA-TAK
TA-TA-TA-TAK
WHUMP
NH ...!

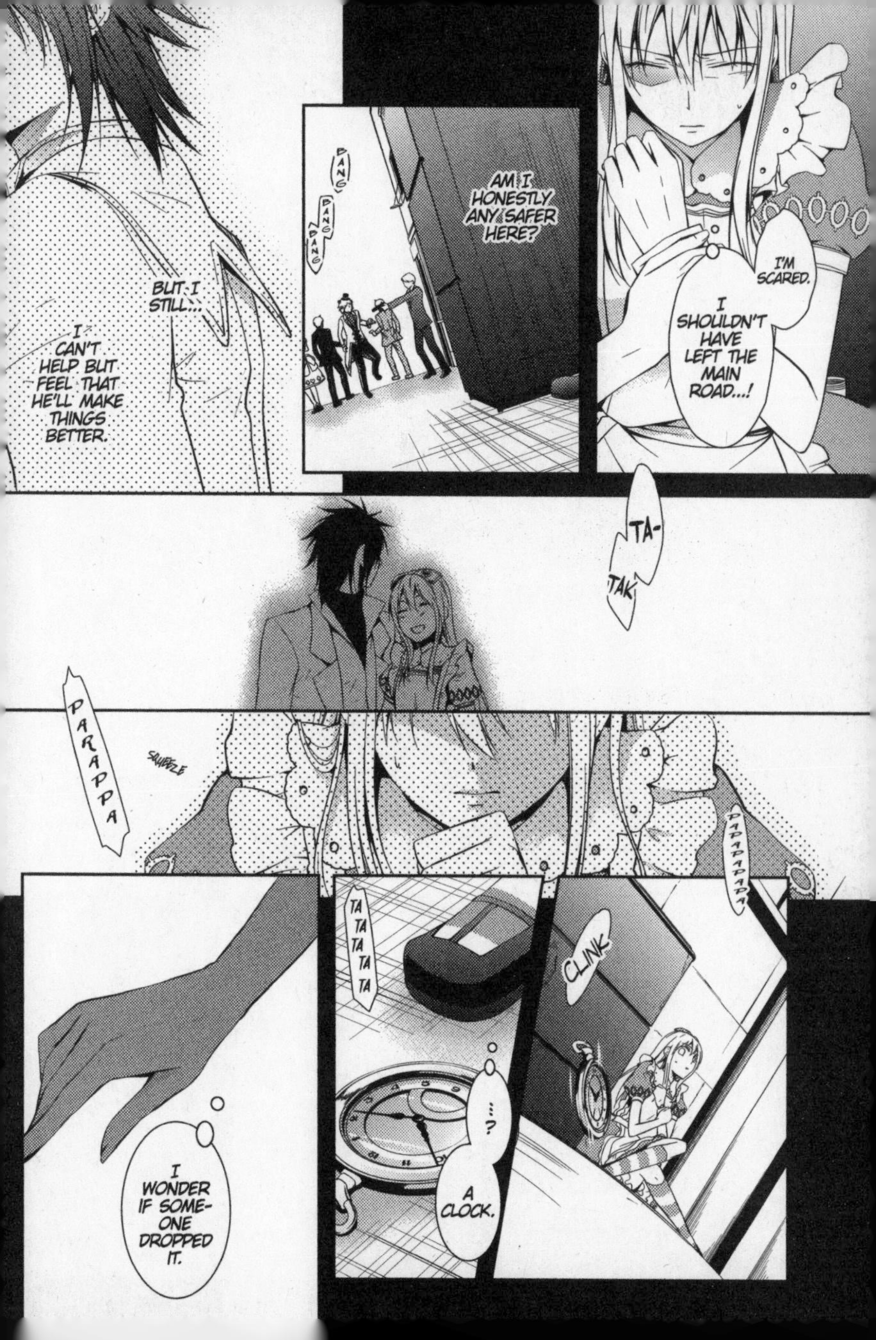
I'M SCARED.
I SHOULDN'T HAVE LEFT THE MAIN ROAD...!
BANG BANG BANG
AM I HONESTLY ANY SAFER HERE?
BUT I STILL...
I CAN'T HELP BUT FEEL THAT HE'LL MAKE THINGS BETTER.
TA-TAK
PAPAPAPAPA
SQUEEZE
PARAPPA
CLINK
...?
TA TA TA TA TA
A CLOCK.
I WONDER IF SOME-ONE DROPPED IT.

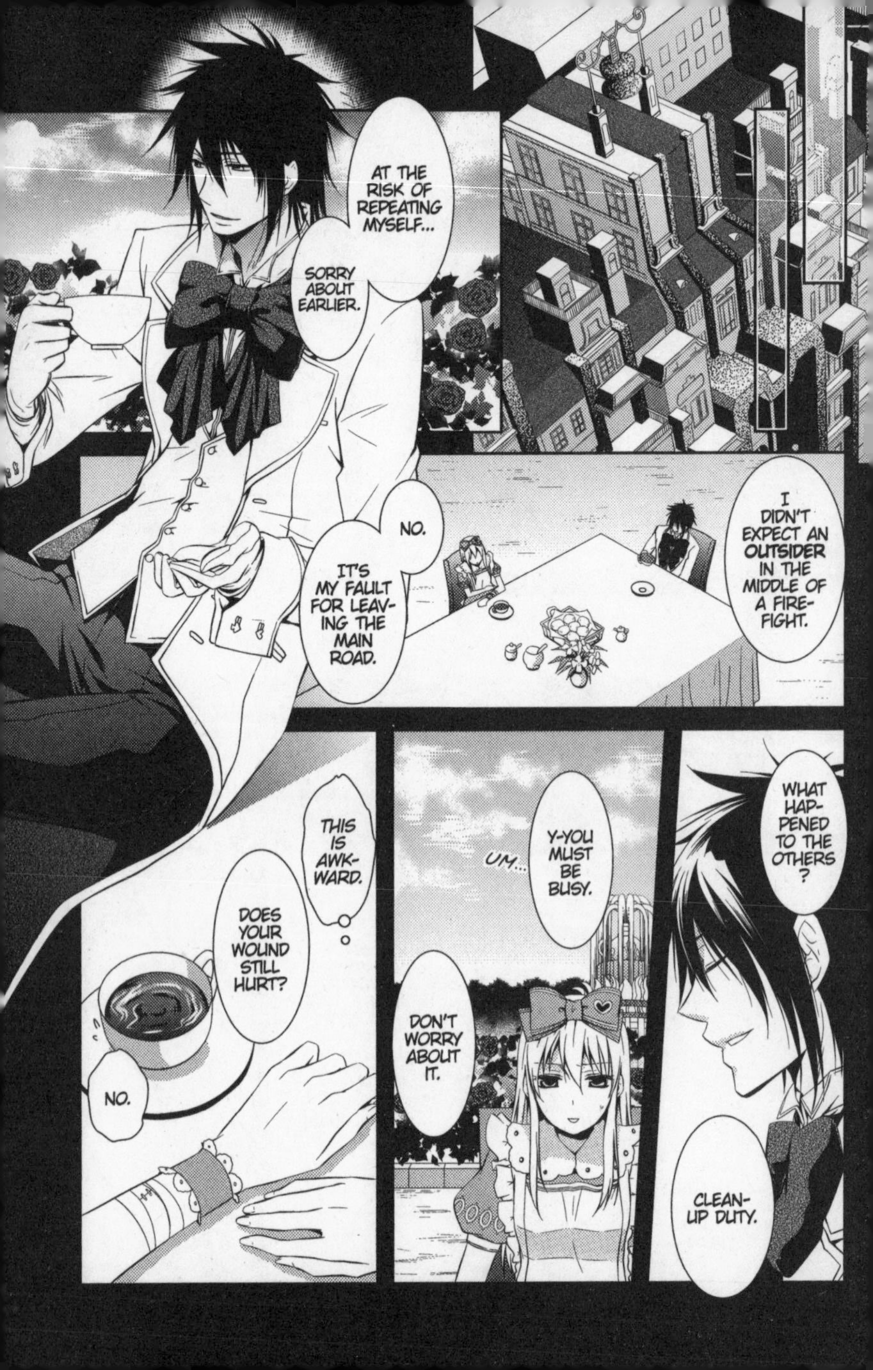

AT THE RISK OF REPEATING MYSELF...
SORRY ABOUT EARLIER.
I DIDN'T EXPECT AN OUTSIDER IN THE MIDDLE OF A FIRE-FIGHT.
NO.
IT'S MY FAULT FOR LEAVING THE MAIN ROAD.
WHAT HAPPENED TO THE OTHERS?
CLEAN-UP DUTY.
UM...
Y-YOU MUST BE BUSY.
DON'T WORRY ABOUT IT.
THIS IS AWKWARD.
DOES YOUR WOUND STILL HURT?
NO.

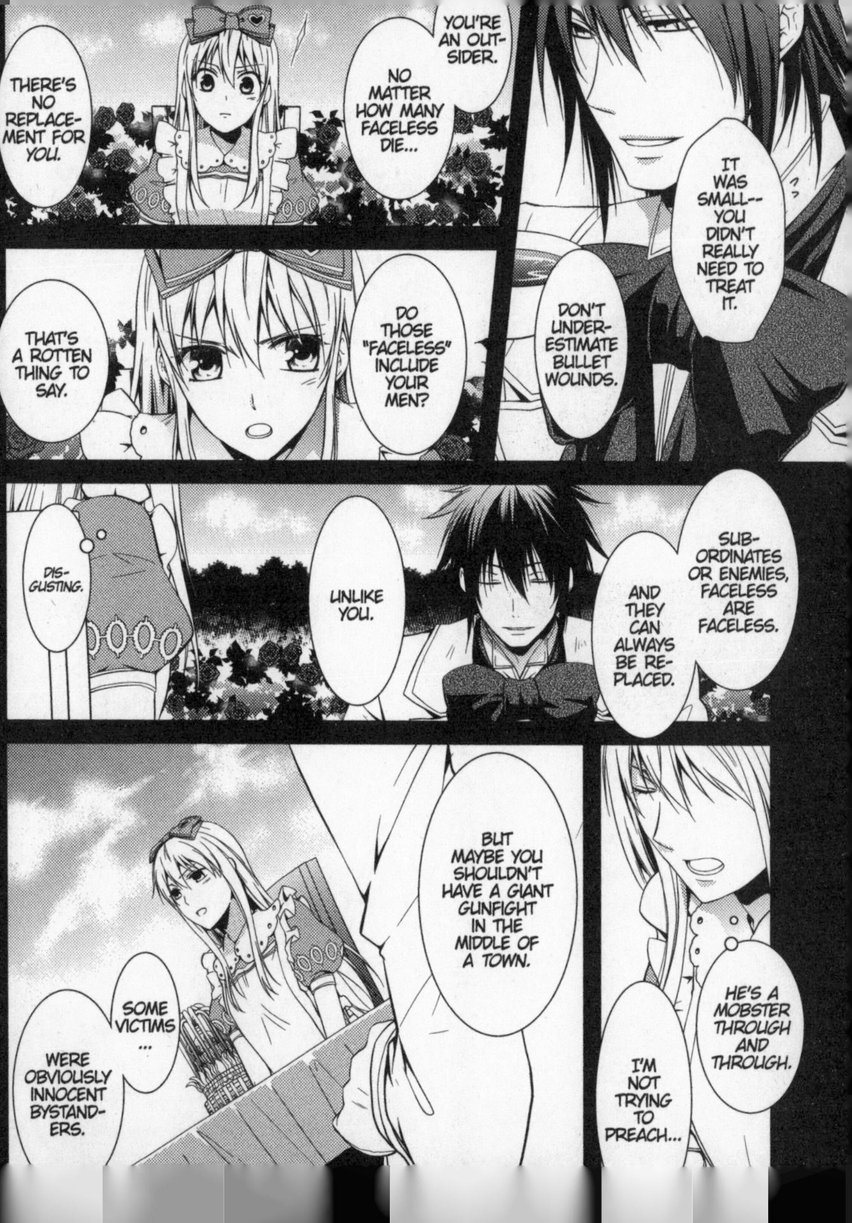
IT WAS SMALL--YOU DIDN'T REALLY NEED TO TREAT IT.
DON'T UNDER-ESTIMATE BULLET WOUNDS.
YOU'RE AN OUT-SIDER.
NO MATTER HOW MANY FACELESS DIE...
THERE'S NO REPLACE-MENT FOR YOU.
DO THOSE "FACELESS" INCLUDE YOUR MEN?
THAT'S A ROTTEN THING TO SAY.
SUB-ORDINATES OR ENEMIES, FACELESS ARE FACELESS.
AND THEY CAN ALWAYS BE RE-PLACED.
UNLIKE YOU.
DIS-GUSTING.
HE'S A MOBSTER THROUGH AND THROUGH.
I'M NOT TRYING TO PREACH...
BUT MAYBE YOU SHOULDN'T HAVE A GIANT GUNFIGHT IN THE MIDDLE OF A TOWN.
SOME VICTIMS...
WERE OBVIOUSLY INNOCENT BYSTAND-ERS.

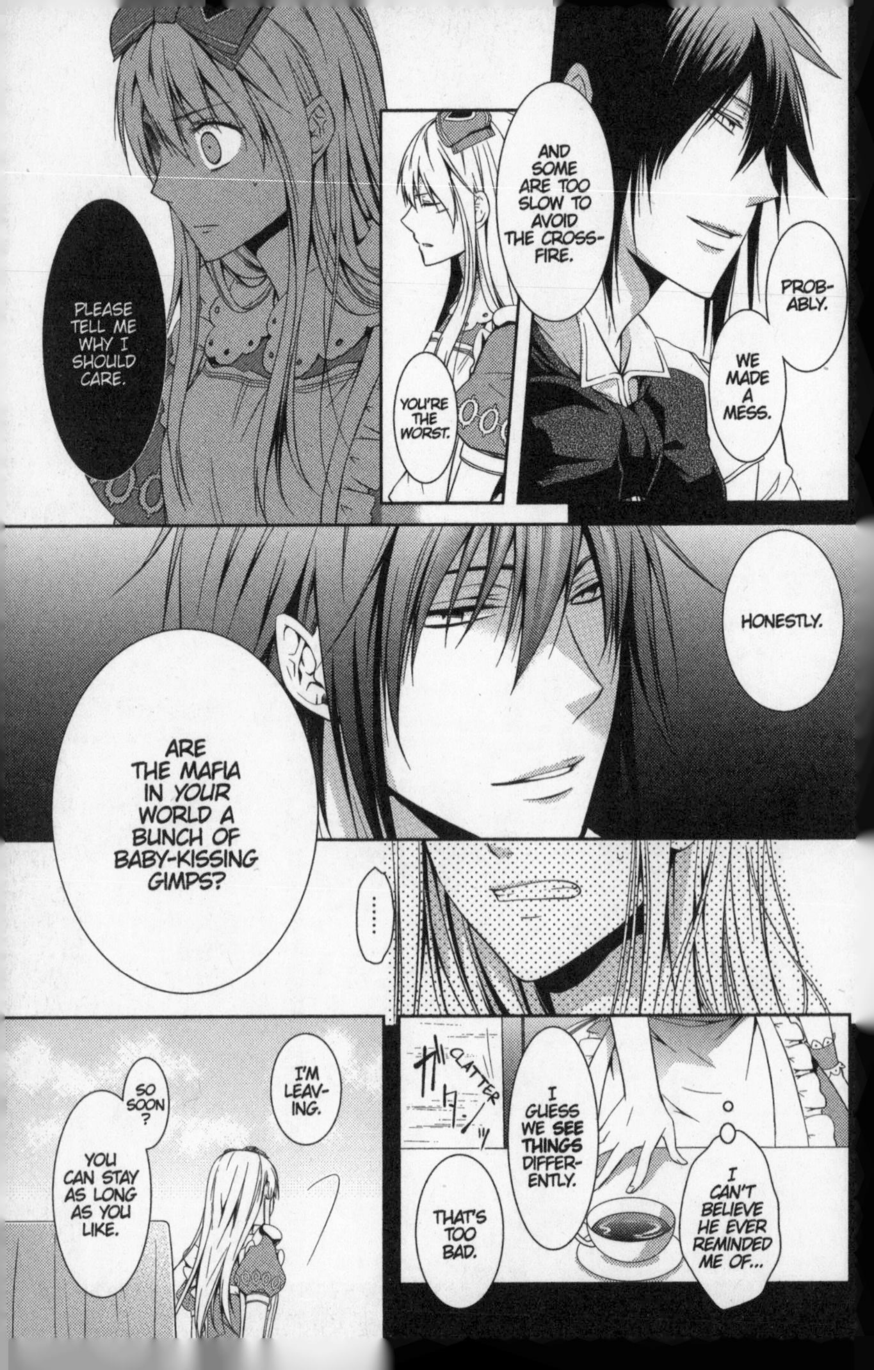
PROBABLY.
WE MADE A MESS.
AND SOME ARE TOO SLOW TO AVOID THE CROSS-FIRE.
YOU'RE THE WORST.
PLEASE TELL ME WHY I SHOULD CARE.
HONESTLY.
ARE THE MAFIA IN YOUR WORLD A BUNCH OF BABY-KISSING GIMPS?
......
CLATTER
I GUESS WE SEE THINGS DIFFERENTLY.
I CAN'T BELIEVE HE EVER REMINDED ME OF...
THAT'S TOO BAD.
I'M LEAVING.
SO SOON?
YOU CAN STAY AS LONG AS YOU LIKE.

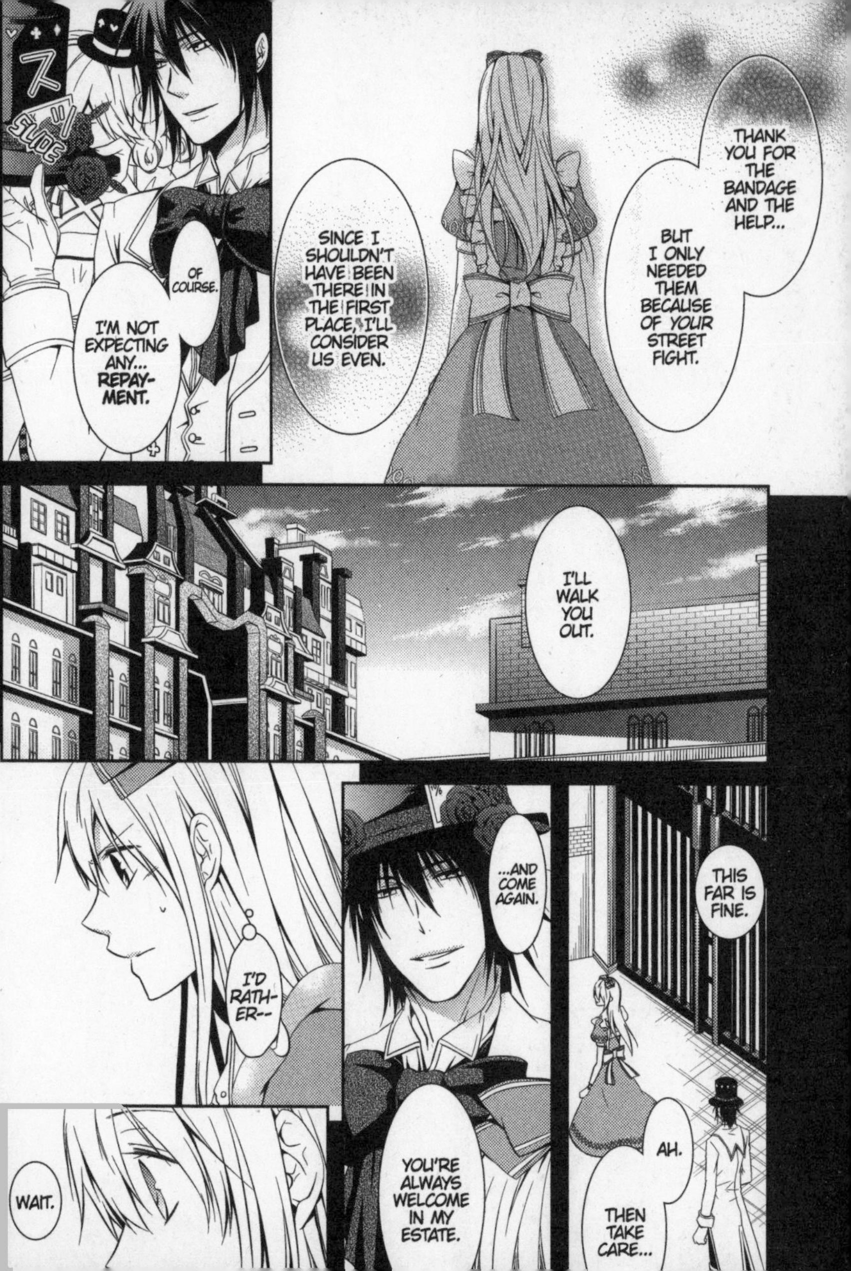
THANK YOU FOR THE BANDAGE AND THE HELP...
BUT I ONLY NEEDED THEM BECAUSE OF YOUR STREET FIGHT.
SINCE I SHOULDN'T HAVE BEEN THERE IN THE FIRST PLACE, I'LL CONSIDER US EVEN.
スッ
SLIDE
OF COURSE.
I'M NOT EXPECTING ANY... REPAYMENT.
I'LL WALK YOU OUT.
THIS FAR IS FINE.
AH.
THEN TAKE CARE...
YOU'RE ALWAYS WELCOME IN MY ESTATE.
...AND COME AGAIN.
I'D RATHER--
WAIT.

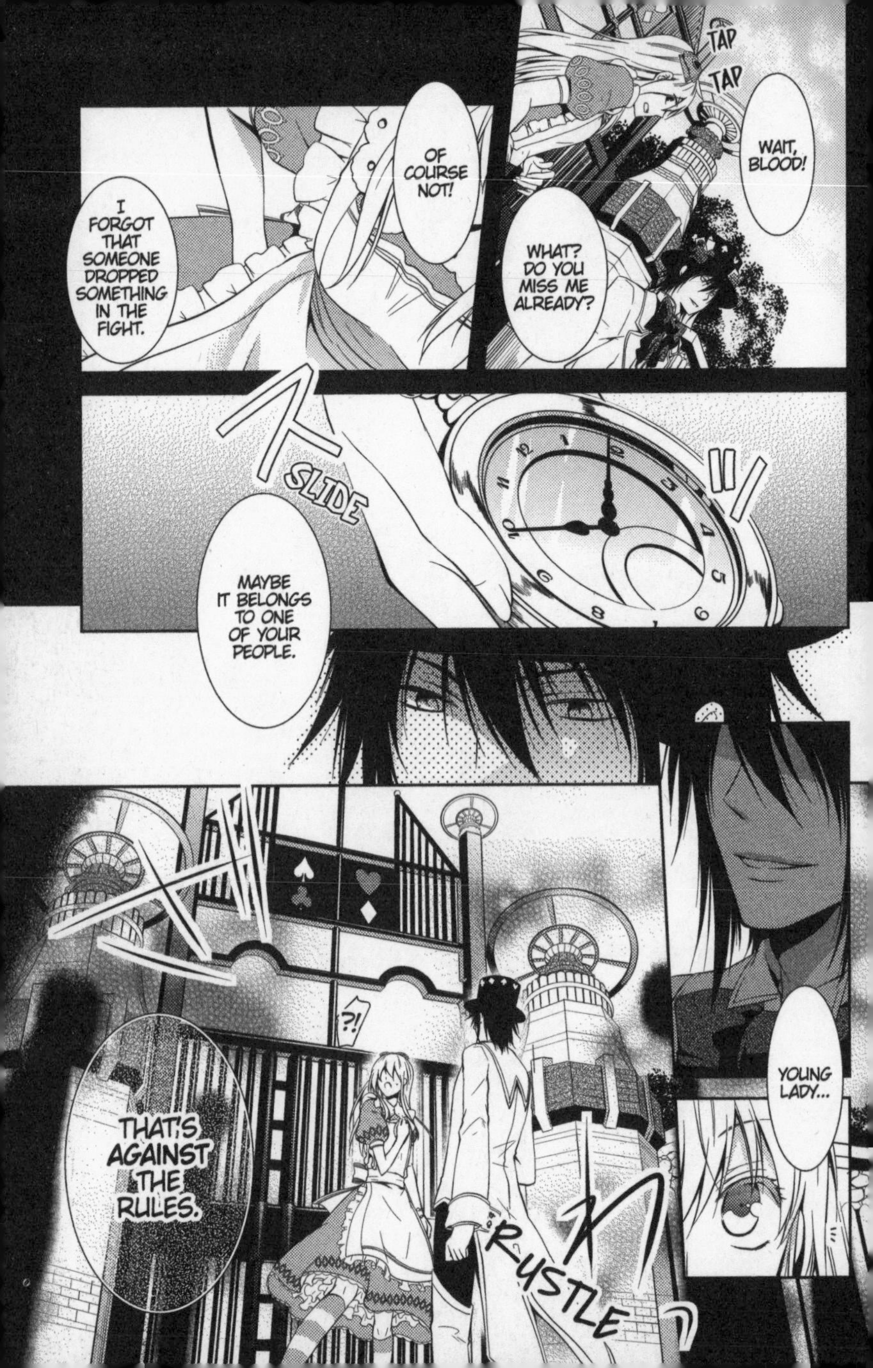

TAP
TAP
WAIT, BLOOD!
WHAT? DO YOU MISS ME ALREADY?
OF COURSE NOT!
I FORGOT THAT SOMEONE DROPPED SOMETHING IN THE FIGHT.
SLIDE
MAYBE IT BELONGS TO ONE OF YOUR PEOPLE.
YOUNG LADY...
?!
RUSTLE
THAT'S AGAINST THE RULES.

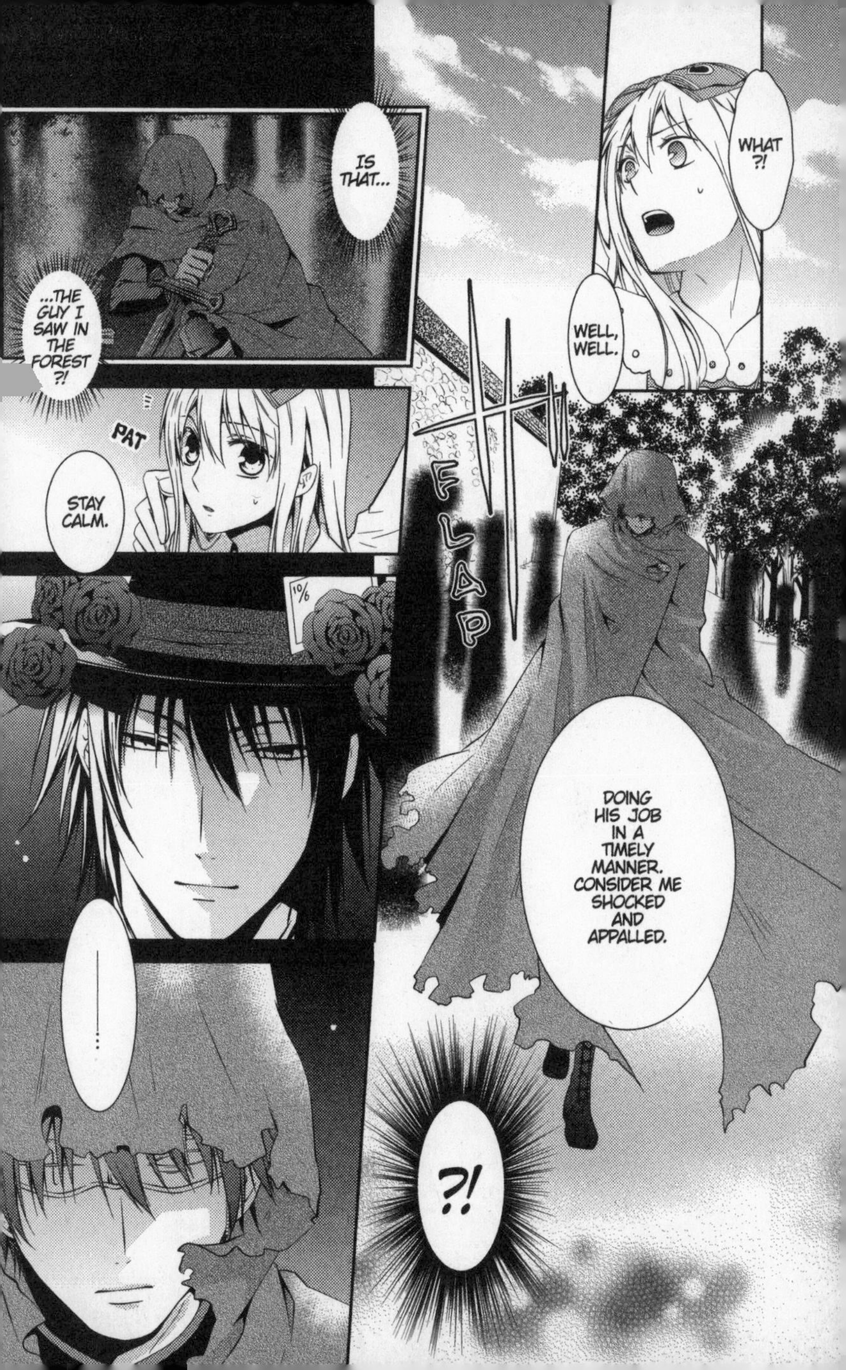
WHAT ?!
WELL, WELL.
FLAP
DOING HIS JOB IN A TIMELY MANNER. CONSIDER ME SHOCKED AND APPALLED.
?!
IS THAT...
...THE GUY I SAW IN THE FOREST ?!
PAT
...
STAY CALM.
10/6
......

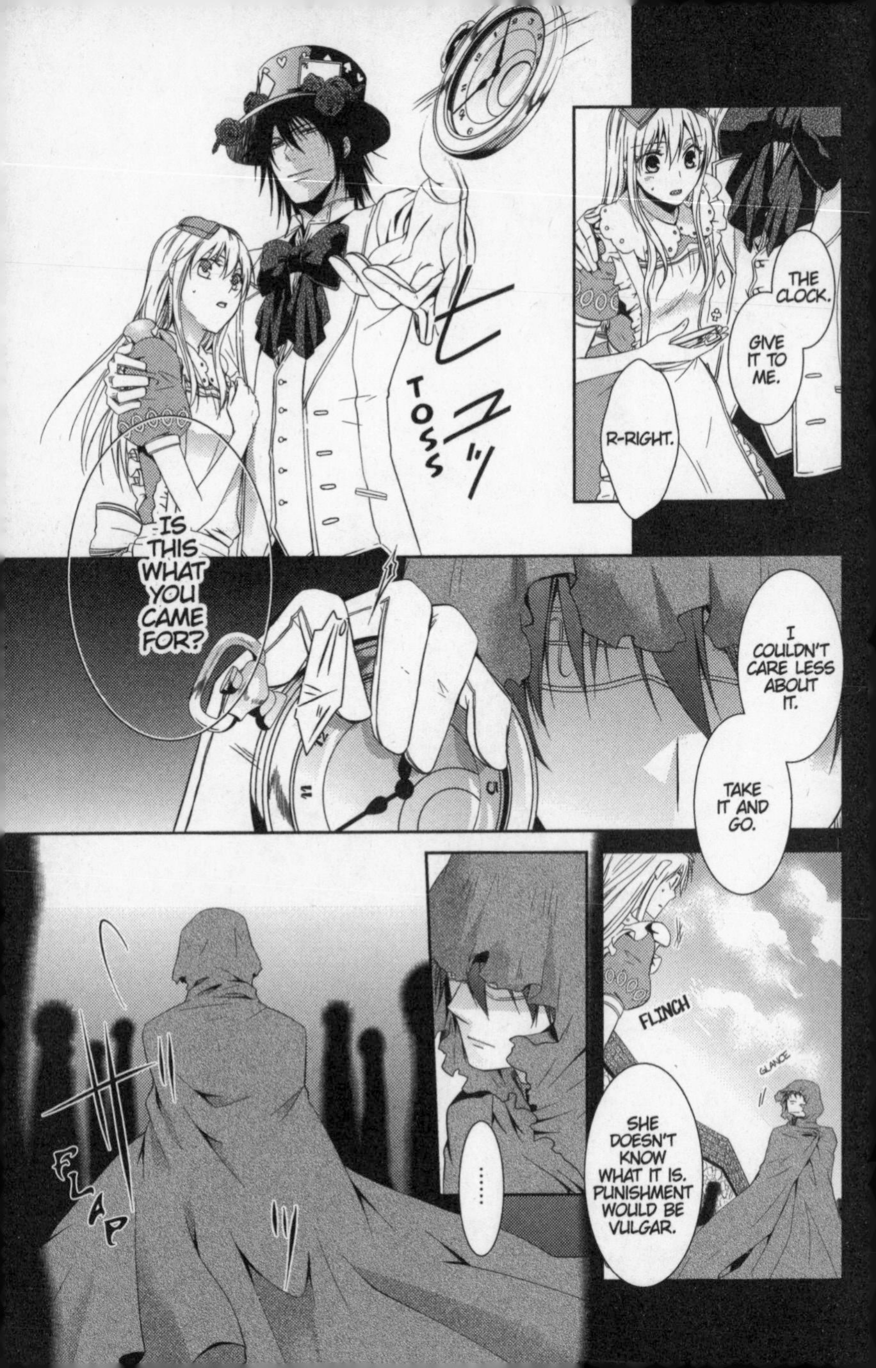
THE CLOCK.
GIVE IT TO ME.
R-RIGHT.
TOSS
IS THIS WHAT YOU CAME FOR?
I COULDN'T CARE LESS ABOUT IT.
TAKE IT AND GO.
FLINCH
GLANCE
SHE DOESN'T KNOW WHAT IT IS. PUNISHMENT WOULD BE VULGAR.
......
FLAP

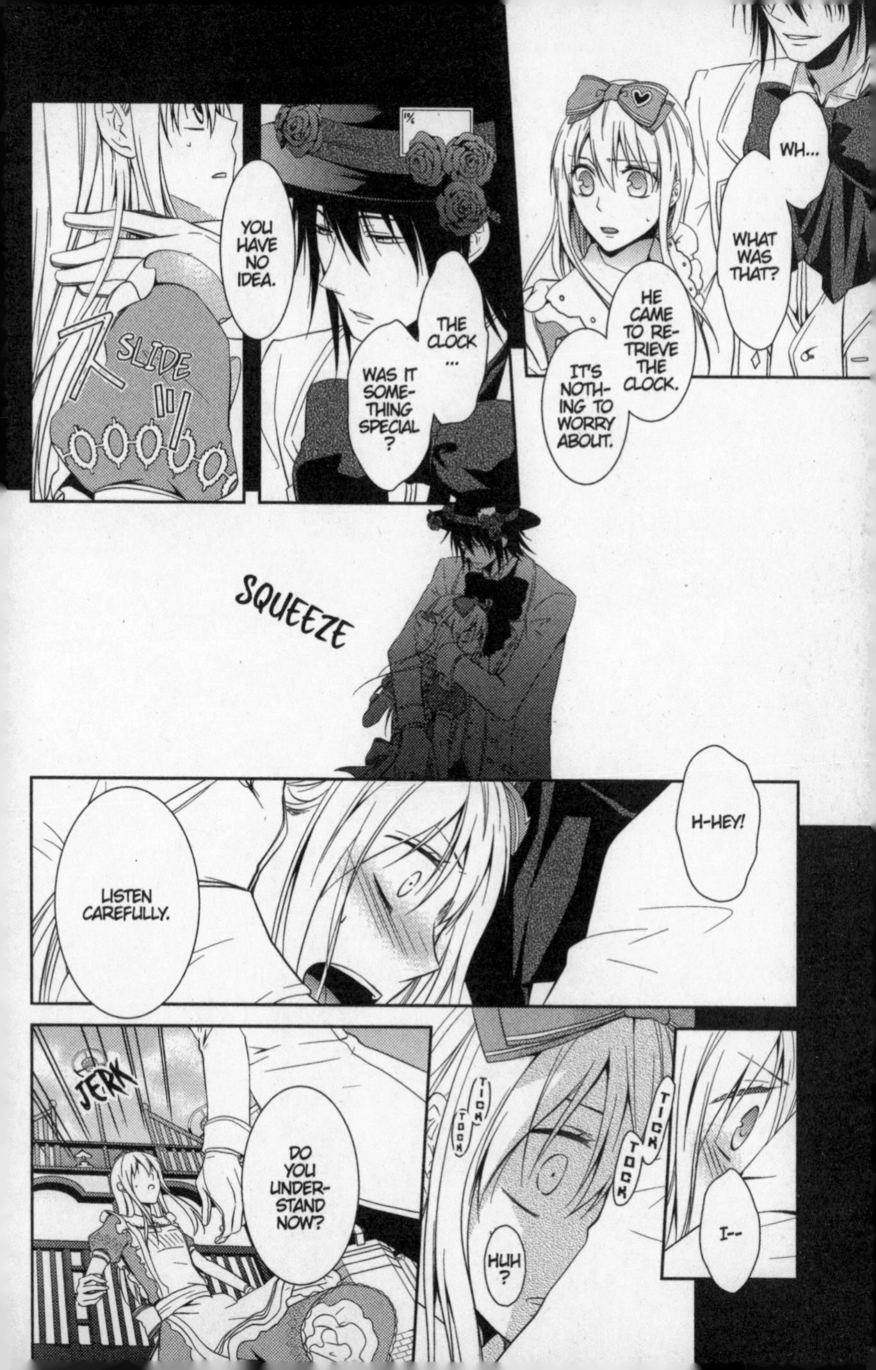
WH...
WHAT WAS THAT?
HE CAME TO RE-TRIEVE THE CLOCK.
IT'S NOTH-ING TO WORRY ABOUT.
THE CLOCK ...
WAS IT SOME-THING SPECIAL ?
YOU HAVE NO IDEA.
SLIDE
SQUEEZE
H-HEY!
LISTEN CAREFULLY.
I--
TICK TOCK
TICK TOCK
HUH ?
DO YOU UNDER-STAND NOW?
JERK

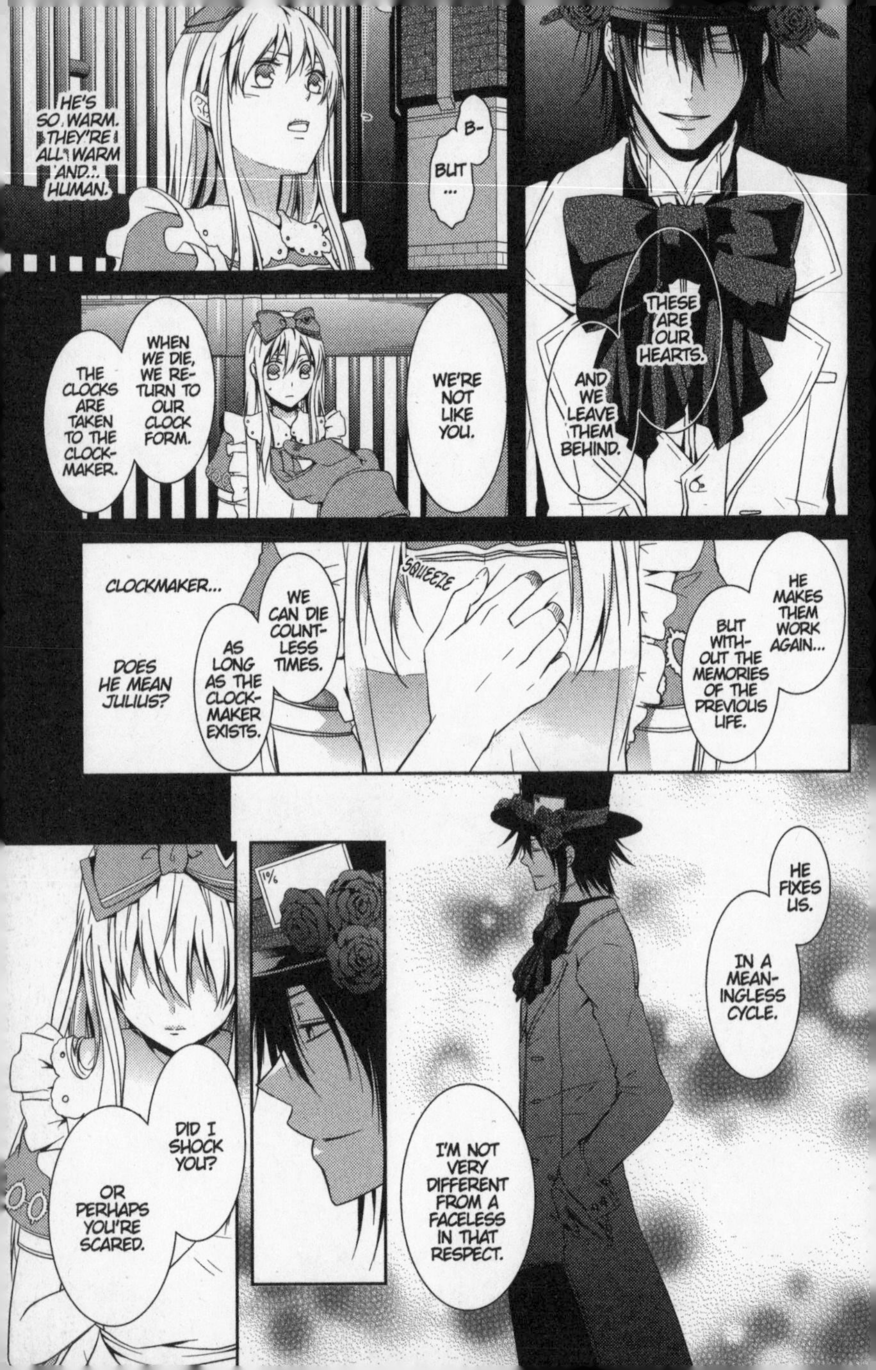
THESE ARE OUR HEARTS.
AND WE LEAVE THEM BEHIND.
B- BUT ...
HE'S SO WARM. THEY'RE ALL WARM AND... HUMAN.
WE'RE NOT LIKE YOU.
WHEN WE DIE, WE RE-TURN TO OUR CLOCK FORM.
THE CLOCKS ARE TAKEN TO THE CLOCK-MAKER.
HE MAKES THEM WORK AGAIN...
BUT WITH-OUT THE MEMORIES OF THE PREVIOUS LIFE.
SQUEEZE
WE CAN DIE COUNT-LESS TIMES.
AS LONG AS THE CLOCK-MAKER EXISTS.
CLOCKMAKER...
DOES HE MEAN JULIUS?
HE FIXES US.
IN A MEAN-INGLESS CYCLE.
I'M NOT VERY DIFFERENT FROM A FACELESS IN THAT RESPECT.
DID I SHOCK YOU?
OR PERHAPS YOU'RE SCARED.

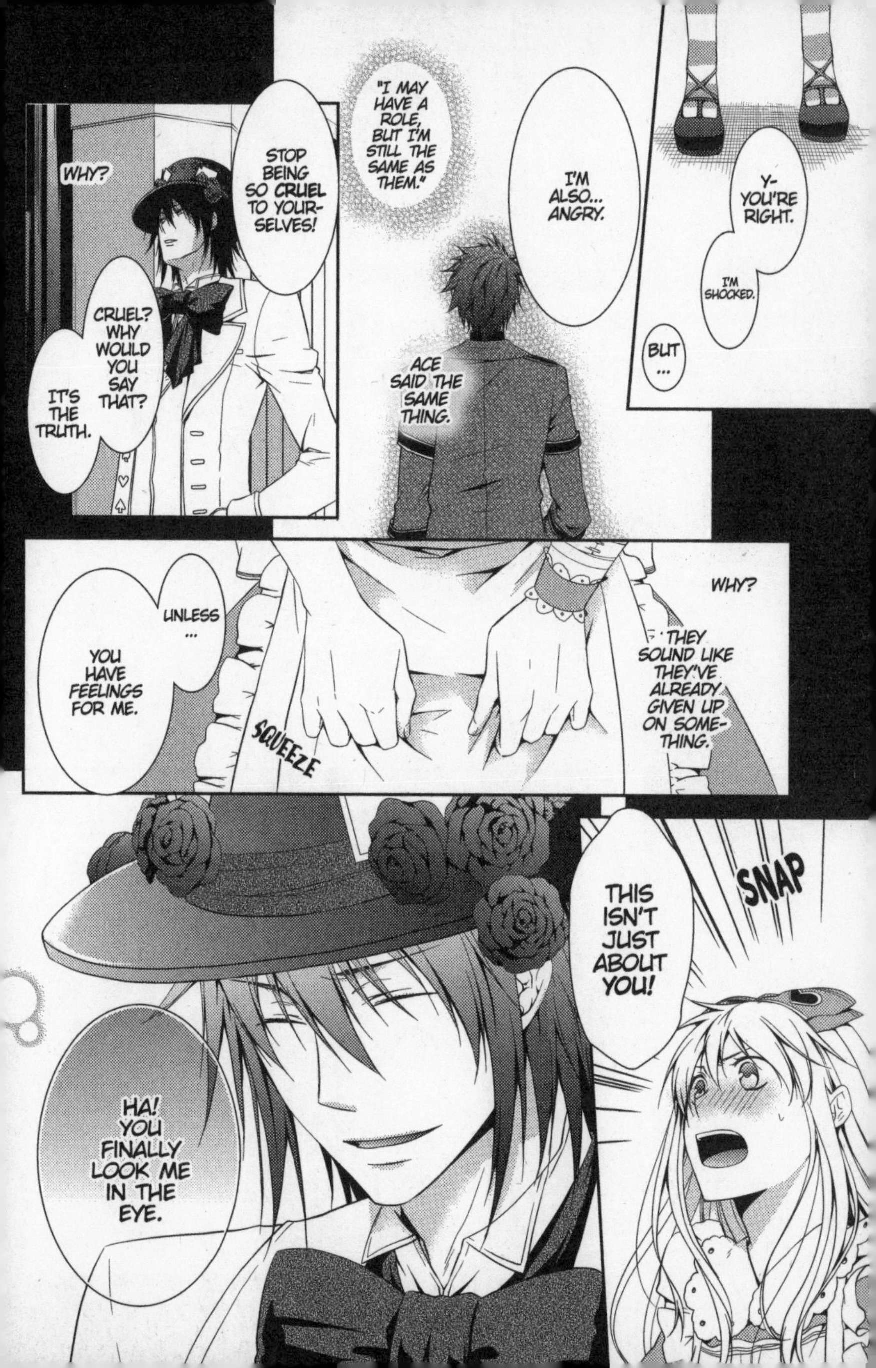
Y-YOU'RE RIGHT.
I'M SHOCKED.
BUT ...
I'M ALSO... ANGRY.
"I MAY HAVE A ROLE, BUT I'M STILL THE SAME AS THEM."
ACE SAID THE SAME THING.
STOP BEING SO CRUEL TO YOUR-SELVES!
WHY?
CRUEL? WHY WOULD YOU SAY THAT?
IT'S THE TRUTH.
WHY?
THEY SOUND LIKE THEY'VE ALREADY GIVEN UP ON SOME-THING.
SQUEEZE
UNLESS ...
YOU HAVE FEELINGS FOR ME.
SNAP
THIS ISN'T JUST ABOUT YOU!
HA! YOU FINALLY LOOK ME IN THE EYE.

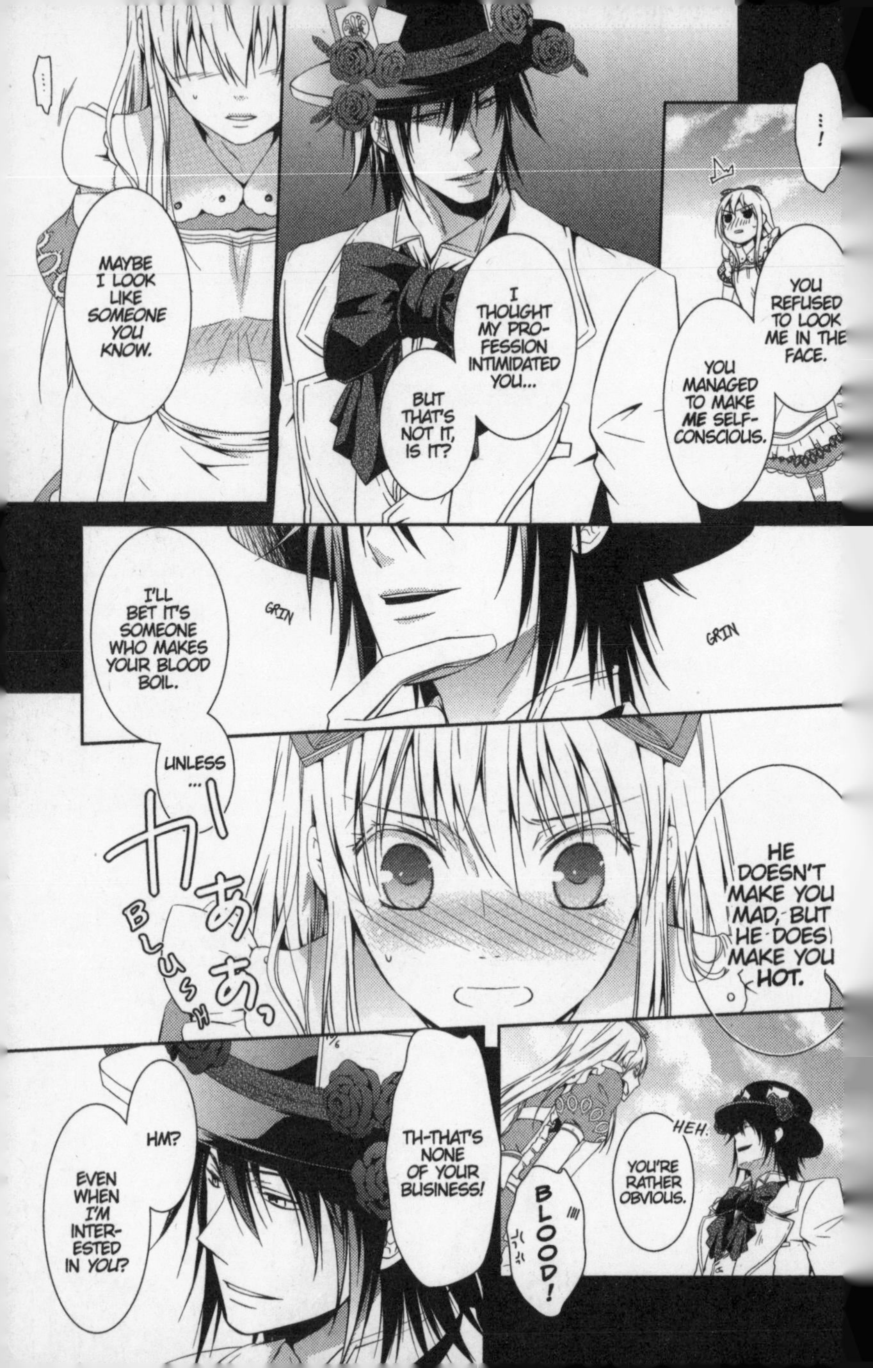
...!
YOU REFUSED TO LOOK ME IN THE FACE.
YOU MANAGED TO MAKE ME SELF-CONSCIOUS.
I THOUGHT MY PROFESSION INTIMIDATED YOU...
BUT THAT'S NOT IT, IS IT?
...
MAYBE I LOOK LIKE SOMEONE YOU KNOW.
GRIN
GRIN
I'LL BET IT'S SOMEONE WHO MAKES YOUR BLOOD BOIL.
HE DOESN'T MAKE YOU MAD, BUT HE DOES MAKE YOU HOT.
UNLESS...
カーあ、あ、
BLUSH
HEH.
YOU'RE RATHER OBVIOUS.
BLOOD!
TH-THAT'S NONE OF YOUR BUSINESS!
HM?
EVEN WHEN I'M INTERESTED IN YOU?

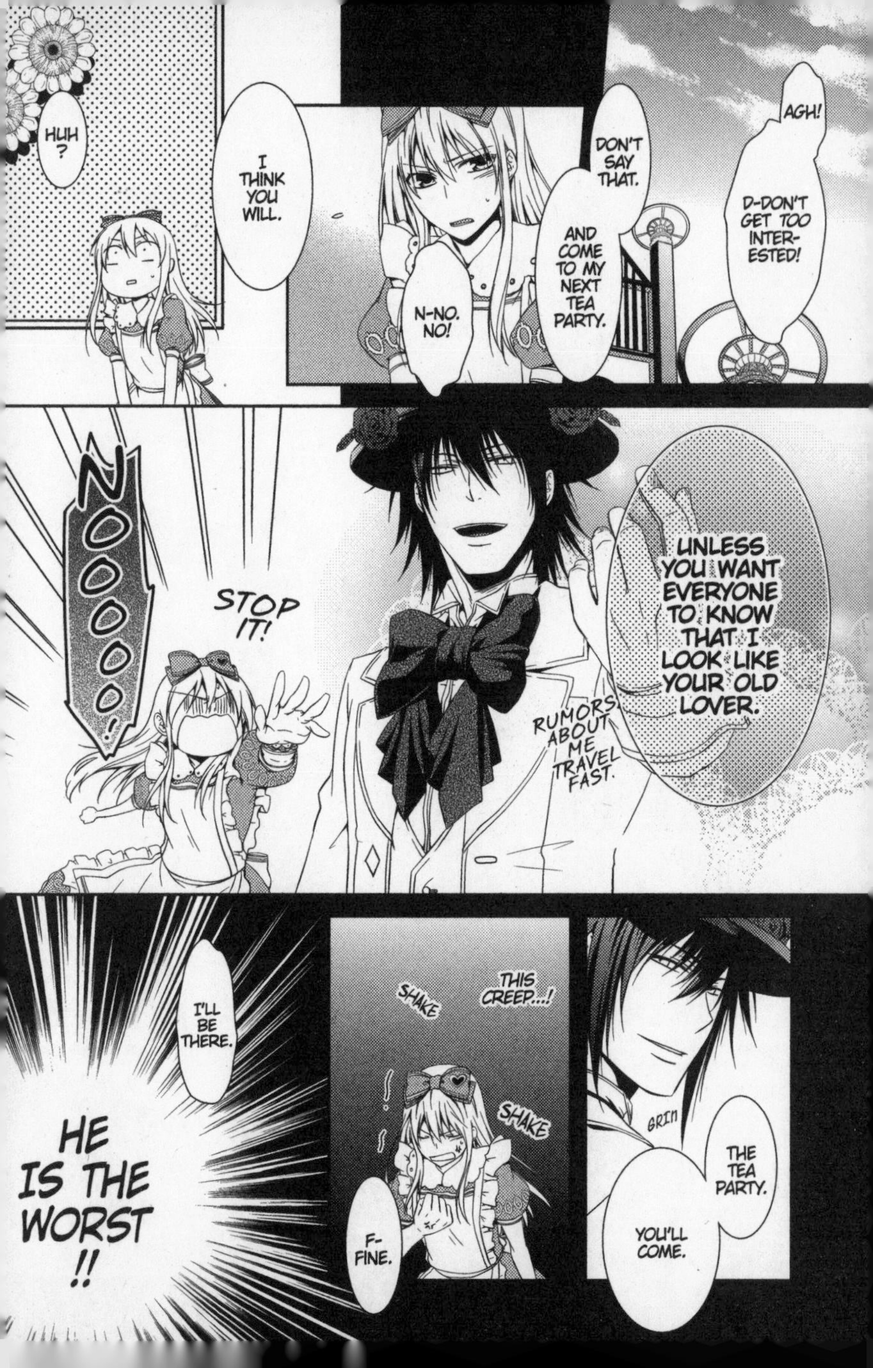
AGH!
D-DON'T GET TOO INTER-ESTED!
DON'T SAY THAT.
AND COME TO MY NEXT TEA PARTY.
N-NO. NO!
I THINK YOU WILL.
HUH?
UNLESS YOU WANT EVERYONE TO KNOW THAT I LOOK LIKE YOUR OLD LOVER.
RUMORS ABOUT ME TRAVEL FAST.
STOP IT!
NOOOOOO!
GRIN
THE TEA PARTY.
YOU'LL COME.
THIS CREEP...!
SHAKE
SHAKE
F-FINE.
I'LL BE THERE.
HE IS THE WORST!!

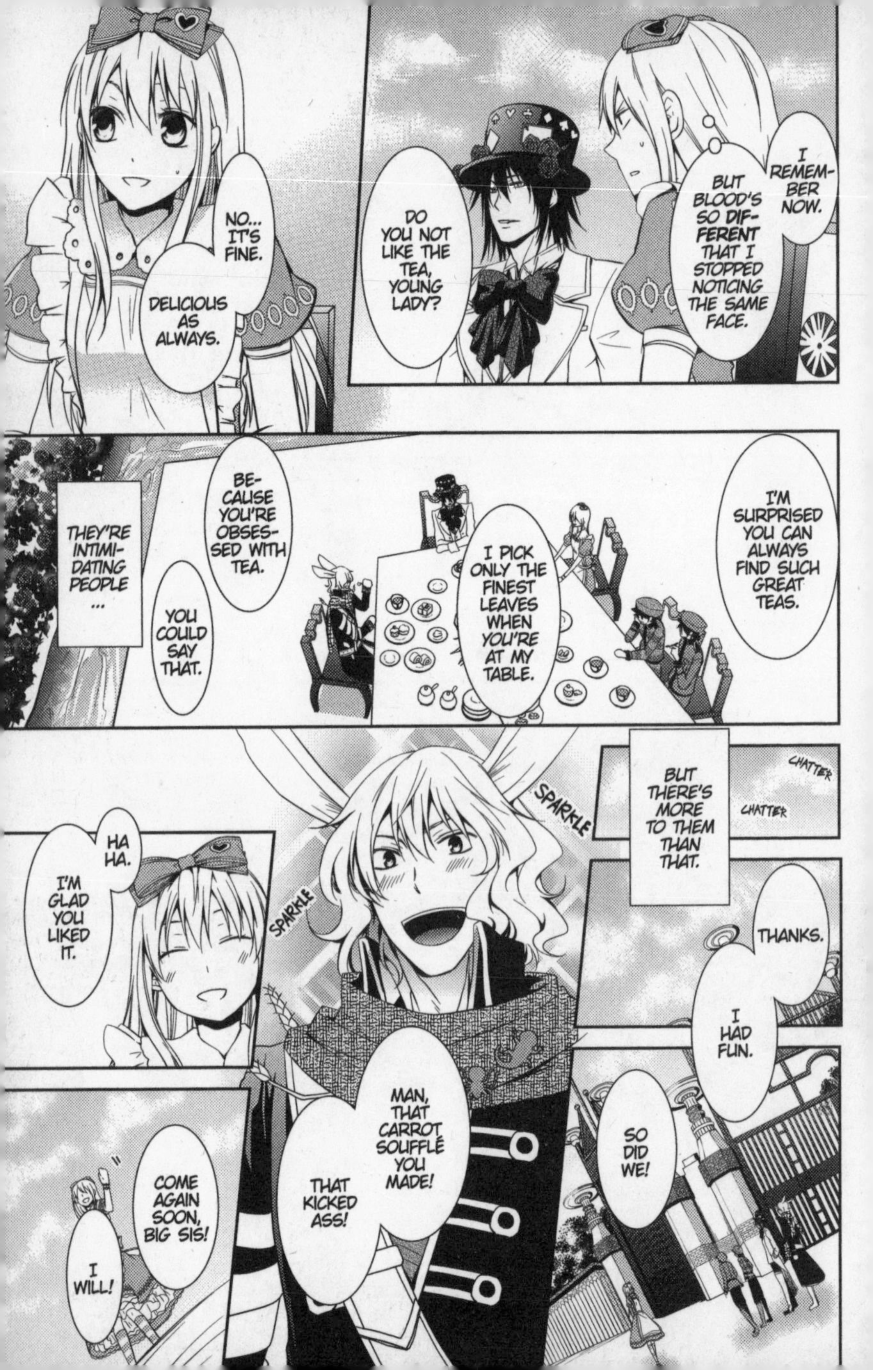
I REMEMBER NOW.
BUT BLOOD'S SO DIFFERENT THAT I STOPPED NOTICING THE SAME FACE.
DO YOU NOT LIKE THE TEA, YOUNG LADY?
NO... IT'S FINE.
DELICIOUS AS ALWAYS.
I'M SURPRISED YOU CAN ALWAYS FIND SUCH GREAT TEAS.
I PICK ONLY THE FINEST LEAVES WHEN YOU'RE AT MY TABLE.
BECAUSE YOU'RE OBSESSED WITH TEA.
YOU COULD SAY THAT.
THEY'RE INTIMIDATING PEOPLE ...
BUT THERE'S MORE TO THEM THAN THAT.
CHATTER
CHATTER
THANKS.
I HAD FUN.
SO DID WE!
SPARKLE
SPARKLE
MAN, THAT CARROT SOUFFLÉ YOU MADE!
THAT KICKED ASS!
HA HA.
I'M GLAD YOU LIKED IT.
COME AGAIN SOON, BIG SIS!
I WILL!

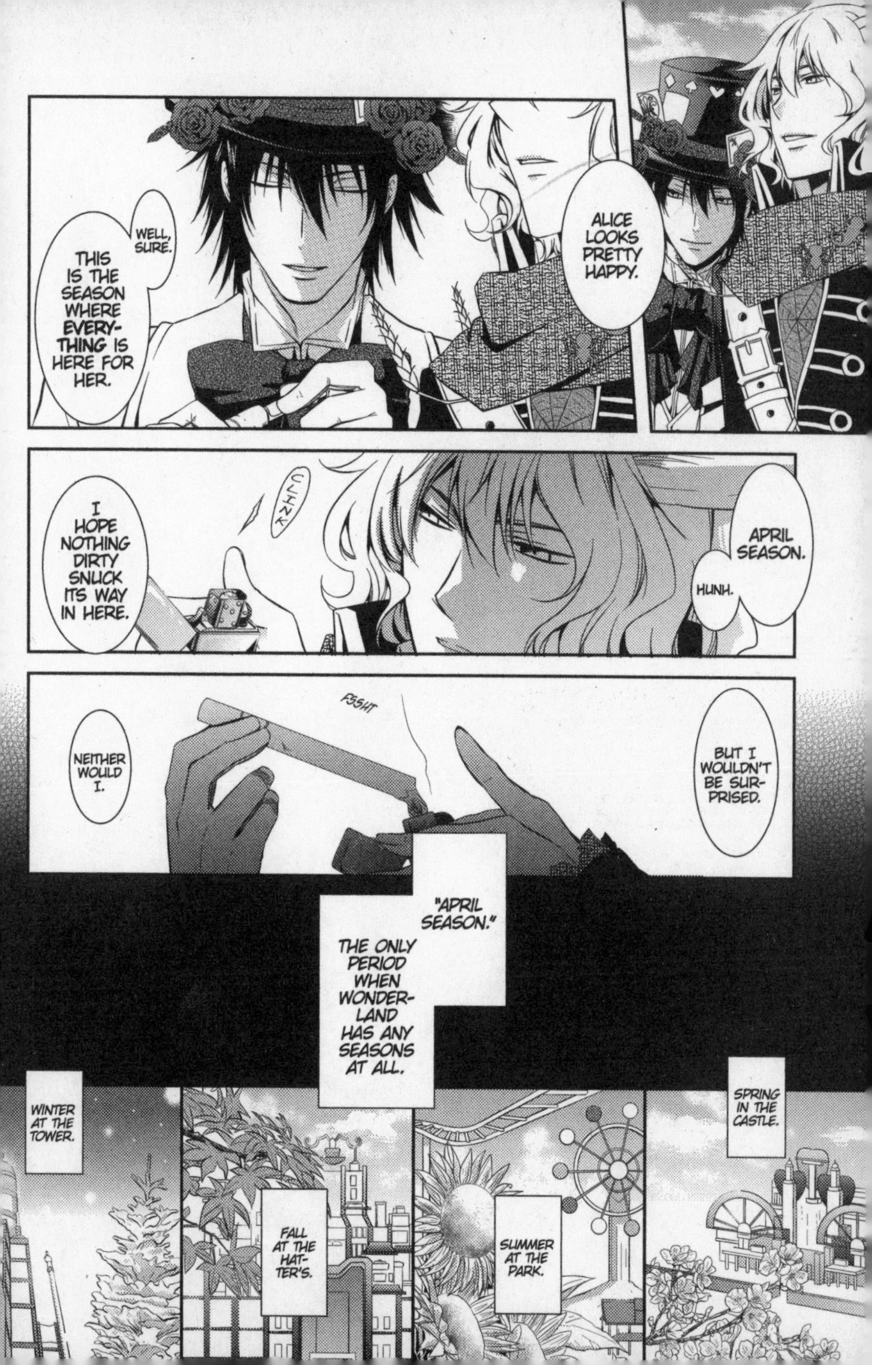
ALICE LOOKS PRETTY HAPPY.
WELL, SURE.
THIS IS THE SEASON WHERE EVERY-THING IS HERE FOR HER.
APRIL SEASON.
HUNH.
CLINK
I HOPE NOTHING DIRTY SNUCK ITS WAY IN HERE.
BUT I WOULDN'T BE SUR-PRISED.
FSSHT
NEITHER WOULD I.
"APRIL SEASON."
THE ONLY PERIOD WHEN WONDER-LAND HAS ANY SEASONS AT ALL.
SPRING IN THE CASTLE.
SUMMER AT THE PARK.
FALL AT THE HAT-TER'S.
WINTER AT THE TOWER.

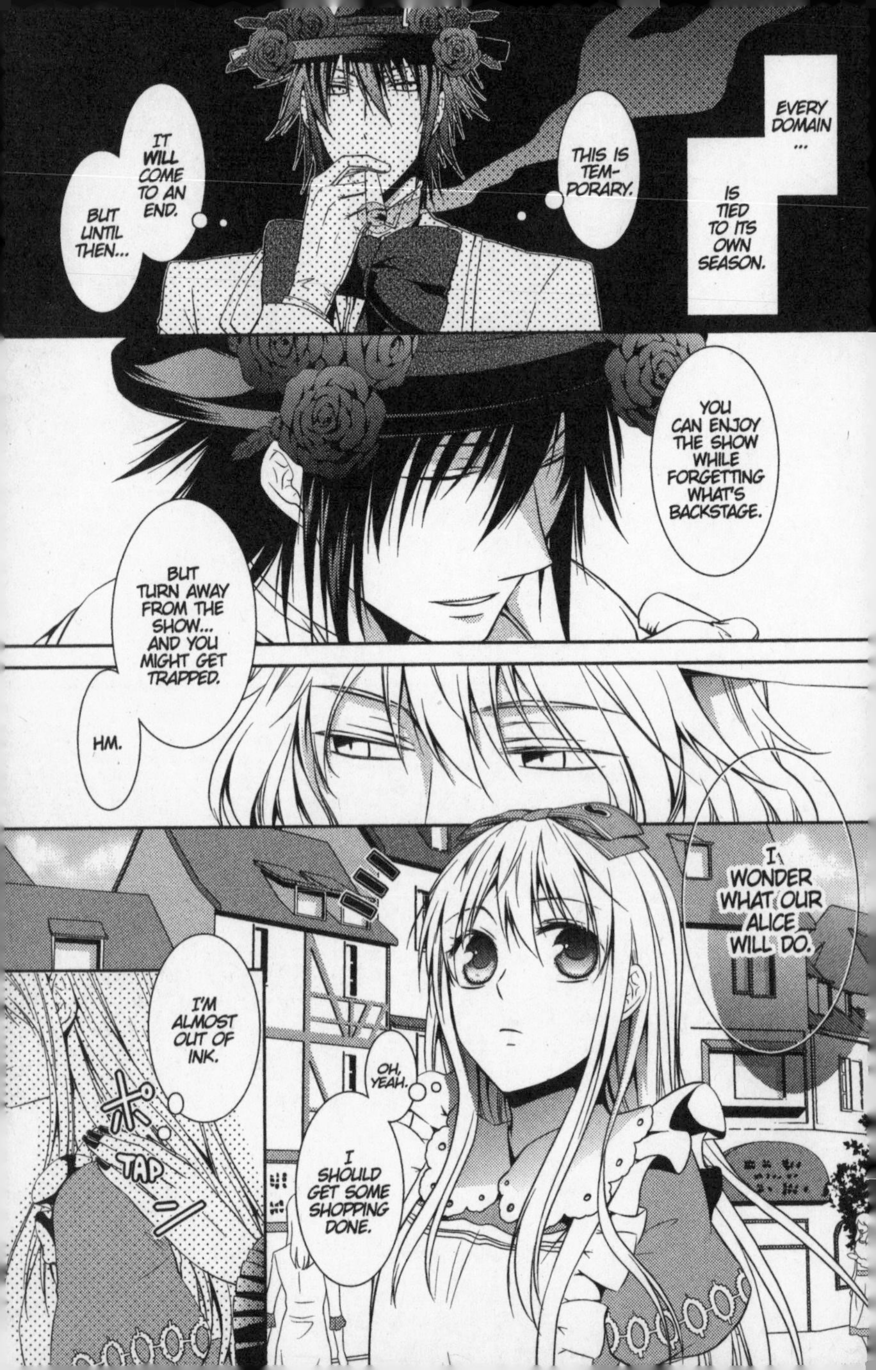
EVERY DOMAIN...
IS TIED TO ITS OWN SEASON.
THIS IS TEMPORARY.
IT WILL COME TO AN END.
BUT UNTIL THEN...
YOU CAN ENJOY THE SHOW WHILE FORGETTING WHAT'S BACKSTAGE.
BUT TURN AWAY FROM THE SHOW... AND YOU MIGHT GET TRAPPED.
HM.
I WONDER WHAT OUR ALICE WILL DO.
OH, YEAH.
I SHOULD GET SOME SHOPPING DONE.
I'M ALMOST OUT OF INK.
TAP

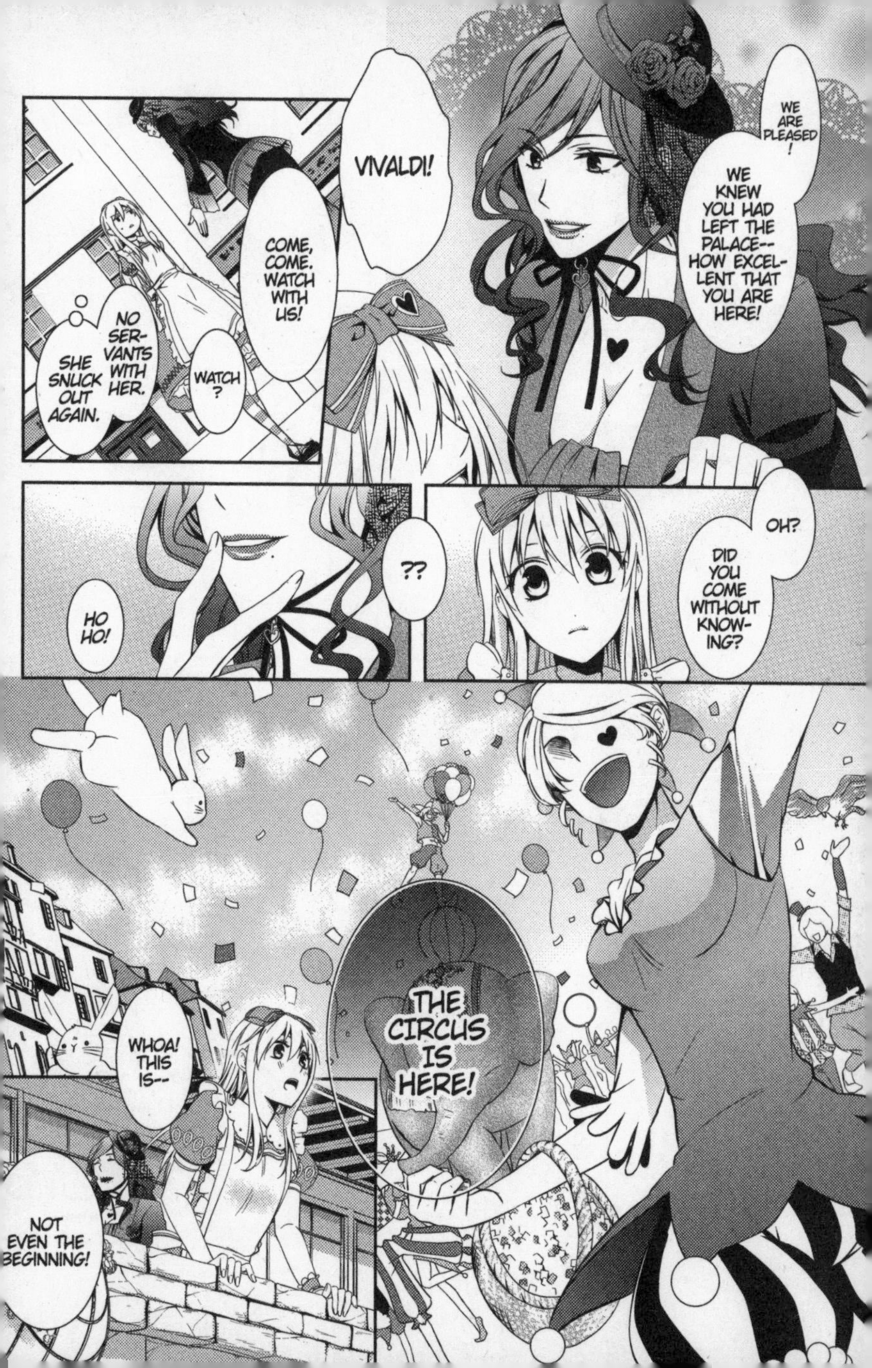
VIVALDI!
WE ARE PLEASED!
WE KNEW YOU HAD LEFT THE PALACE--HOW EXCEL-LENT THAT YOU ARE HERE!
COME, COME. WATCH WITH US!
WATCH?
NO SER-VANTS WITH HER.
SHE SNUCK OUT AGAIN.
OH?
DID YOU COME WITHOUT KNOW-ING?
??
HO HO!
THE CIRCUS IS HERE!
WHOA! THIS IS--
NOT EVEN THE BEGINNING!

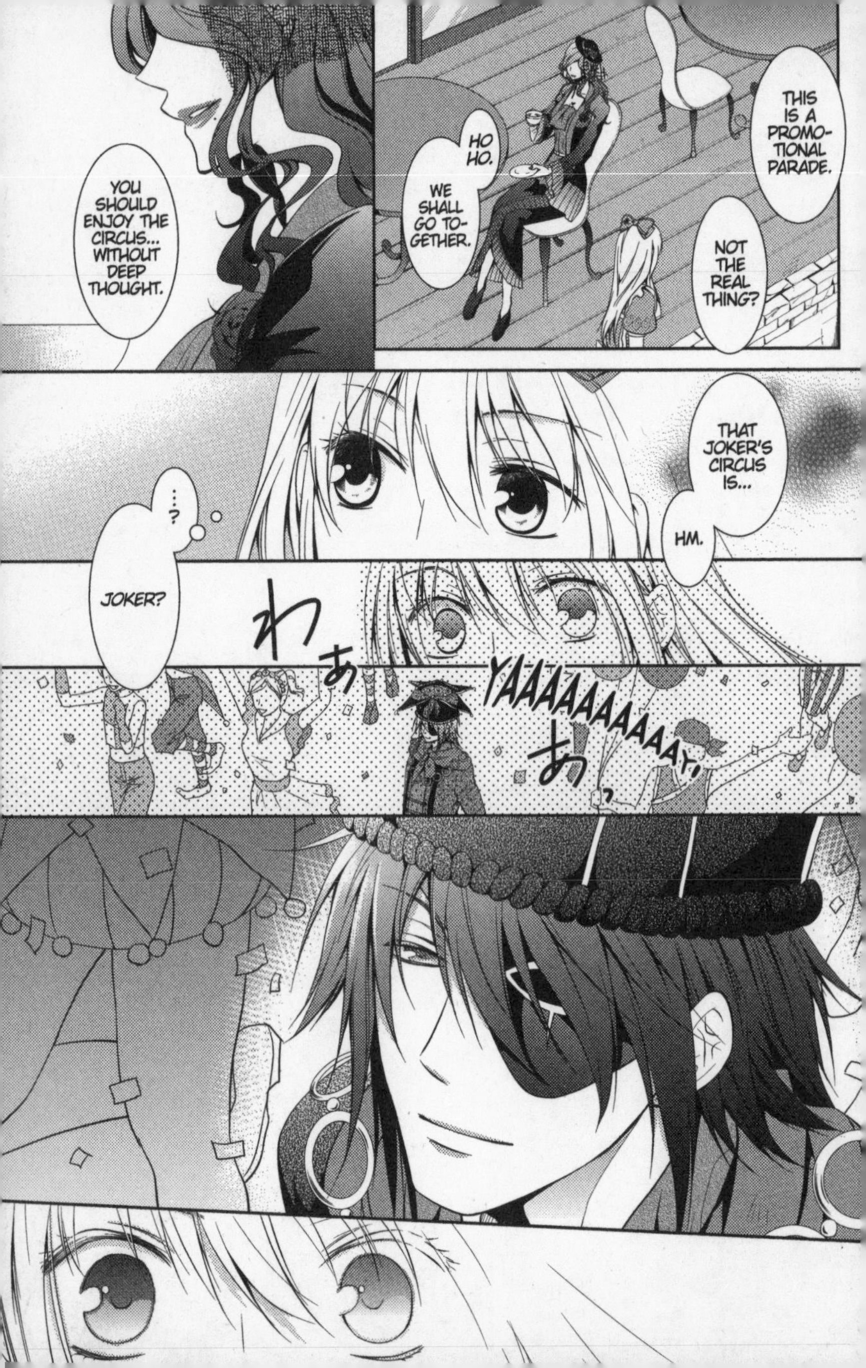
THIS IS A PROMOTIONAL PARADE.
NOT THE REAL THING?
HO HO.
WE SHALL GO TOGETHER.
YOU SHOULD ENJOY THE CIRCUS... WITHOUT DEEP THOUGHT.
THAT JOKER'S CIRCUS IS...
HM.
...?
JOKER?
わあ
YAAAAAAAAAAAY!
あっ

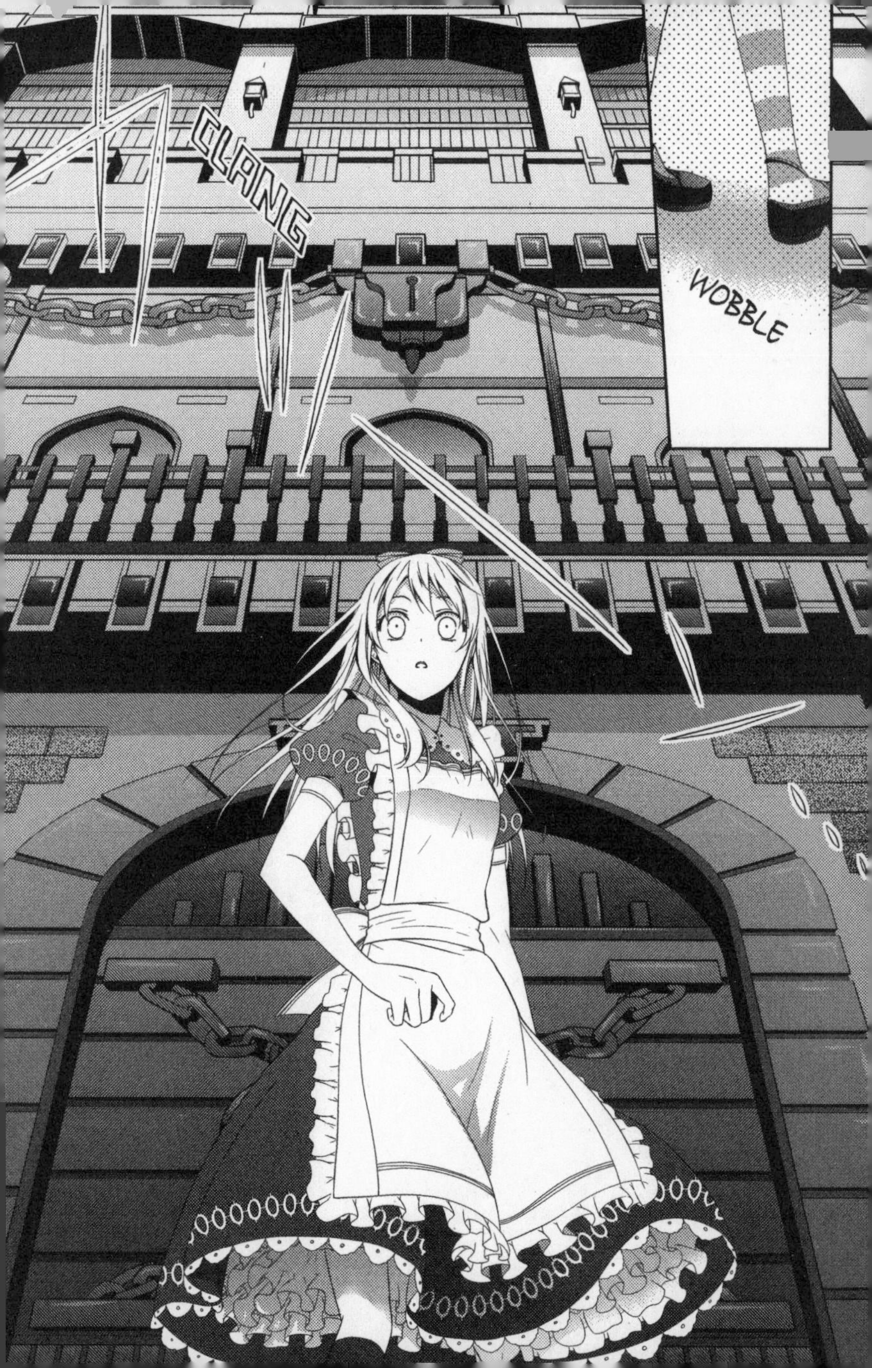
WOBBLE
CLANG

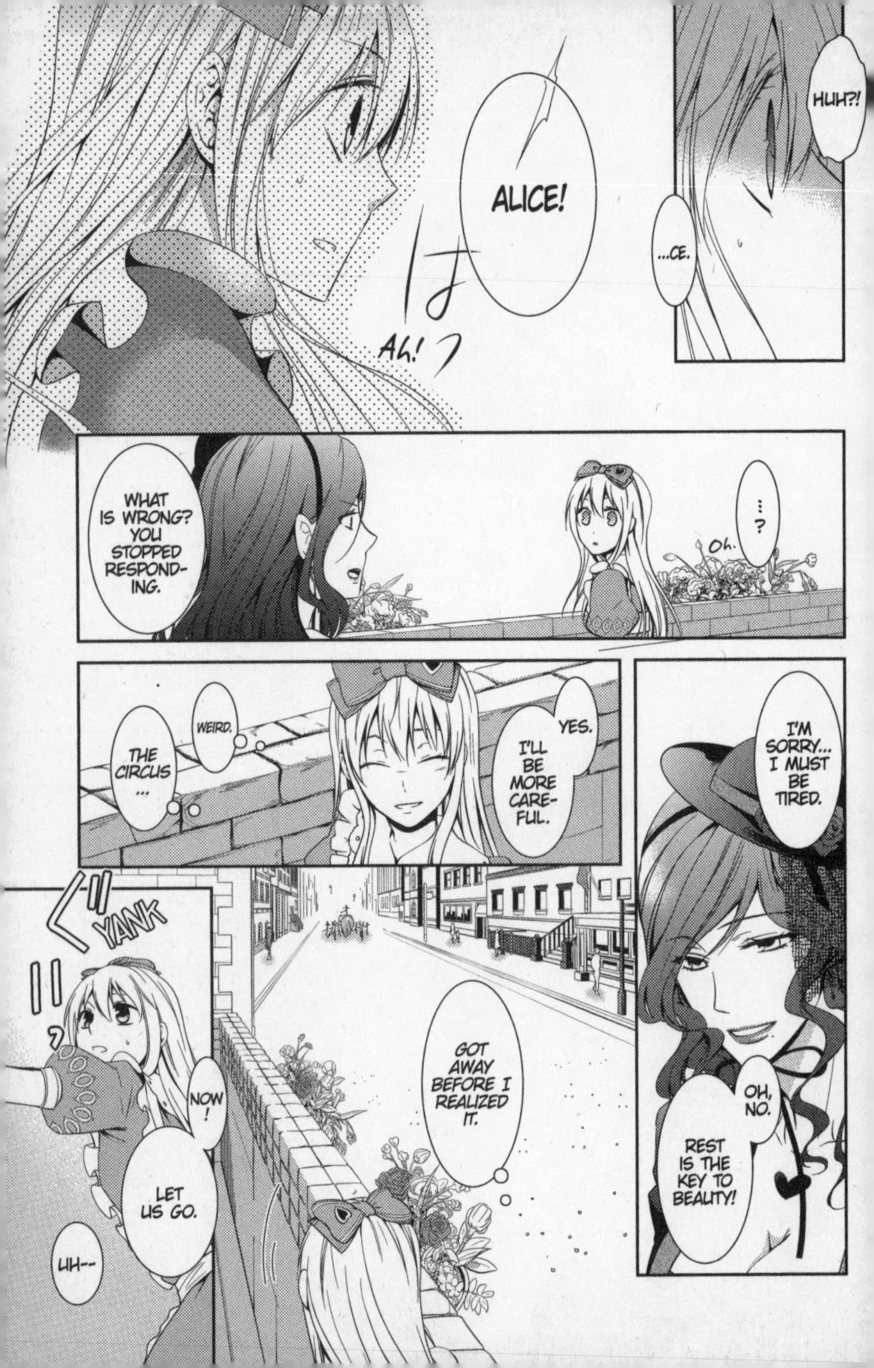
HUH?!
...CE.
ALICE!
Ah!
...?
Oh.
WHAT IS WRONG? YOU STOPPED RESPOND-ING.
I'M SORRY... I MUST BE TIRED.
OH, NO.
REST IS THE KEY TO BEAUTY!
YES.
I'LL BE MORE CARE-FUL.
WEIRD.
THE CIRCUS ...
GOT AWAY BEFORE I REALIZED IT.
YANK
NOW!
LET US GO.
UH--

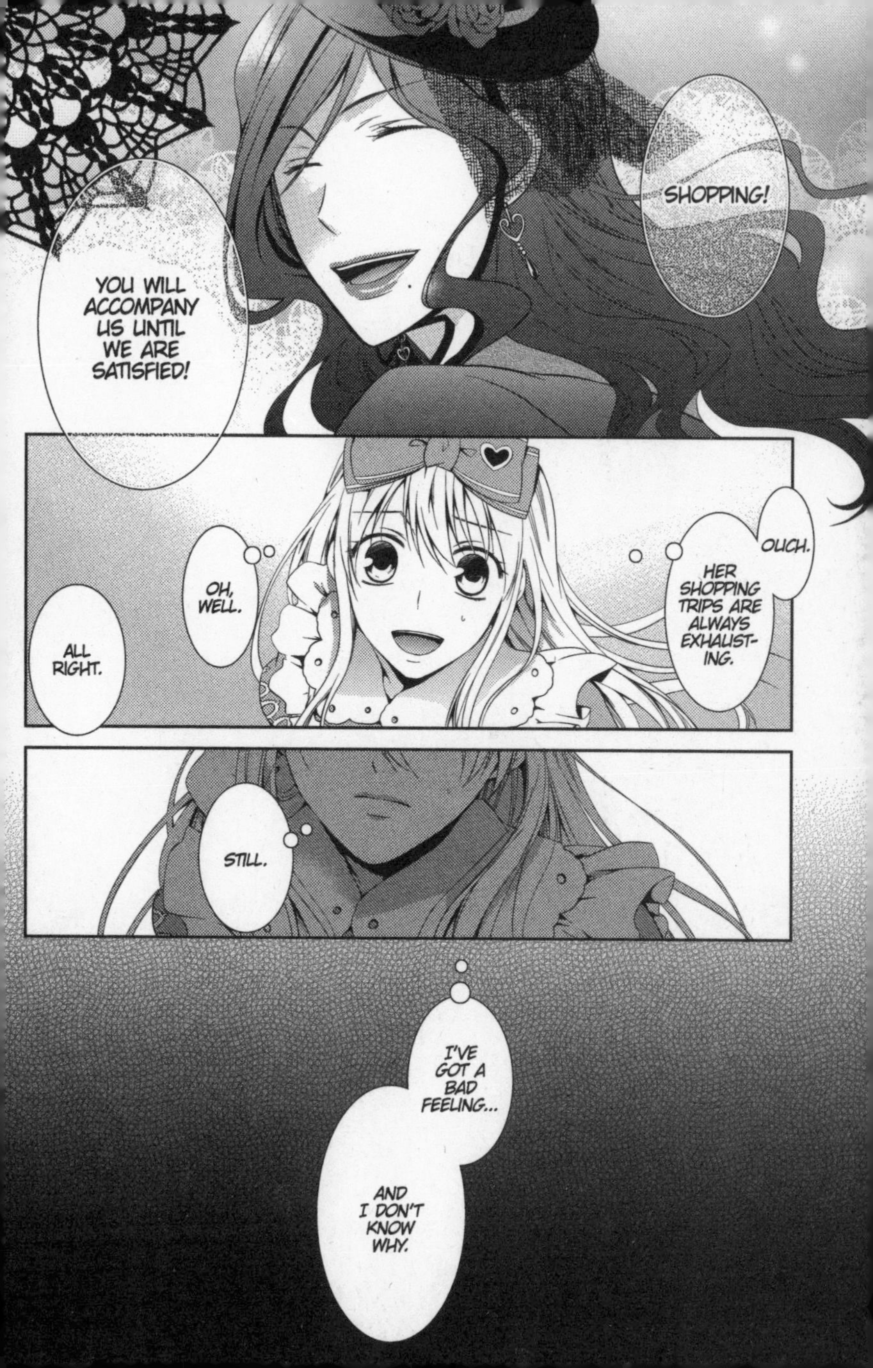
SHOPPING!
YOU WILL ACCOMPANY US UNTIL WE ARE SATISFIED!
OUCH. HER SHOPPING TRIPS ARE ALWAYS EXHAUSTING.
OH, WELL.
ALL RIGHT.
STILL.
I'VE GOT A BAD FEELING...
AND I DON'T KNOW WHY.

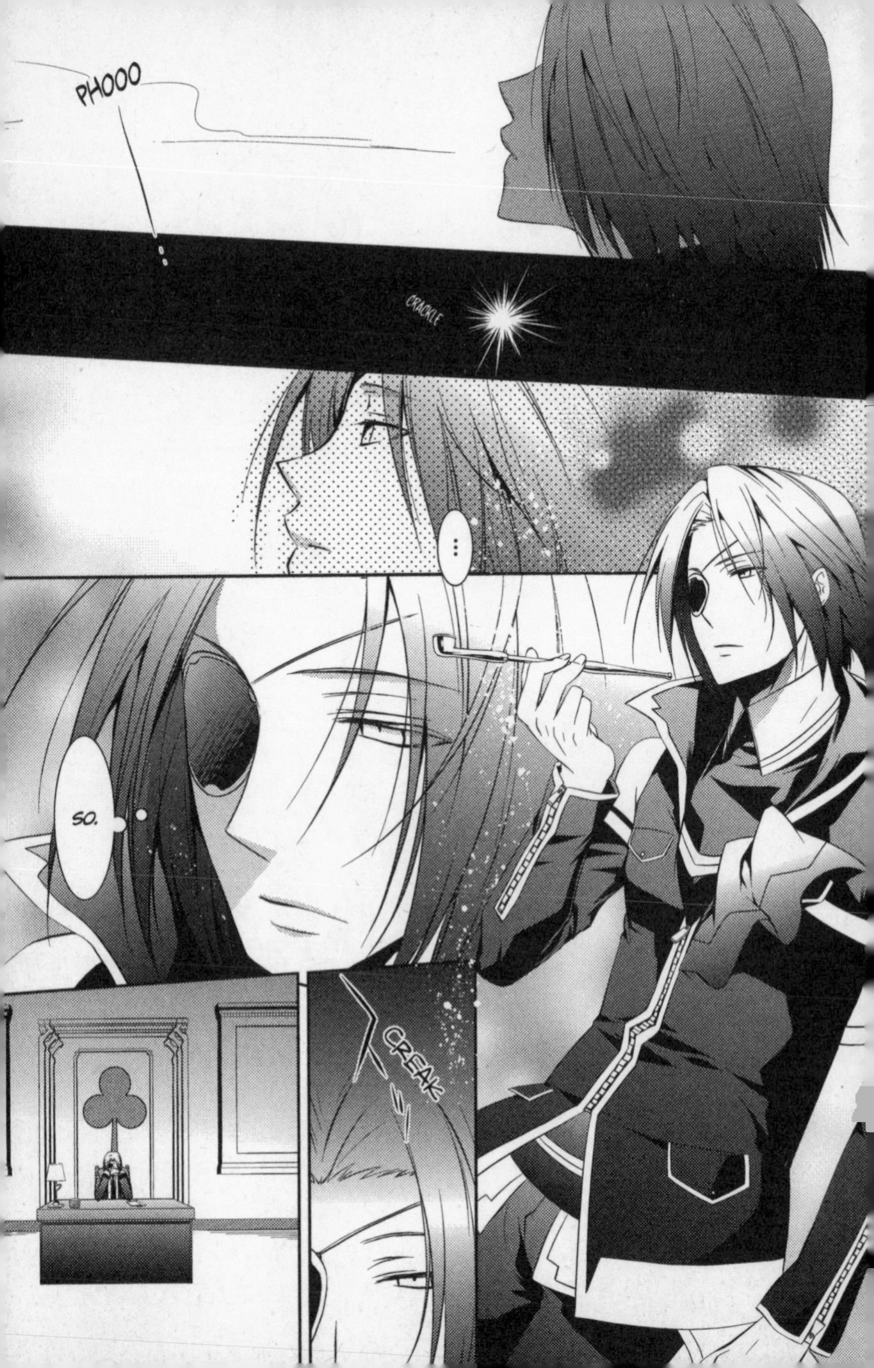
PHOOO
CRACKLE
...
SO.
CREAK

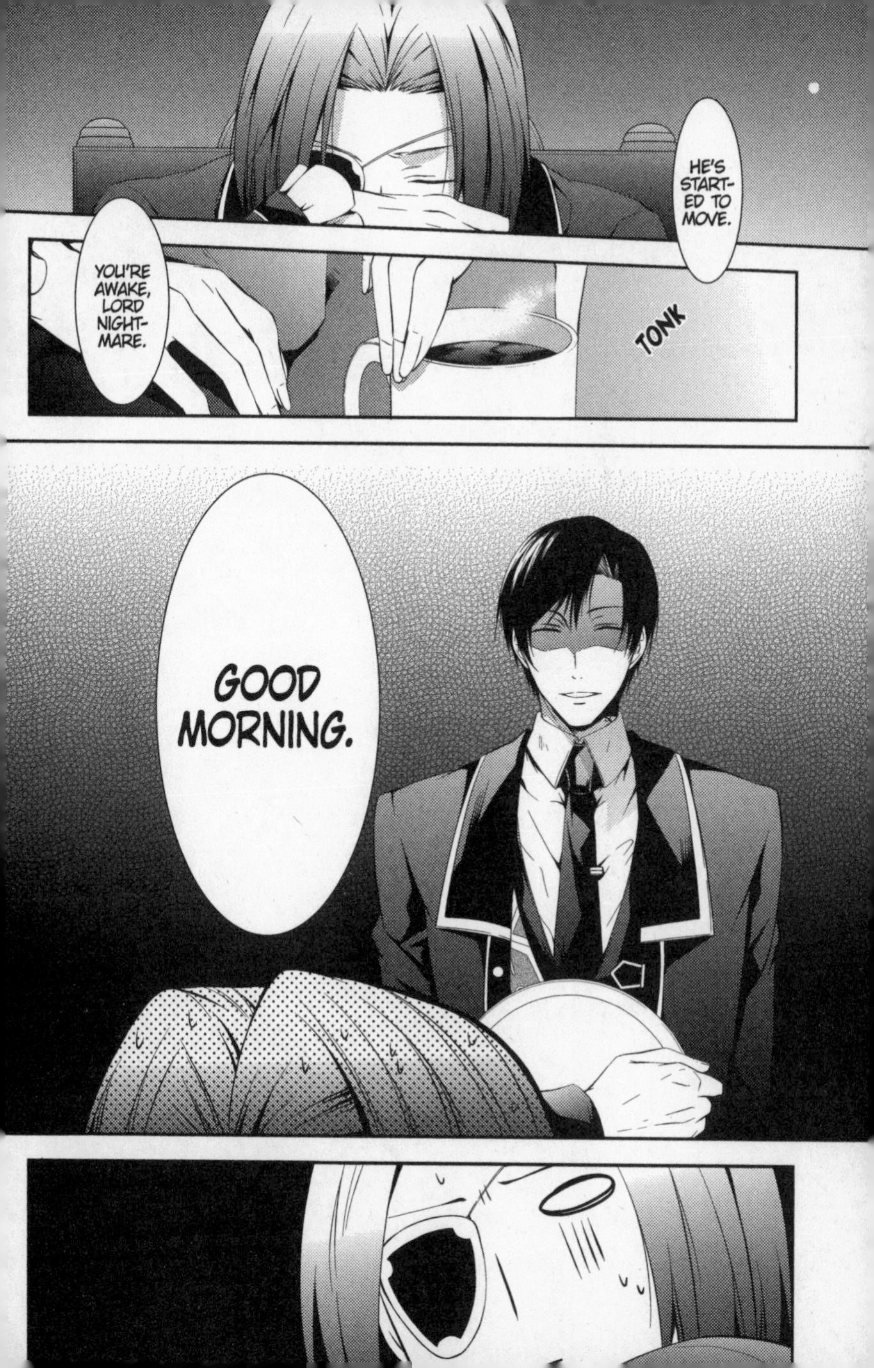
HE'S START-ED TO MOVE.
YOU'RE AWAKE, LORD NIGHT-MARE.
TONK
GOOD MORNING.

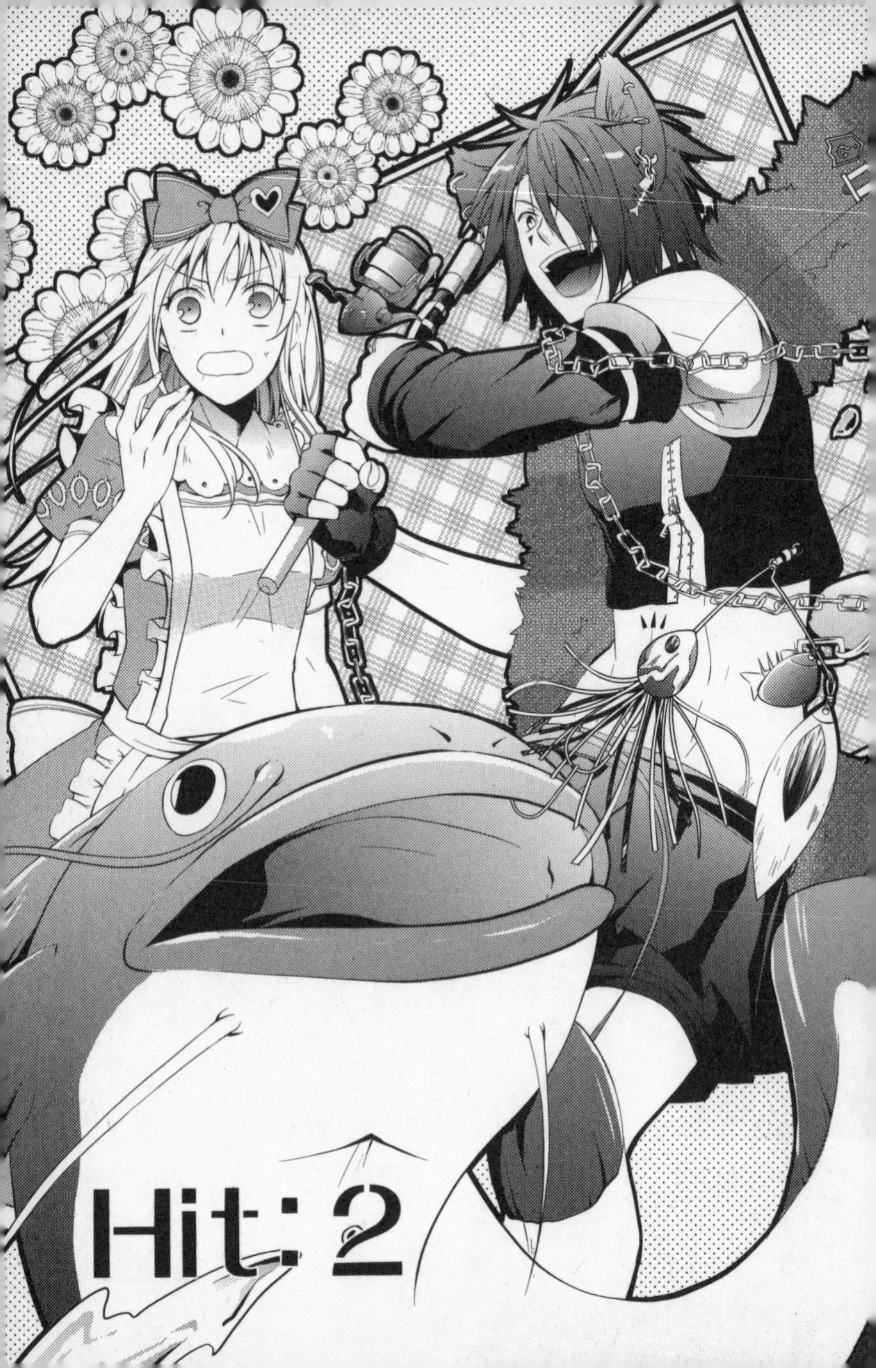
Hit: 2

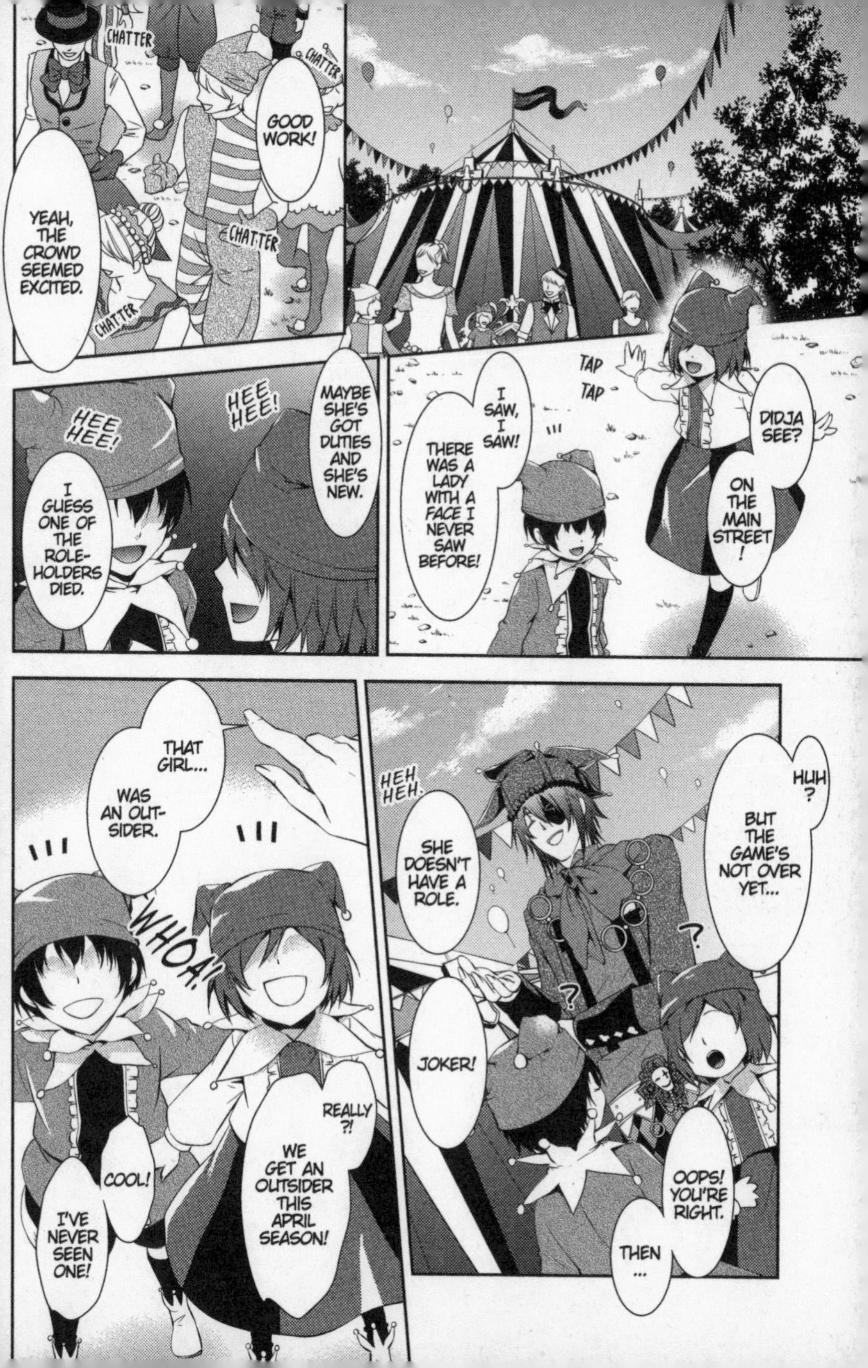
CHATTER
CHATTER
GOOD WORK!
CHATTER
YEAH, THE CROWD SEEMED EXCITED.
CHATTER
TAP TAP
DIDJA SEE?
ON THE MAIN STREET!
I SAW, I SAW!
THERE WAS A LADY WITH A FACE I NEVER SAW BEFORE!
MAYBE SHE'S GOT DUTIES AND SHE'S NEW.
HEE HEE!
HEE HEE!
I GUESS ONE OF THE ROLE-HOLDERS DIED.
HUH?
BUT THE GAME'S NOT OVER YET...
HEH HEH.
SHE DOESN'T HAVE A ROLE.
JOKER!
OOPS! YOU'RE RIGHT.
THEN...
THAT GIRL...
WAS AN OUT-SIDER.
WHOA!
REALLY?!
WE GET AN OUTSIDER THIS APRIL SEASON!
COOL!
I'VE NEVER SEEN ONE!

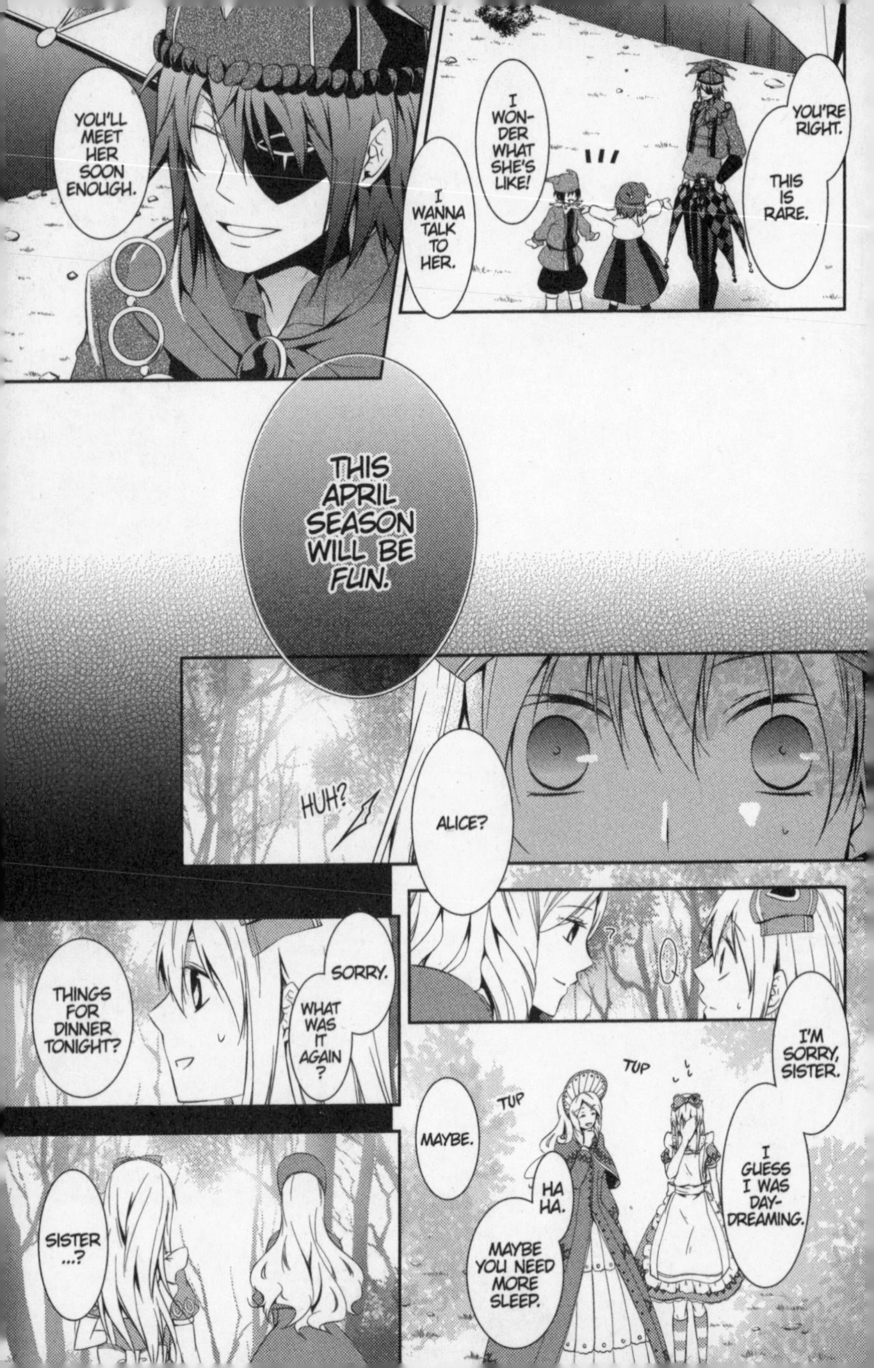
YOU'RE RIGHT.
THIS IS RARE.
I WONDER WHAT SHE'S LIKE!
!!!
I WANNA TALK TO HER.
YOU'LL MEET HER SOON ENOUGH.
THIS APRIL SEASON WILL BE FUN.
ALICE?
HUH?
?
I'M SORRY, SISTER.
TUP
I GUESS I WAS DAY-DREAMING.
TUP
MAYBE.
HA HA.
MAYBE YOU NEED MORE SLEEP.
SORRY.
WHAT WAS IT AGAIN?
THINGS FOR DINNER TONIGHT?
SISTER ...?

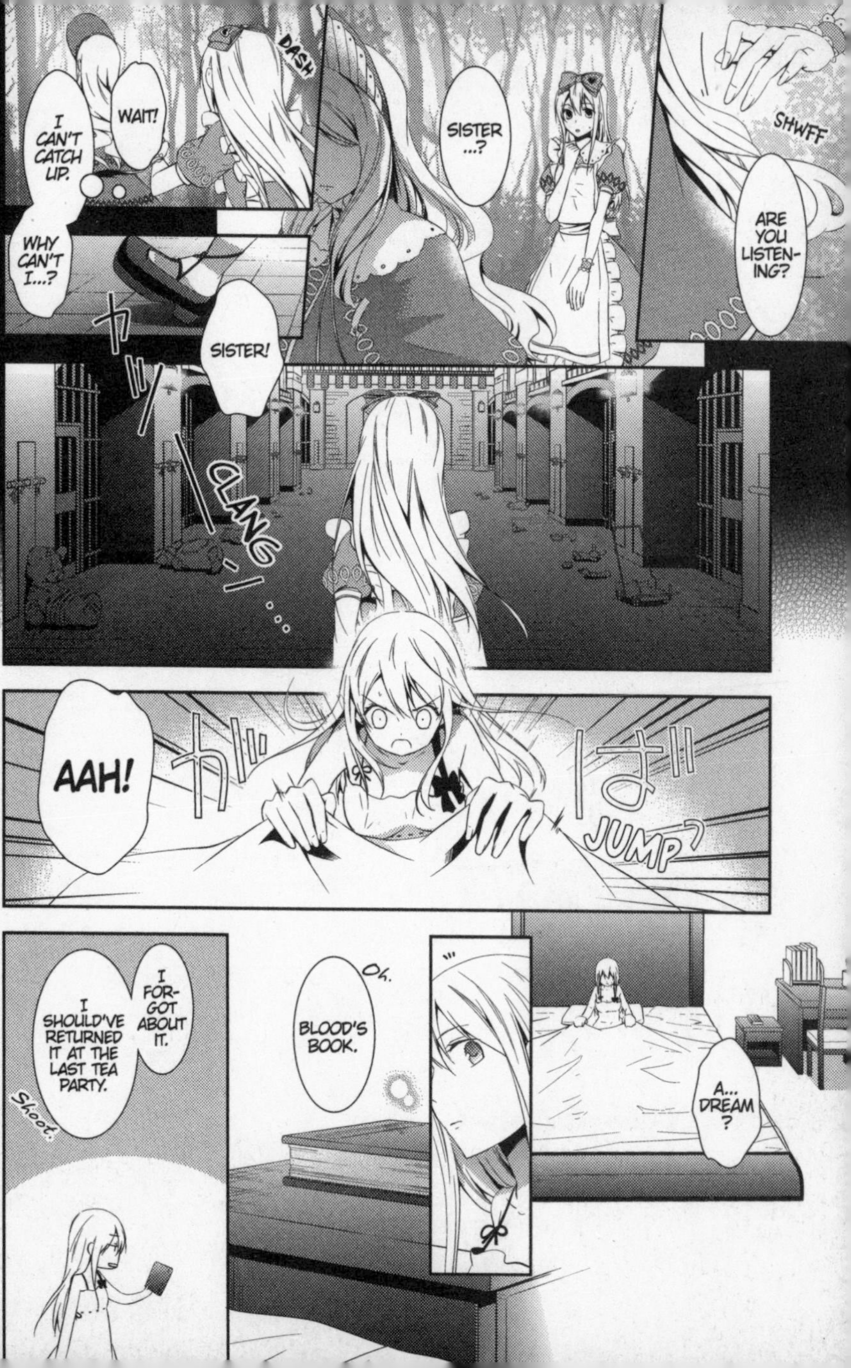
SHWFF
ARE YOU LISTENING?
SISTER ...?
DASH
WAIT!
I CAN'T CATCH UP.
WHY CAN'T I...?
SISTER!
CLANG
AAH!
JUMP
A... DREAM?
Oh.
BLOOD'S BOOK.
I FORGOT ABOUT IT.
I SHOULD'VE RETURNED IT AT THE LAST TEA PARTY.
Shoot.

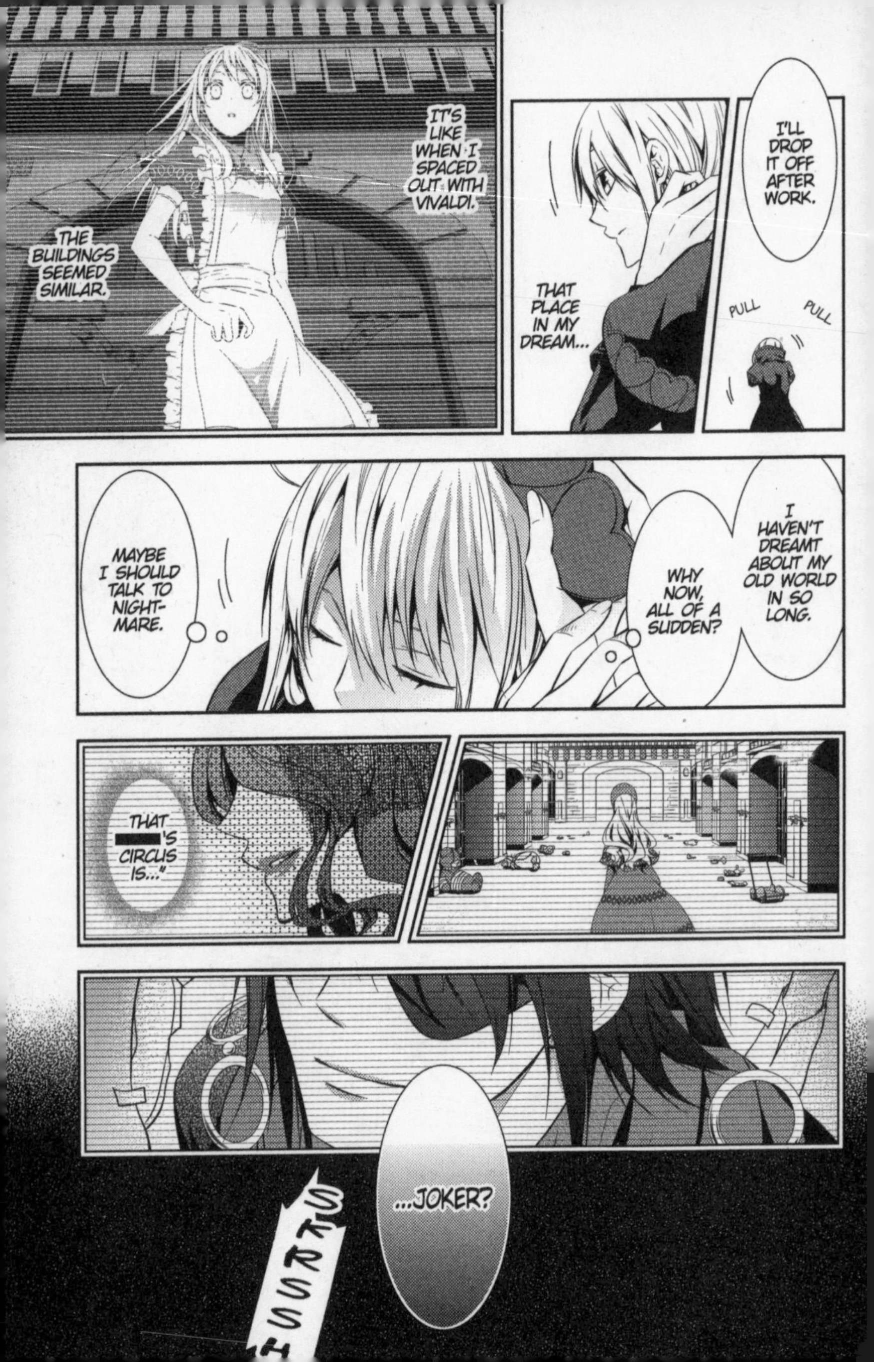
I'LL DROP IT OFF AFTER WORK.
PULL
PULL
THAT PLACE IN MY DREAM...
IT'S LIKE WHEN I SPACED OUT WITH VIVALDI.
THE BUILDINGS SEEMED SIMILAR.
I HAVEN'T DREAMT ABOUT MY OLD WORLD IN SO LONG.
WHY NOW, ALL OF A SUDDEN?
MAYBE I SHOULD TALK TO NIGHT-MARE.
THAT [redacted]'S CIRCUS IS..."
...JOKER?
SKRSSH

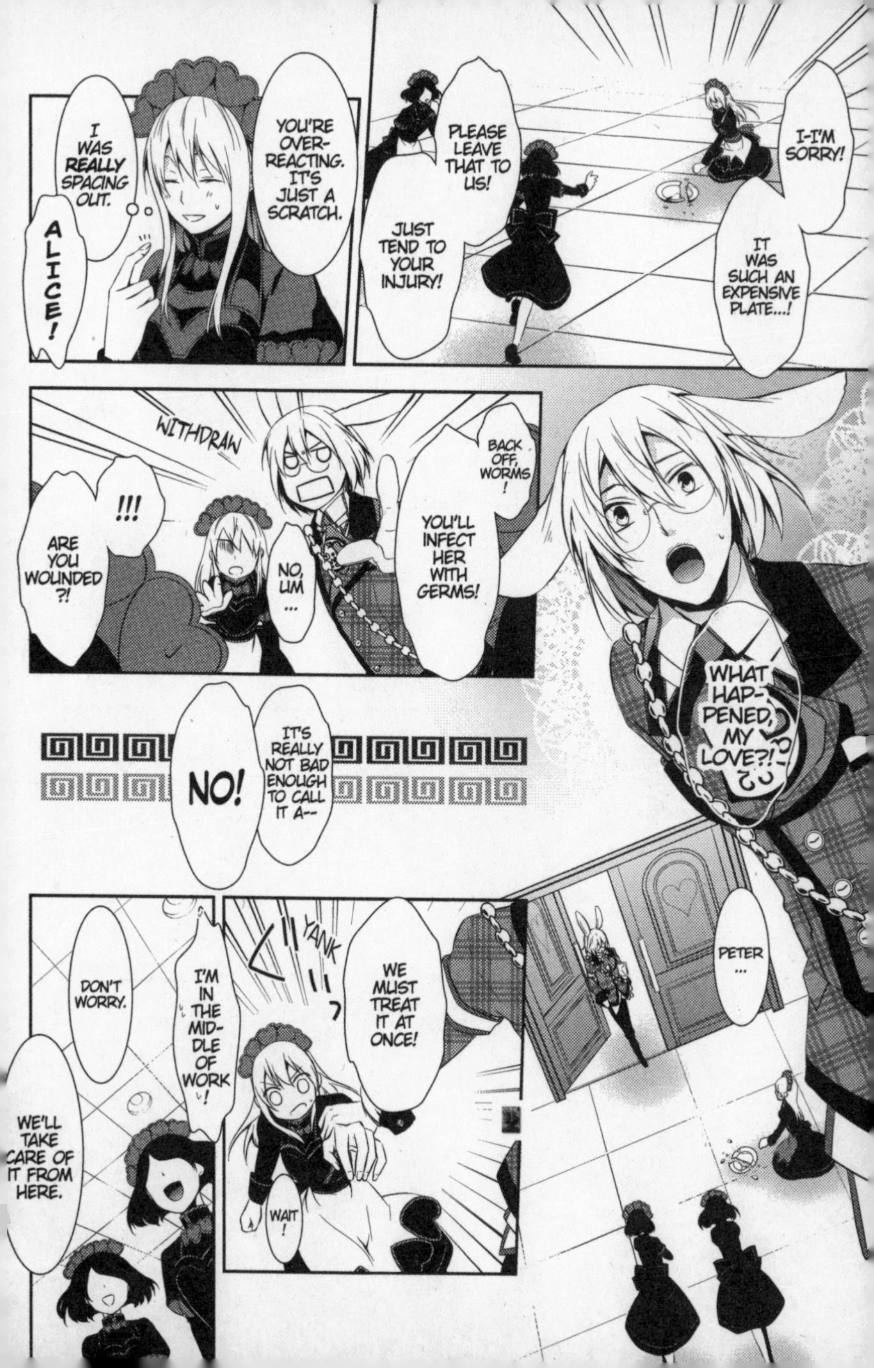
I-I'M SORRY!
IT WAS SUCH AN EXPENSIVE PLATE...!
PLEASE LEAVE THAT TO US!
JUST TEND TO YOUR INJURY!
YOU'RE OVER-REACTING. IT'S JUST A SCRATCH.
I WAS REALLY SPACING OUT.
ALICE!
WHAT HAP-PENED, MY LOVE?!
PETER ...
BACK OFF, WORMS!
YOU'LL INFECT HER WITH GERMS!
WITHDRAW
!!!
ARE YOU WOUNDED?!
NO, UM ...
IT'S REALLY NOT BAD ENOUGH TO CALL IT A--
NO!
WE MUST TREAT IT AT ONCE!
YANK
I'M IN THE MID-DLE OF WORK!
WAIT!
DON'T WORRY.
WE'LL TAKE CARE OF IT FROM HERE.

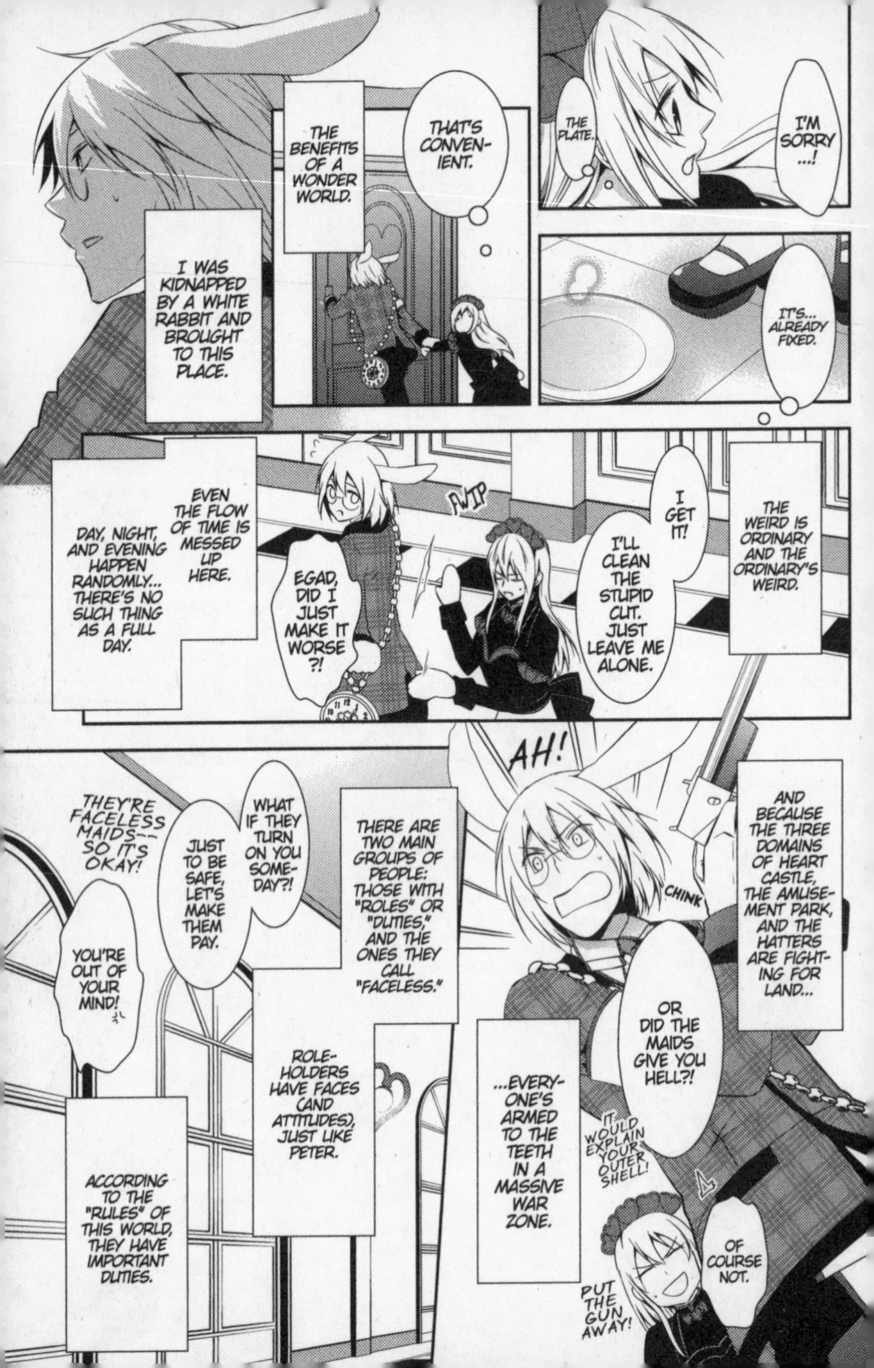
I'M SORRY ...!
THE PLATE.
IT'S... ALREADY FIXED.
THAT'S CONVEN-IENT.
THE BENEFITS OF A WONDER WORLD.
I WAS KIDNAPPED BY A WHITE RABBIT AND BROUGHT TO THIS PLACE.
THE WEIRD IS ORDINARY AND THE ORDINARY'S WEIRD.
I GET IT!
I'LL CLEAN THE STUPID CUT. JUST LEAVE ME ALONE.
FWIP
EGAD, DID I JUST MAKE IT WORSE?!
EVEN THE FLOW OF TIME IS MESSED UP HERE.
DAY, NIGHT, AND EVENING HAPPEN RANDOMLY... THERE'S NO SUCH THING AS A FULL DAY.
AH!
AND BECAUSE THE THREE DOMAINS OF HEART CASTLE, THE AMUSE-MENT PARK, AND THE HATTERS ARE FIGHT-ING FOR LAND...
CHINK
OR DID THE MAIDS GIVE YOU HELL?!
IT WOULD EXPLAIN YOUR OUTER SHELL!
...EVERY-ONE'S ARMED TO THE TEETH IN A MASSIVE WAR ZONE.
OF COURSE NOT.
PUT THE GUN AWAY!
THERE ARE TWO MAIN GROUPS OF PEOPLE: THOSE WITH "ROLES" OR "DUTIES," AND THE ONES THEY CALL "FACELESS."
ROLE-HOLDERS HAVE FACES (AND ATTITUDES), JUST LIKE PETER.
WHAT IF THEY TURN ON YOU SOME-DAY?!
JUST TO BE SAFE, LET'S MAKE THEM PAY.
THEY'RE FACELESS MAIDS-- SO IT'S OKAY!
YOU'RE OUT OF YOUR MIND!
ACCORDING TO THE "RULES" OF THIS WORLD, THEY HAVE IMPORTANT DUTIES.

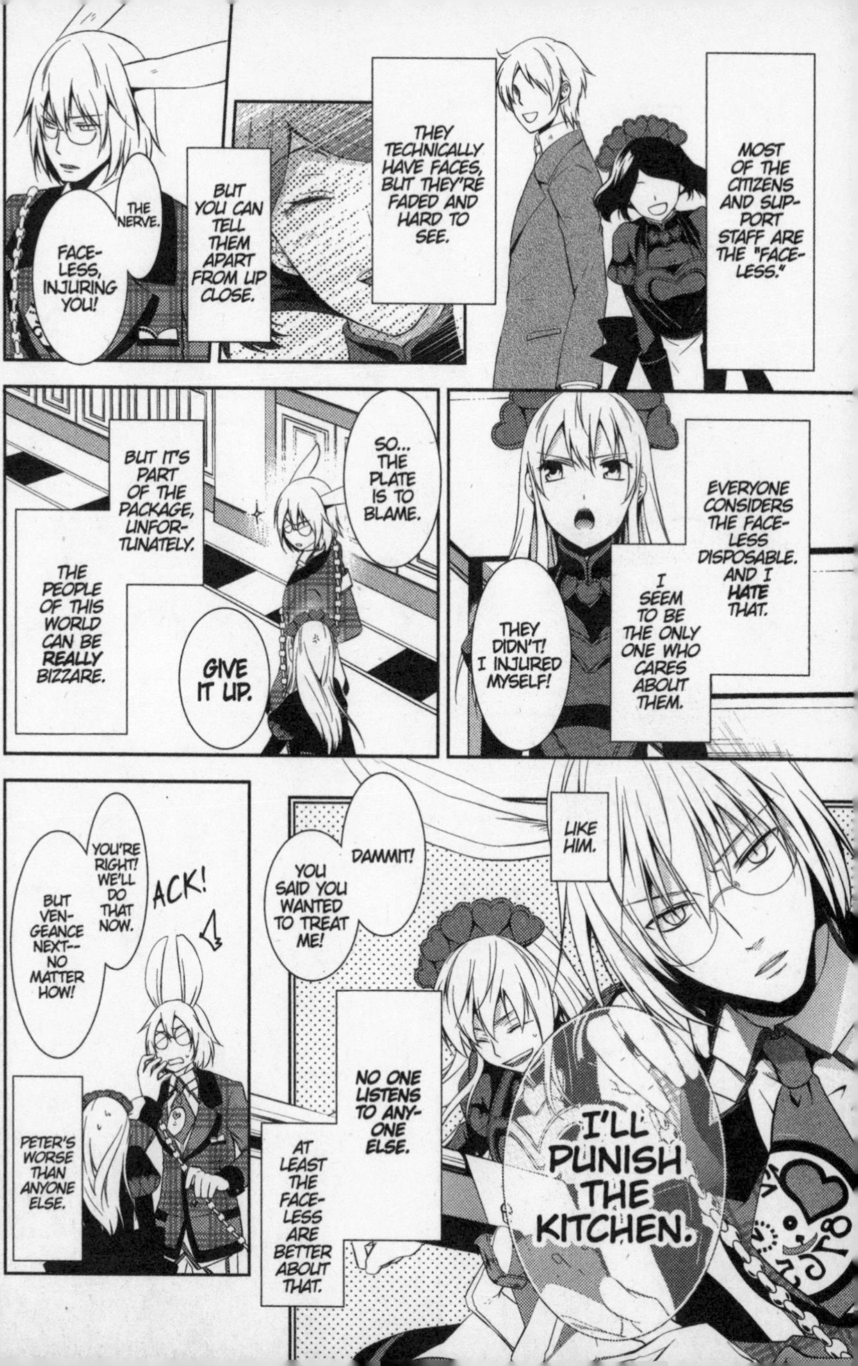
MOST OF THE CITIZENS AND SUP-PORT STAFF ARE THE "FACE-LESS."
THEY TECHNICALLY HAVE FACES, BUT THEY'RE FADED AND HARD TO SEE.
BUT YOU CAN TELL THEM APART FROM UP CLOSE.
THE NERVE.
FACE-LESS, INJURING YOU!
EVERYONE CONSIDERS THE FACE-LESS DISPOSABLE. AND I HATE THAT.
I SEEM TO BE THE ONLY ONE WHO CARES ABOUT THEM.
THEY DIDN'T! I INJURED MYSELF!
SO... THE PLATE IS TO BLAME.
BUT IT'S PART OF THE PACKAGE, UNFORTUNATELY.
GIVE IT UP.
THE PEOPLE OF THIS WORLD CAN BE REALLY BIZZARE.
LIKE HIM.
I'LL PUNISH THE KITCHEN.
DAMMIT!
YOU SAID YOU WANTED TO TREAT ME!
NO ONE LISTENS TO ANY-ONE ELSE.
AT LEAST THE FACE-LESS ARE BETTER ABOUT THAT.
ACK!
YOU'RE RIGHT! WE'LL DO THAT NOW.
BUT VEN-GEANCE NEXT-- NO MATTER HOW!
PETER'S WORSE THAN ANYONE ELSE.

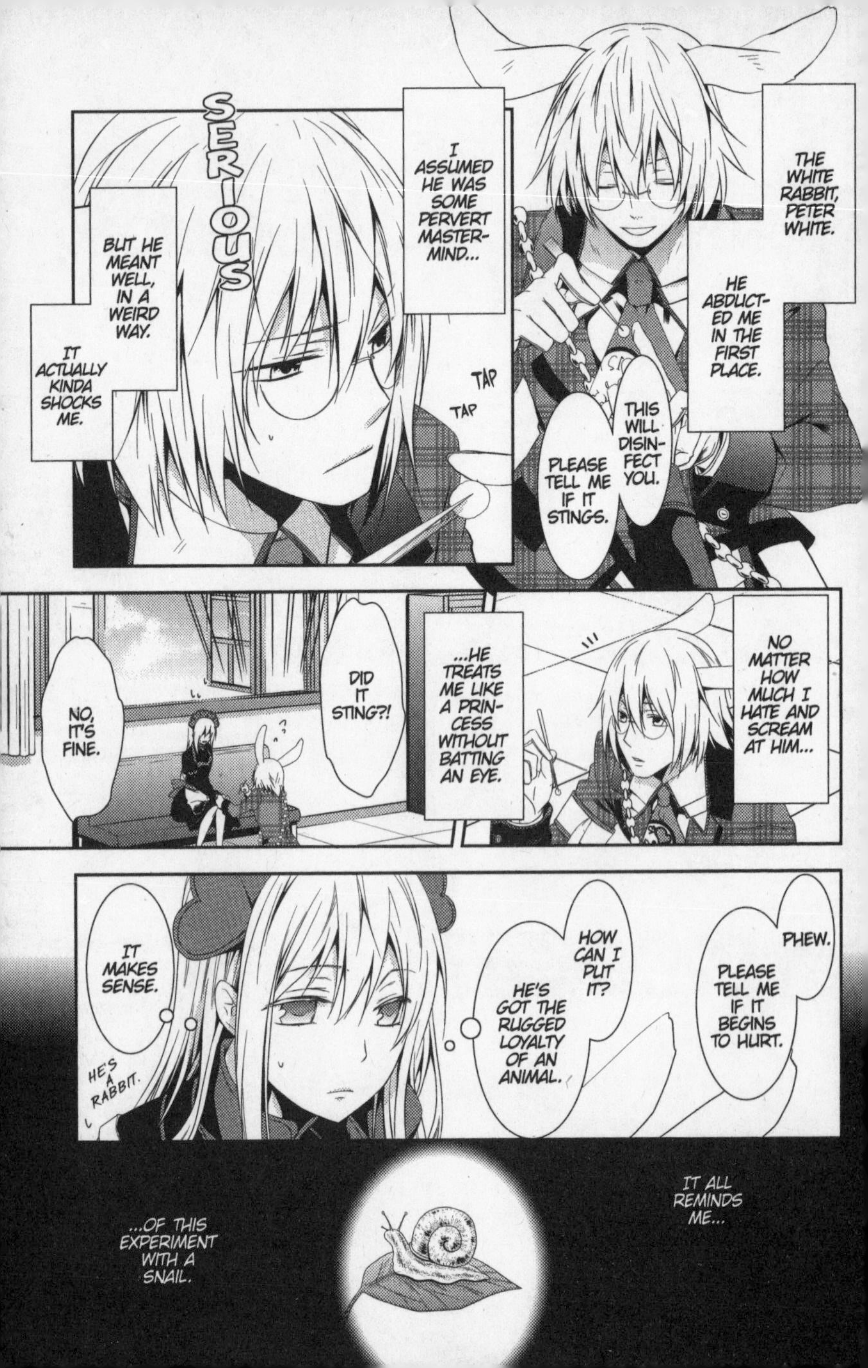
THE WHITE RABBIT, PETER WHITE.
HE ABDUCTED ME IN THE FIRST PLACE.
THIS WILL DISINFECT YOU.
PLEASE TELL ME IF IT STINGS.
I ASSUMED HE WAS SOME PERVERT MASTERMIND...
SERIOUS
BUT HE MEANT WELL, IN A WEIRD WAY.
TAP
TAP
IT ACTUALLY KINDA SHOCKS ME.
NO MATTER HOW MUCH I HATE AND SCREAM AT HIM...
...HE TREATS ME LIKE A PRINCESS WITHOUT BATTING AN EYE.
DID IT STING?!
NO, IT'S FINE.
PHEW.
PLEASE TELL ME IF IT BEGINS TO HURT.
HOW CAN I PUT IT?
HE'S GOT THE RUGGED LOYALTY OF AN ANIMAL.
IT MAKES SENSE.
HE'S A RABBIT.
IT ALL REMINDS ME...
...OF THIS EXPERIMENT WITH A SNAIL.

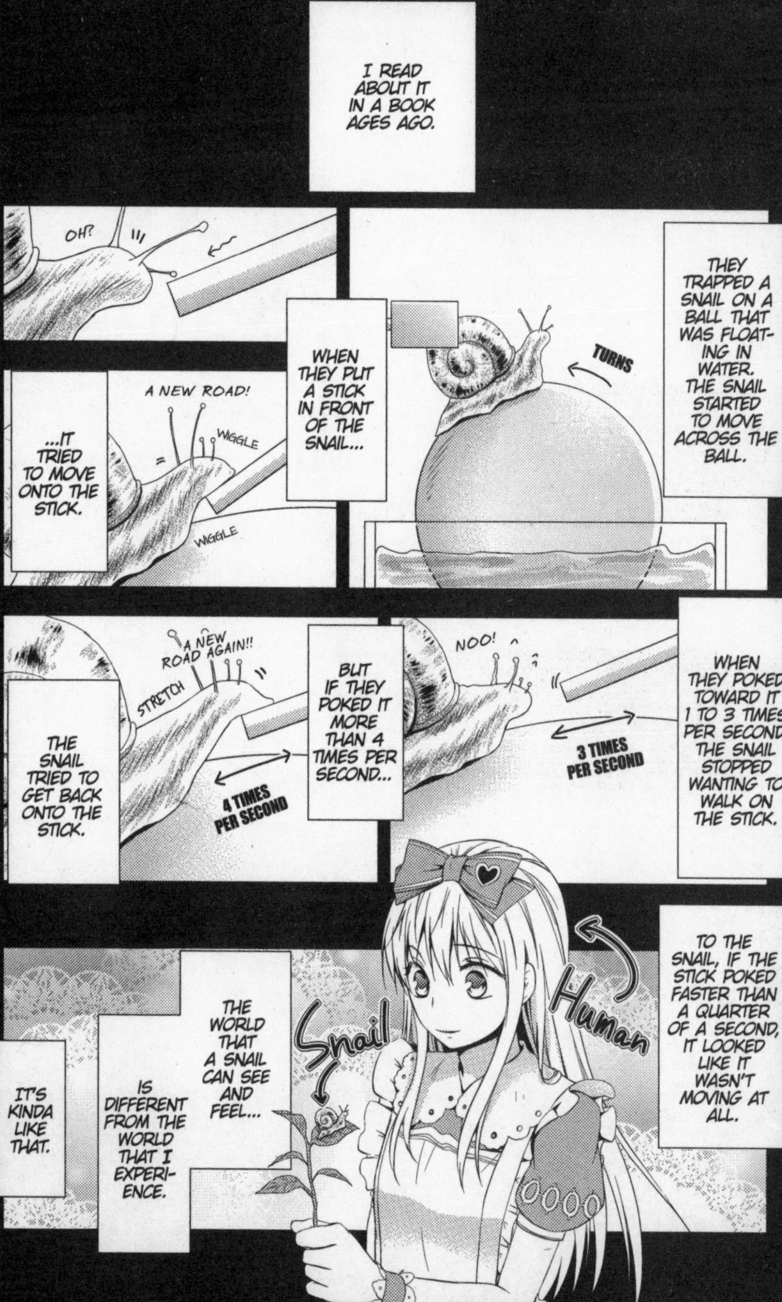
I READ ABOUT IT IN A BOOK AGES AGO.
THEY TRAPPED A SNAIL ON A BALL THAT WAS FLOATING IN WATER. THE SNAIL STARTED TO MOVE ACROSS THE BALL.
TURNS
WHEN THEY PUT A STICK IN FRONT OF THE SNAIL...
OH?
A NEW ROAD!
WIGGLE
...IT TRIED TO MOVE ONTO THE STICK.
WIGGLE
WHEN THEY POKED TOWARD IT 1 TO 3 TIMES PER SECOND, THE SNAIL STOPPED WANTING TO WALK ON THE STICK.
NOO!
3 TIMES PER SECOND
BUT IF THEY POKED IT MORE THAN 4 TIMES PER SECOND...
A NEW ROAD AGAIN!!
STRETCH
4 TIMES PER SECOND
THE SNAIL TRIED TO GET BACK ONTO THE STICK.
TO THE SNAIL, IF THE STICK POKED FASTER THAN A QUARTER OF A SECOND, IT LOOKED LIKE IT WASN'T MOVING AT ALL.
Human
Snail
THE WORLD THAT A SNAIL CAN SEE AND FEEL...
IS DIFFERENT FROM THE WORLD THAT I EXPERIENCE.
IT'S KINDA LIKE THAT.

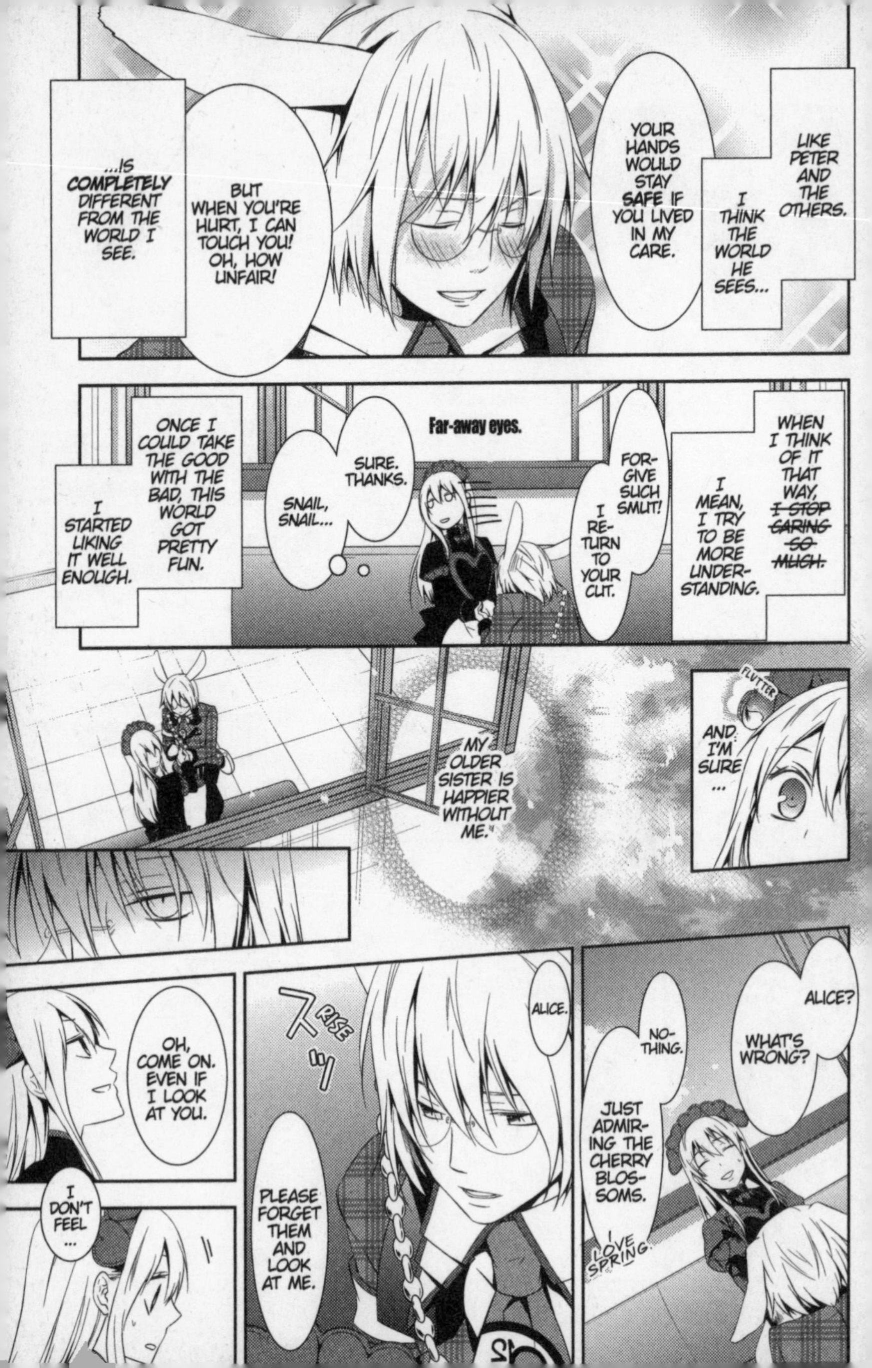
LIKE PETER AND THE OTHERS.
I THINK THE WORLD HE SEES...
YOUR HANDS WOULD STAY SAFE IF YOU LIVED IN MY CARE.
BUT WHEN YOU'RE HURT, I CAN TOUCH YOU! OH, HOW UNFAIR!
...IS COMPLETELY DIFFERENT FROM THE WORLD I SEE.
WHEN I THINK OF IT THAT WAY, ~~I STOP CARING SO MUCH.~~
I MEAN, I TRY TO BE MORE UNDERSTANDING.
FOR-GIVE SUCH SMUT!
I RE-TURN TO YOUR CUT.
Far-away eyes.
SURE. THANKS.
SNAIL, SNAIL...
ONCE I COULD TAKE THE GOOD WITH THE BAD, THIS WORLD GOT PRETTY FUN.
I STARTED LIKING IT WELL ENOUGH.
FLUTTER
AND I'M SURE ...
MY OLDER SISTER IS HAPPIER WITHOUT ME.
ALICE?
WHAT'S WRONG?
NO-THING.
JUST ADMIR-ING THE CHERRY BLOS-SOMS.
I LOVE SPRING.
ALICE.
RISE
PLEASE FORGET THEM AND LOOK AT ME.
OH, COME ON. EVEN IF I LOOK AT YOU.
I DON'T FEEL ...

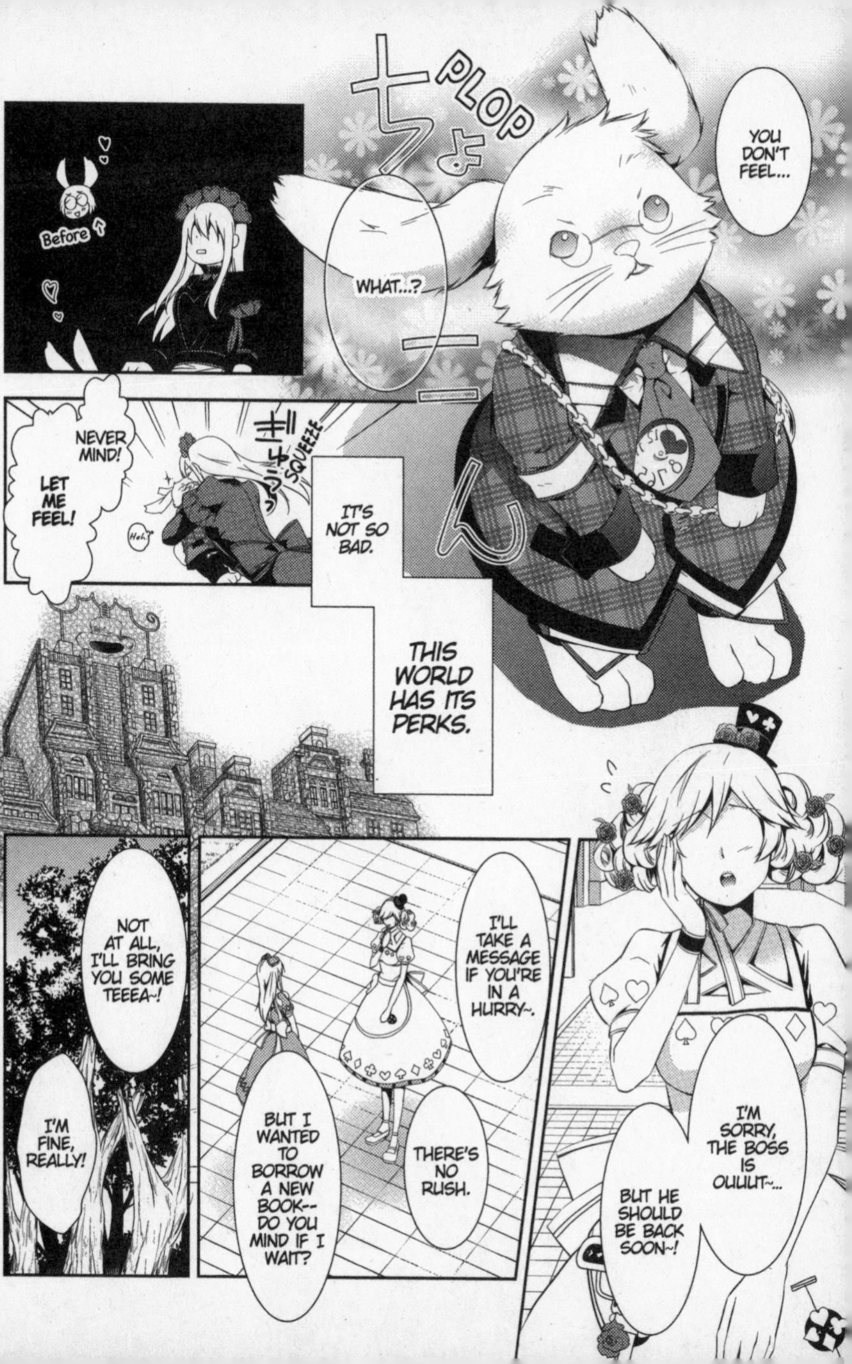
YOU DON'T FEEL...
PLOP
WHAT...?
Before
IT'S NOT SO BAD.
SQUEEZE
NEVER MIND! LET ME FEEL!
THIS WORLD HAS ITS PERKS.
I'M SORRY, THE BOSS IS OUUUT~...
BUT HE SHOULD BE BACK SOON~!
I'LL TAKE A MESSAGE IF YOU'RE IN A HURRY~.
THERE'S NO RUSH.
BUT I WANTED TO BORROW A NEW BOOK-- DO YOU MIND IF I WAIT?
NOT AT ALL, I'LL BRING YOU SOME TEEEA~!
I'M FINE, REALLY!

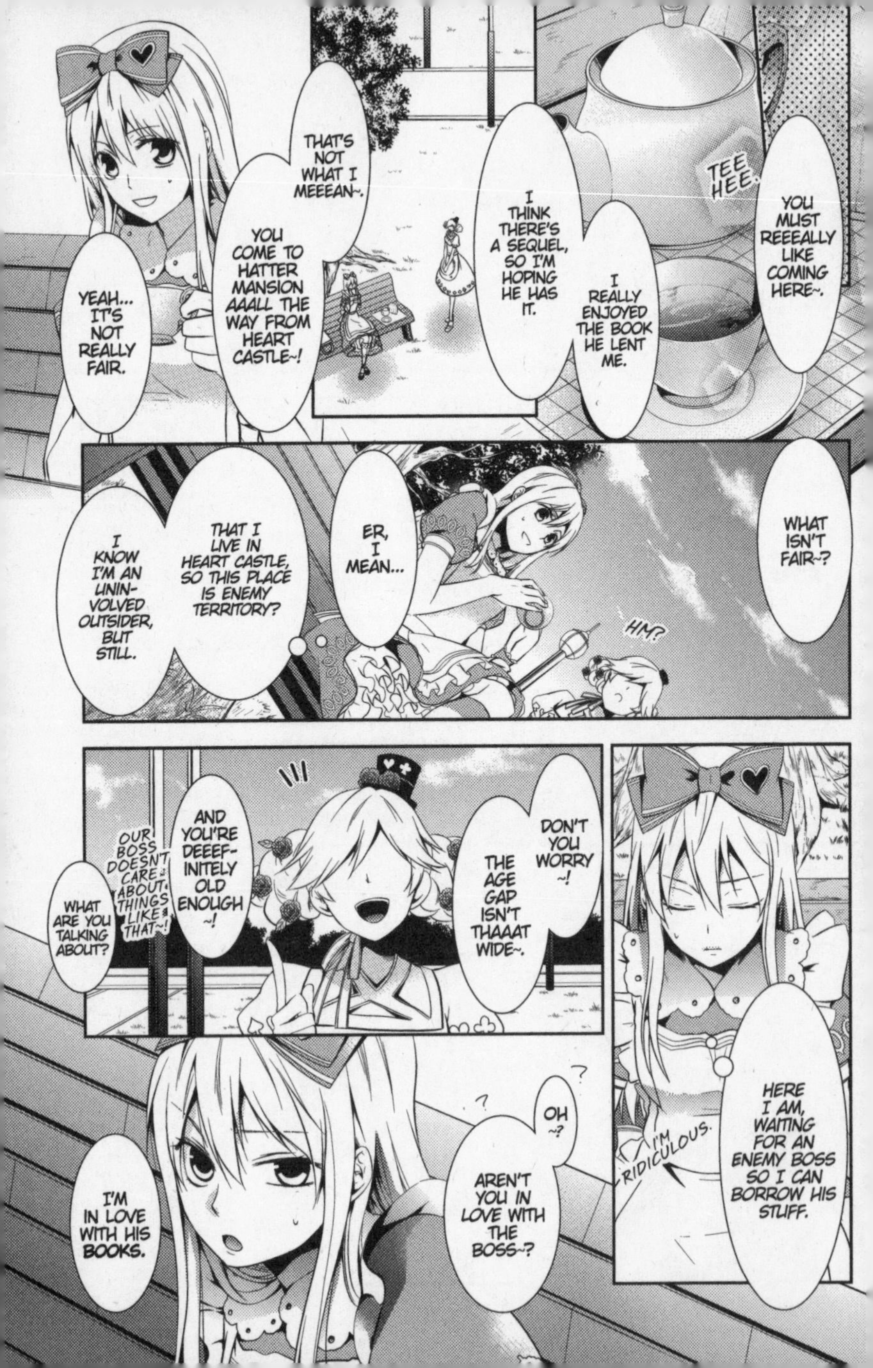
TEE HEE.
YOU MUST REEEALLY LIKE COMING HERE~.
I REALLY ENJOYED THE BOOK HE LENT ME.
I THINK THERE'S A SEQUEL, SO I'M HOPING HE HAS IT.
THAT'S NOT WHAT I MEEEAN~.
YOU COME TO HATTER MANSION AAALL THE WAY FROM HEART CASTLE~!
YEAH... IT'S NOT REALLY FAIR.
WHAT ISN'T FAIR~?
HM?
ER, I MEAN...
THAT I LIVE IN HEART CASTLE, SO THIS PLACE IS ENEMY TERRITORY?
I KNOW I'M AN UNIN-VOLVED OUTSIDER, BUT STILL.
HERE I AM, WAITING FOR AN ENEMY BOSS SO I CAN BORROW HIS STUFF.
I'M RIDICULOUS.
DON'T YOU WORRY~!
THE AGE GAP ISN'T THAAAT WIDE~.
AND YOU'RE DEEEF-INITELY OLD ENOUGH~!
OUR BOSS DOESN'T CARE ABOUT THINGS LIKE THAT~!
WHAT ARE YOU TALKING ABOUT?
OH~?
AREN'T YOU IN LOVE WITH THE BOSS~?
I'M IN LOVE WITH HIS BOOKS.

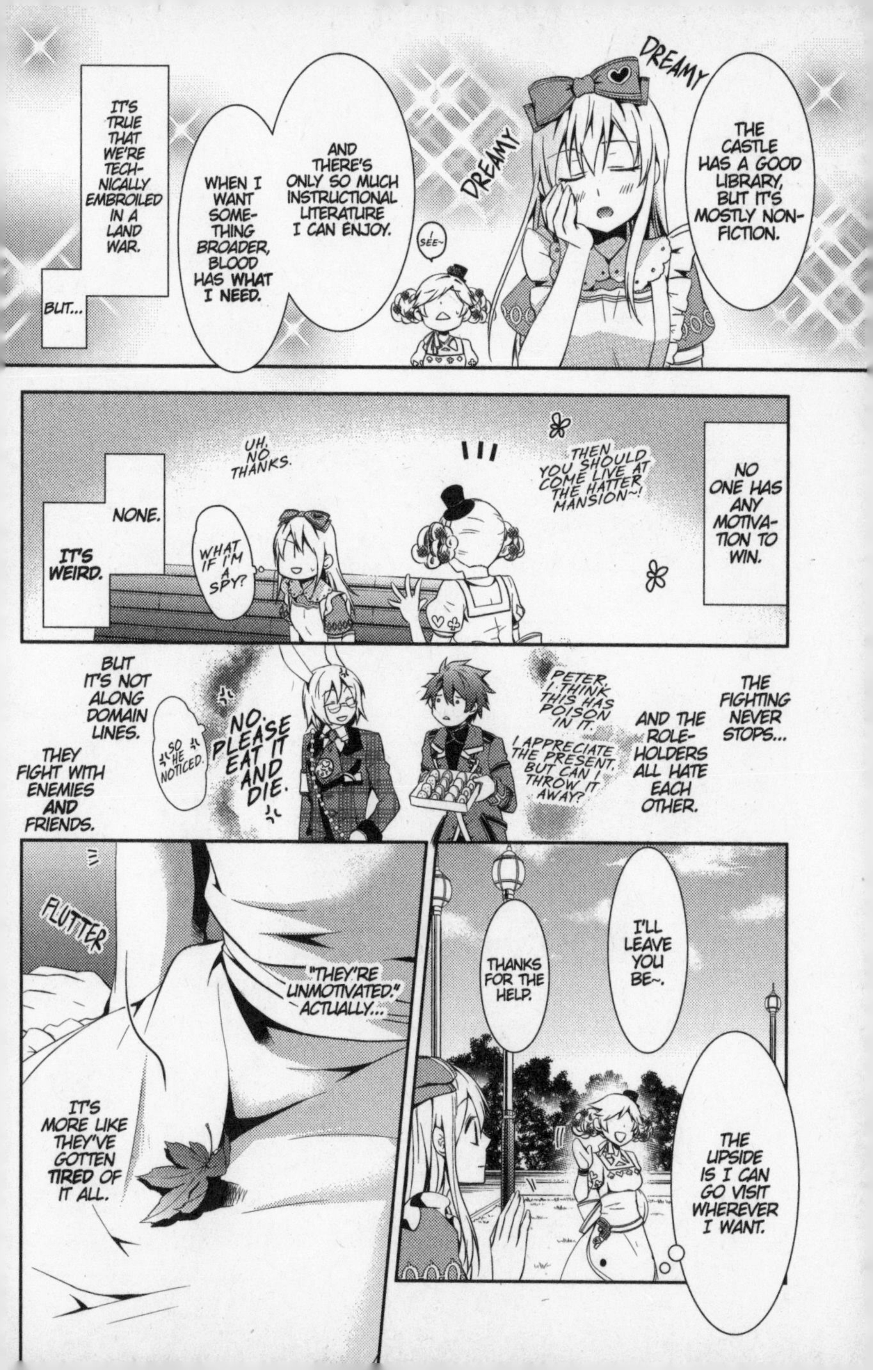
DREAMY
THE CASTLE HAS A GOOD LIBRARY, BUT IT'S MOSTLY NON-FICTION.
DREAMY
I SEE~
AND THERE'S ONLY SO MUCH INSTRUCTIONAL LITERATURE I CAN ENJOY.
WHEN I WANT SOMETHING BROADER, BLOOD HAS WHAT I NEED.
IT'S TRUE THAT WE'RE TECHNICALLY EMBROILED IN A LAND WAR.
BUT...
NO ONE HAS ANY MOTIVATION TO WIN.
THEN YOU SHOULD COME LIVE AT THE HATTER MANSION~!
UH, NO THANKS.
WHAT IF I'M A SPY?
NONE.
IT'S WEIRD.
THE FIGHTING NEVER STOPS...
AND THE ROLE-HOLDERS ALL HATE EACH OTHER.
PETER, I THINK THIS HAS POISON IN IT.
I APPRECIATE THE PRESENT, BUT CAN I THROW IT AWAY?
NO. PLEASE EAT IT AND DIE.
SO HE NOTICED.
BUT IT'S NOT ALONG DOMAIN LINES.
THEY FIGHT WITH ENEMIES AND FRIENDS.
I'LL LEAVE YOU BE~.
THANKS FOR THE HELP.
THE UPSIDE IS I CAN GO VISIT WHEREVER I WANT.
FLUTTER
"THEY'RE UNMOTIVATED," ACTUALLY...
IT'S MORE LIKE THEY'VE GOTTEN TIRED OF IT ALL.

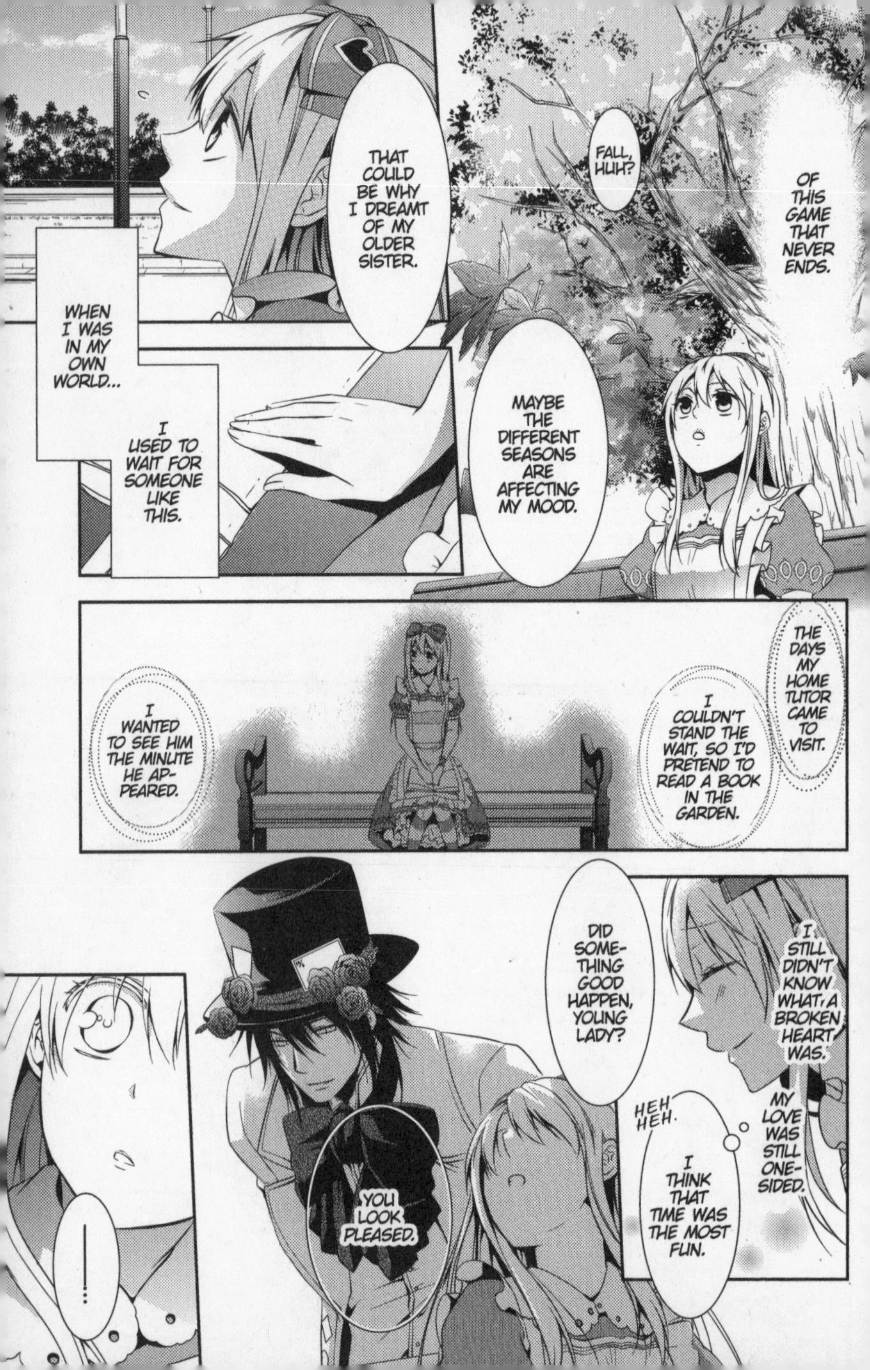
OF THIS GAME THAT NEVER ENDS.
FALL, HUH?
MAYBE THE DIFFERENT SEASONS ARE AFFECTING MY MOOD.
THAT COULD BE WHY I DREAMT OF MY OLDER SISTER.
WHEN I WAS IN MY OWN WORLD...
I USED TO WAIT FOR SOMEONE LIKE THIS.
THE DAYS MY HOME TUTOR CAME TO VISIT.
I COULDN'T STAND THE WAIT, SO I'D PRETEND TO READ A BOOK IN THE GARDEN.
I WANTED TO SEE HIM THE MINUTE HE AP-PEARED.
I STILL DIDN'T KNOW WHAT A BROKEN HEART WAS.
MY LOVE WAS STILL ONE-SIDED.
I THINK THAT TIME WAS THE MOST FUN.
HEH HEH.
DID SOME-THING GOOD HAPPEN, YOUNG LADY?
YOU LOOK PLEASED.
......!

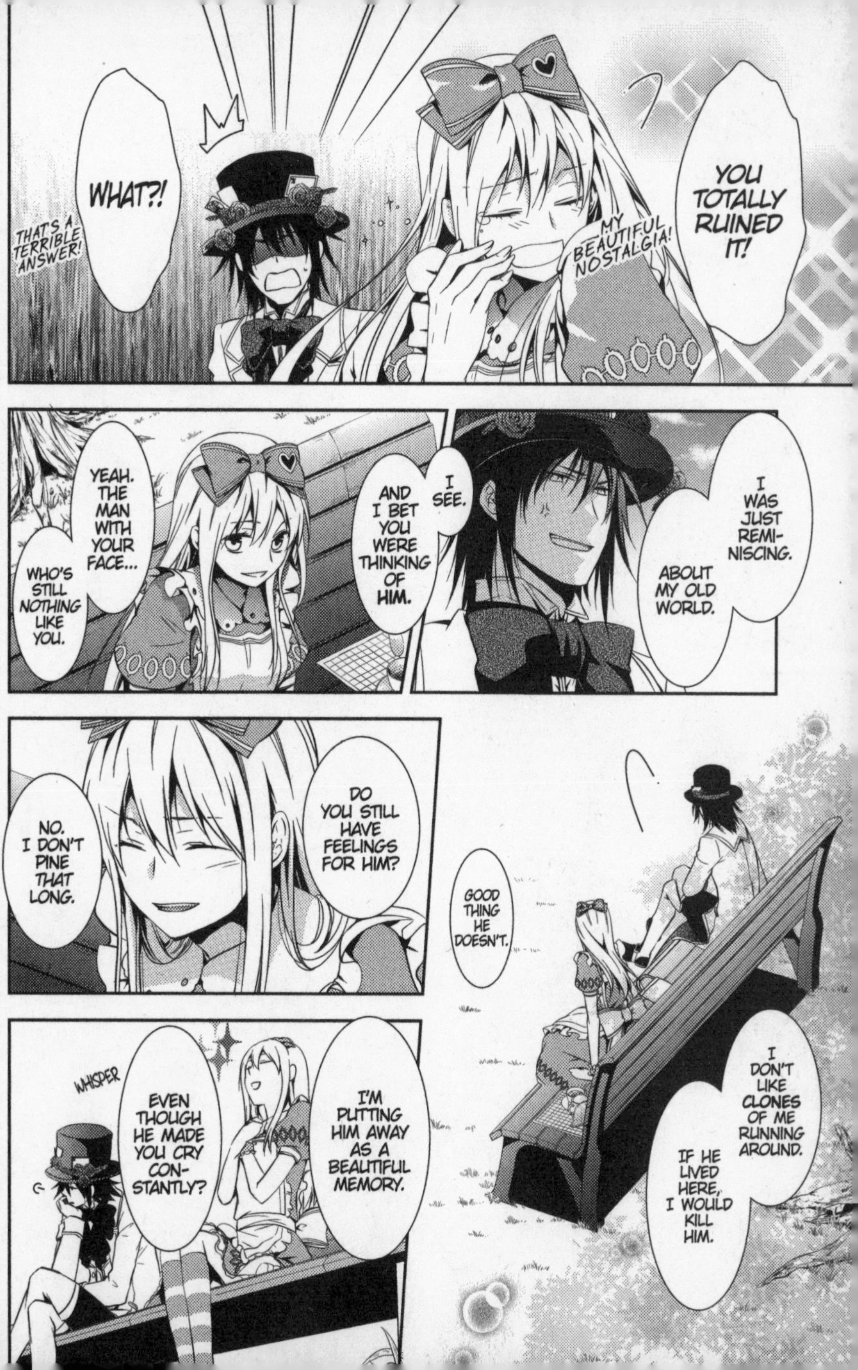
YOU TOTALLY RUINED IT!
MY BEAUTIFUL NOSTALGIA!
WHAT?!
THAT'S A TERRIBLE ANSWER!
I WAS JUST REMI-NISCING.
ABOUT MY OLD WORLD.
I SEE.
AND I BET YOU WERE THINKING OF HIM.
YEAH. THE MAN WITH YOUR FACE...
WHO'S STILL NOTHING LIKE YOU.
GOOD THING HE DOESN'T.
I DON'T LIKE CLONES OF ME RUNNING AROUND.
IF HE LIVED HERE, I WOULD KILL HIM.
DO YOU STILL HAVE FEELINGS FOR HIM?
NO. I DON'T PINE THAT LONG.
I'M PUTTING HIM AWAY AS A BEAUTIFUL MEMORY.
EVEN THOUGH HE MADE YOU CRY CON-STANTLY?
WHISPER

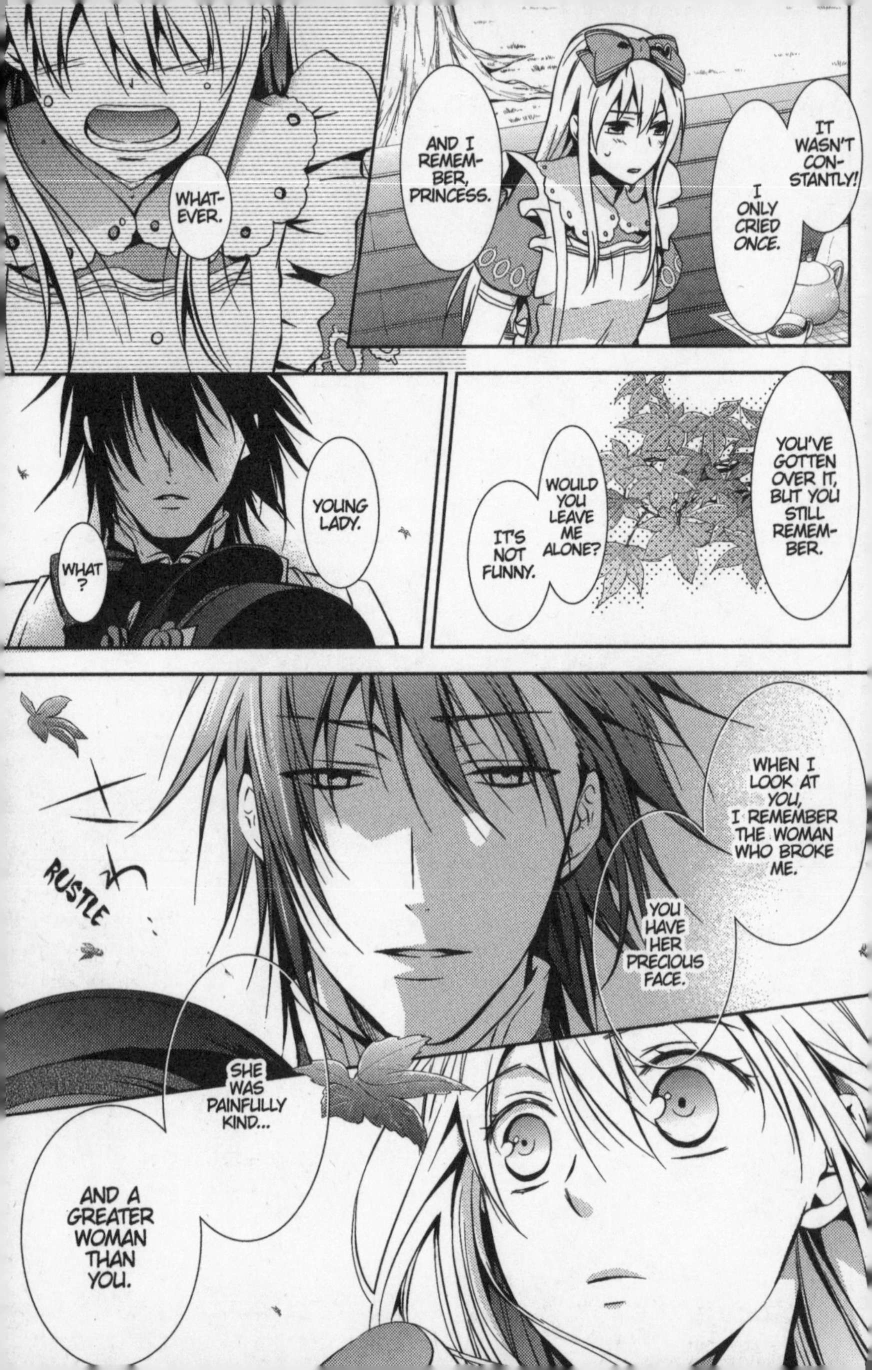
IT WASN'T CONSTANTLY!
I ONLY CRIED ONCE.
AND I REMEMBER, PRINCESS.
WHAT-EVER.
YOU'VE GOTTEN OVER IT, BUT YOU STILL REMEMBER.
WOULD YOU LEAVE ME ALONE?
IT'S NOT FUNNY.
YOUNG LADY.
WHAT?
WHEN I LOOK AT YOU, I REMEMBER THE WOMAN WHO BROKE ME.
YOU HAVE HER PRECIOUS FACE.
RUSTLE
SHE WAS PAINFULLY KIND...
AND A GREATER WOMAN THAN YOU.

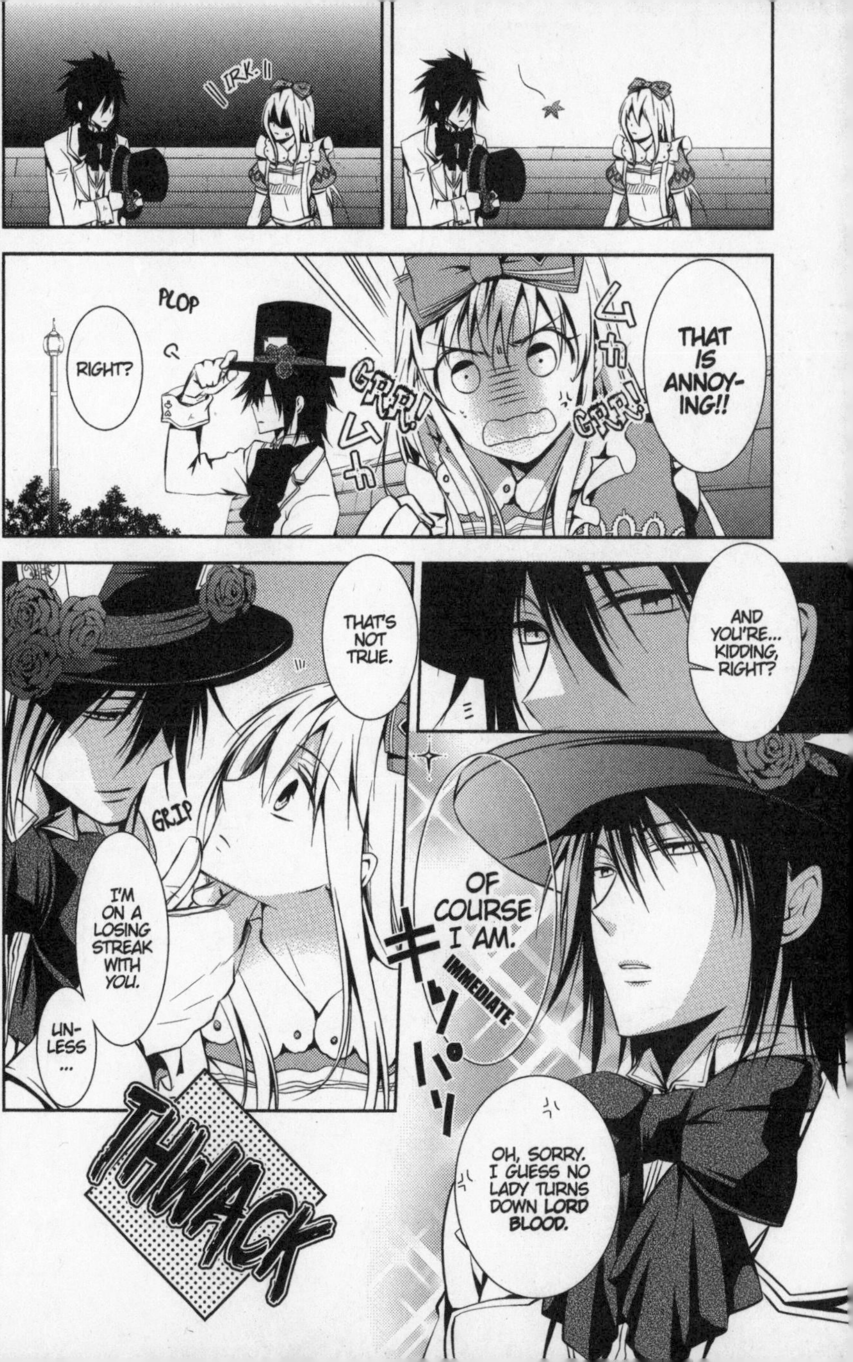

IRK.
THAT IS ANNOYING!!
ムカ
GRR!
GRR!
ムカ
PLOP
RIGHT?
AND YOU'RE... KIDDING, RIGHT?
OF COURSE I AM.
IMMEDIATE
OH, SORRY. I GUESS NO LADY TURNS DOWN LORD BLOOD.
THAT'S NOT TRUE.
GRIP
I'M ON A LOSING STREAK WITH YOU.
UN-LESS ...
THWACK

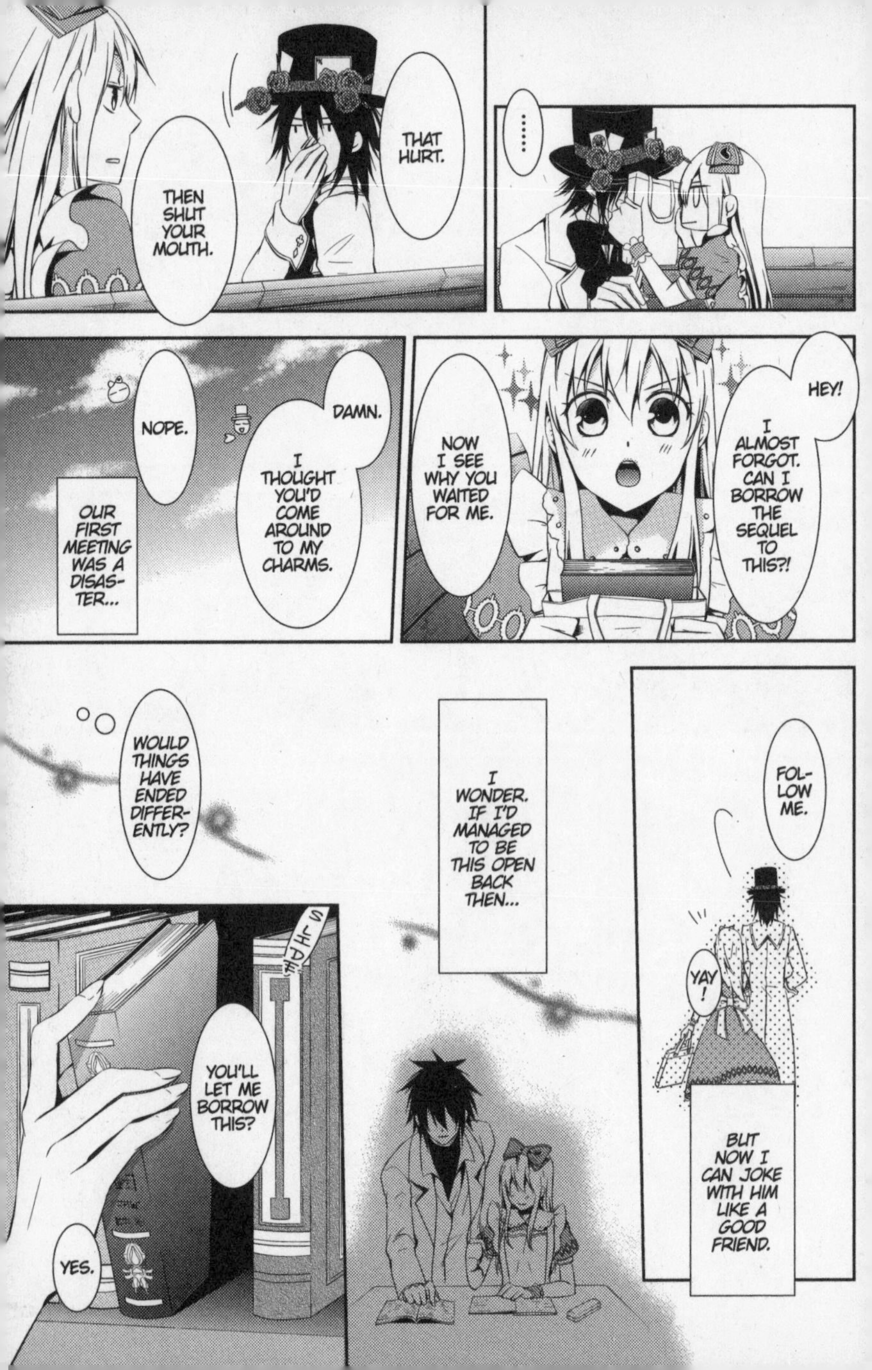
......
THAT HURT.
THEN SHUT YOUR MOUTH.
HEY! I ALMOST FORGOT. CAN I BORROW THE SEQUEL TO THIS?!
NOW I SEE WHY YOU WAITED FOR ME.
DAMN. I THOUGHT YOU'D COME AROUND TO MY CHARMS.
NOPE.
OUR FIRST MEETING WAS A DISASTER...
FOL-LOW ME.
YAY!
BUT NOW I CAN JOKE WITH HIM LIKE A GOOD FRIEND.
I WONDER. IF I'D MANAGED TO BE THIS OPEN BACK THEN...
WOULD THINGS HAVE ENDED DIFFERENTLY?
SLIDE!
YOU'LL LET ME BORROW THIS?
YES.

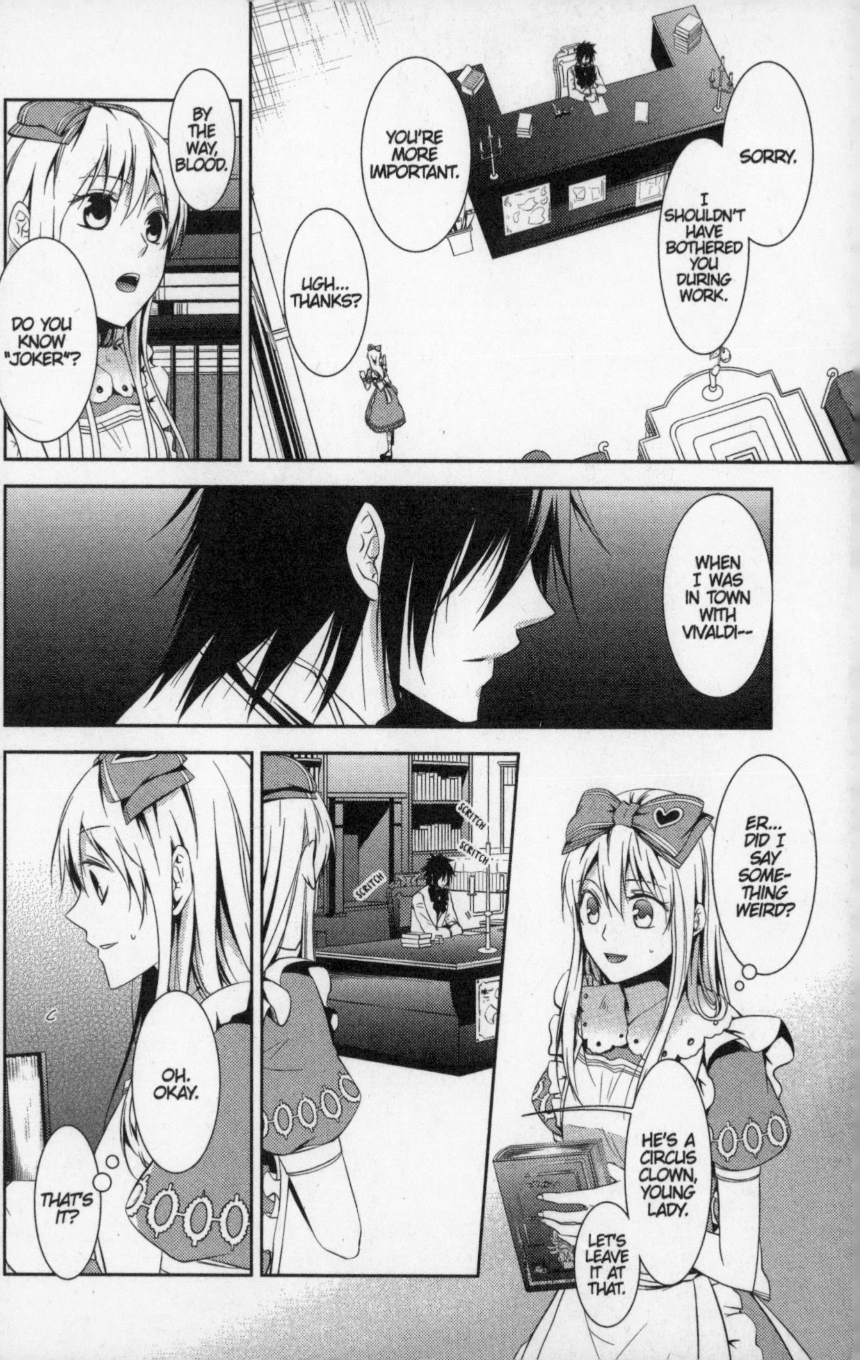
SORRY.
I SHOULDN'T HAVE BOTHERED YOU DURING WORK.
YOU'RE MORE IMPORTANT.
UGH... THANKS?
BY THE WAY, BLOOD.
DO YOU KNOW "JOKER"?
WHEN I WAS IN TOWN WITH VIVALDI--
ER... DID I SAY SOMETHING WEIRD?
HE'S A CIRCUS CLOWN, YOUNG LADY.
LET'S LEAVE IT AT THAT.
SCRITCH
SCRITCH
SCRITCH
OH. OKAY.
THAT'S IT?

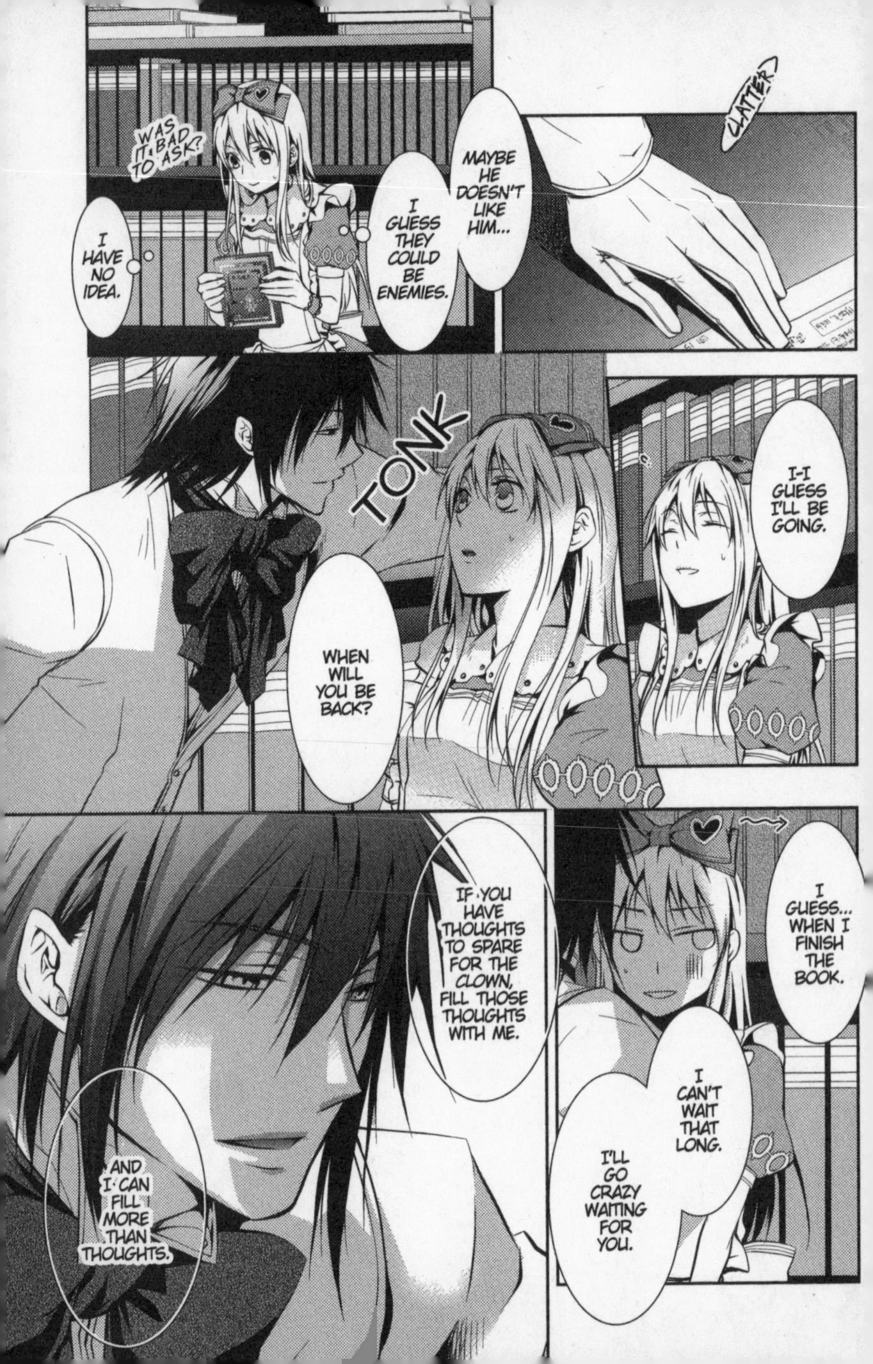
CLATTER
MAYBE HE DOESN'T LIKE HIM...
I GUESS THEY COULD BE ENEMIES.
WAS IT BAD TO ASK?
I HAVE NO IDEA.
I-I GUESS I'LL BE GOING.
TONK
WHEN WILL YOU BE BACK?
I GUESS... WHEN I FINISH THE BOOK.
I CAN'T WAIT THAT LONG.
I'LL GO CRAZY WAITING FOR YOU.
IF YOU HAVE THOUGHTS TO SPARE FOR THE CLOWN, FILL THOSE THOUGHTS WITH ME.
AND I CAN FILL MORE THAN THOUGHTS.

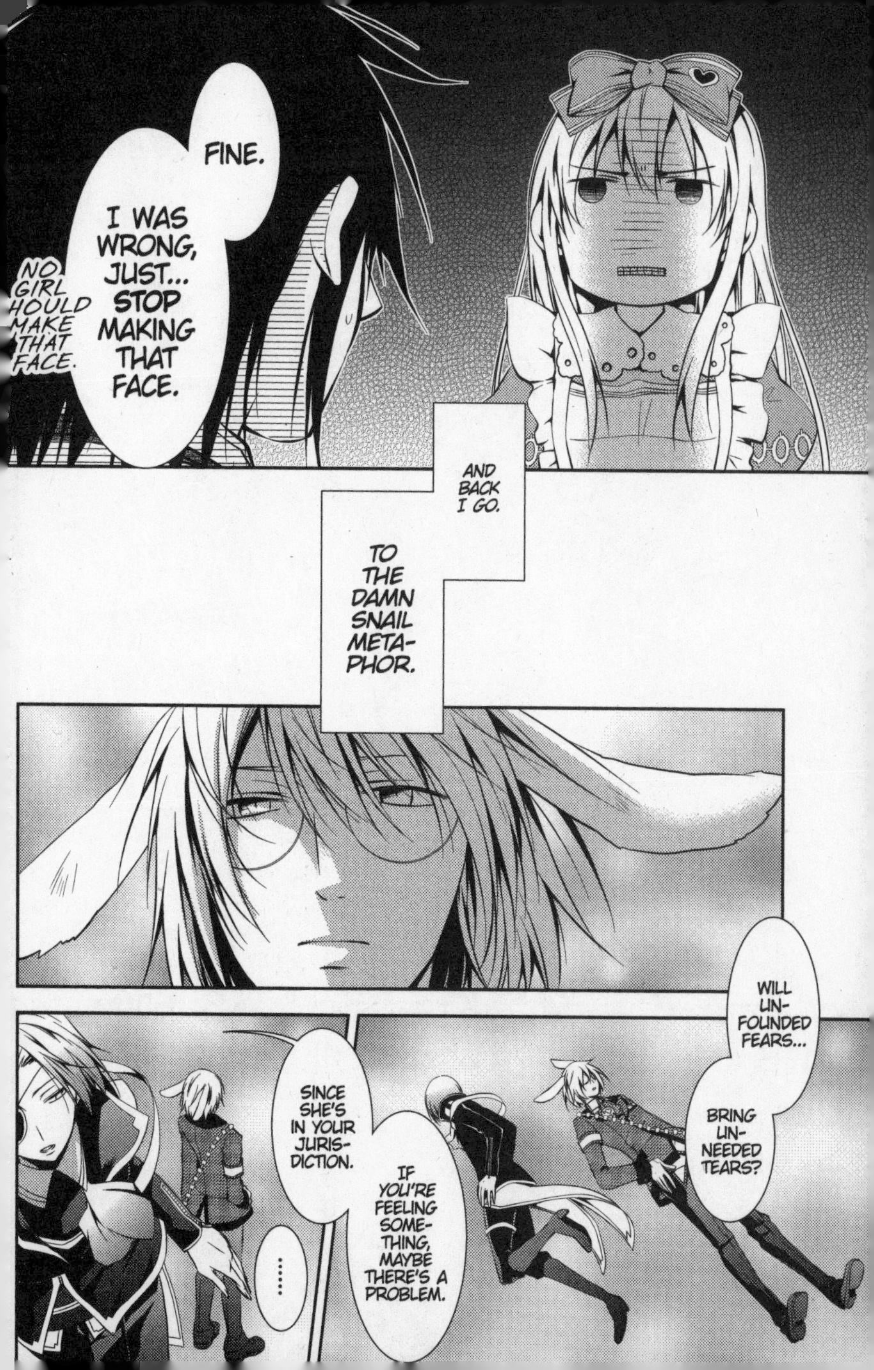
FINE.
I WAS WRONG, JUST... STOP MAKING THAT FACE.
NO GIRL HOULD MAKE THAT FACE.
AND BACK I GO.
TO THE DAMN SNAIL METAPHOR.
WILL UN-FOUNDED FEARS...
BRING UN-NEEDED TEARS?
IF YOU'RE FEELING SOME-THING, MAYBE THERE'S A PROBLEM.
SINCE SHE'S IN YOUR JURIS-DICTION.
......

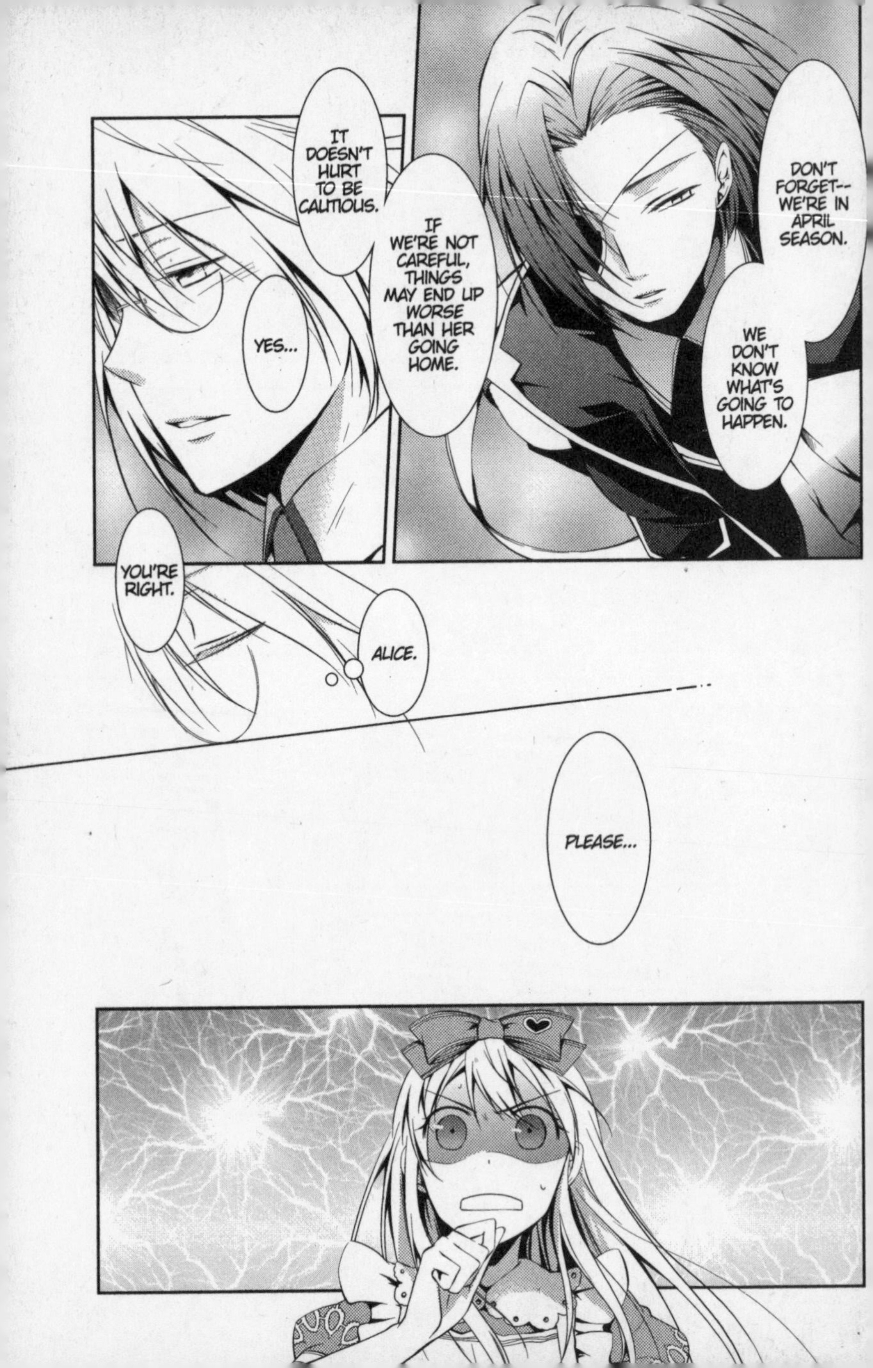
DON'T FORGET-- WE'RE IN APRIL SEASON.
WE DON'T KNOW WHAT'S GOING TO HAPPEN.
IF WE'RE NOT CAREFUL, THINGS MAY END UP WORSE THAN HER GOING HOME.
IT DOESN'T HURT TO BE CAUTIOUS.
YES...
YOU'RE RIGHT.
ALICE.
PLEASE...

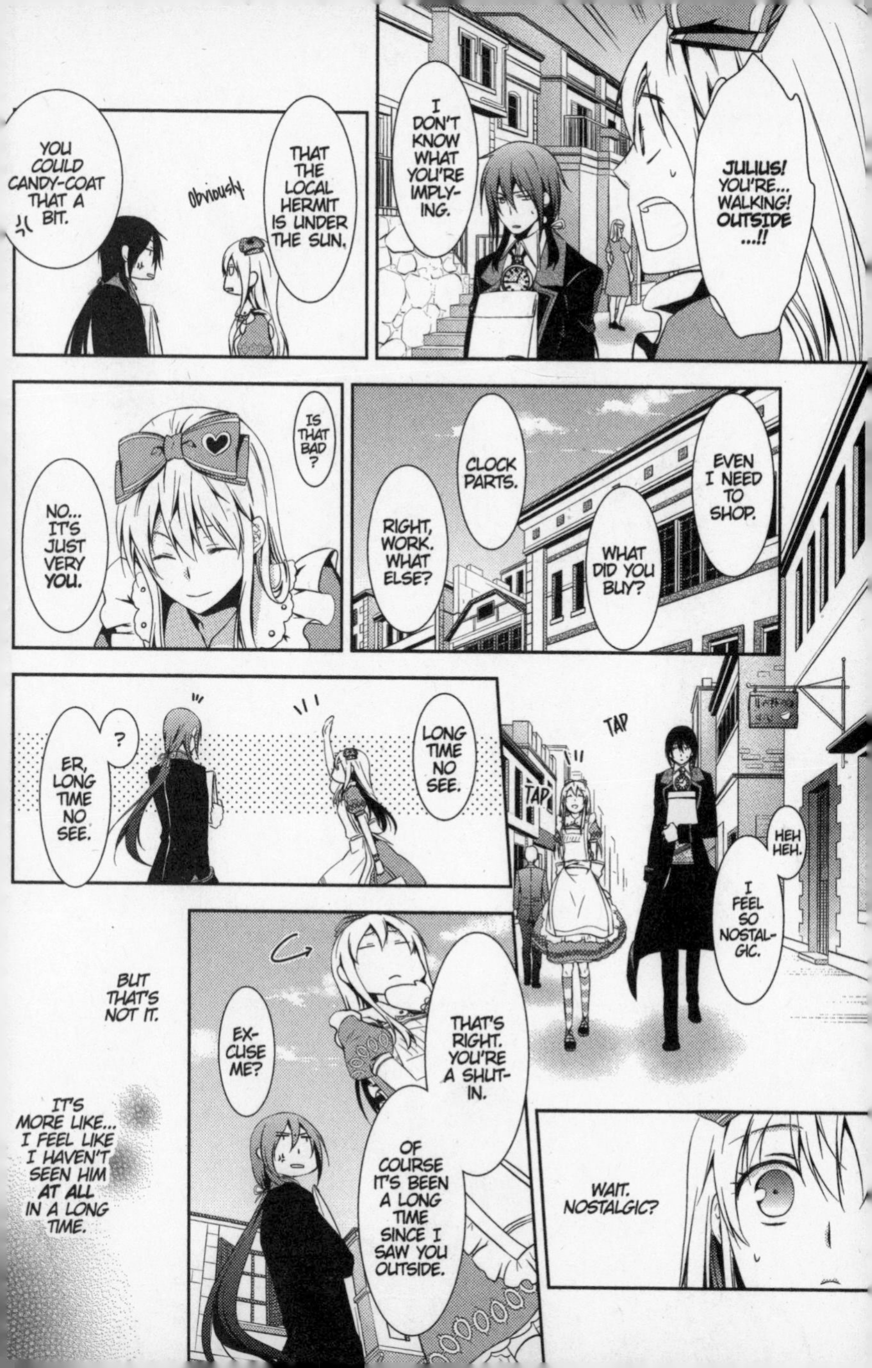
JULIUS! YOU'RE... WALKING! OUTSIDE ...!!
I DON'T KNOW WHAT YOU'RE IMPLYING.
THAT THE LOCAL HERMIT IS UNDER THE SUN.
Obviously.
YOU COULD CANDY-COAT THAT A BIT.
EVEN I NEED TO SHOP.
WHAT DID YOU BUY?
CLOCK PARTS.
RIGHT, WORK. WHAT ELSE?
IS THAT BAD?
NO... IT'S JUST VERY YOU.
LONG TIME NO SEE.
?
ER, LONG TIME NO SEE.
TAP
TAP
HEH HEH.
I FEEL SO NOSTALGIC.
WAIT. NOSTALGIC?
THAT'S RIGHT. YOU'RE A SHUT-IN.
EXCUSE ME?
OF COURSE IT'S BEEN A LONG TIME SINCE I SAW YOU OUTSIDE.
BUT THAT'S NOT IT.
IT'S MORE LIKE... I FEEL LIKE I HAVEN'T SEEN HIM AT ALL IN A LONG TIME.

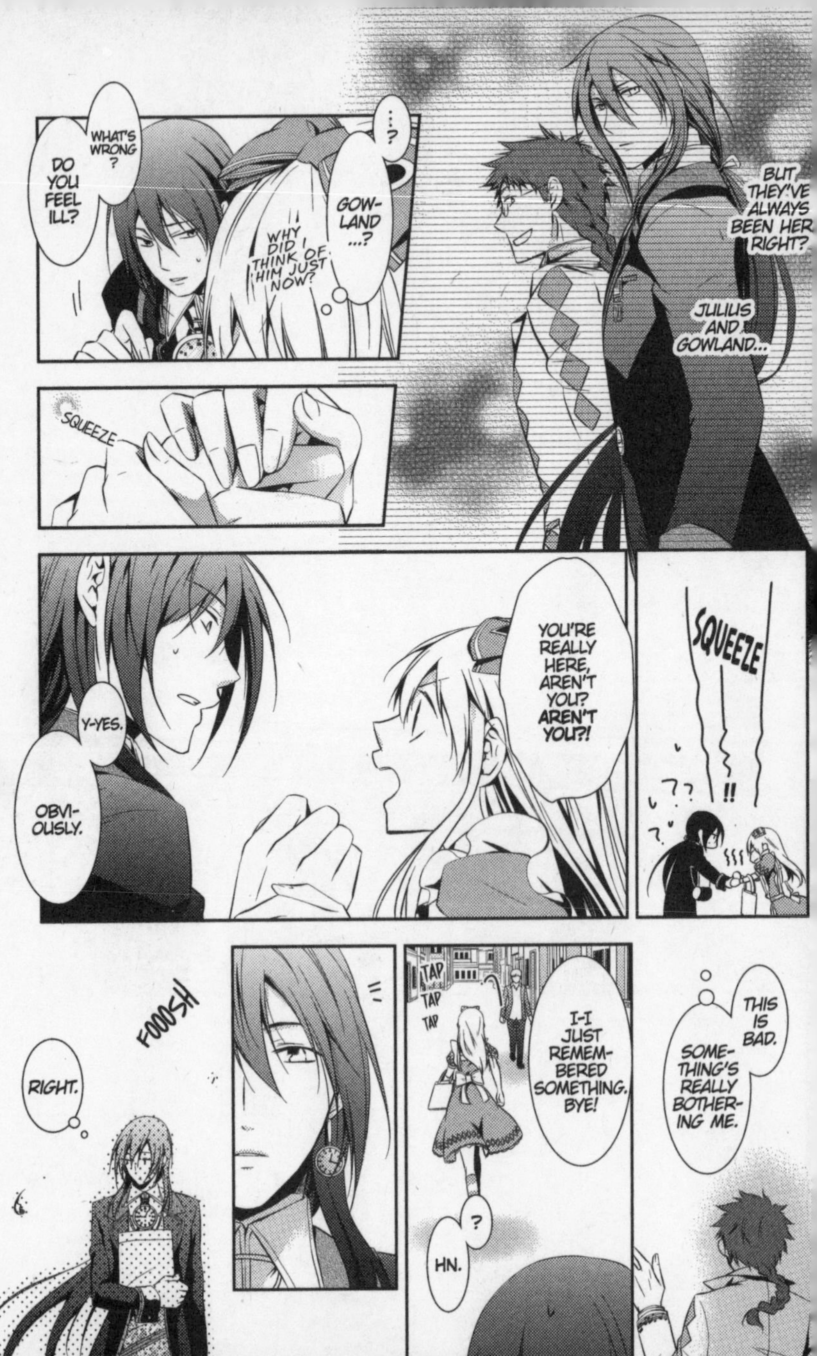
BUT THEY'VE ALWAYS BEEN HER RIGHT?
JULIUS AND GOWLAND...
...?
GOW-LAND ...?
WHY DID I THINK OF HIM JUST NOW?
WHAT'S WRONG?
DO YOU FEEL ILL?
SQUEEZE
SQUEEZE
!!
YOU'RE REALLY HERE, AREN'T YOU? AREN'T YOU?!
Y-YES.
OBVI-OUSLY.
THIS IS BAD.
SOME-THING'S REALLY BOTHER-ING ME.
TAP
TAP
TAP
I-I JUST REMEM-BERED SOMETHING. BYE!
?
HN.
FOOOSH
RIGHT.

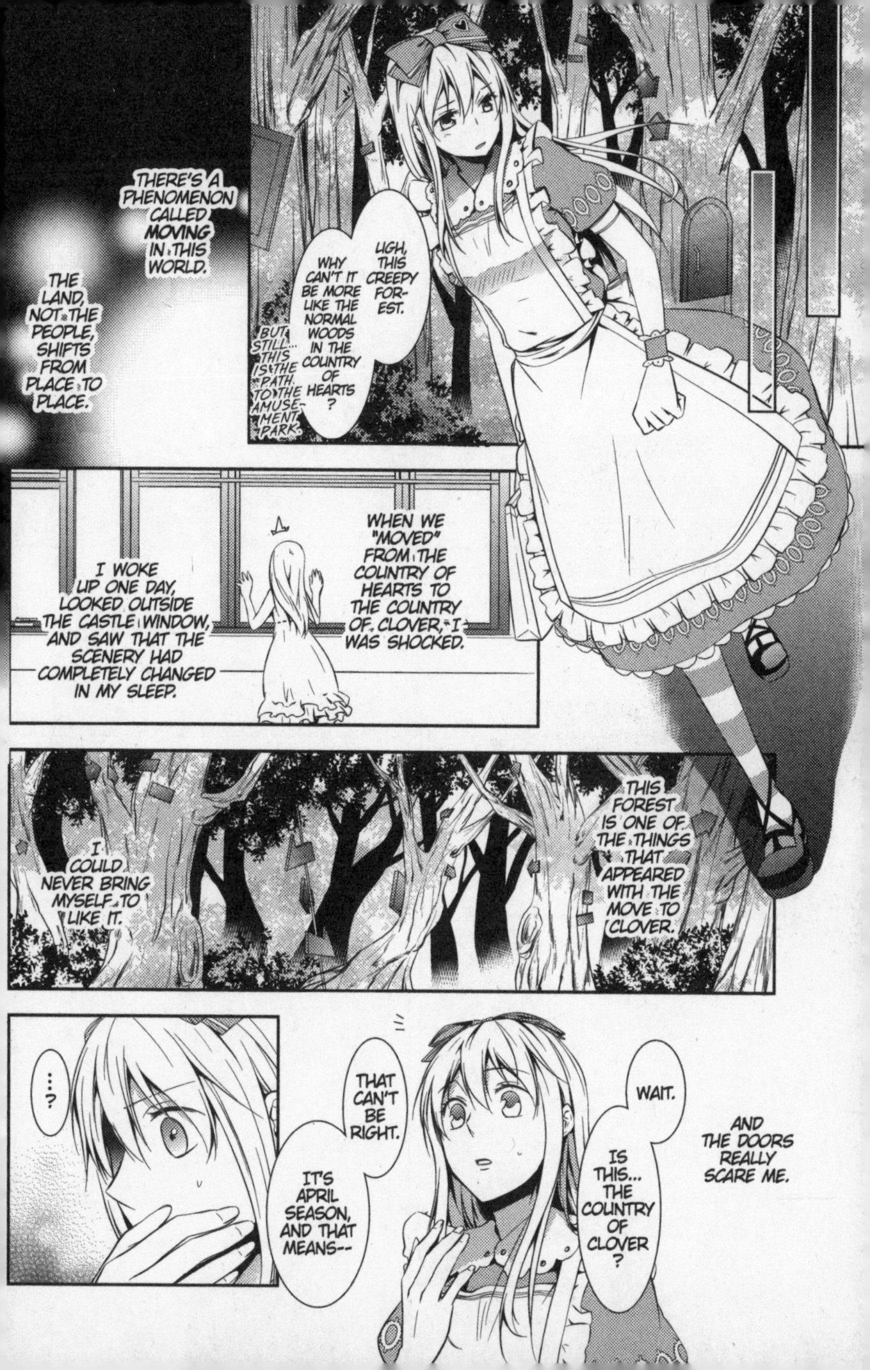
UGH, THIS CREEPY FOREST.
WHY CAN'T IT BE MORE LIKE THE NORMAL WOODS IN THE COUNTRY OF HEARTS?
BUT STILL... THIS IS THE PATH TO THE AMUSEMENT PARK.
THERE'S A PHENOMENON CALLED MOVING IN THIS WORLD.
THE LAND, NOT THE PEOPLE, SHIFTS FROM PLACE TO PLACE.
WHEN WE "MOVED" FROM THE COUNTRY OF HEARTS TO THE COUNTRY OF CLOVER, I WAS SHOCKED.
I WOKE UP ONE DAY, LOOKED OUTSIDE THE CASTLE WINDOW, AND SAW THAT THE SCENERY HAD COMPLETELY CHANGED IN MY SLEEP.
THIS FOREST IS ONE OF THE THINGS THAT APPEARED WITH THE MOVE TO CLOVER.
I COULD NEVER BRING MYSELF TO LIKE IT.
AND THE DOORS REALLY SCARE ME.
WAIT.
IS THIS... THE COUNTRY OF CLOVER?
THAT CAN'T BE RIGHT.
IT'S APRIL SEASON, AND THAT MEANS--
...?

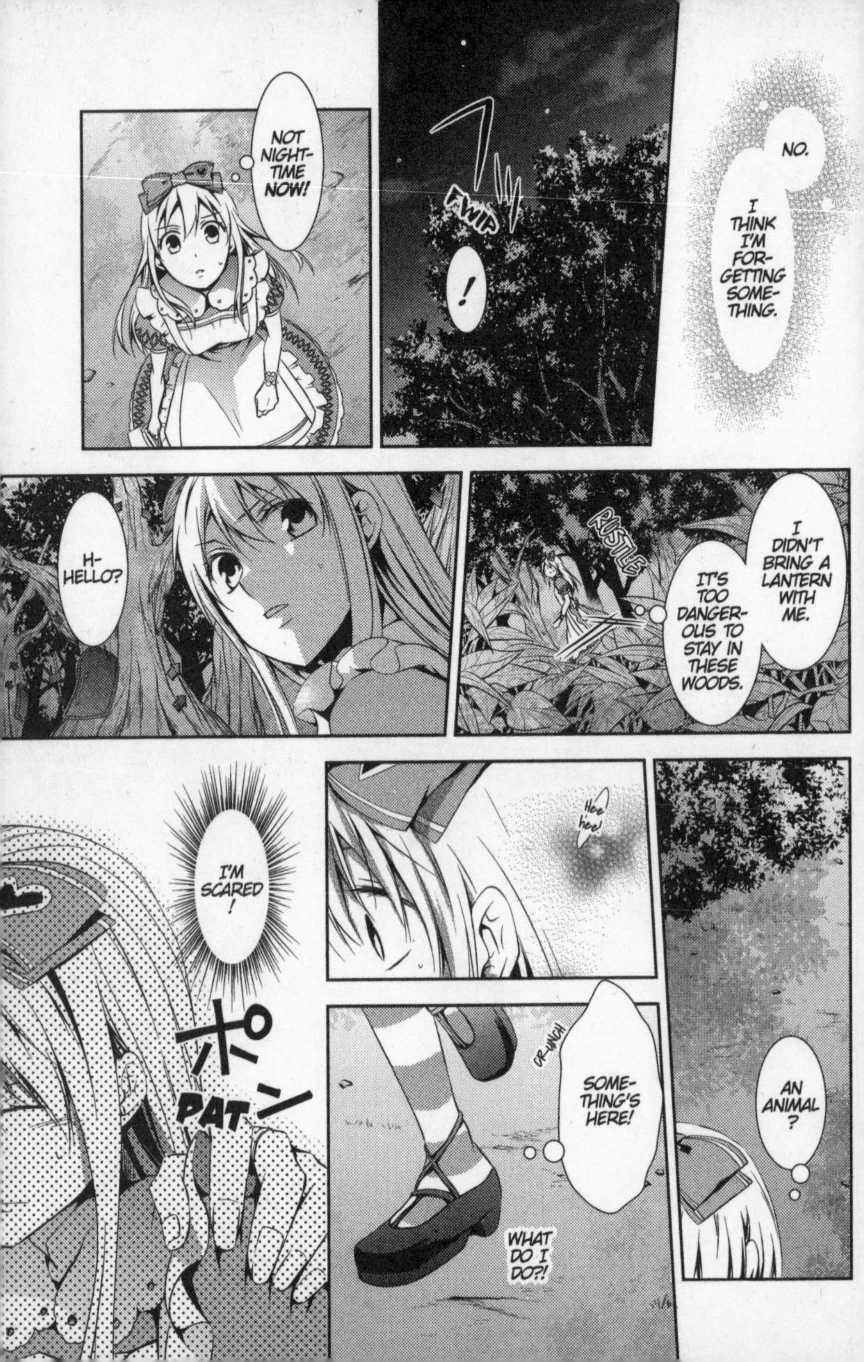
NO.
I THINK I'M FOR-GETTING SOME-THING.
FWIP
!
NOT NIGHT-TIME NOW!
I DIDN'T BRING A LANTERN WITH ME.
IT'S TOO DANGER-OUS TO STAY IN THESE WOODS.
RUSTLE
H-HELLO?
AN ANIMAL?
Hee hee!
CR-UNCH
SOME-THING'S HERE!
WHAT DO I DO?!
I'M SCARED!
ポン
PAT

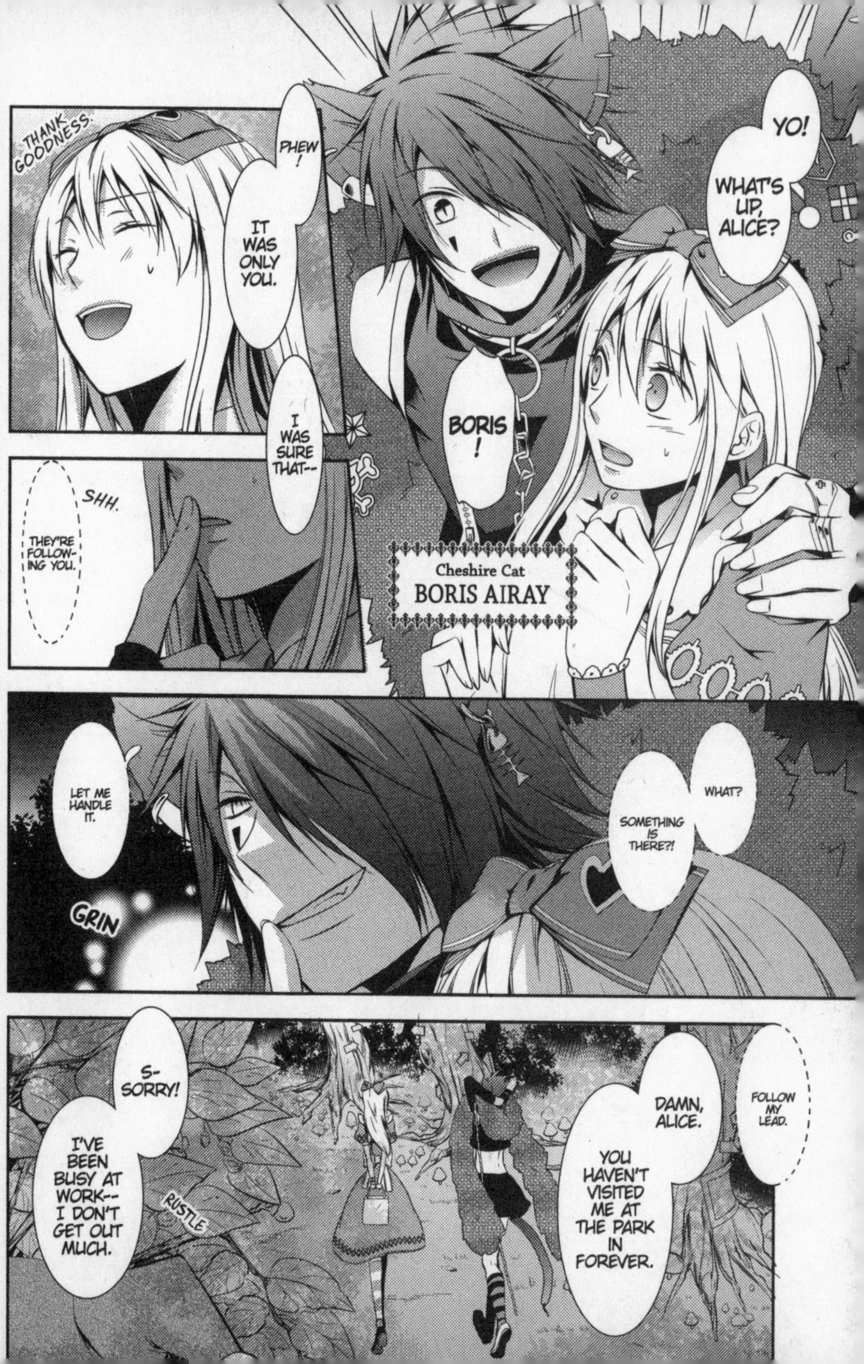
YO!
WHAT'S UP, ALICE?
BORIS!
Cheshire Cat
BORIS AIRAY
PHEW!
IT WAS ONLY YOU.
THANK GOODNESS.
I WAS SURE THAT--
SHH.
THEY'RE FOLLOWING YOU.
WHAT?
SOMETHING IS THERE?!
LET ME HANDLE IT.
GRIN
FOLLOW MY LEAD.
DAMN, ALICE.
YOU HAVEN'T VISITED ME AT THE PARK IN FOREVER.
S-SORRY!
I'VE BEEN BUSY AT WORK-- I DON'T GET OUT MUCH.
RUSTLE

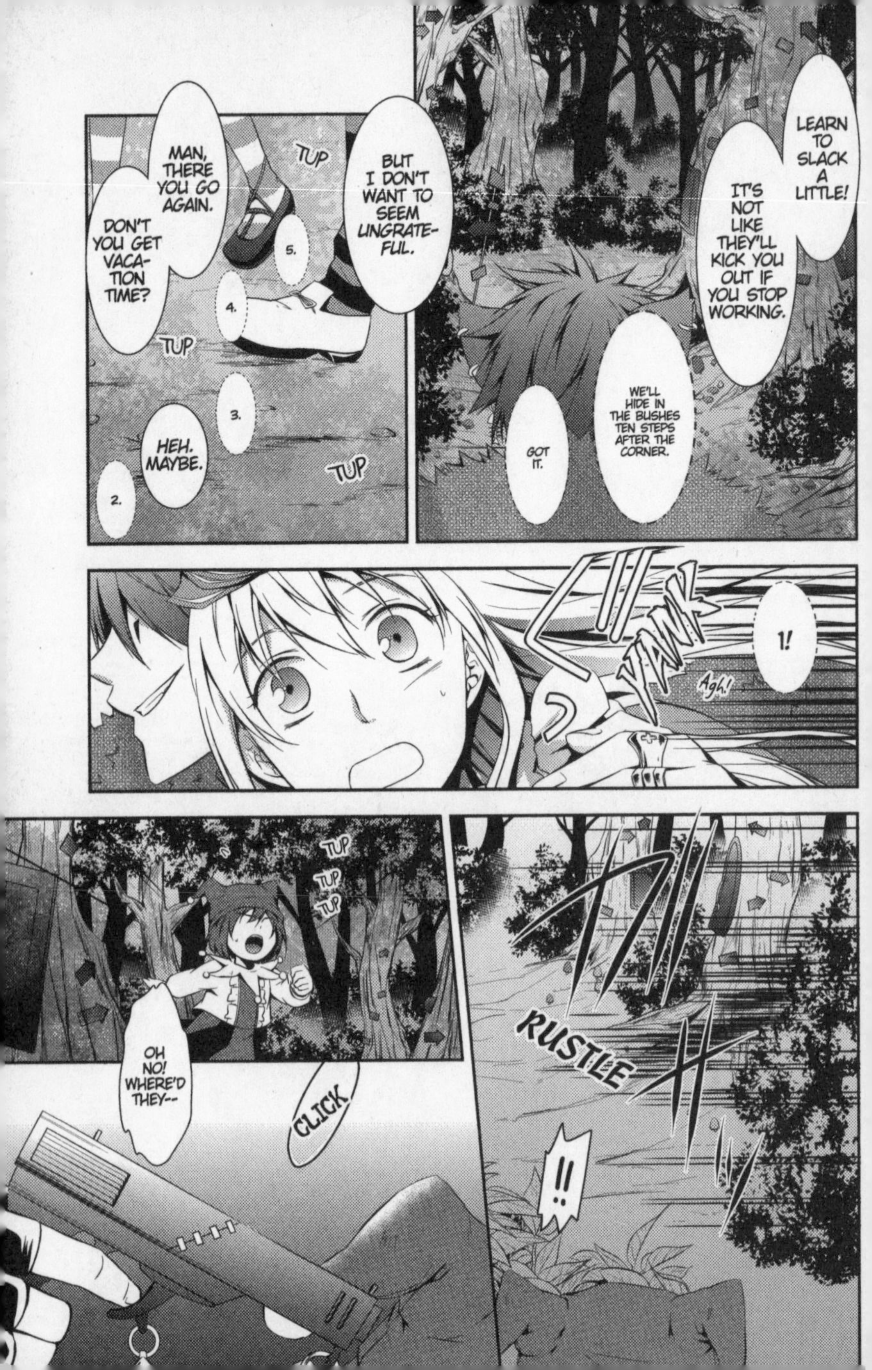
LEARN TO SLACK A LITTLE!
IT'S NOT LIKE THEY'LL KICK YOU OUT IF YOU STOP WORKING.
WE'LL HIDE IN THE BUSHES TEN STEPS AFTER THE CORNER.
GOT IT.
BUT I DON'T WANT TO SEEM UNGRATE-FUL.
MAN, THERE YOU GO AGAIN.
TUP
DON'T YOU GET VACA-TION TIME?
5.
4.
TUP
3.
HEH. MAYBE.
TUP
2.
YANK
1!
Agh!
RUSTLE
!!
TUP
TUP
TUP
OH NO! WHERE'D THEY--
CLICK

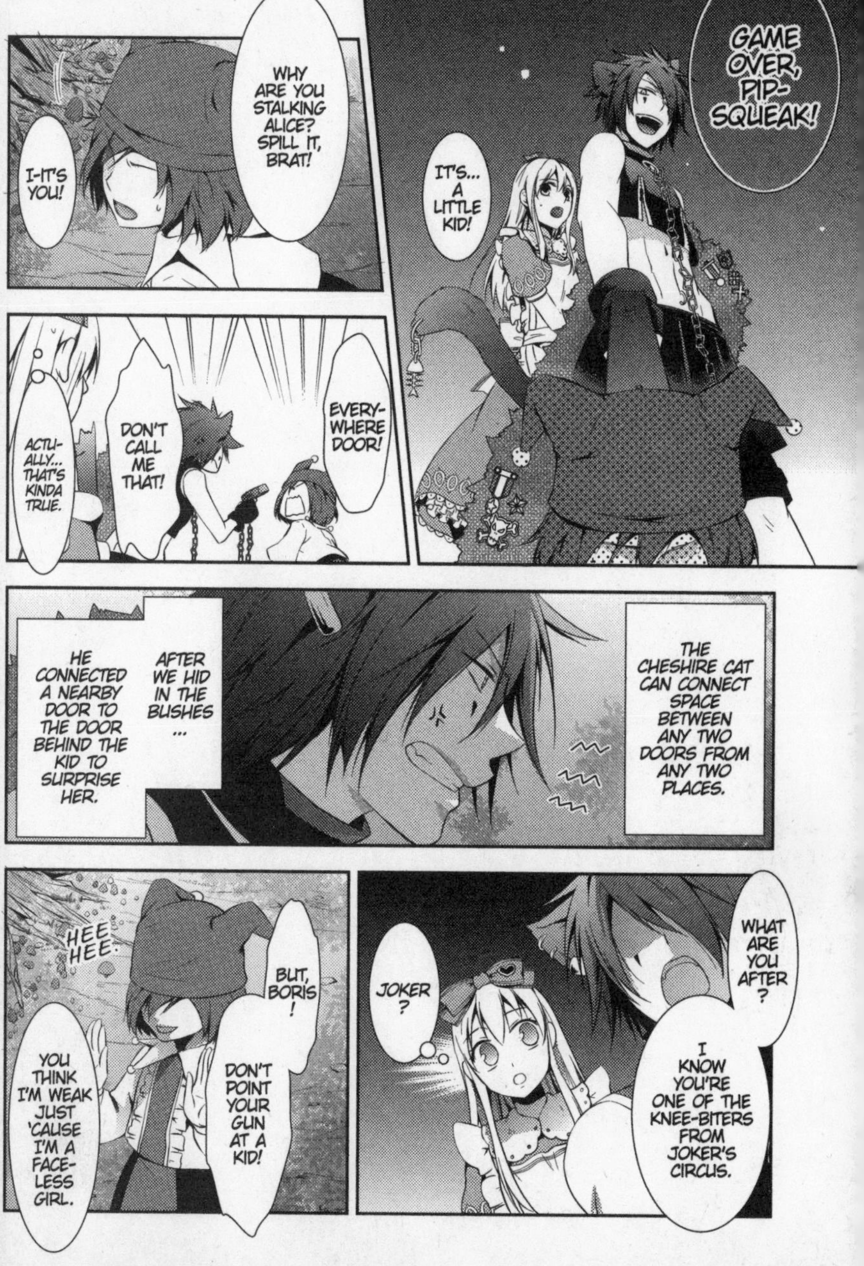
GAME OVER, PIP-SQUEAK!
IT'S... A LITTLE KID!
WHY ARE YOU STALKING ALICE? SPILL IT, BRAT!
I-IT'S YOU!
EVERY-WHERE DOOR!
DON'T CALL ME THAT!
ACTU-ALLY... THAT'S KINDA TRUE.
THE CHESHIRE CAT CAN CONNECT SPACE BETWEEN ANY TWO DOORS FROM ANY TWO PLACES.
AFTER WE HID IN THE BUSHES ...
HE CONNECTED A NEARBY DOOR TO THE DOOR BEHIND THE KID TO SURPRISE HER.
WHAT ARE YOU AFTER ?
I KNOW YOU'RE ONE OF THE KNEE-BITERS FROM JOKER'S CIRCUS.
JOKER ?
BUT, BORIS !
DON'T POINT YOUR GUN AT A KID!
HEE HEE.
YOU THINK I'M WEAK JUST 'CAUSE I'M A FACE-LESS GIRL.

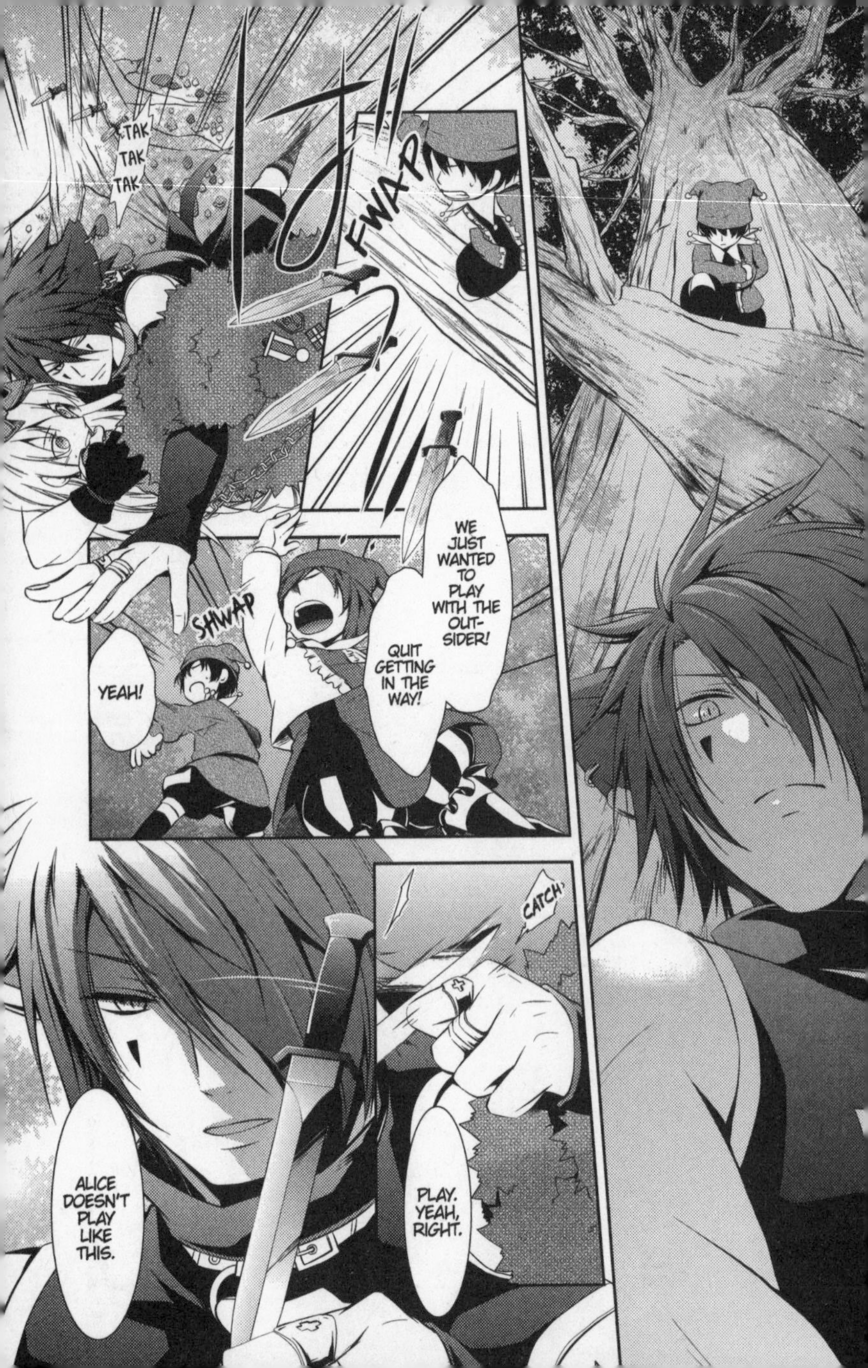
FWAP
TAK TAK TAK
WE JUST WANTED TO PLAY WITH THE OUT-SIDER!
QUIT GETTING IN THE WAY!
SHWAP
YEAH!
CATCH
PLAY. YEAH, RIGHT.
ALICE DOESN'T PLAY LIKE THIS.

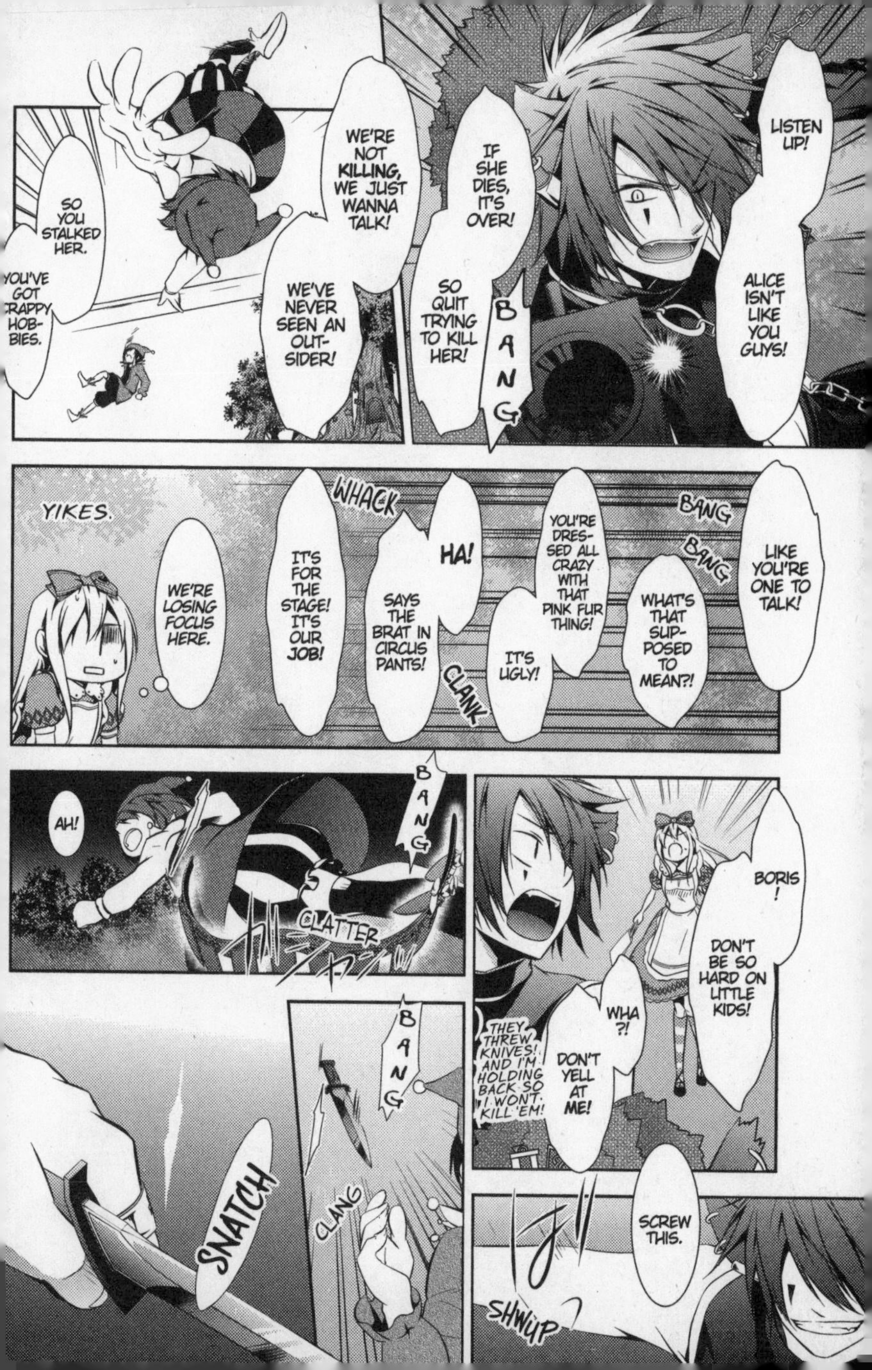
LISTEN UP!
ALICE ISN'T LIKE YOU GUYS!
BANG
IF SHE DIES, IT'S OVER!
SO QUIT TRYING TO KILL HER!
WE'RE NOT KILLING, WE JUST WANNA TALK!
WE'VE NEVER SEEN AN OUT-SIDER!
SO YOU STALKED HER.
YOU'VE GOT CRAPPY HOB-BIES.
LIKE YOU'RE ONE TO TALK!
BANG
BANG
WHAT'S THAT SUP-POSED TO MEAN?!
YOU'RE DRES-SED ALL CRAZY WITH THAT PINK FUR THING!
IT'S UGLY!
HA!
WHACK
SAYS THE BRAT IN CIRCUS PANTS!
CLANK
IT'S FOR THE STAGE! IT'S OUR JOB!
WE'RE LOSING FOCUS HERE.
YIKES.
BORIS!
DON'T BE SO HARD ON LITTLE KIDS!
WHA?!
DON'T YELL AT ME!
THEY THREW KNIVES! AND I'M HOLDING BACK SO I WON'T KILL 'EM!
BANG
AH!
CLATTER
BANG
CLANG
SNATCH
SCREW THIS.
SHWUP

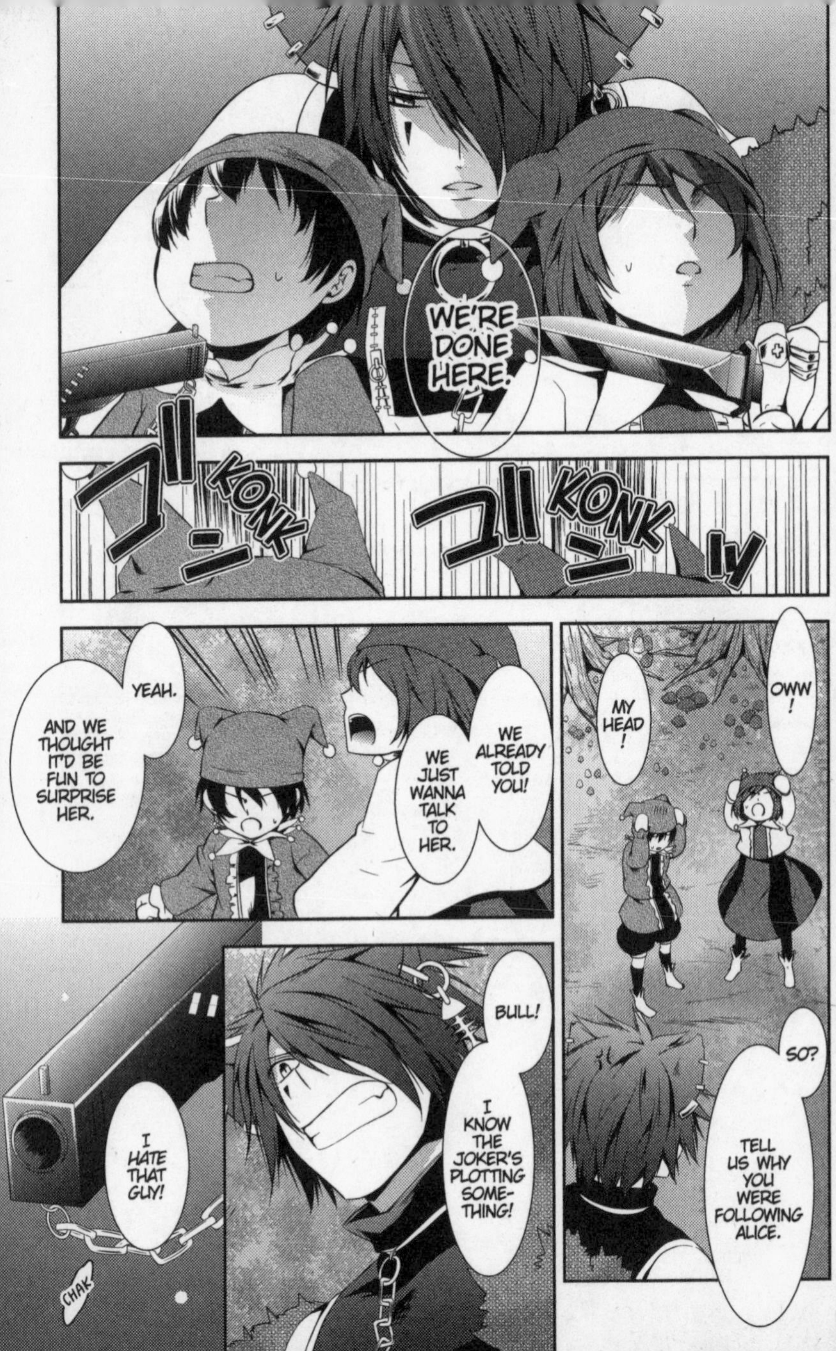
WE'RE DONE HERE.
KONK
KONK
OWW!
MY HEAD!
WE ALREADY TOLD YOU!
WE JUST WANNA TALK TO HER.
YEAH.
AND WE THOUGHT IT'D BE FUN TO SURPRISE HER.
SO?
TELL US WHY YOU WERE FOLLOWING ALICE.
BULL!
I KNOW THE JOKER'S PLOTTING SOME-THING!
I HATE THAT GUY!
CHAK

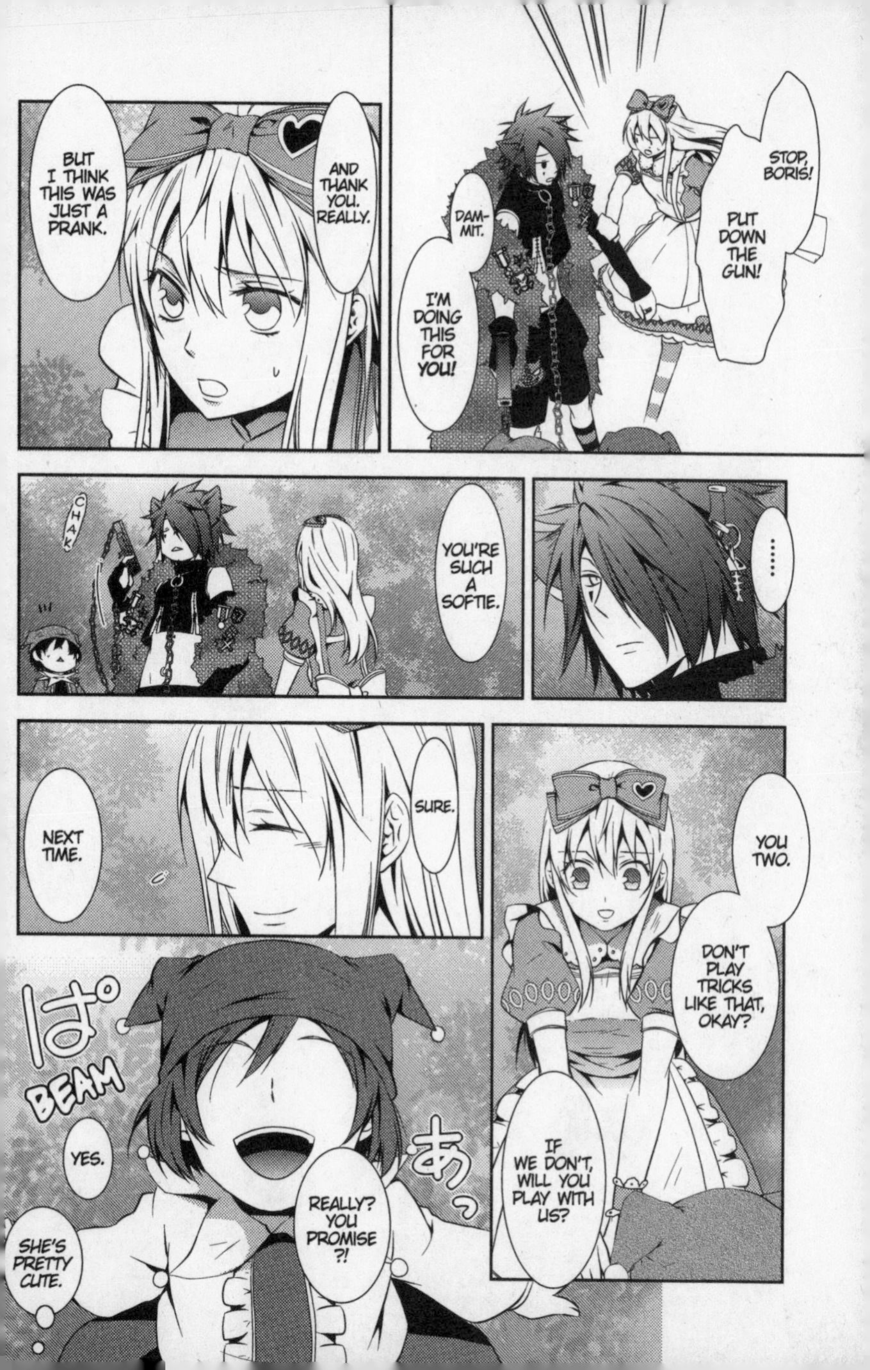
STOP, BORIS!
PUT DOWN THE GUN!
DAM-MIT.
I'M DOING THIS FOR YOU!
AND THANK YOU. REALLY.
BUT I THINK THIS WAS JUST A PRANK.
......
YOU'RE SUCH A SOFTIE.
CHAK
YOU TWO.
DON'T PLAY TRICKS LIKE THAT, OKAY?
IF WE DON'T, WILL YOU PLAY WITH US?
SURE.
NEXT TIME.
あっ
REALLY? YOU PROMISE?!
ぱっ
BEAM
YES.
SHE'S PRETTY CUTE.

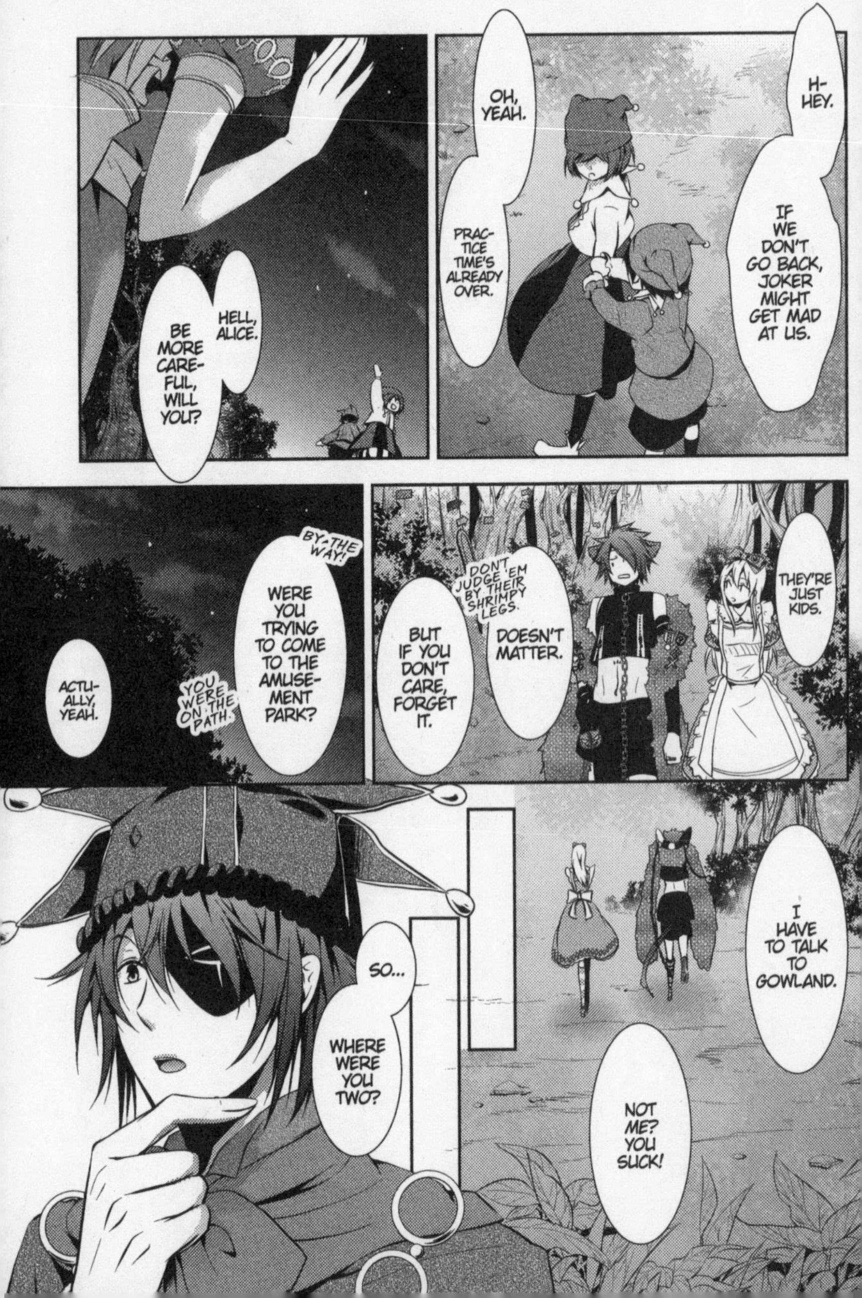
H-HEY.
IF WE DON'T GO BACK, JOKER MIGHT GET MAD AT US.
OH, YEAH.
PRACTICE TIME'S ALREADY OVER.
HELL, ALICE.
BE MORE CAREFUL, WILL YOU?
THEY'RE JUST KIDS.
DOESN'T MATTER.
DON'T JUDGE 'EM BY THEIR SHRIMPY LEGS.
BUT IF YOU DON'T CARE, FORGET IT.
BY THE WAY!
WERE YOU TRYING TO COME TO THE AMUSEMENT PARK?
YOU WERE ON THE PATH.
ACTUALLY, YEAH.
I HAVE TO TALK TO GOWLAND.
NOT ME? YOU SUCK!
SO...
WHERE WERE YOU TWO?

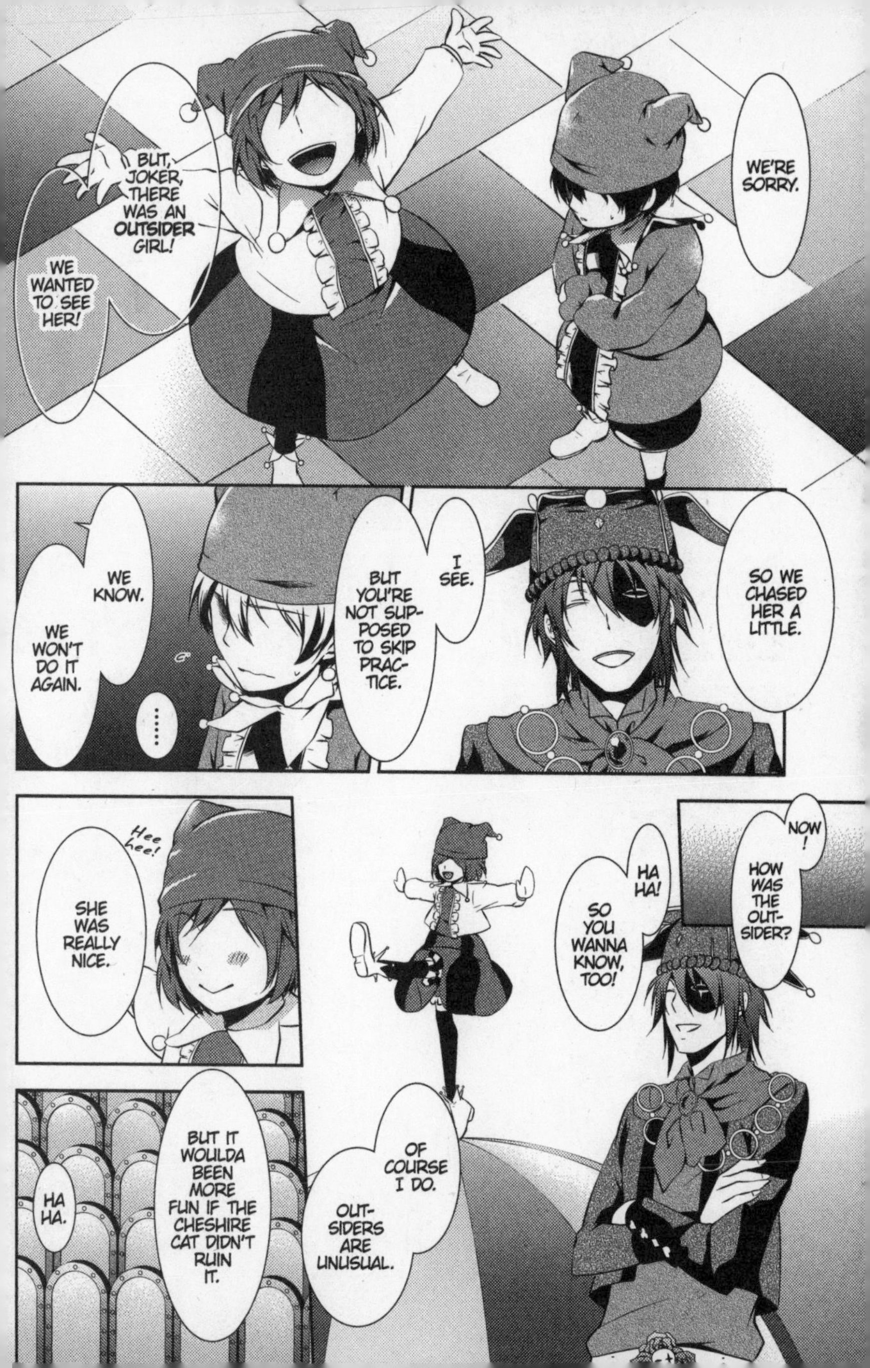
WE'RE SORRY.
BUT, JOKER, THERE WAS AN OUTSIDER GIRL!
WE WANTED TO SEE HER!
SO WE CHASED HER A LITTLE.
I SEE.
BUT YOU'RE NOT SUP-POSED TO SKIP PRAC-TICE.
WE KNOW.
WE WON'T DO IT AGAIN.
......
NOW!
HOW WAS THE OUT-SIDER?
HA HA!
SO YOU WANNA KNOW, TOO!
Hee hee!
SHE WAS REALLY NICE.
OF COURSE I DO.
OUT-SIDERS ARE UNUSUAL.
BUT IT WOULDA BEEN MORE FUN IF THE CHESHIRE CAT DIDN'T RUIN IT.
HA HA.

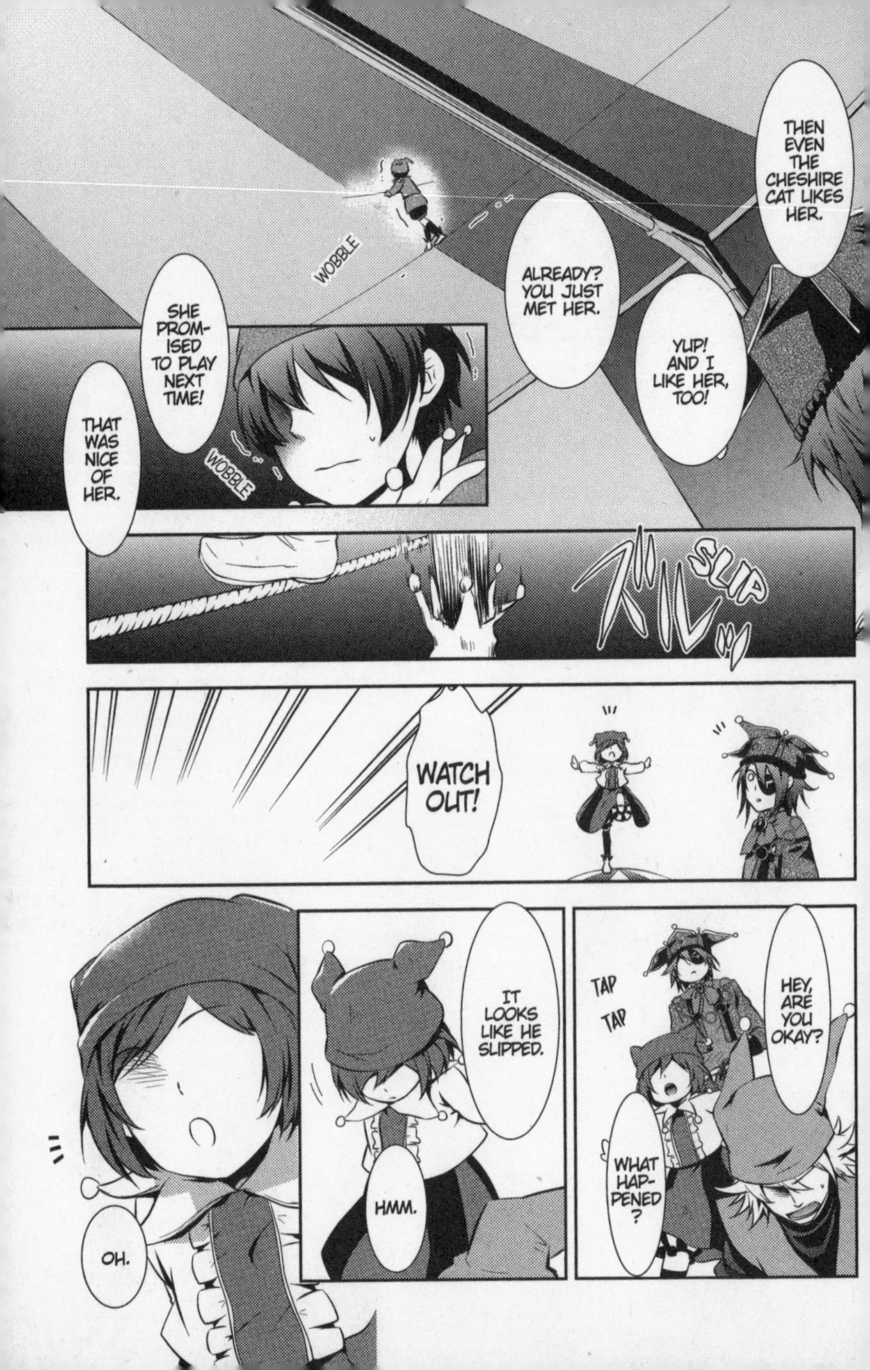
THEN EVEN THE CHESHIRE CAT LIKES HER.
ALREADY? YOU JUST MET HER.
YUP! AND I LIKE HER, TOO!
WOBBLE
SHE PROMISED TO PLAY NEXT TIME!
WOBBLE
THAT WAS NICE OF HER.
SLIP
WATCH OUT!
TAP
TAP
HEY, ARE YOU OKAY?
WHAT HAP-PENED?
IT LOOKS LIKE HE SLIPPED.
HMM.
OH.

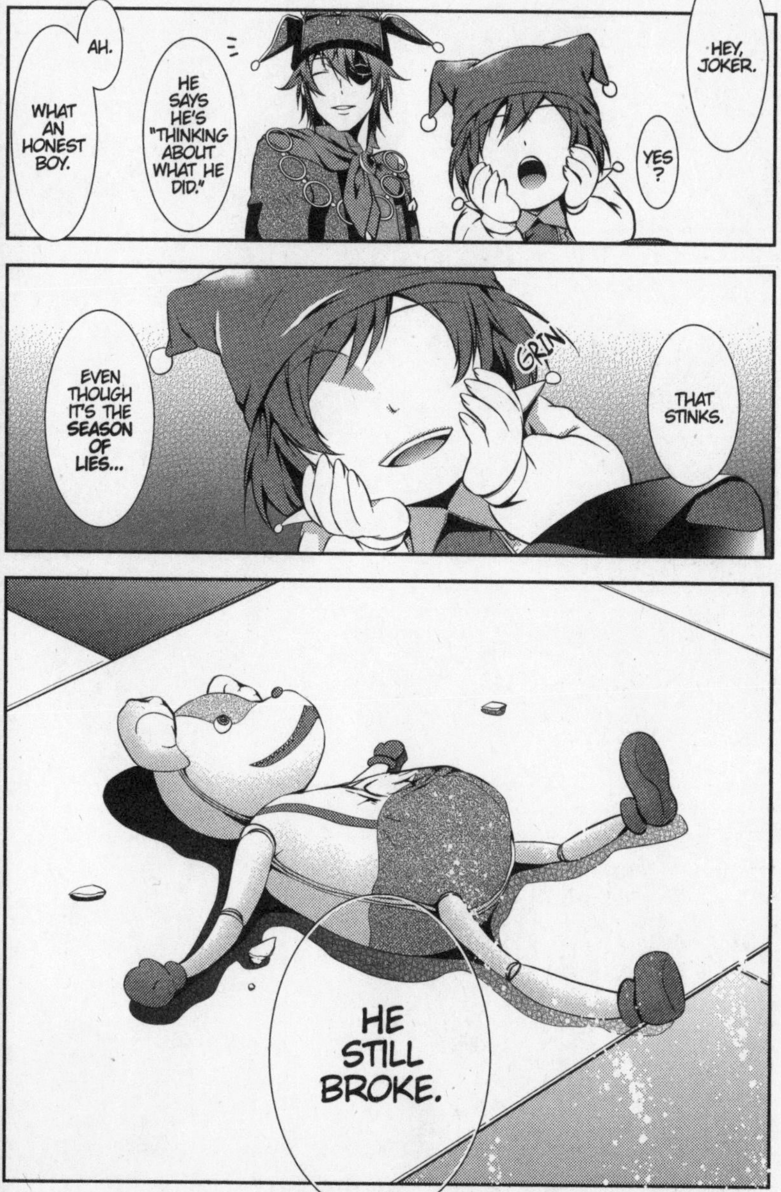
HEY, JOKER.
YES?
HE SAYS HE'S "THINKING ABOUT WHAT HE DID."
AH.
WHAT AN HONEST BOY.
THAT STINKS.
GRIN
EVEN THOUGH IT'S THE SEASON OF LIES...
HE STILL BROKE.

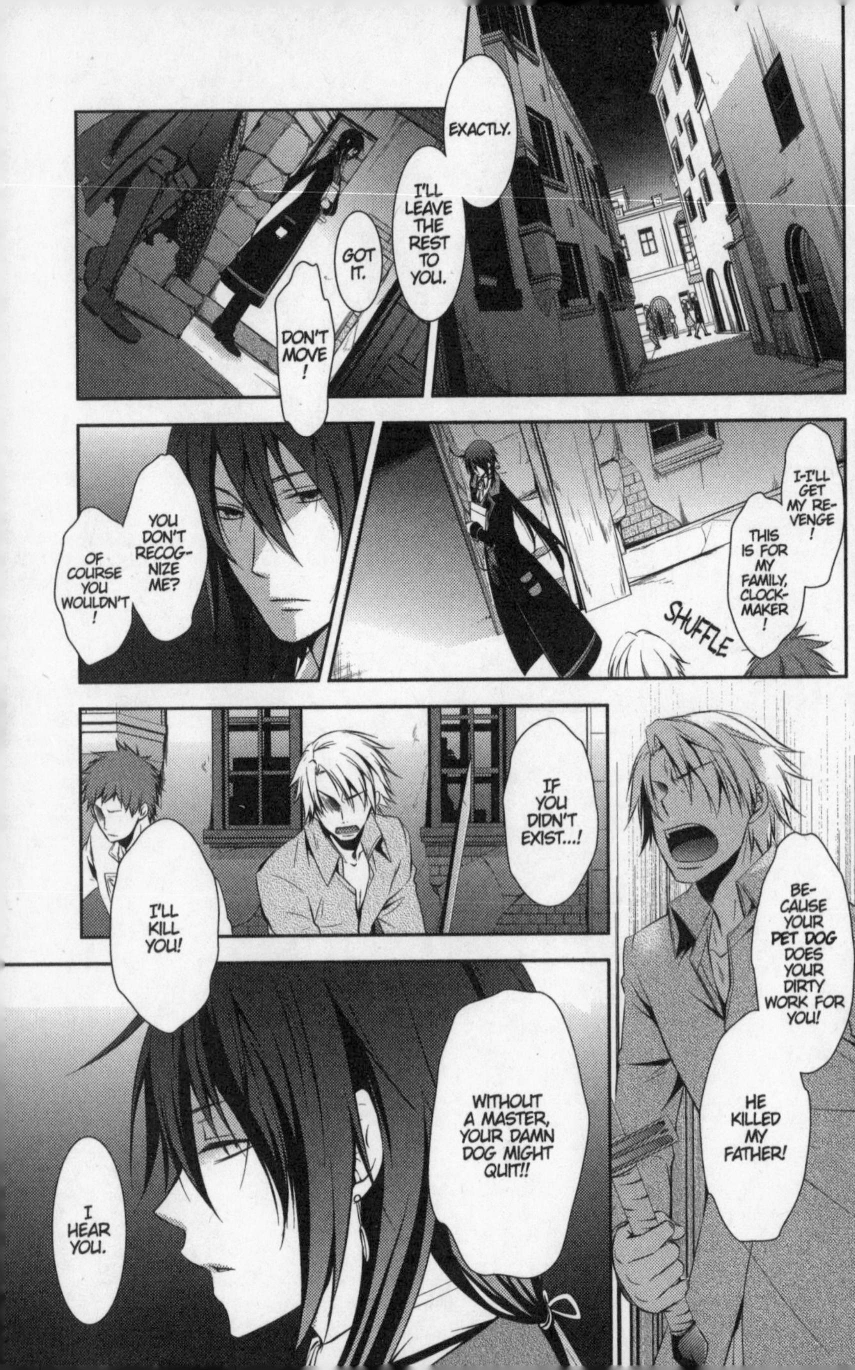
EXACTLY.
I'LL LEAVE THE REST TO YOU.
GOT IT.
DON'T MOVE!
I-I'LL GET MY REVENGE!
THIS IS FOR MY FAMILY, CLOCKMAKER!
SHUFFLE
YOU DON'T RECOGNIZE ME?
OF COURSE YOU WOULDN'T!
BECAUSE YOUR PET DOG DOES YOUR DIRTY WORK FOR YOU!
HE KILLED MY FATHER!
IF YOU DIDN'T EXIST...!
I'LL KILL YOU!
WITHOUT A MASTER, YOUR DAMN DOG MIGHT QUIT!!
I HEAR YOU.

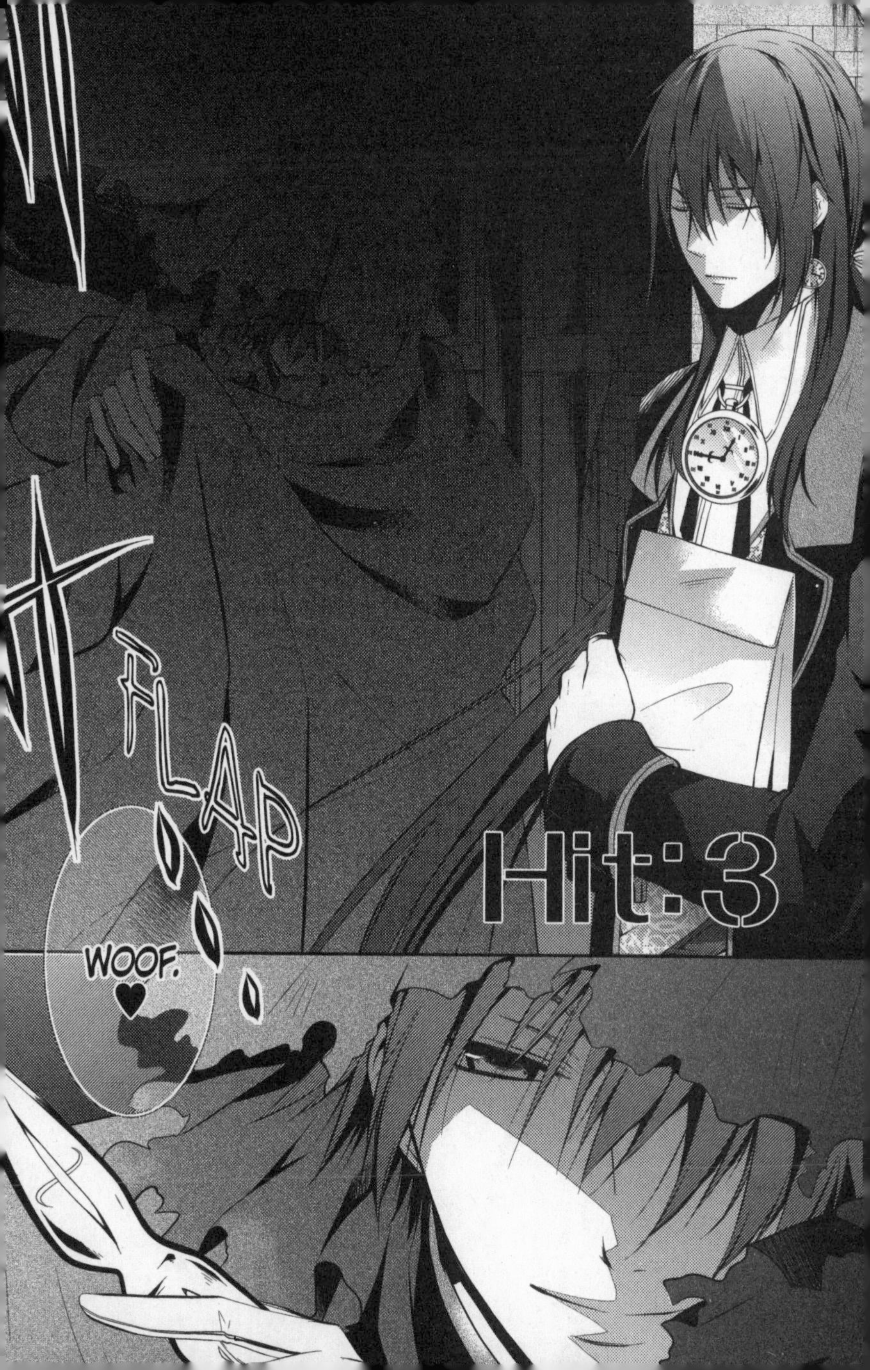
Hit:3
FLAP
WOOF.
♥

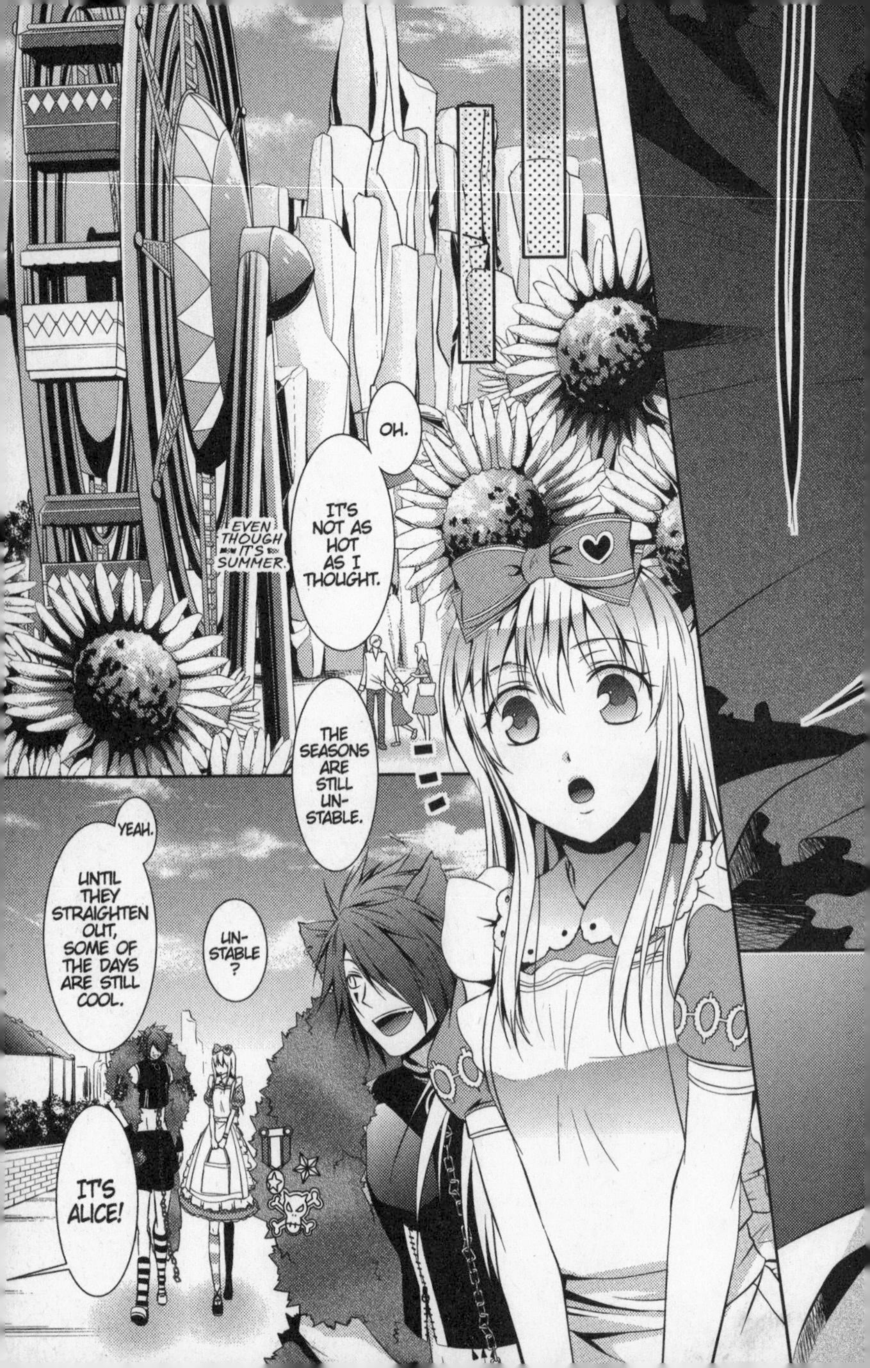
OH.
IT'S NOT AS HOT AS I THOUGHT.
EVEN THOUGH IT'S SUMMER.
THE SEASONS ARE STILL UN-STABLE.
...
UN-STABLE?
YEAH.
UNTIL THEY STRAIGHTEN OUT, SOME OF THE DAYS ARE STILL COOL.
IT'S ALICE!

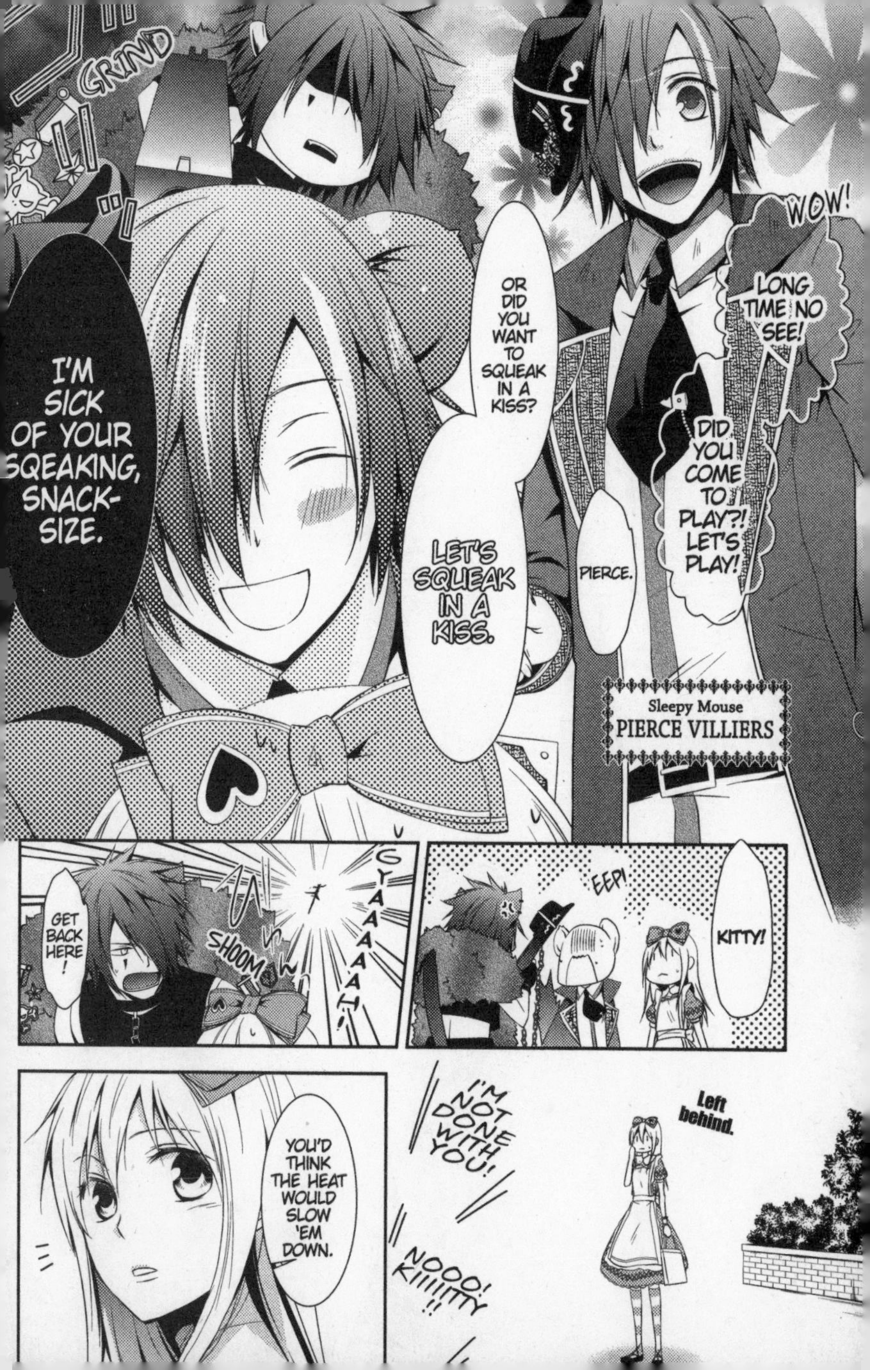
WOW!
LONG TIME NO SEE!
DID YOU COME TO PLAY?! LET'S PLAY!
PIERCE.
Sleepy Mouse
PIERCE VILLIERS
OR DID YOU WANT TO SQUEAK IN A KISS?
LET'S SQUEAK IN A KISS.
GRIND
I'M SICK OF YOUR SQEAKING, SNACK-SIZE.
KITTY!
EEP!
GYAAAAAAH!
SHOOM
GET BACK HERE!
Left behind.
I'M NOT DONE WITH YOU!
NOOO! KIIIIITTY!!
YOU'D THINK THE HEAT WOULD SLOW 'EM DOWN.

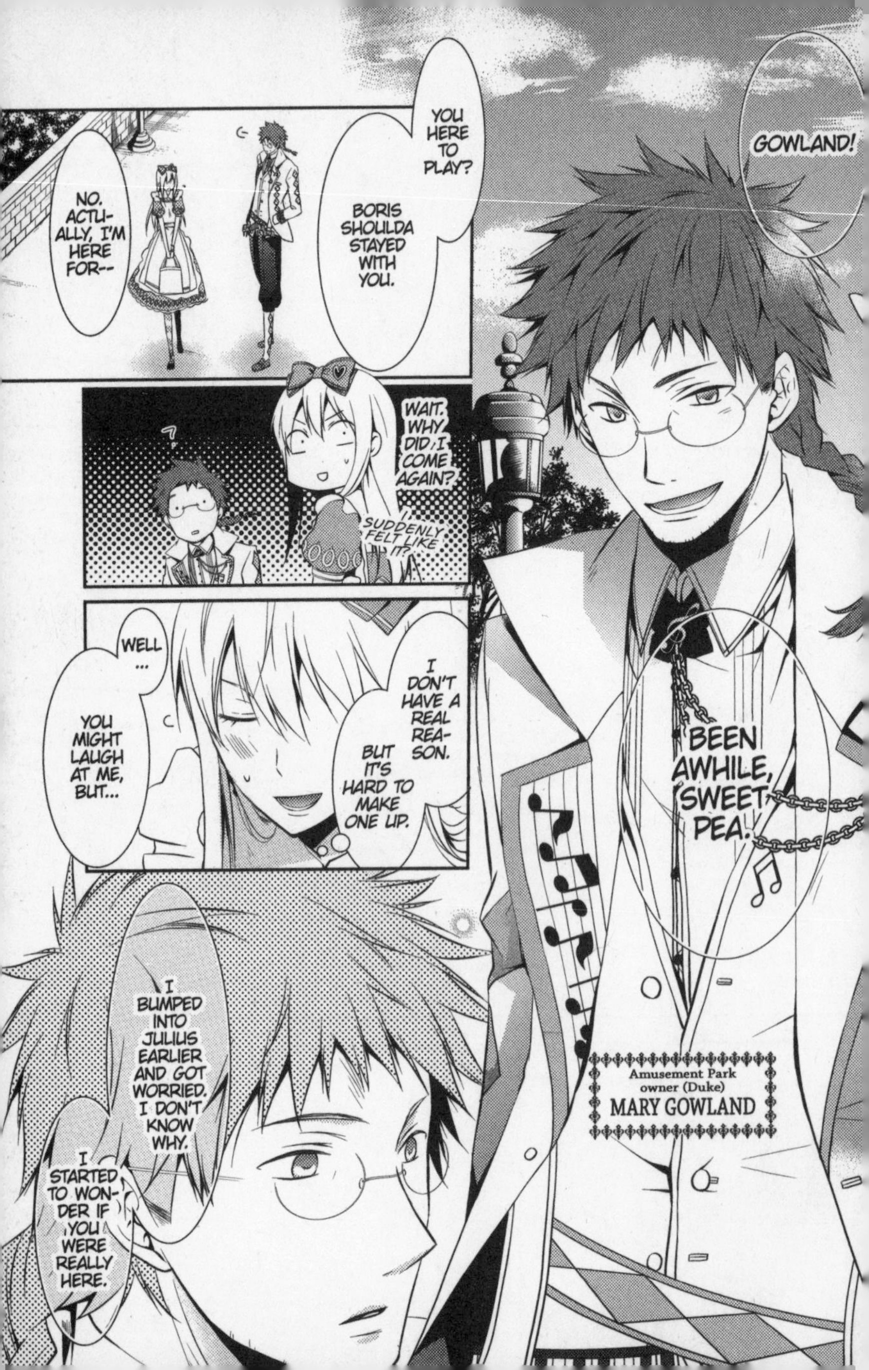
GOWLAND!
BEEN AWHILE, SWEET PEA.
Amusement Park owner (Duke)
MARY GOWLAND
YOU HERE TO PLAY?
BORIS SHOULDA STAYED WITH YOU.
NO. ACTUALLY, I'M HERE FOR--
WAIT. WHY DID I COME AGAIN?
I SUDDENLY FELT LIKE IT?
I DON'T HAVE A REAL REASON.
BUT IT'S HARD TO MAKE ONE UP.
WELL...
YOU MIGHT LAUGH AT ME, BUT...
I BUMPED INTO JULIUS EARLIER AND GOT WORRIED. I DON'T KNOW WHY.
I STARTED TO WONDER IF YOU WERE REALLY HERE.

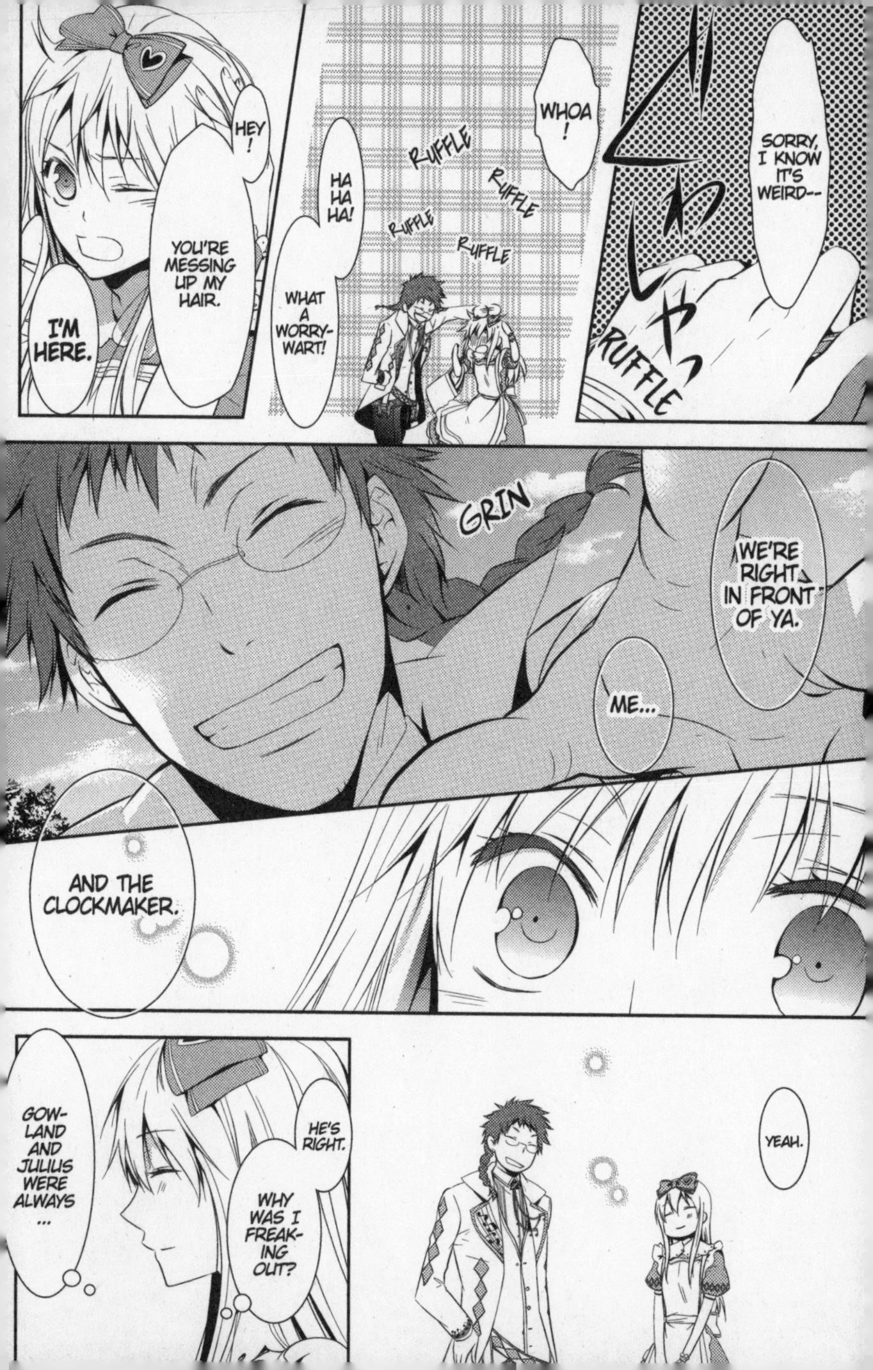
SORRY, I KNOW IT'S WEIRD--
RUFFLE
WHOA!
RUFFLE
RUFFLE
RUFFLE
RUFFLE
HA HA HA!
WHAT A WORRY-WART!
HEY!
YOU'RE MESSING UP MY HAIR.
I'M HERE.
GRIN
WE'RE RIGHT IN FRONT OF YA.
ME...
AND THE CLOCKMAKER.
YEAH.
HE'S RIGHT.
WHY WAS I FREAKING OUT?
GOWLAND AND JULIUS WERE ALWAYS ...

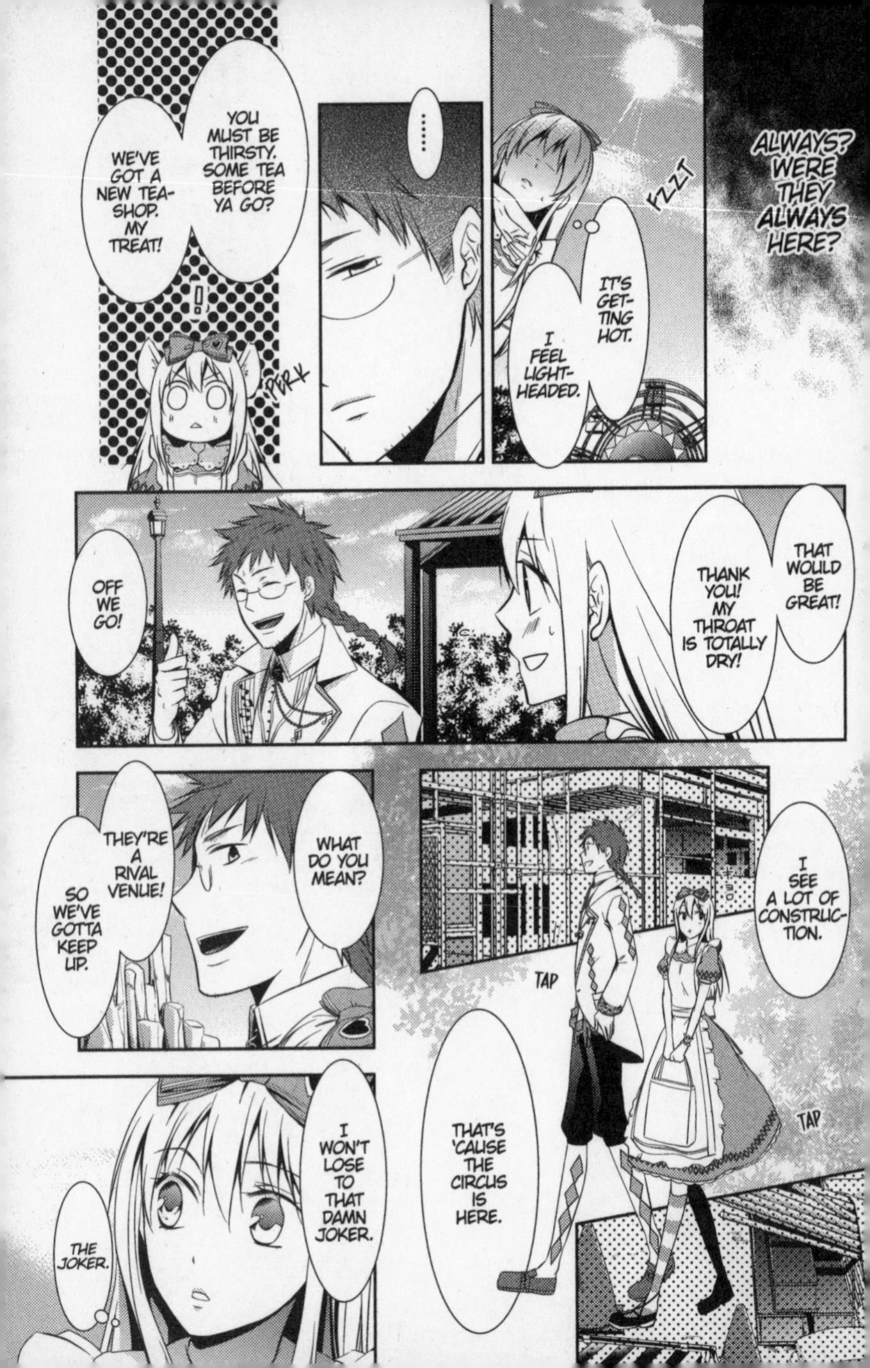
ALWAYS? WERE THEY ALWAYS HERE?
IT'S GETTING HOT.
I FEEL LIGHT-HEADED.
FZZT
......
YOU MUST BE THIRSTY. SOME TEA BEFORE YA GO?
WE'VE GOT A NEW TEA-SHOP. MY TREAT!
!
PERK
THAT WOULD BE GREAT!
THANK YOU! MY THROAT IS TOTALLY DRY!
OFF WE GO!
I SEE A LOT OF CONSTRUCTION.
TAP
TAP
THAT'S 'CAUSE THE CIRCUS IS HERE.
WHAT DO YOU MEAN?
THEY'RE A RIVAL VENUE!
SO WE'VE GOTTA KEEP UP.
I WON'T LOSE TO THAT DAMN JOKER.
THE JOKER.

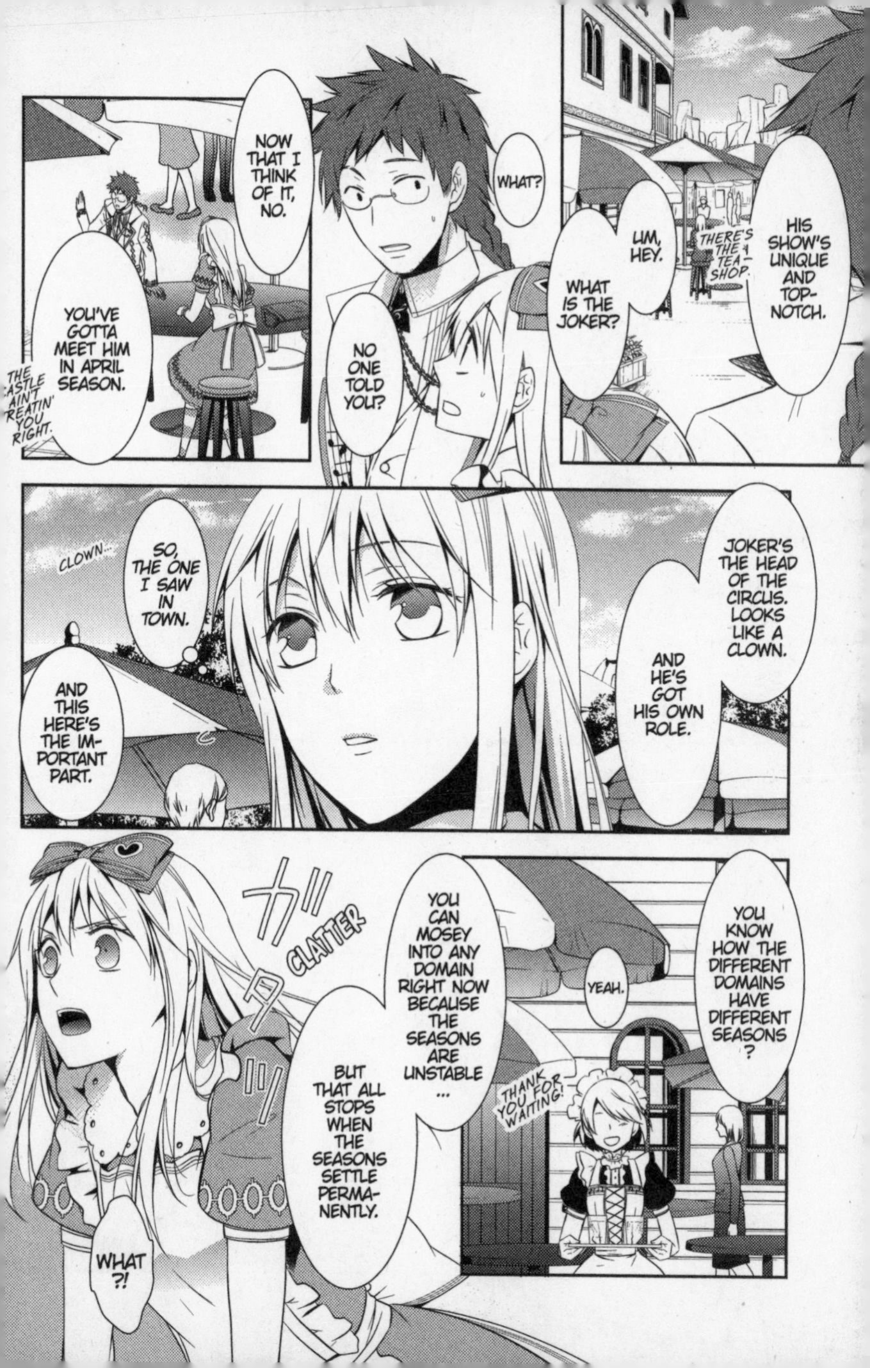
HIS SHOW'S UNIQUE AND TOP-NOTCH.
THERE'S THE TEA-SHOP.
UM, HEY. WHAT IS THE JOKER?
WHAT?
NO ONE TOLD YOU?
NOW THAT I THINK OF IT, NO.
YOU'VE GOTTA MEET HIM IN APRIL SEASON.
THE CASTLE AIN'T TREATIN' YOU RIGHT.
JOKER'S THE HEAD OF THE CIRCUS. LOOKS LIKE A CLOWN.
AND HE'S GOT HIS OWN ROLE.
SO, THE ONE I SAW IN TOWN.
CLOWN...
AND THIS HERE'S THE IMPORTANT PART.
YOU KNOW HOW THE DIFFERENT DOMAINS HAVE DIFFERENT SEASONS?
YEAH.
THANK YOU FOR WAITING!
YOU CAN MOSEY INTO ANY DOMAIN RIGHT NOW BECAUSE THE SEASONS ARE UNSTABLE...
BUT THAT ALL STOPS WHEN THE SEASONS SETTLE PERMANENTLY.
CLATTER
WHAT?!

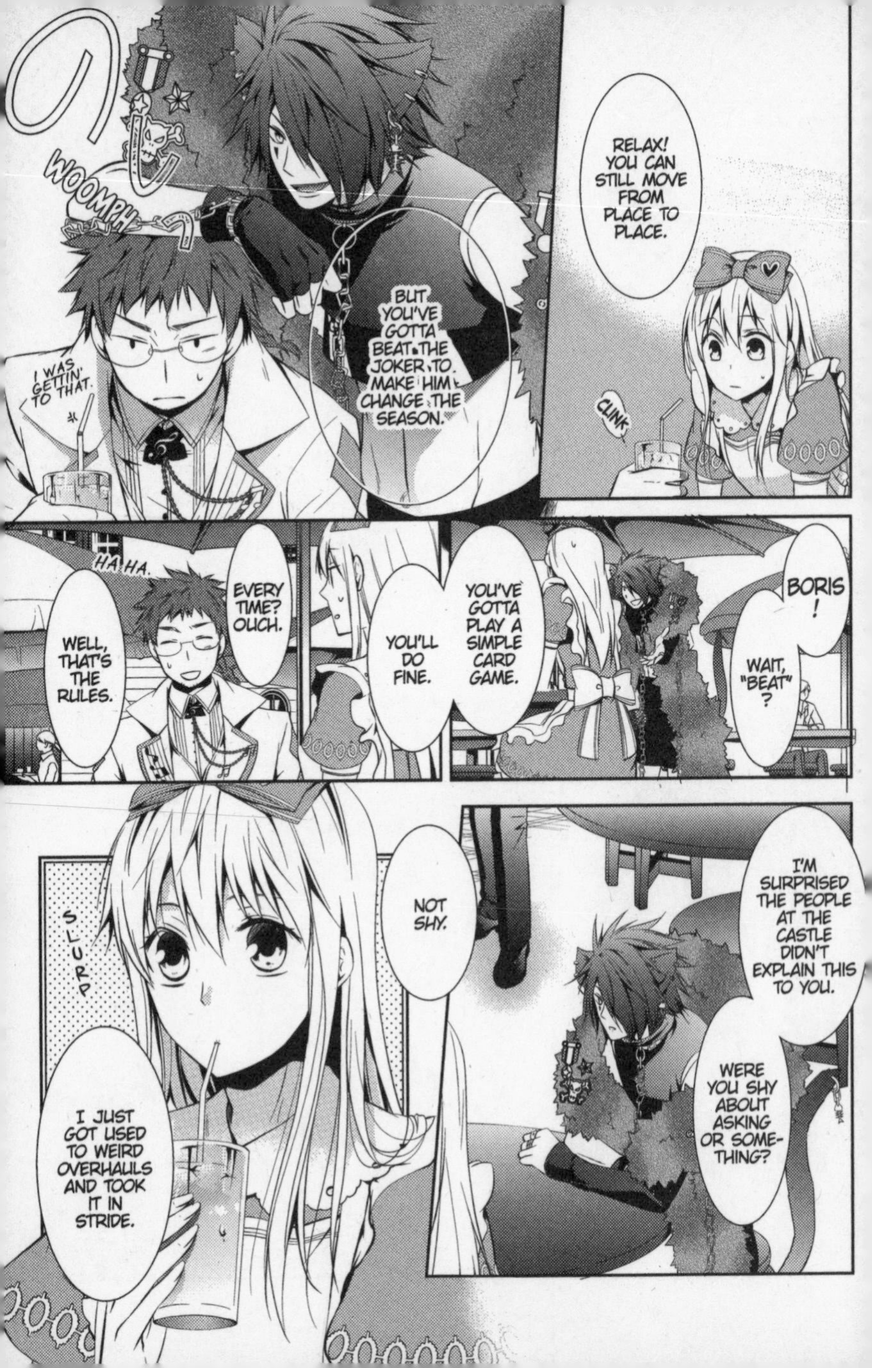
RELAX! YOU CAN STILL MOVE FROM PLACE TO PLACE.
CLINK
BUT YOU'VE GOTTA BEAT THE JOKER TO MAKE HIM CHANGE THE SEASON.
WOOMPH
I WAS GETTIN' TO THAT.
BORIS!
WAIT, "BEAT"?
YOU'VE GOTTA PLAY A SIMPLE CARD GAME.
YOU'LL DO FINE.
EVERY TIME? OUCH.
HA HA.
WELL, THAT'S THE RULES.
I'M SURPRISED THE PEOPLE AT THE CASTLE DIDN'T EXPLAIN THIS TO YOU.
WERE YOU SHY ABOUT ASKING OR SOME-THING?
NOT SHY.
SLURP
I JUST GOT USED TO WEIRD OVERHAULS AND TOOK IT IN STRIDE.

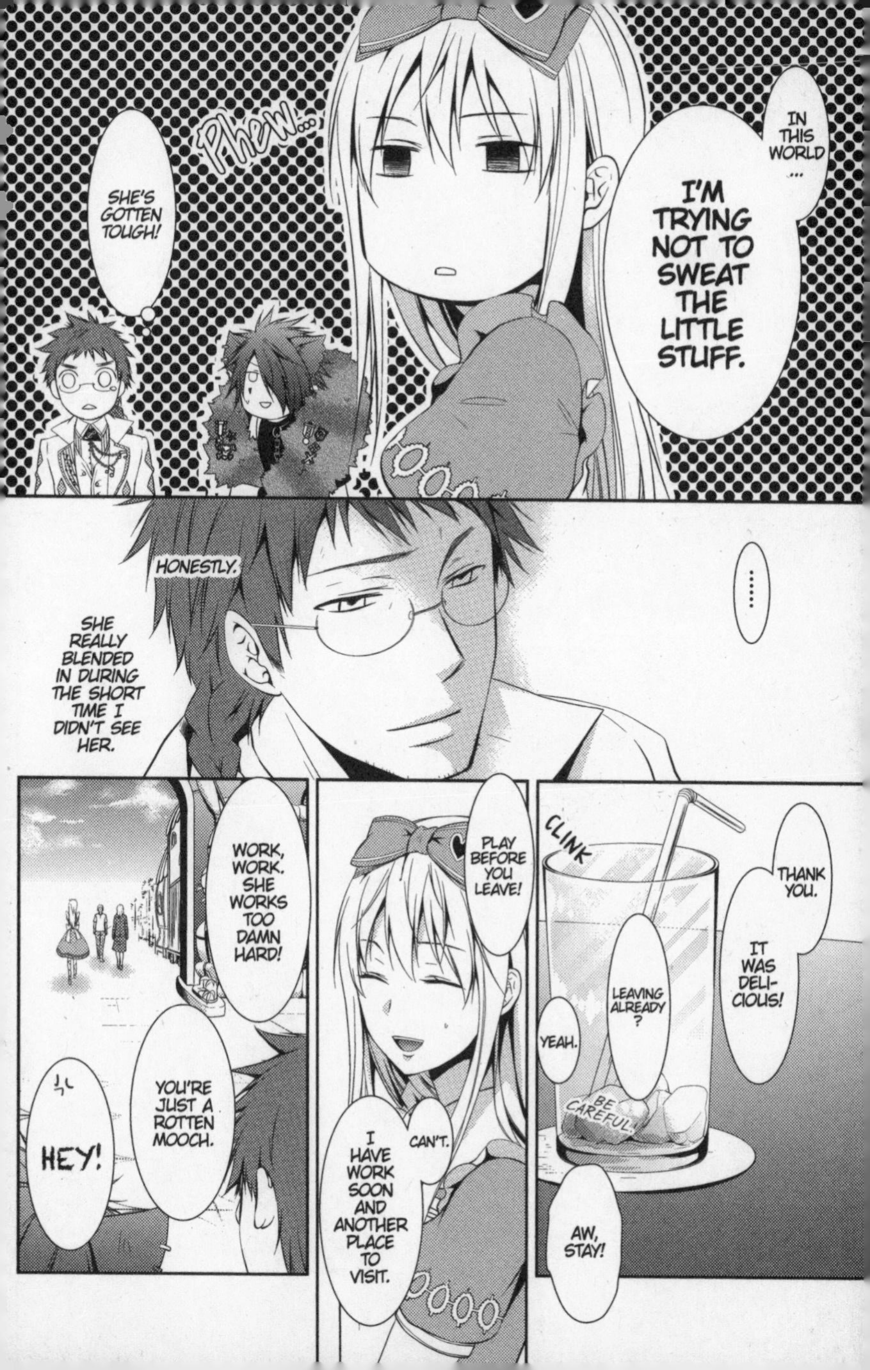
IN THIS WORLD ...
I'M TRYING NOT TO SWEAT THE LITTLE STUFF.
Phew...
SHE'S GOTTEN TOUGH!
......
HONESTLY.
SHE REALLY BLENDED IN DURING THE SHORT TIME I DIDN'T SEE HER.
CLINK
THANK YOU.
IT WAS DELICIOUS!
LEAVING ALREADY ?
YEAH.
BE CAREFUL.
AW, STAY!
PLAY BEFORE YOU LEAVE!
CAN'T.
I HAVE WORK SOON AND ANOTHER PLACE TO VISIT.
WORK, WORK. SHE WORKS TOO DAMN HARD!
YOU'RE JUST A ROTTEN MOOCH.
HEY!

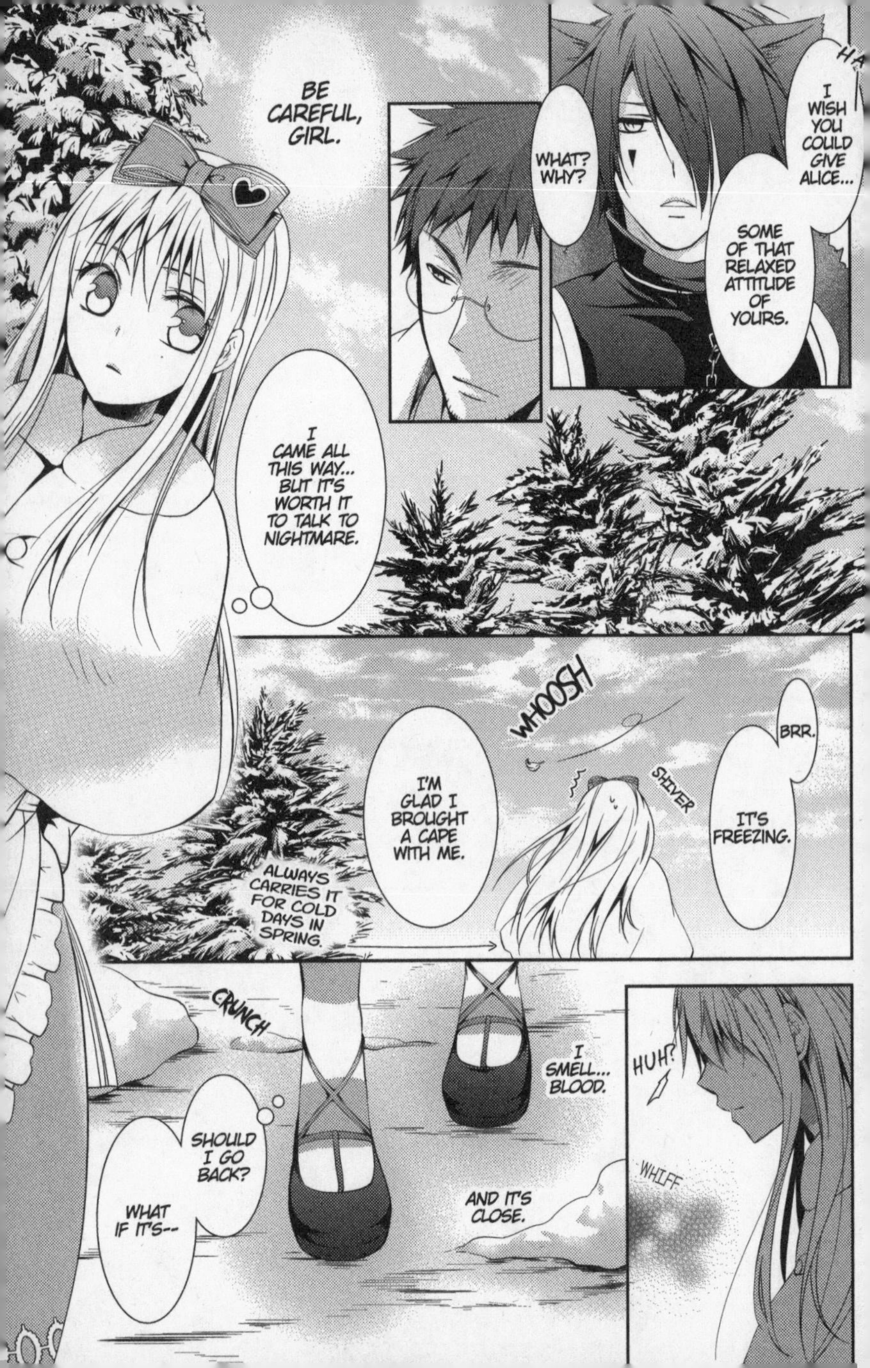
HA
I WISH YOU COULD GIVE ALICE...
SOME OF THAT RELAXED ATTITUDE OF YOURS.
WHAT? WHY?
BE CAREFUL, GIRL.
I CAME ALL THIS WAY... BUT IT'S WORTH IT TO TALK TO NIGHTMARE.
BRR.
IT'S FREEZING.
SHIVER
WHOOSH
I'M GLAD I BROUGHT A CAPE WITH ME.
ALWAYS CARRIES IT FOR COLD DAYS IN SPRING.
HUH?
I SMELL... BLOOD.
WHIFF
AND IT'S CLOSE.
CRUNCH
SHOULD I GO BACK?
WHAT IF IT'S--

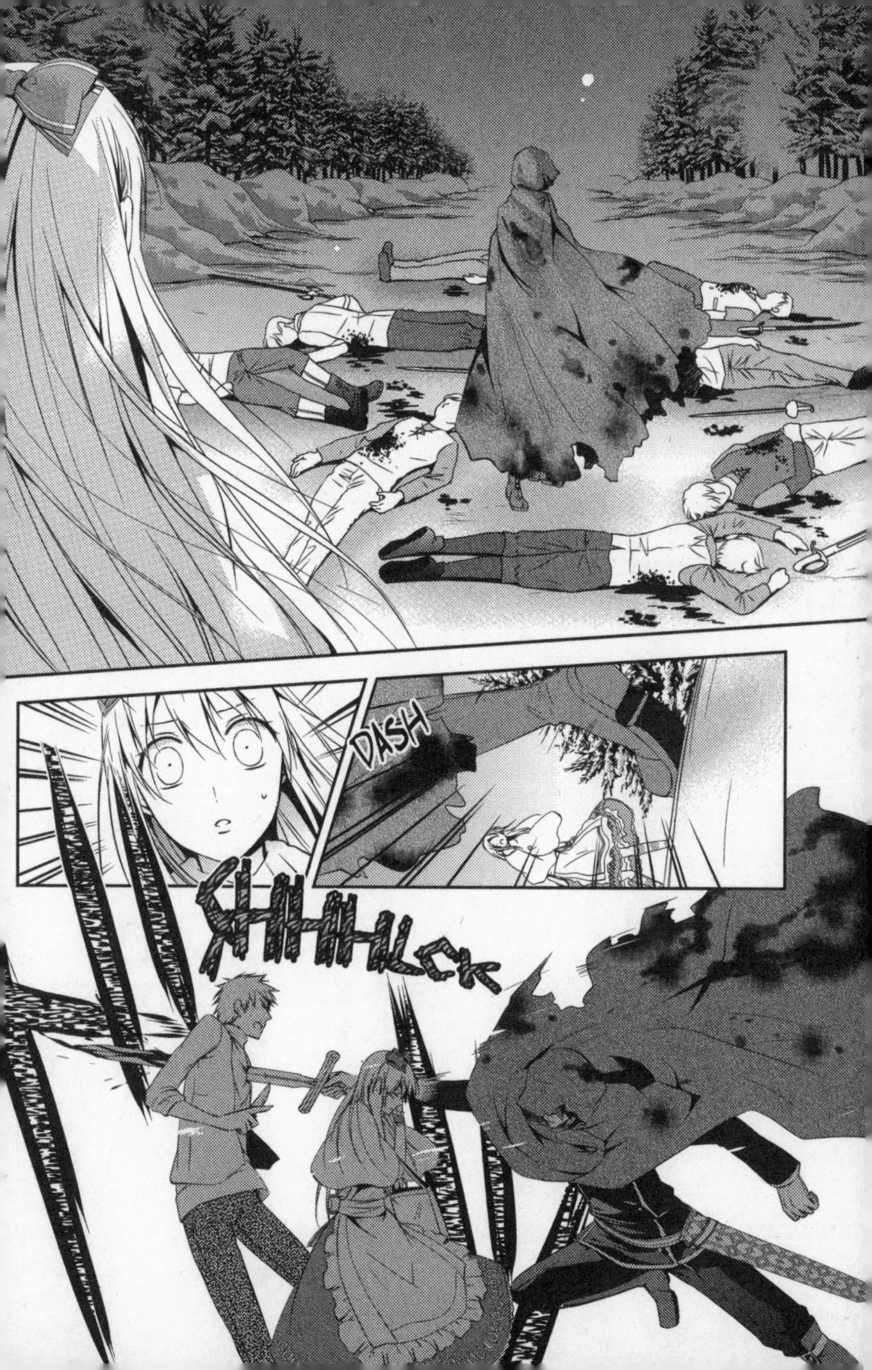
DASH
SHHHHLCK

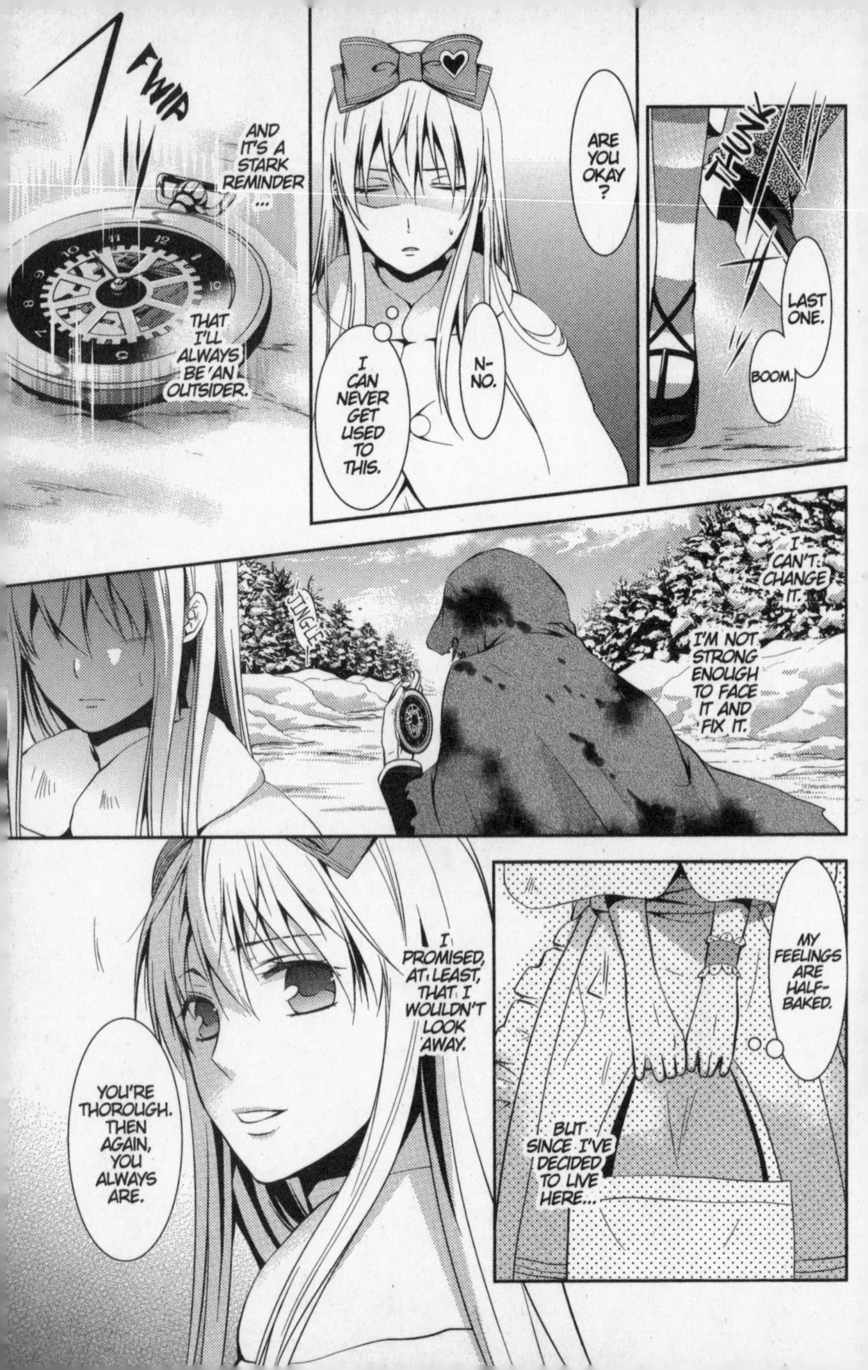
THUNK
LAST ONE.
BOOM.
ARE YOU OKAY?
N-NO.
I CAN NEVER GET USED TO THIS.
FWIP
AND IT'S A STARK REMINDER...
THAT I'LL ALWAYS BE AN OUTSIDER.
I CAN'T CHANGE IT.
I'M NOT STRONG ENOUGH TO FACE IT AND FIX IT.
JINGLE
MY FEELINGS ARE HALF-BAKED.
BUT SINCE I'VE DECIDED TO LIVE HERE...
I PROMISED, AT LEAST, THAT I WOULDN'T LOOK AWAY.
YOU'RE THOROUGH. THEN AGAIN, YOU ALWAYS ARE.

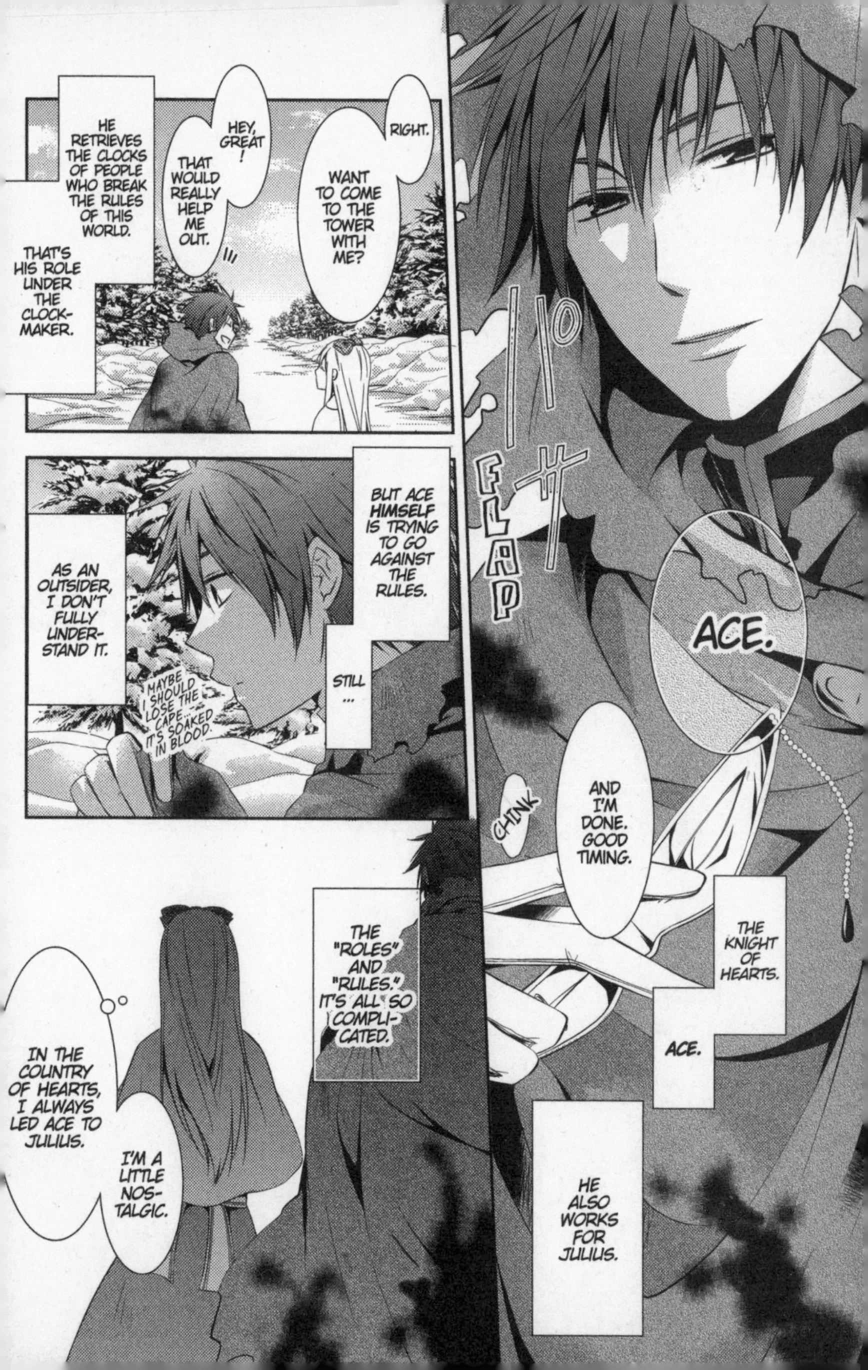
FLAP
ACE.
AND I'M DONE. GOOD TIMING.
CHINK
THE KNIGHT OF HEARTS.
ACE.
HE ALSO WORKS FOR JULIUS.
RIGHT.
WANT TO COME TO THE TOWER WITH ME?
HEY, GREAT! THAT WOULD REALLY HELP ME OUT.
HE RETRIEVES THE CLOCKS OF PEOPLE WHO BREAK THE RULES OF THIS WORLD.
THAT'S HIS ROLE UNDER THE CLOCK-MAKER.
BUT ACE HIMSELF IS TRYING TO GO AGAINST THE RULES.
STILL...
MAYBE I SHOULD LOSE THE CAPE... IT'S SOAKED IN BLOOD.
AS AN OUTSIDER, I DON'T FULLY UNDER-STAND IT.
THE "ROLES" AND "RULES." IT'S ALL SO COMPLI-CATED.
IN THE COUNTRY OF HEARTS, I ALWAYS LED ACE TO JULIUS.
I'M A LITTLE NOS-TALGIC.

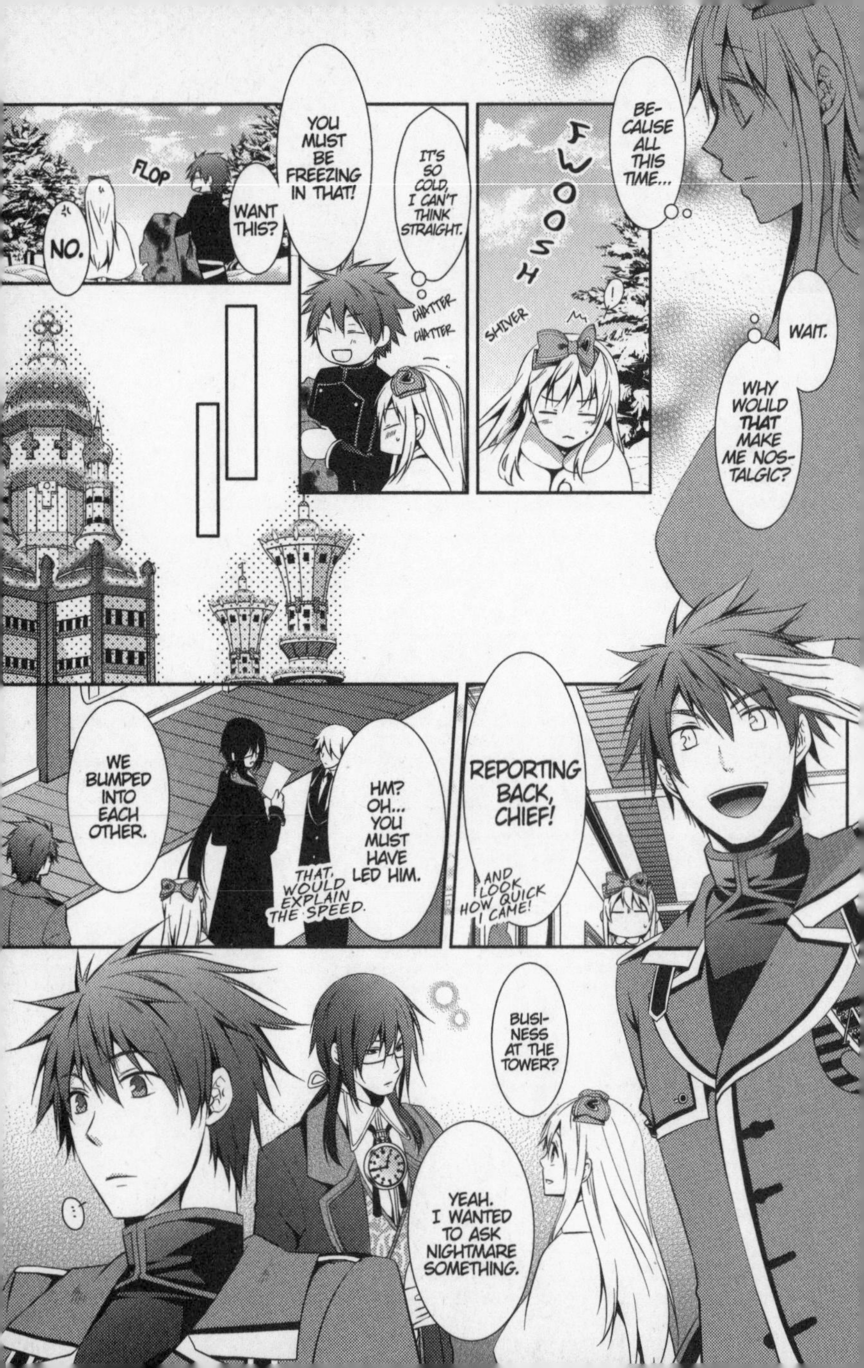
BE-CAUSE ALL THIS TIME...
WAIT.
WHY WOULD THAT MAKE ME NOS-TALGIC?
FWOOSH
!
SHIVER
IT'S SO COLD, I CAN'T THINK STRAIGHT.
YOU MUST BE FREEZING IN THAT!
CHATTER CHATTER
WANT THIS?
FLOP
NO.
REPORTING BACK, CHIEF!
AND LOOK HOW QUICK I CAME!
HM? OH... YOU MUST HAVE LED HIM.
THAT WOULD EXPLAIN THE SPEED.
WE BUMPED INTO EACH OTHER.
BUSI-NESS AT THE TOWER?
YEAH. I WANTED TO ASK NIGHTMARE SOMETHING.
...

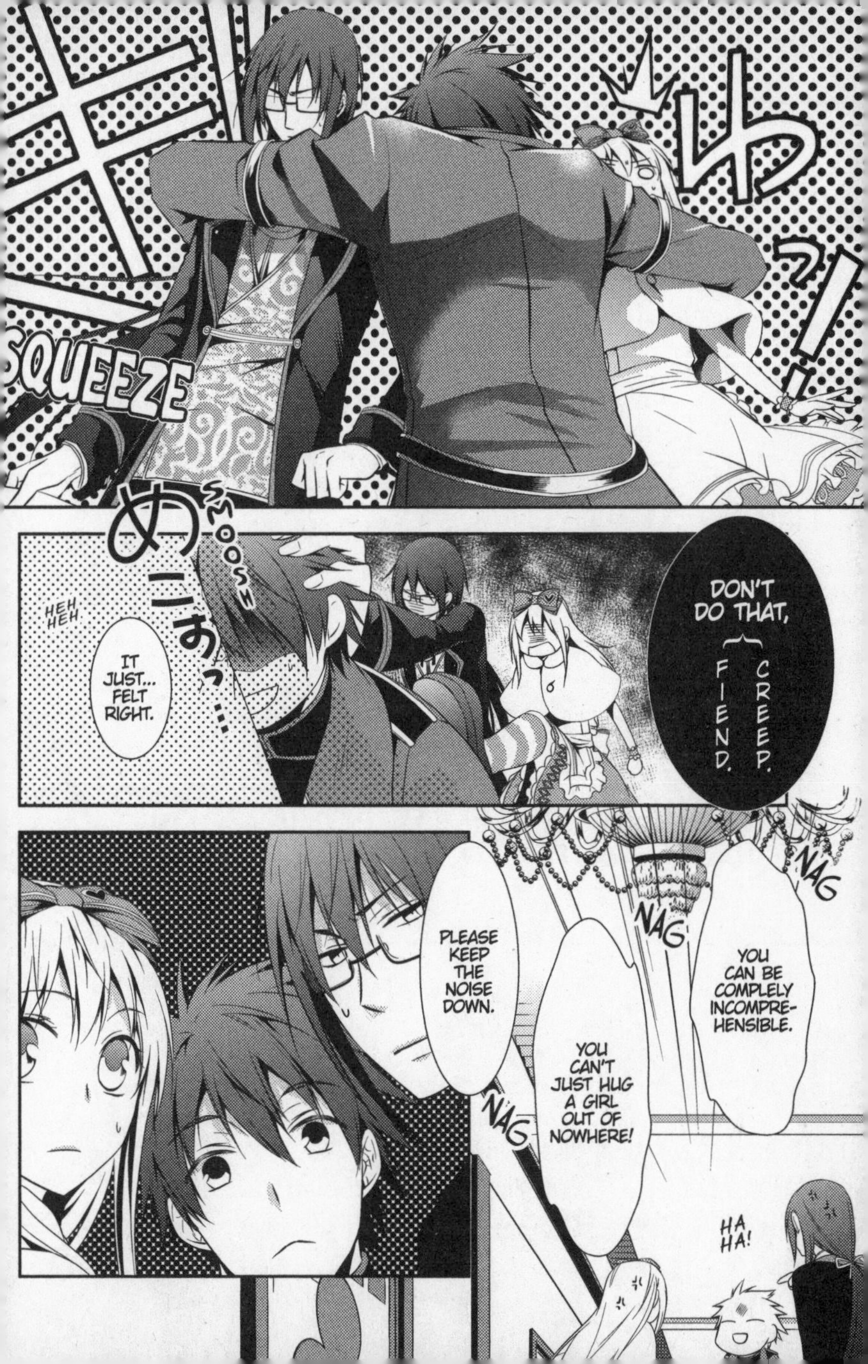

SQUEEZE
DON'T DO THAT, CREEP. FIEND.
HEH HEH
IT JUST... FELT RIGHT.
めこぉっ...
SMOOSH
NAG
YOU CAN BE COMPLEY INCOMPRE-HENSIBLE.
NAG
PLEASE KEEP THE NOISE DOWN.
YOU CAN'T JUST HUG A GIRL OUT OF NOWHERE!
NAG
HA HA!

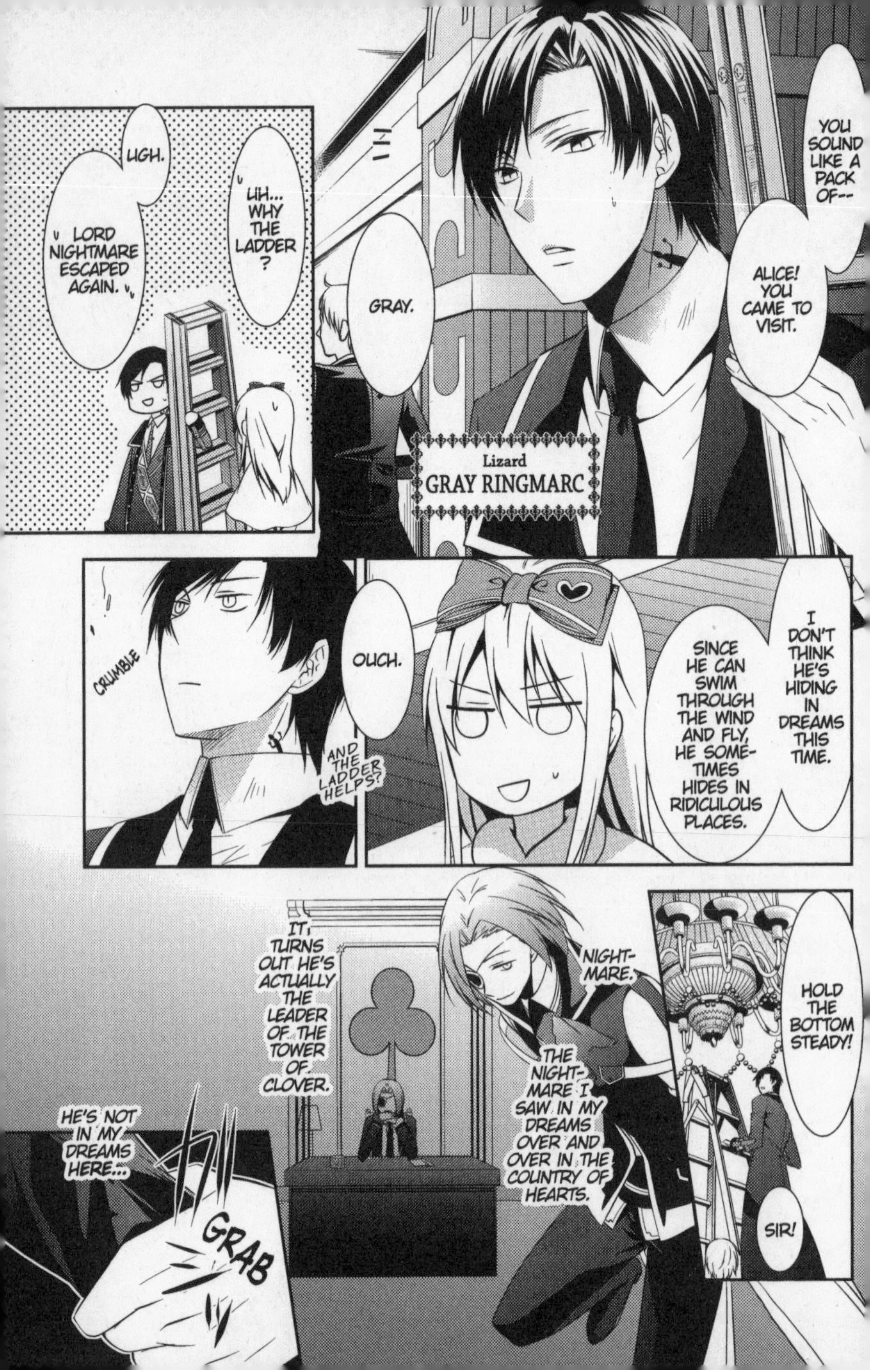
YOU SOUND LIKE A PACK OF--
ALICE! YOU CAME TO VISIT.
GRAY.
Lizard
GRAY RINGMARC
UH... WHY THE LADDER?
UGH.
LORD NIGHTMARE ESCAPED AGAIN.
I DON'T THINK HE'S HIDING IN DREAMS THIS TIME.
SINCE HE CAN SWIM THROUGH THE WIND AND FLY, HE SOMETIMES HIDES IN RIDICULOUS PLACES.
OUCH.
AND THE LADDER HELPS?
CRUMBLE
HOLD THE BOTTOM STEADY!
SIR!
NIGHTMARE.
IT TURNS OUT HE'S ACTUALLY THE LEADER OF THE TOWER OF CLOVER.
THE NIGHTMARE I SAW IN MY DREAMS OVER AND OVER IN THE COUNTRY OF HEARTS.
HE'S NOT IN MY DREAMS HERE...
GRAB

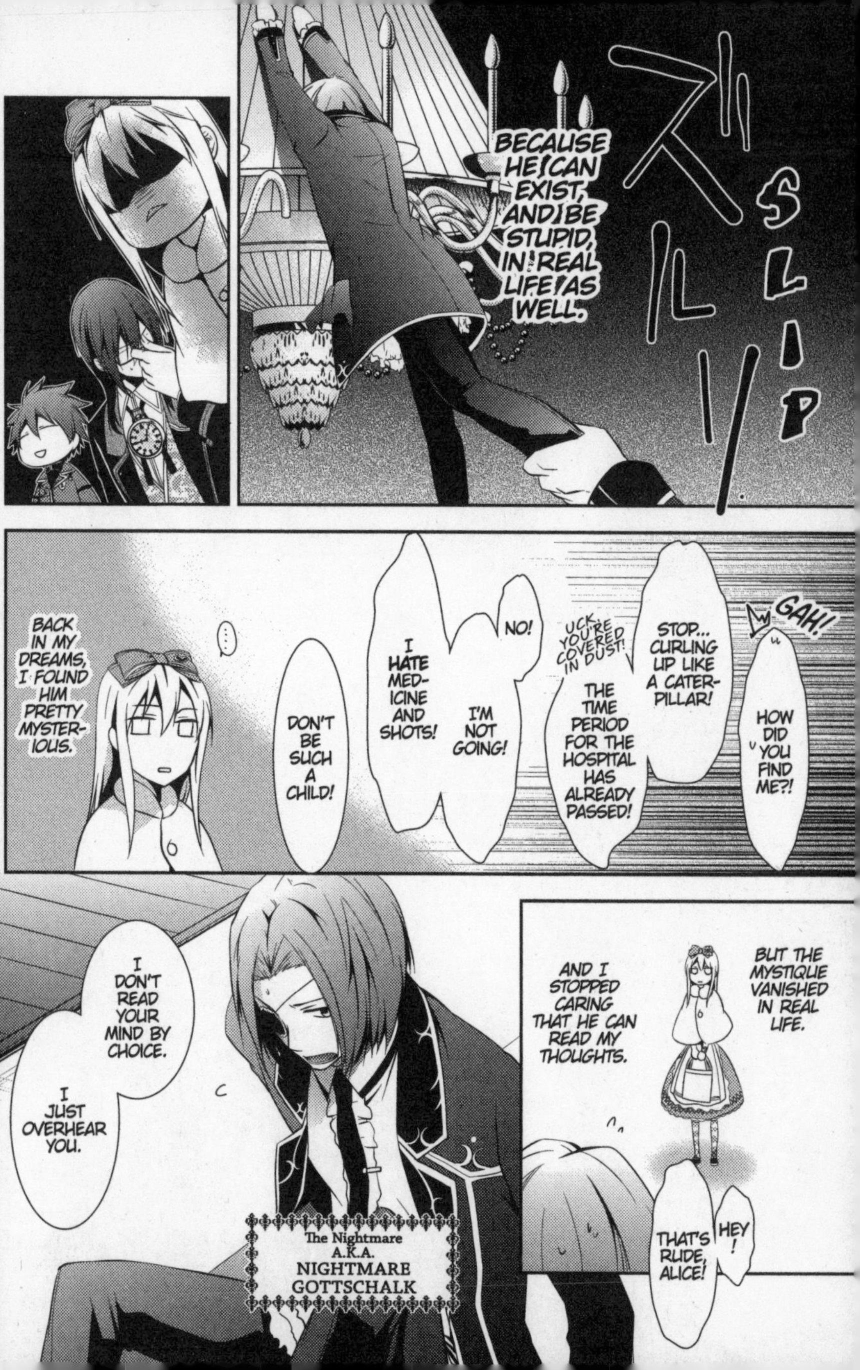
ズルッ
SLIP
BECAUSE HE CAN EXIST, AND BE STUPID, IN REAL LIFE AS WELL.
GAH!
HOW DID YOU FIND ME?!
STOP... CURLING UP LIKE A CATER-PILLAR!
UCK. YOU'RE COVERED IN DUST!
THE TIME PERIOD FOR THE HOSPITAL HAS ALREADY PASSED!
NO!
I'M NOT GOING!
I HATE MEDI-CINE AND SHOTS!
DON'T BE SUCH A CHILD!
...
BACK IN MY DREAMS, I FOUND HIM PRETTY MYSTER-IOUS.
BUT THE MYSTIQUE VANISHED IN REAL LIFE.
AND I STOPPED CARING THAT HE CAN READ MY THOUGHTS.
HEY!
THAT'S RUDE, ALICE!
I DON'T READ YOUR MIND BY CHOICE.
I JUST OVERHEAR YOU.
The Nightmare A.K.A. NIGHTMARE GOTTSCHALK

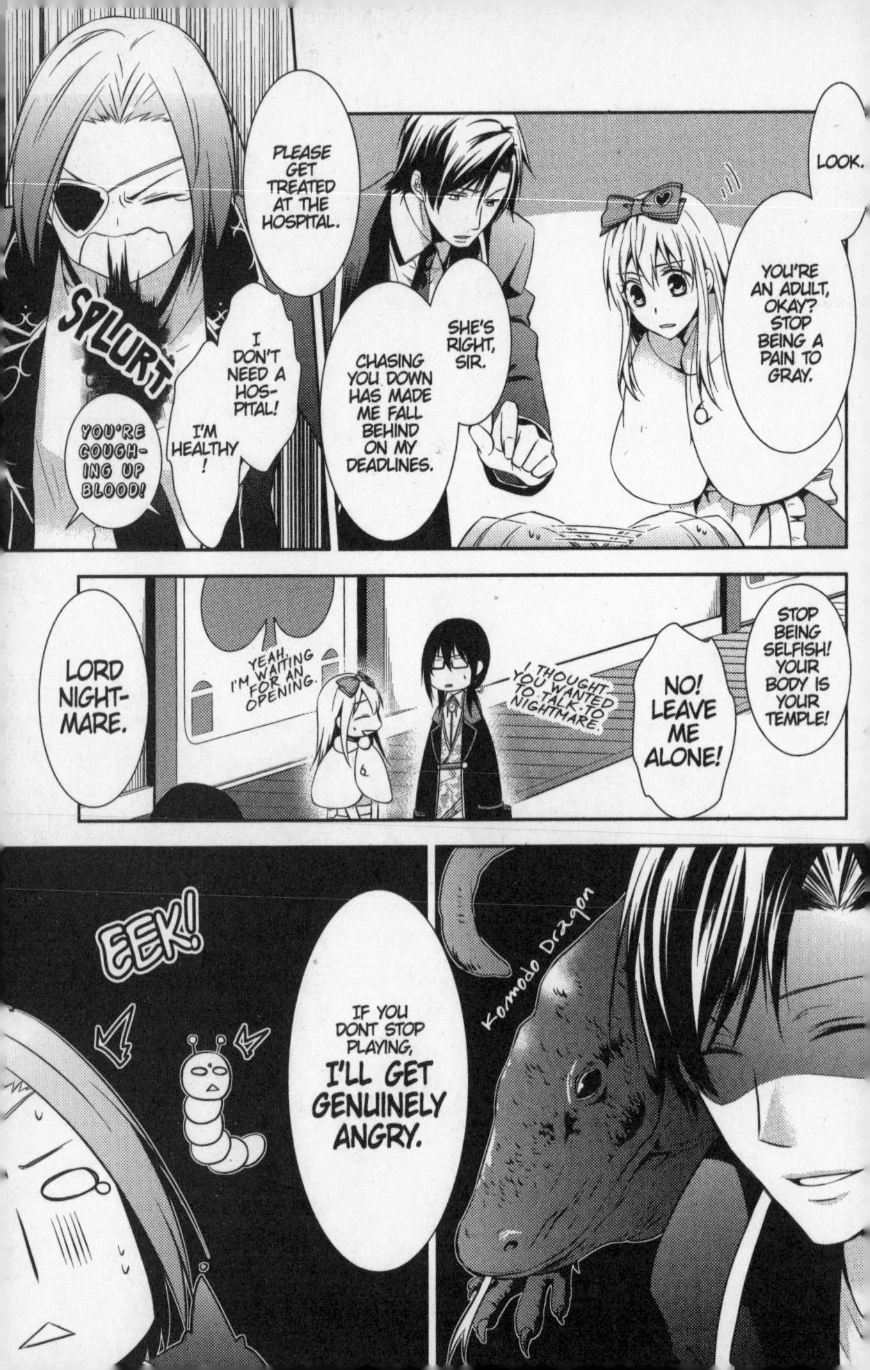
LOOK.
YOU'RE AN ADULT, OKAY? STOP BEING A PAIN TO GRAY.
SHE'S RIGHT, SIR.
CHASING YOU DOWN HAS MADE ME FALL BEHIND ON MY DEADLINES.
PLEASE GET TREATED AT THE HOSPITAL.
I DON'T NEED A HOS-PITAL!
I'M HEALTHY!
SPLURT
YOU'RE COUGH-ING UP BLOOD!
STOP BEING SELFISH! YOUR BODY IS YOUR TEMPLE!
NO! LEAVE ME ALONE!
I THOUGHT YOU WANTED TO TALK TO NIGHTMARE.
YEAH, I'M WAITING FOR AN OPENING.
LORD NIGHT-MARE.
Komodo Dragon
IF YOU DONT STOP PLAYING, I'LL GET GENUINELY ANGRY.
EEK!

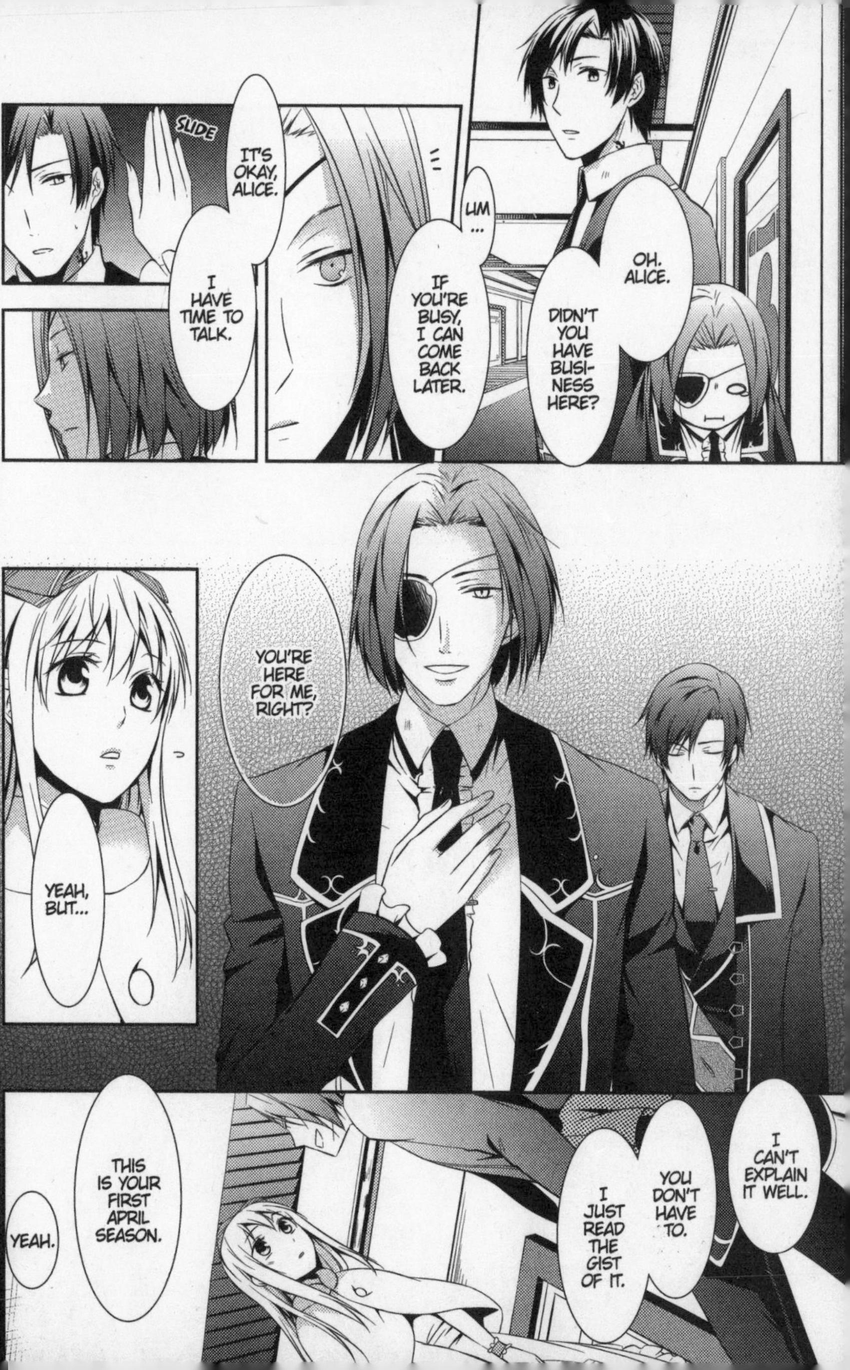
OH. ALICE.
DIDN'T YOU HAVE BUSINESS HERE?
UM...
IF YOU'RE BUSY, I CAN COME BACK LATER.
SLIDE
IT'S OKAY, ALICE.
I HAVE TIME TO TALK.
YOU'RE HERE FOR ME, RIGHT?
YEAH, BUT...
I CAN'T EXPLAIN IT WELL.
YOU DON'T HAVE TO.
I JUST READ THE GIST OF IT.
THIS IS YOUR FIRST APRIL SEASON.
YEAH.

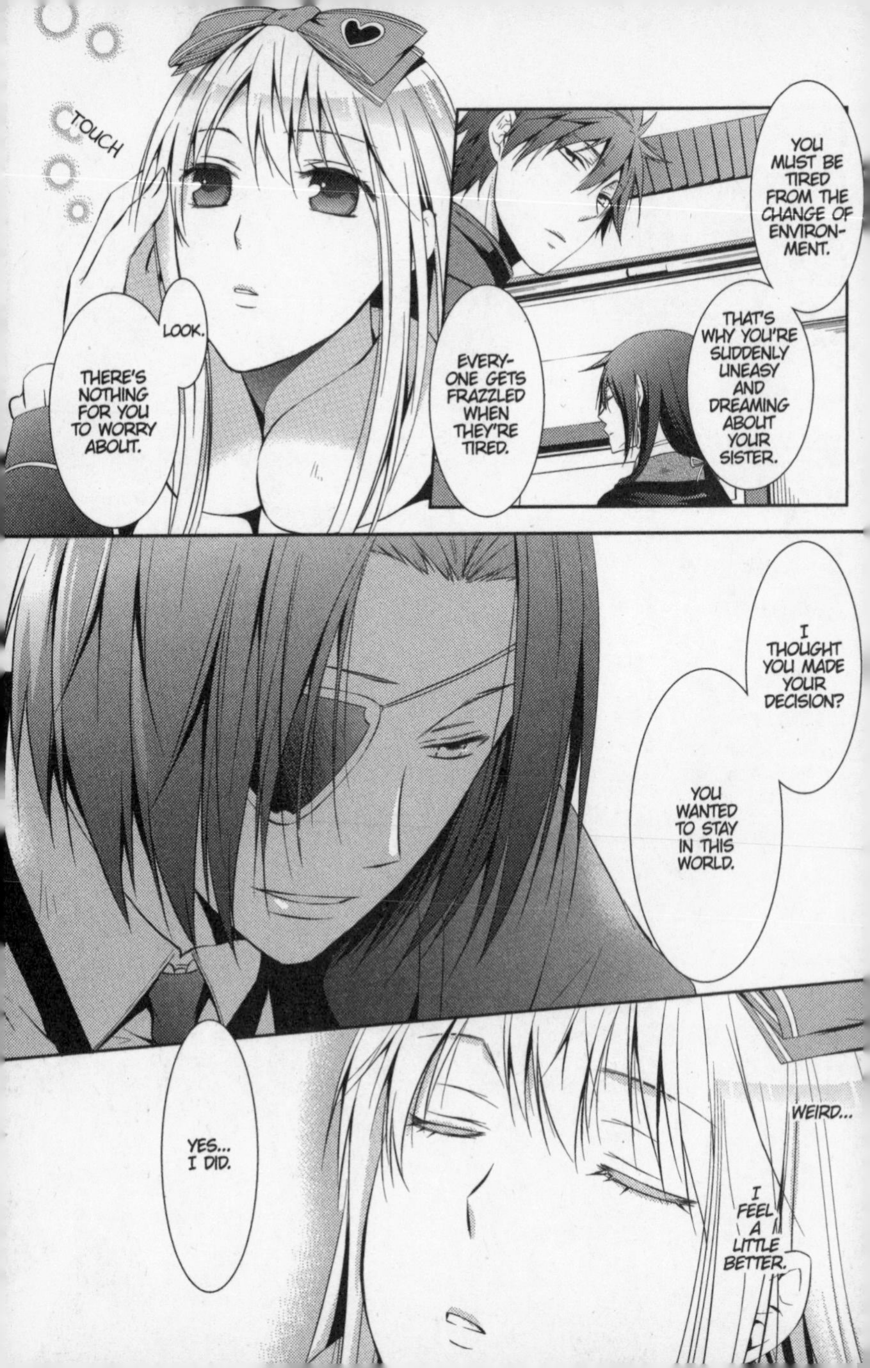
YOU MUST BE TIRED FROM THE CHANGE OF ENVIRON-MENT.
THAT'S WHY YOU'RE SUDDENLY UNEASY AND DREAMING ABOUT YOUR SISTER.
EVERY-ONE GETS FRAZZLED WHEN THEY'RE TIRED.
TOUCH
LOOK.
THERE'S NOTHING FOR YOU TO WORRY ABOUT.
I THOUGHT YOU MADE YOUR DECISION?
YOU WANTED TO STAY IN THIS WORLD.
YES... I DID.
WEIRD...
I FEEL A LITTLE BETTER.

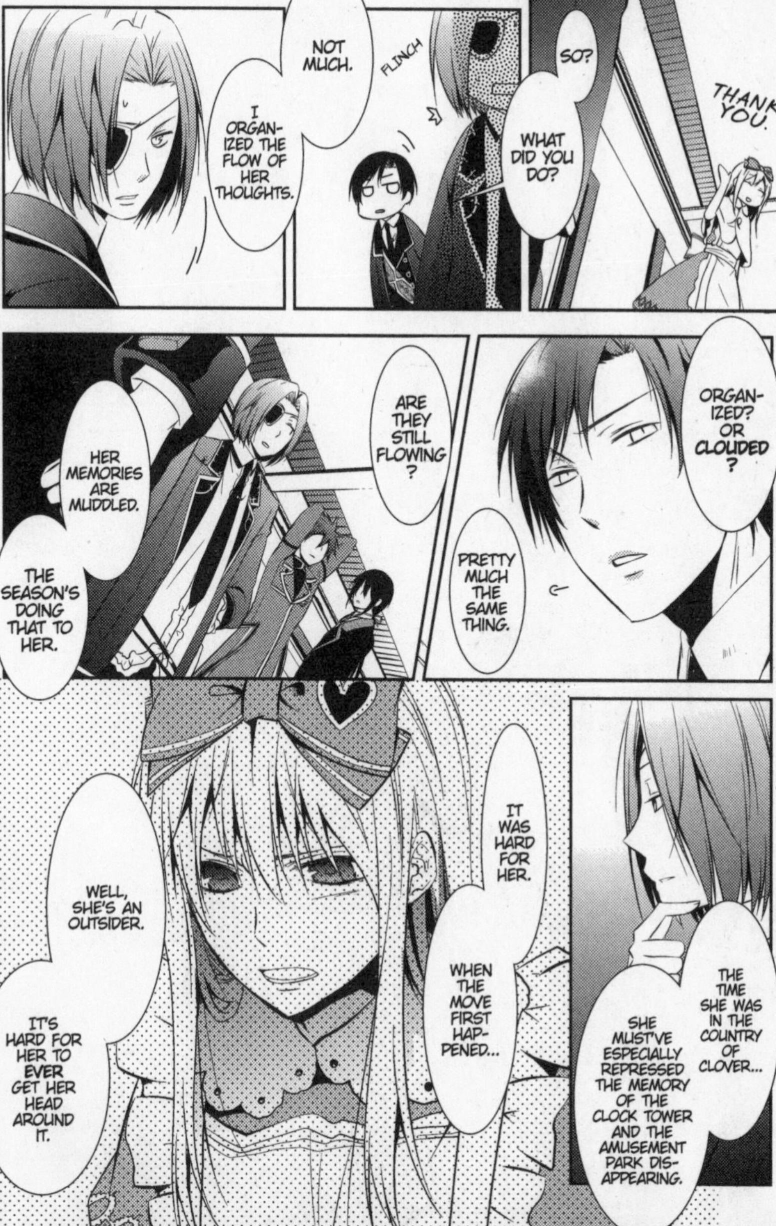
THANK YOU.
SO?
WHAT DID YOU DO?
FLINCH
NOT MUCH.
I ORGANIZED THE FLOW OF HER THOUGHTS.
ORGANIZED? OR CLOUDED?
PRETTY MUCH THE SAME THING.
ARE THEY STILL FLOWING?
HER MEMORIES ARE MUDDLED.
THE SEASON'S DOING THAT TO HER.
THE TIME SHE WAS IN THE COUNTRY OF CLOVER...
SHE MUST'VE ESPECIALLY REPRESSED THE MEMORY OF THE CLOCK TOWER AND THE AMUSEMENT PARK DISAPPEARING.
IT WAS HARD FOR HER.
WHEN THE MOVE FIRST HAPPENED...
WELL, SHE'S AN OUTSIDER.
IT'S HARD FOR HER TO EVER GET HER HEAD AROUND IT.

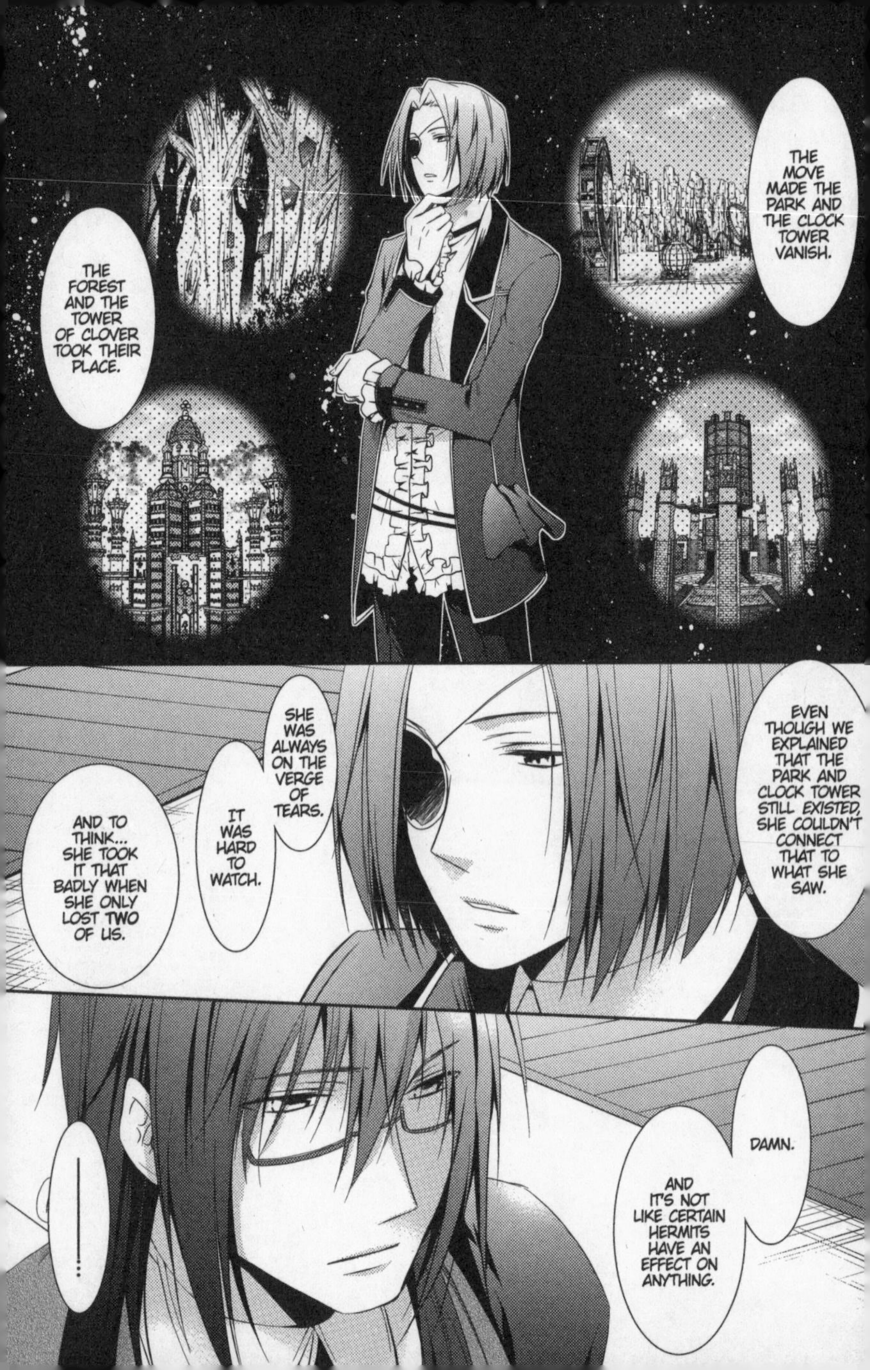
THE MOVE MADE THE PARK AND THE CLOCK TOWER VANISH.
THE FOREST AND THE TOWER OF CLOVER TOOK THEIR PLACE.
EVEN THOUGH WE EXPLAINED THAT THE PARK AND CLOCK TOWER STILL *EXISTED*, SHE COULDN'T CONNECT THAT TO WHAT SHE SAW.
SHE WAS ALWAYS ON THE VERGE OF TEARS.
IT WAS HARD TO WATCH.
AND TO THINK... SHE TOOK IT THAT BADLY WHEN SHE ONLY LOST TWO OF US.
DAMN.
AND IT'S NOT LIKE CERTAIN HERMITS HAVE AN EFFECT ON ANYTHING.
......

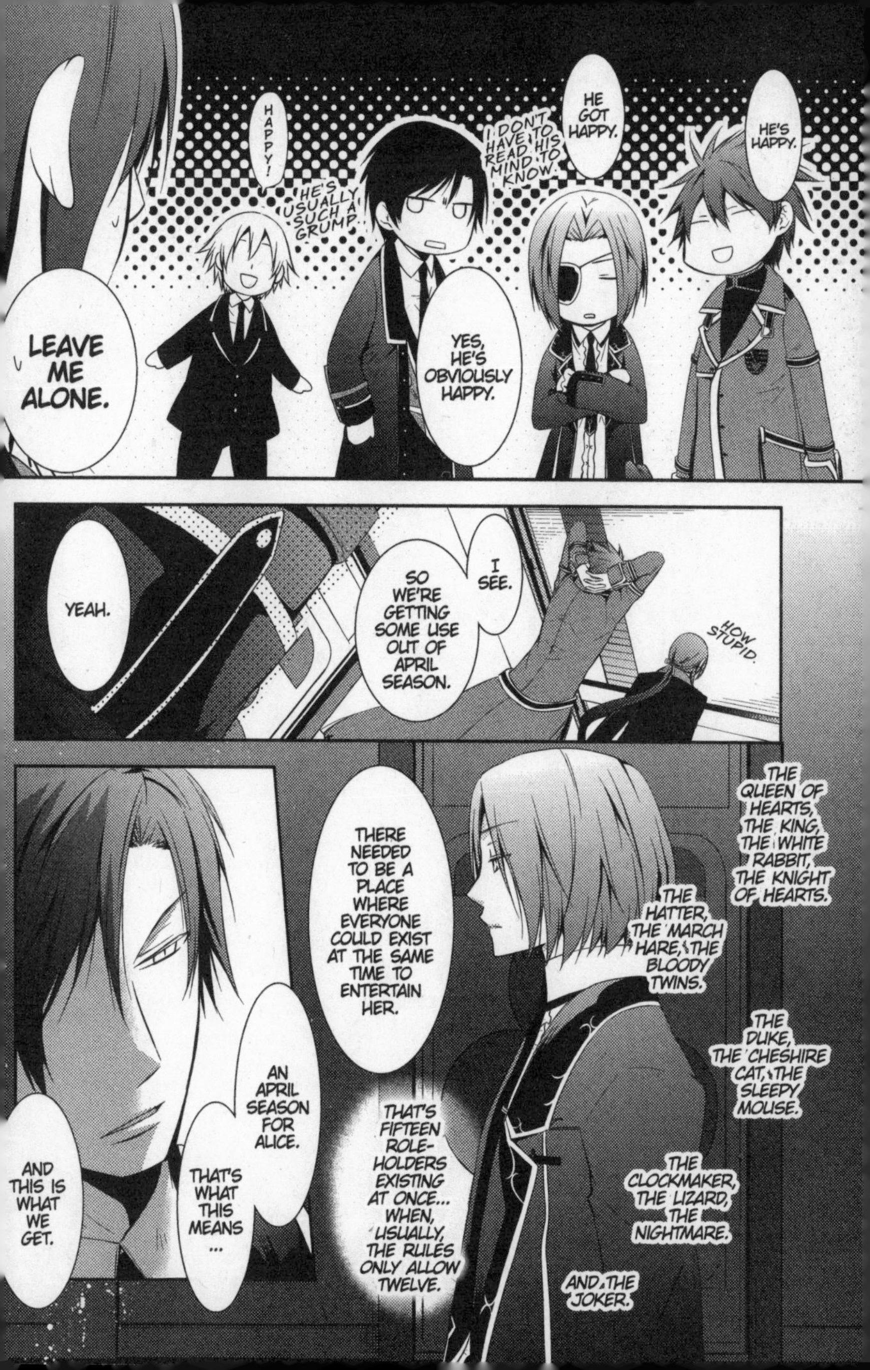
HE'S HAPPY.
HE GOT HAPPY.
I DON'T HAVE TO READ HIS MIND TO KNOW.
HAPPY!
HE'S USUALLY SUCH A GRUMP.
YES, HE'S OBVIOUSLY HAPPY.
LEAVE ME ALONE.
HOW STUPID.
I SEE.
SO WE'RE GETTING SOME USE OUT OF APRIL SEASON.
YEAH.
THE QUEEN OF HEARTS, THE KING, THE WHITE RABBIT, THE KNIGHT OF HEARTS.
THE HATTER, THE MARCH HARE, THE BLOODY TWINS.
THE DUKE, THE CHESHIRE CAT, THE SLEEPY MOUSE.
THE CLOCKMAKER, THE LIZARD, THE NIGHTMARE.
AND THE JOKER.
THERE NEEDED TO BE A PLACE WHERE EVERYONE COULD EXIST AT THE SAME TIME TO ENTERTAIN HER.
THAT'S FIFTEEN ROLE-HOLDERS EXISTING AT ONCE... WHEN, USUALLY, THE RULES ONLY ALLOW TWELVE.
AN APRIL SEASON FOR ALICE.
THAT'S WHAT THIS MEANS...
AND THIS IS WHAT WE GET.

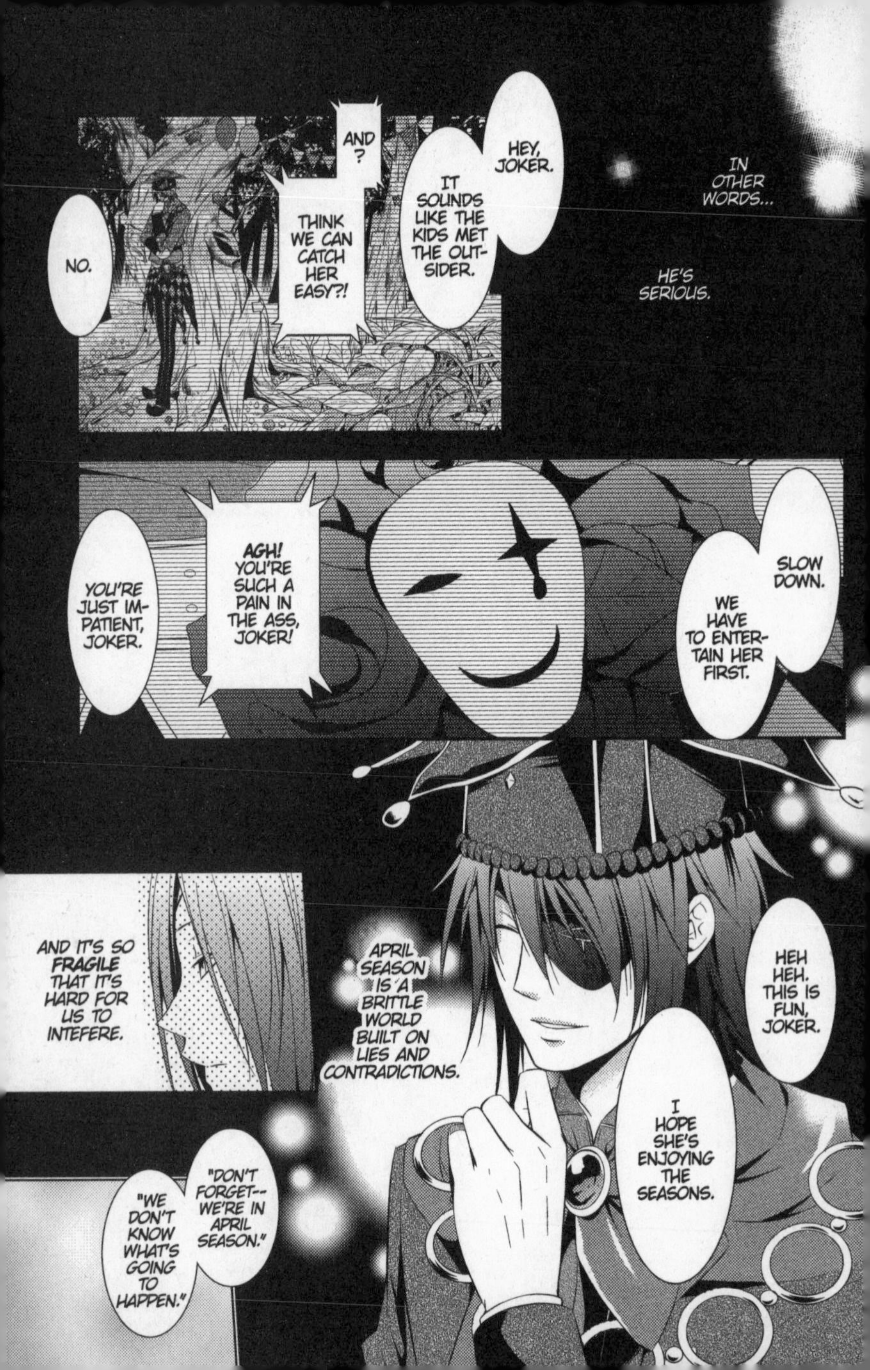
IN OTHER WORDS...
HE'S SERIOUS.
HEY, JOKER.
IT SOUNDS LIKE THE KIDS MET THE OUT-SIDER.
AND ?
THINK WE CAN CATCH HER EASY?!
NO.
SLOW DOWN.
WE HAVE TO ENTER-TAIN HER FIRST.
AGH! YOU'RE SUCH A PAIN IN THE ASS, JOKER!
YOU'RE JUST IM-PATIENT, JOKER.
HEH HEH. THIS IS FUN, JOKER.
I HOPE SHE'S ENJOYING THE SEASONS.
APRIL SEASON IS A BRITTLE WORLD BUILT ON LIES AND CONTRADICTIONS.
AND IT'S SO FRAGILE THAT IT'S HARD FOR US TO INTEFERE.
"DON'T FORGET-- WE'RE IN APRIL SEASON."
"WE DON'T KNOW WHAT'S GOING TO HAPPEN."

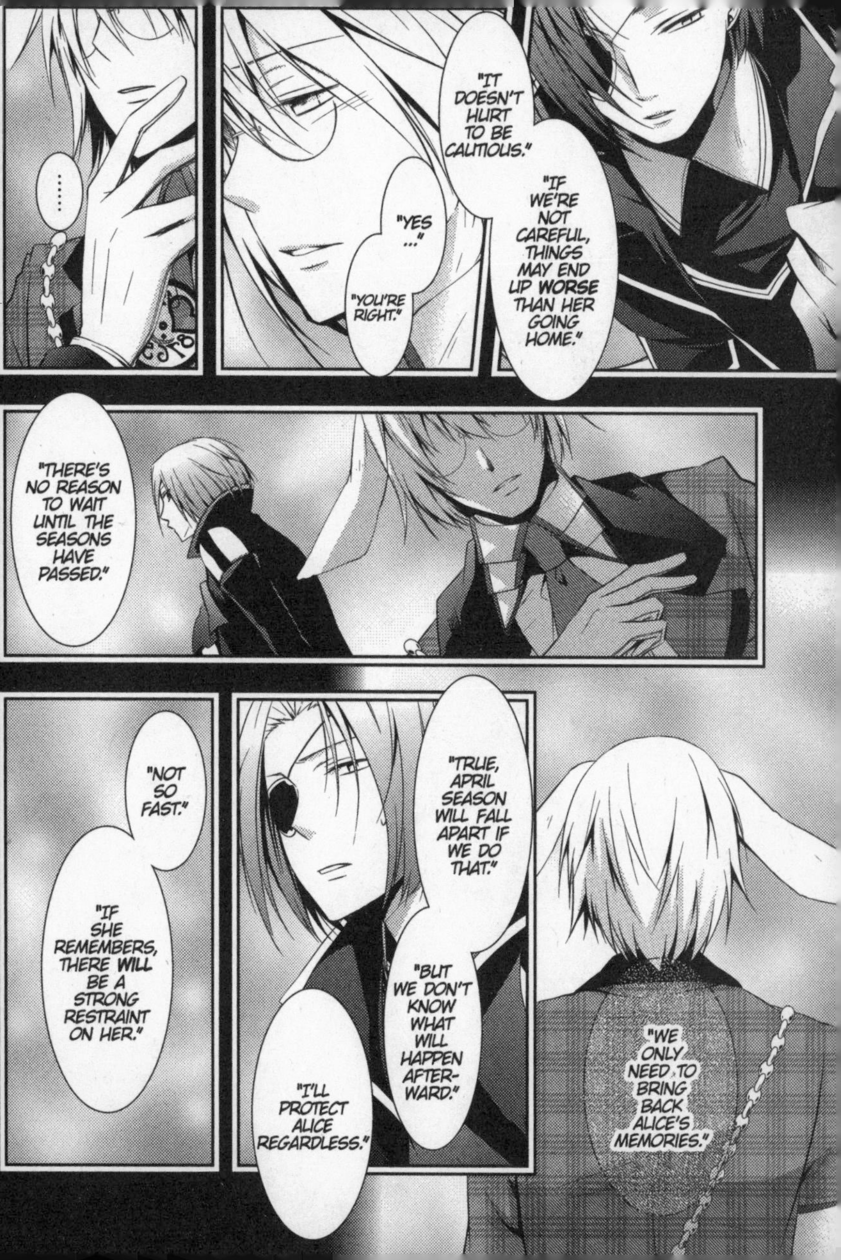
"IT DOESN'T HURT TO BE CAUTIOUS."
"IF WE'RE NOT CAREFUL, THINGS MAY END UP WORSE THAN HER GOING HOME."
"YES ..."
"YOU'RE RIGHT."
......
"THERE'S NO REASON TO WAIT UNTIL THE SEASONS HAVE PASSED."
"WE ONLY NEED TO BRING BACK ALICE'S MEMORIES."
"TRUE, APRIL SEASON WILL FALL APART IF WE DO THAT."
"BUT WE DON'T KNOW WHAT WILL HAPPEN AFTER-WARD."
"I'LL PROTECT ALICE REGARDLESS."
"NOT SO FAST."
"IF SHE REMEMBERS, THERE WILL BE A STRONG RESTRAINT ON HER."

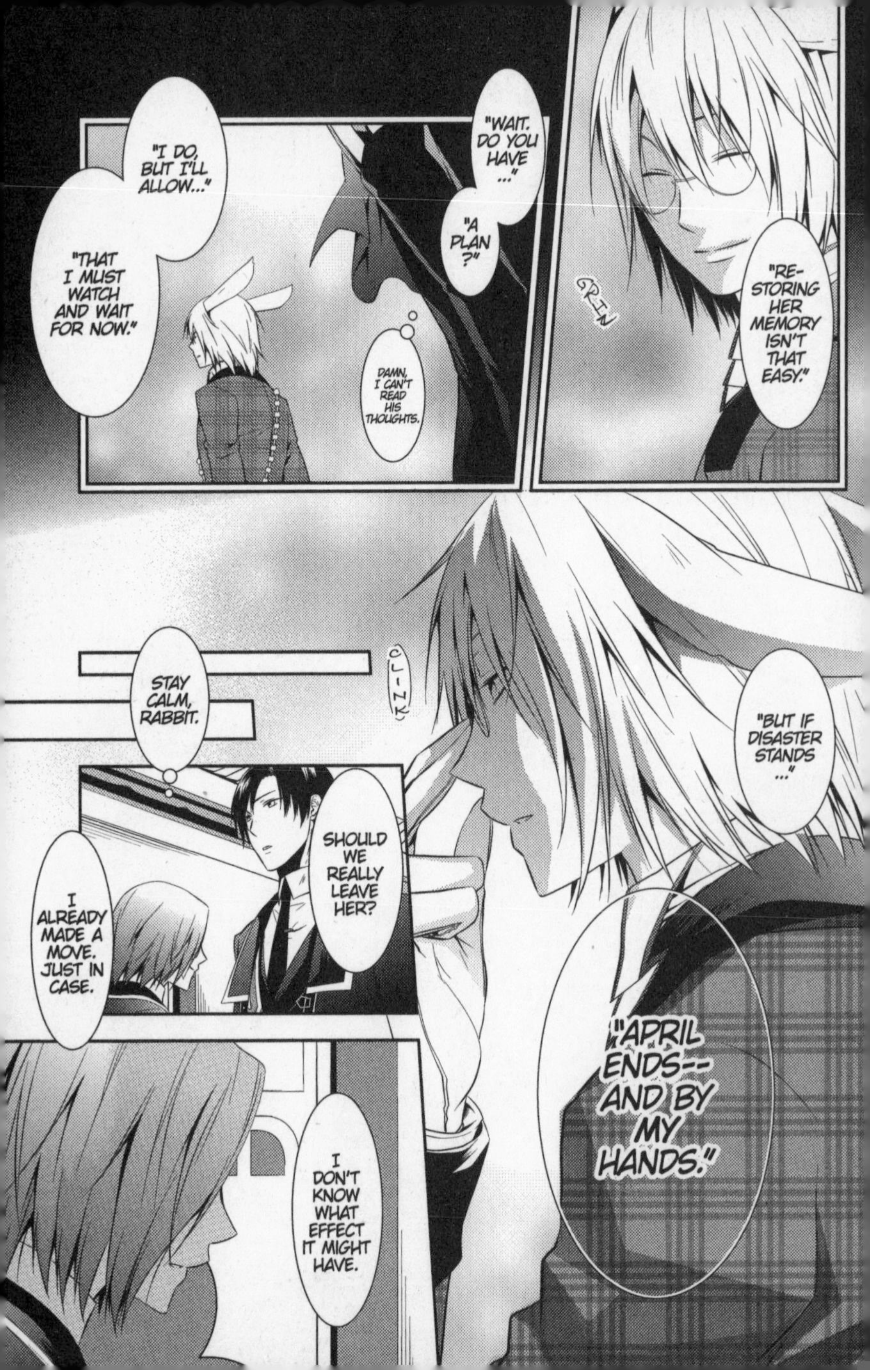
"RE-STORING HER MEMORY ISN'T THAT EASY."
GRIN
"WAIT. DO YOU HAVE ..."
"A PLAN?"
DAMN, I CAN'T READ HIS THOUGHTS.
"I DO, BUT I'LL ALLOW..."
"THAT I MUST WATCH AND WAIT FOR NOW."
"BUT IF DISASTER STANDS ..."
"APRIL ENDS-- AND BY MY HANDS."
CLINK
STAY CALM, RABBIT.
SHOULD WE REALLY LEAVE HER?
I ALREADY MADE A MOVE. JUST IN CASE.
I DON'T KNOW WHAT EFFECT IT MIGHT HAVE.

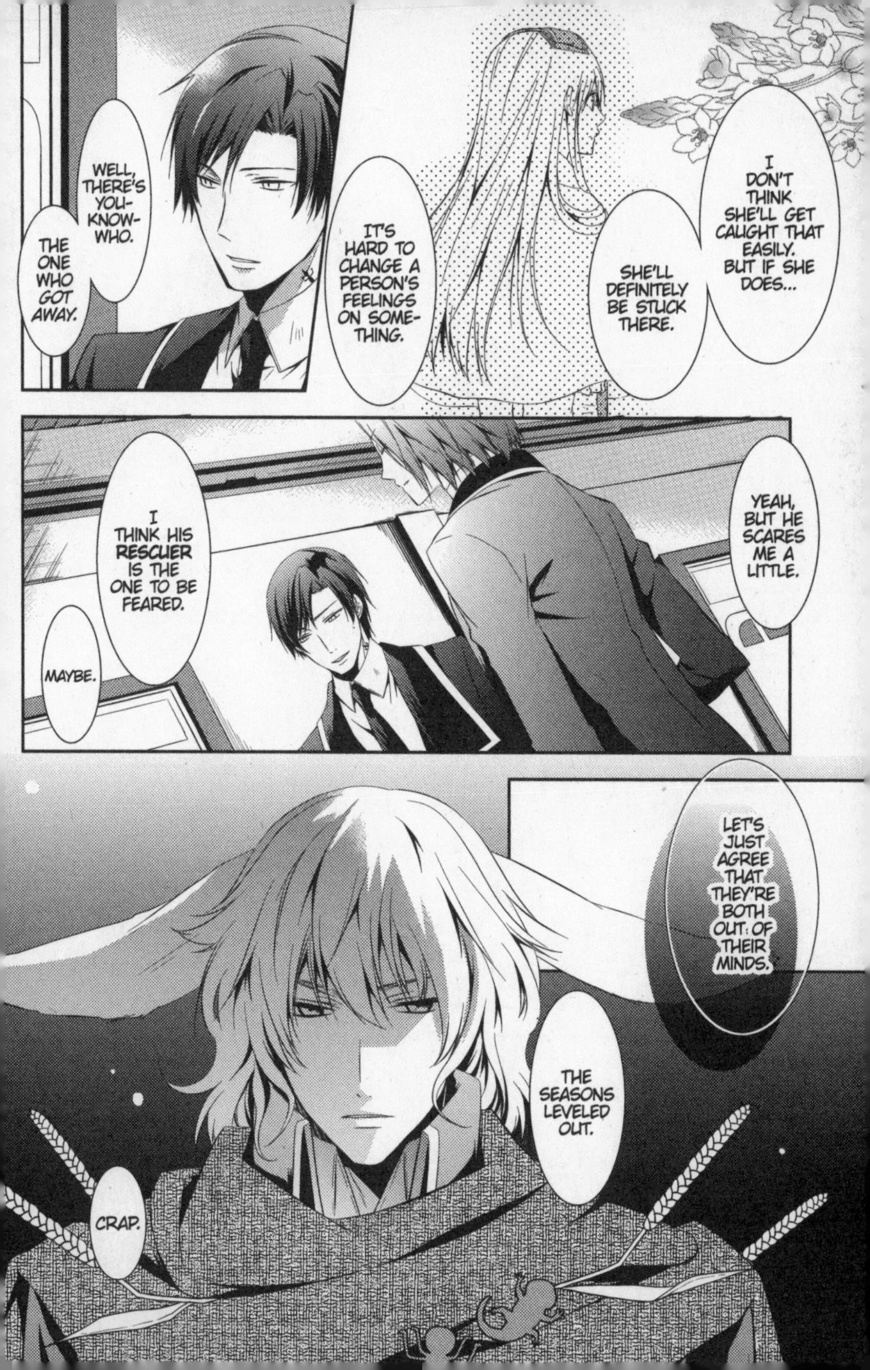
I DON'T THINK SHE'LL GET CAUGHT THAT EASILY. BUT IF SHE DOES...
SHE'LL DEFINITELY BE STUCK THERE.
IT'S HARD TO CHANGE A PERSON'S FEELINGS ON SOME-THING.
WELL, THERE'S YOU-KNOW-WHO.
THE ONE WHO GOT AWAY.
YEAH, BUT HE SCARES ME A LITTLE.
I THINK HIS **RESCUER** IS THE ONE TO BE FEARED.
MAYBE.
LET'S JUST AGREE THAT THEY'RE BOTH OUT OF THEIR MINDS.
THE SEASONS LEVELED OUT.
CRAP.

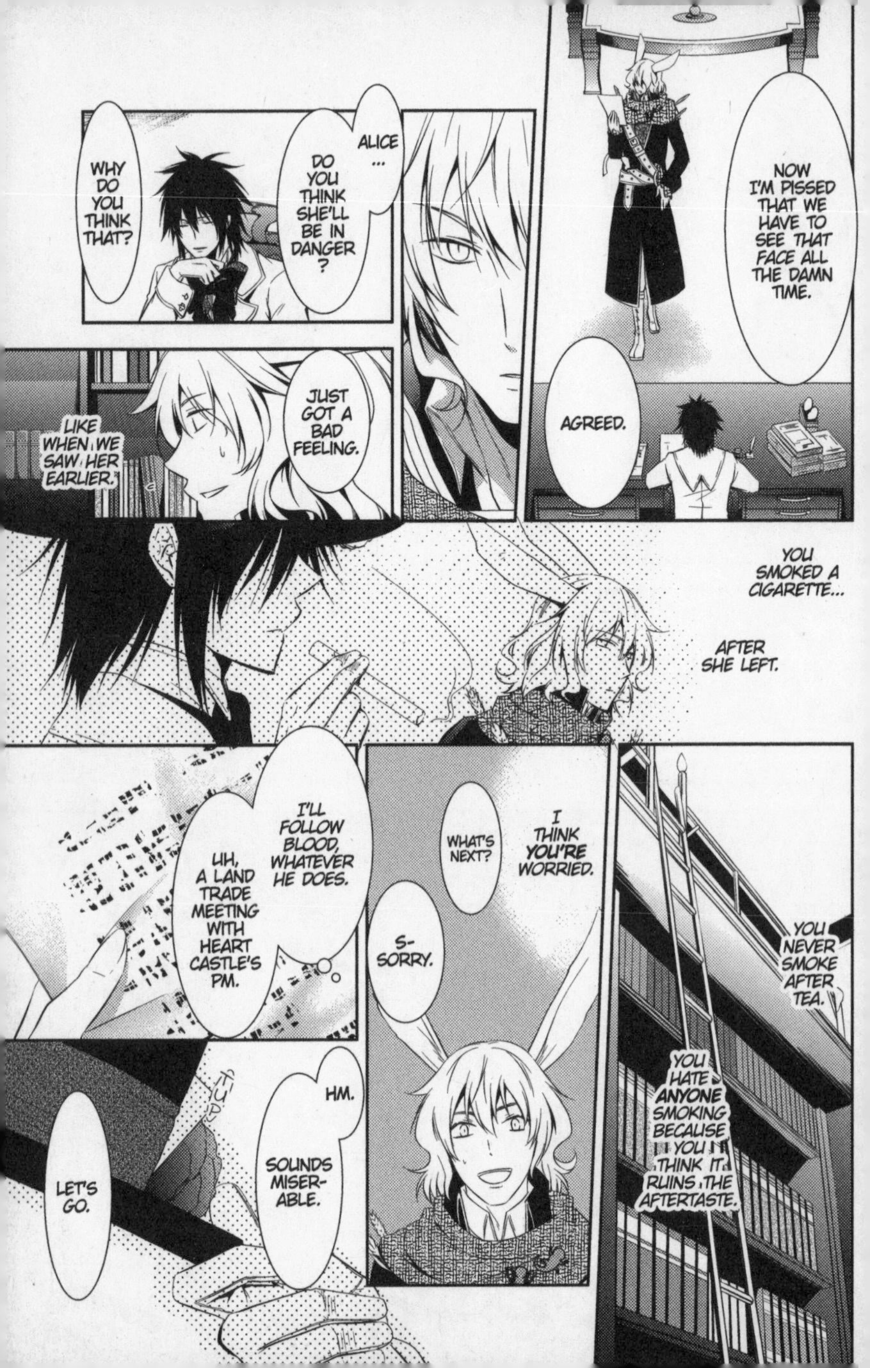

NOW I'M PISSED THAT WE HAVE TO SEE THAT FACE ALL THE DAMN TIME.
AGREED.
ALICE...
DO YOU THINK SHE'LL BE IN DANGER?
WHY DO YOU THINK THAT?
JUST GOT A BAD FEELING.
LIKE WHEN WE SAW HER EARLIER.
YOU SMOKED A CIGARETTE...
AFTER SHE LEFT.
YOU NEVER SMOKE AFTER TEA.
YOU HATE ANYONE SMOKING BECAUSE YOU THINK IT RUINS THE AFTERTASTE.
I THINK YOU'RE WORRIED.
WHAT'S NEXT?
S-SORRY.
I'LL FOLLOW BLOOD, WHATEVER HE DOES.
UH, A LAND TRADE MEETING WITH HEART CASTLE'S PM.
HM.
SOUNDS MISER-ABLE.
THUD
LET'S GO.

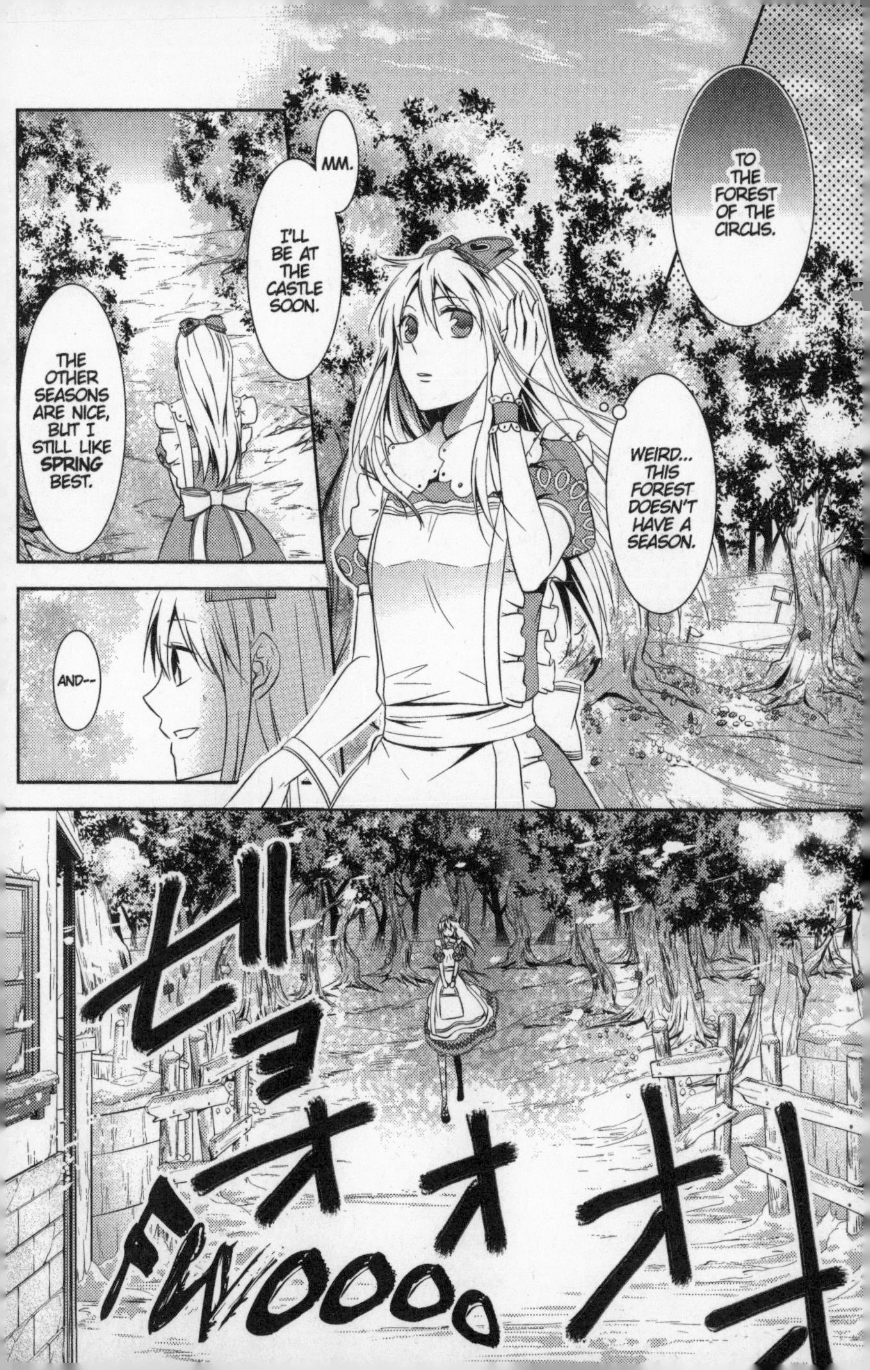

TO THE FOREST OF THE CIRCUS.
WEIRD... THIS FOREST DOESN'T HAVE A SEASON.
MM.
I'LL BE AT THE CASTLE SOON.
THE OTHER SEASONS ARE NICE, BUT I STILL LIKE SPRING BEST.
AND--
ビョオオオ
FWOOOO

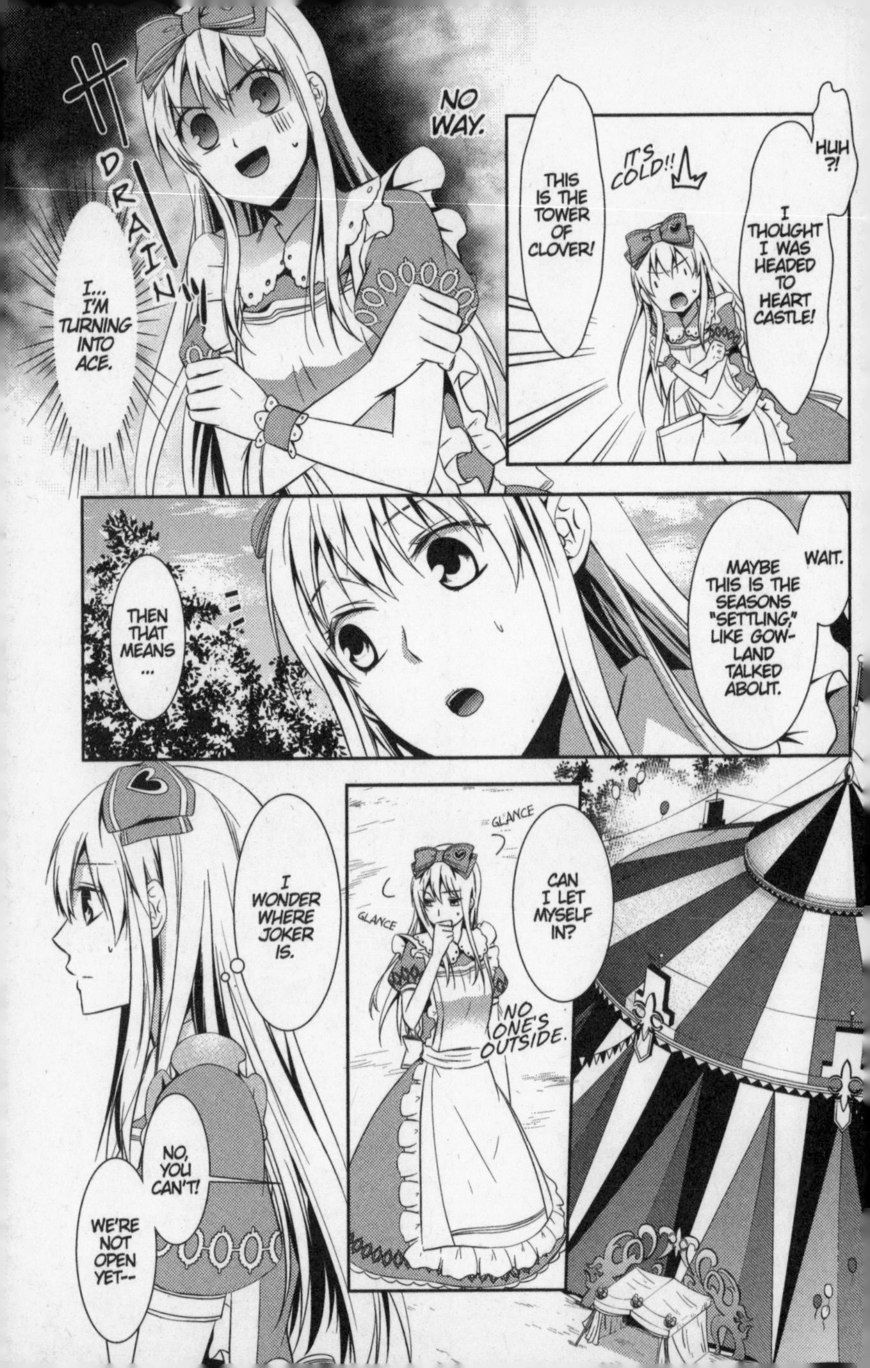
HUH?!
I THOUGHT I WAS HEADED TO HEART CASTLE!
IT'S COLD!!
THIS IS THE TOWER OF CLOVER!
NO WAY.
DRAIN
I... I'M TURNING INTO ACE.
WAIT.
MAYBE THIS IS THE SEASONS "SETTLING," LIKE GOW-LAND TALKED ABOUT.
THEN THAT MEANS...
GLANCE
CAN I LET MYSELF IN?
GLANCE
NO ONE'S OUTSIDE.
I WONDER WHERE JOKER IS.
NO, YOU CAN'T!
WE'RE NOT OPEN YET--

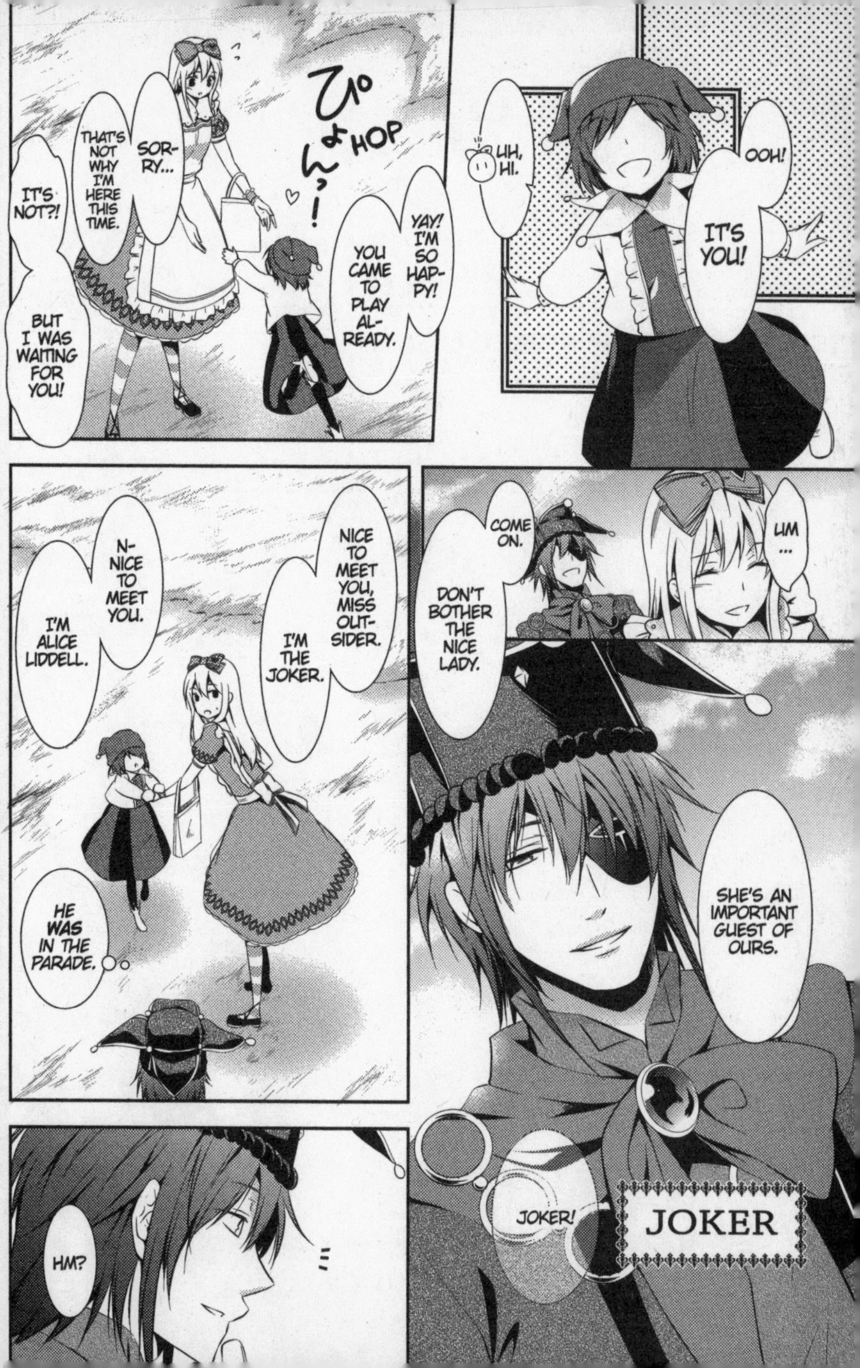
OOH!
IT'S YOU!
UH, HI.
YAY! I'M SO HAP-PY!
YOU CAME TO PLAY AL-READY.
ぴょんっ！ HOP
SOR-RY...
THAT'S NOT WHY I'M HERE THIS TIME.
IT'S NOT?!
BUT I WAS WAITING FOR YOU!
UM ...
COME ON.
DON'T BOTHER THE NICE LADY.
NICE TO MEET YOU, MISS OUT-SIDER.
I'M THE JOKER.
N-NICE TO MEET YOU.
I'M ALICE LIDDELL.
HE WAS IN THE PARADE.
SHE'S AN IMPORTANT GUEST OF OURS.
JOKER!
JOKER
HM?

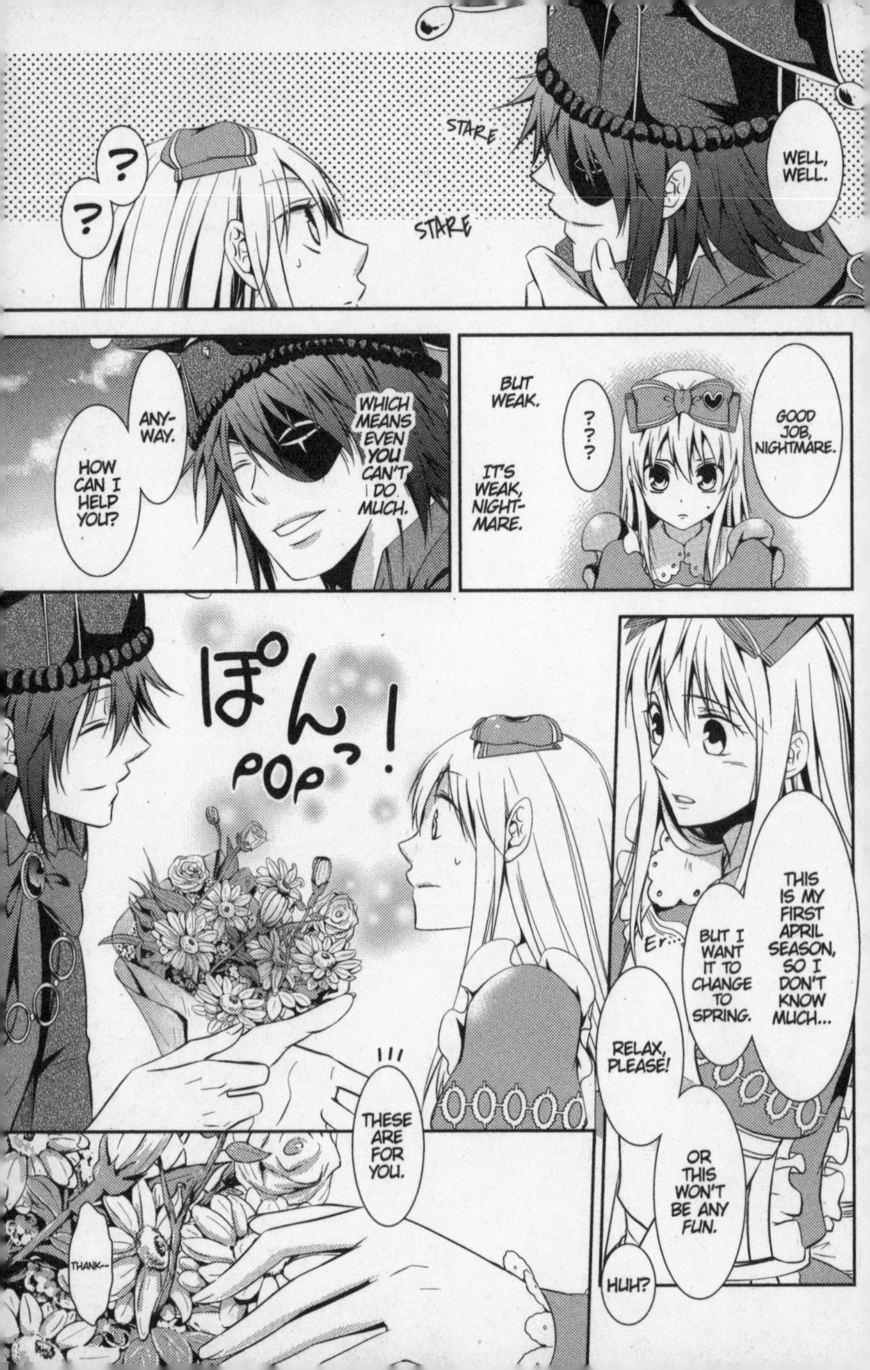
WELL, WELL.
STARE
STARE
?
?
GOOD JOB, NIGHTMARE.
?.?.?
BUT WEAK.
IT'S WEAK, NIGHTMARE.
WHICH MEANS EVEN YOU CAN'T DO MUCH.
ANY-WAY.
HOW CAN I HELP YOU?
THIS IS MY FIRST APRIL SEASON, SO I DON'T KNOW MUCH...
Er...
BUT I WANT IT TO CHANGE TO SPRING.
RELAX, PLEASE!
OR THIS WON'T BE ANY FUN.
HUH?
ぽんっ!
POP
THESE ARE FOR YOU.
THANK--

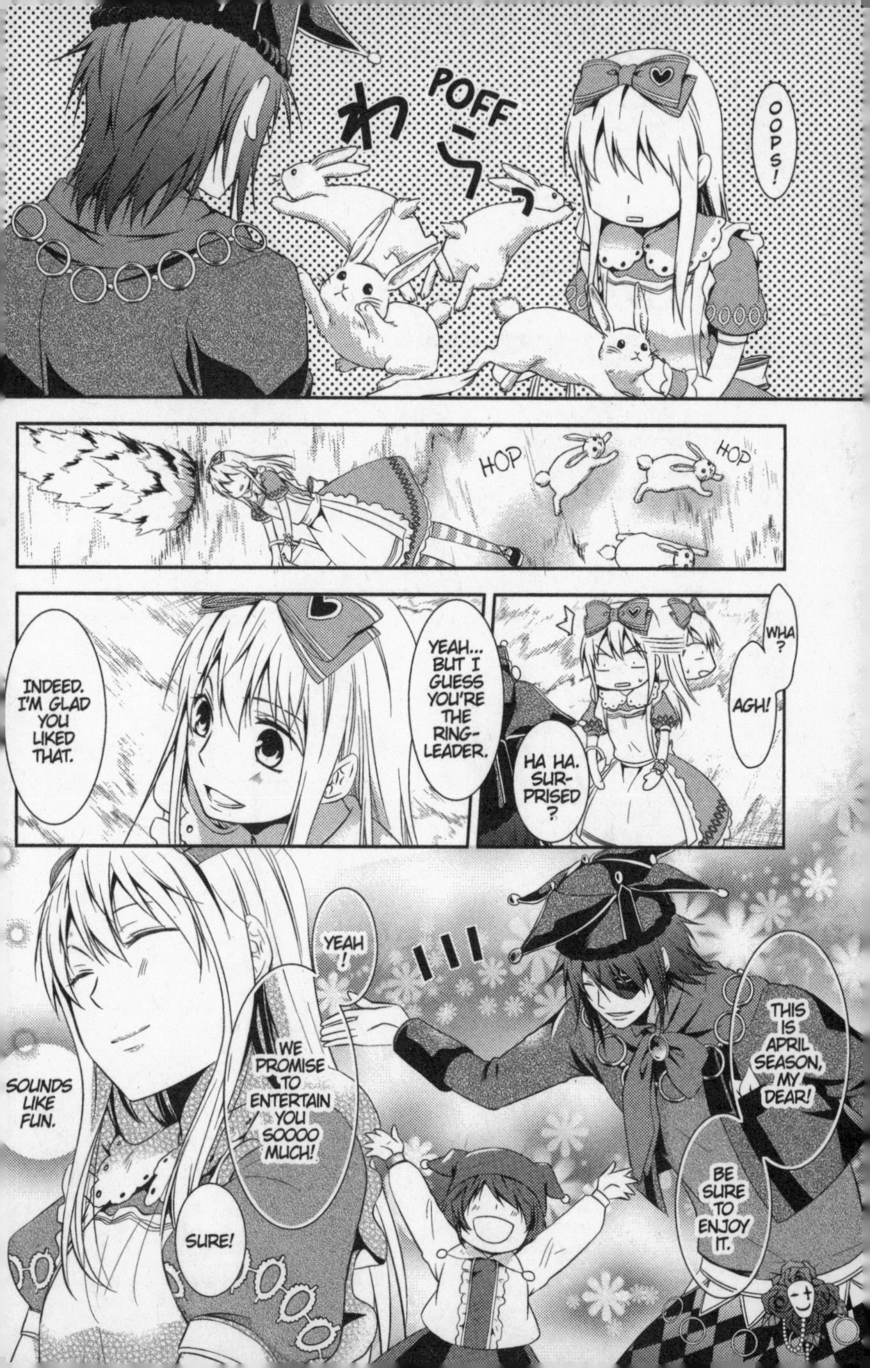
OOPS!
POFF
わ～っ
HOP
HOP
WHA?
AGH!
HA HA. SURPRISED?
YEAH... BUT I GUESS YOU'RE THE RING-LEADER.
INDEED. I'M GLAD YOU LIKED THAT.
THIS IS APRIL SEASON, MY DEAR!
BE SURE TO ENJOY IT.
YEAH!
WE PROMISE TO ENTERTAIN YOU SOOOO MUCH!
SURE!
SOUNDS LIKE FUN.

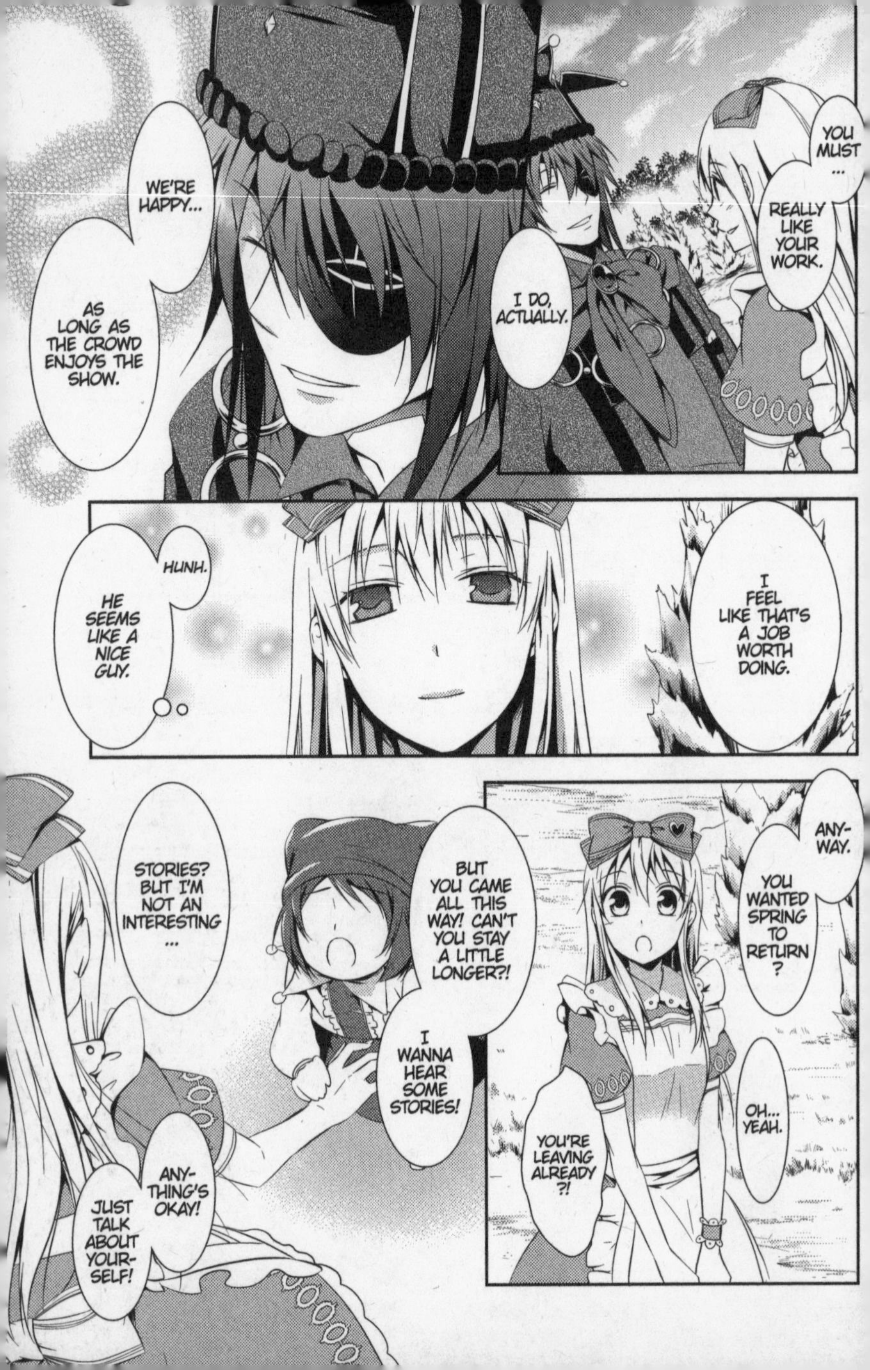
YOU MUST ...
REALLY LIKE YOUR WORK.
I DO, ACTUALLY.
WE'RE HAPPY...
AS LONG AS THE CROWD ENJOYS THE SHOW.
I FEEL LIKE THAT'S A JOB WORTH DOING.
HUNH.
HE SEEMS LIKE A NICE GUY.
ANY-WAY.
YOU WANTED SPRING TO RETURN?
OH... YEAH.
YOU'RE LEAVING ALREADY?!
BUT YOU CAME ALL THIS WAY! CAN'T YOU STAY A LITTLE LONGER?!
I WANNA HEAR SOME STORIES!
STORIES? BUT I'M NOT AN INTERESTING ...
ANY-THING'S OKAY!
JUST TALK ABOUT YOUR-SELF!

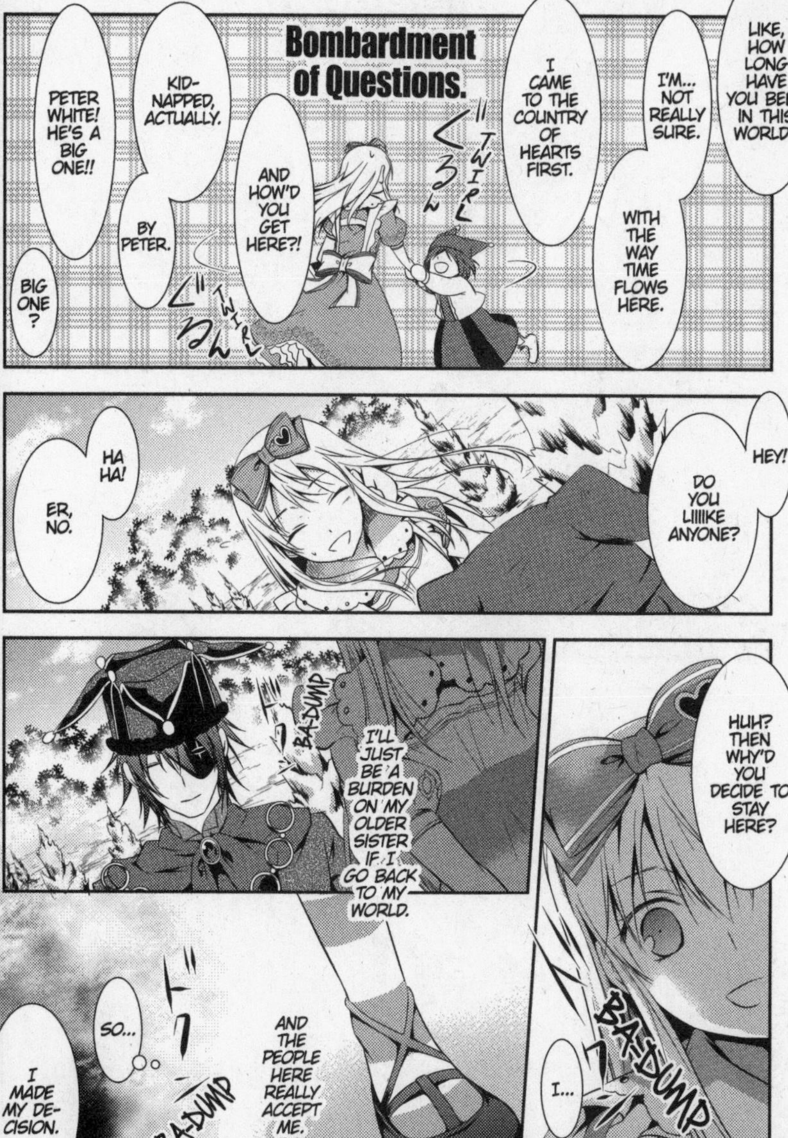
Bombardment of Questions.
LIKE, HOW LONG HAVE YOU BEEN IN THIS WORLD?
I'M... NOT REALLY SURE.
WITH THE WAY TIME FLOWS HERE.
I CAME TO THE COUNTRY OF HEARTS FIRST.
TWIRL
AND HOW'D YOU GET HERE?!
KID-NAPPED, ACTUALLY.
BY PETER.
TWIRL
PETER WHITE! HE'S A BIG ONE!!
BIG ONE?
HEY!
DO YOU LIIIIKE ANYONE?
HA HA!
ER, NO.
HUH? THEN WHY'D YOU DECIDE TO STAY HERE?
BA-DUMP
I...
BA-DUMP
I'LL JUST BE A BURDEN ON MY OLDER SISTER IF I GO BACK TO MY WORLD.
AND THE PEOPLE HERE REALLY ACCEPT ME.
BA-DUMP
SO...
I MADE MY DE-CISION.

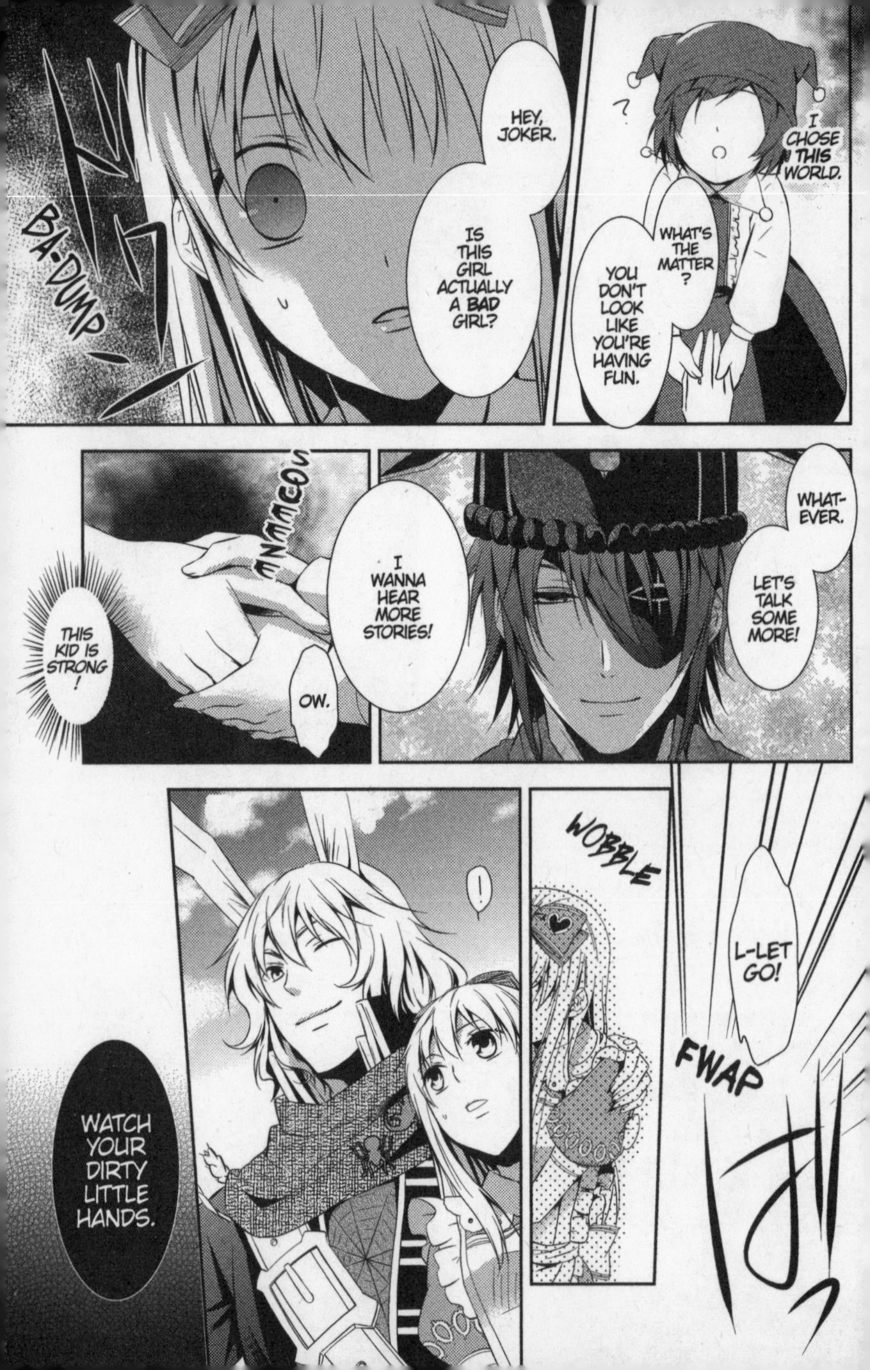
I CHOSE THIS WORLD.
?
WHAT'S THE MATTER?
YOU DON'T LOOK LIKE YOU'RE HAVING FUN.
HEY, JOKER.
IS THIS GIRL ACTUALLY A BAD GIRL?
BA-DUMP
WHATEVER.
LET'S TALK SOME MORE!
I WANNA HEAR MORE STORIES!
SQUEEZE
OW.
THIS KID IS STRONG!
L-LET GO!
FWAP
WOBBLE
!
WATCH YOUR DIRTY LITTLE HANDS.

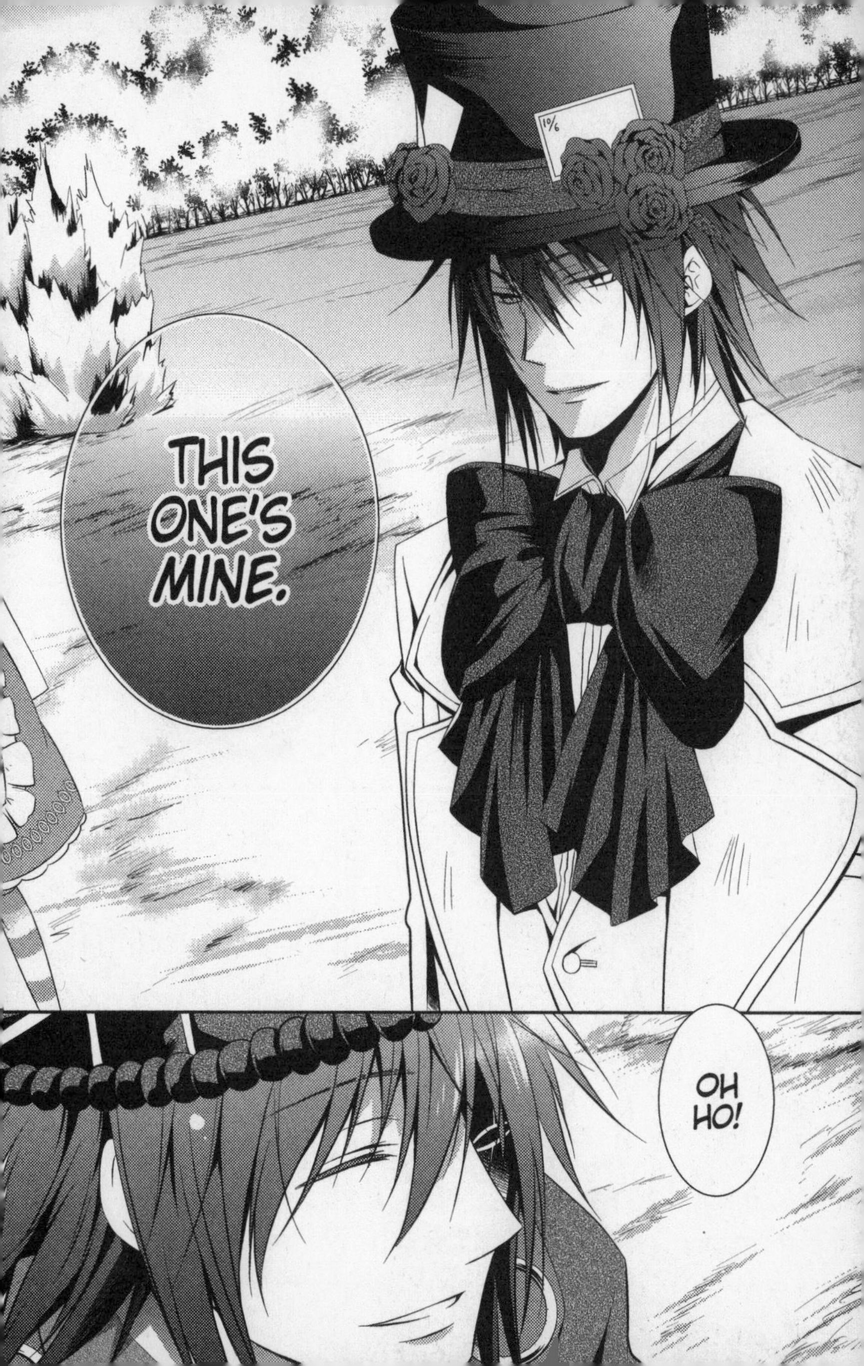
THIS ONE'S MINE.
OH HO!

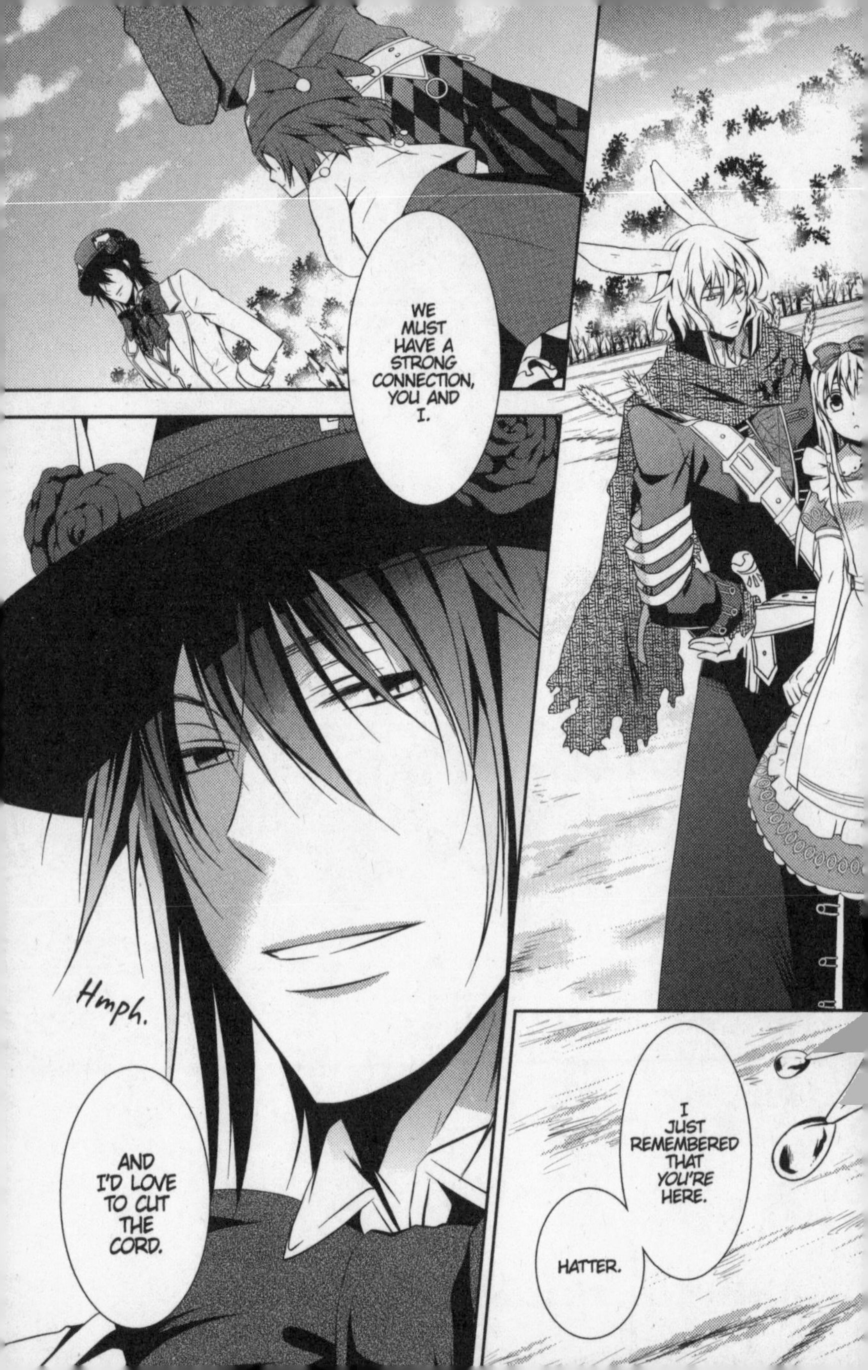
I JUST REMEMBERED THAT YOU'RE HERE.
HATTER.
WE MUST HAVE A STRONG CONNECTION, YOU AND I.
Hmph.
AND I'D LOVE TO CUT THE CORD.

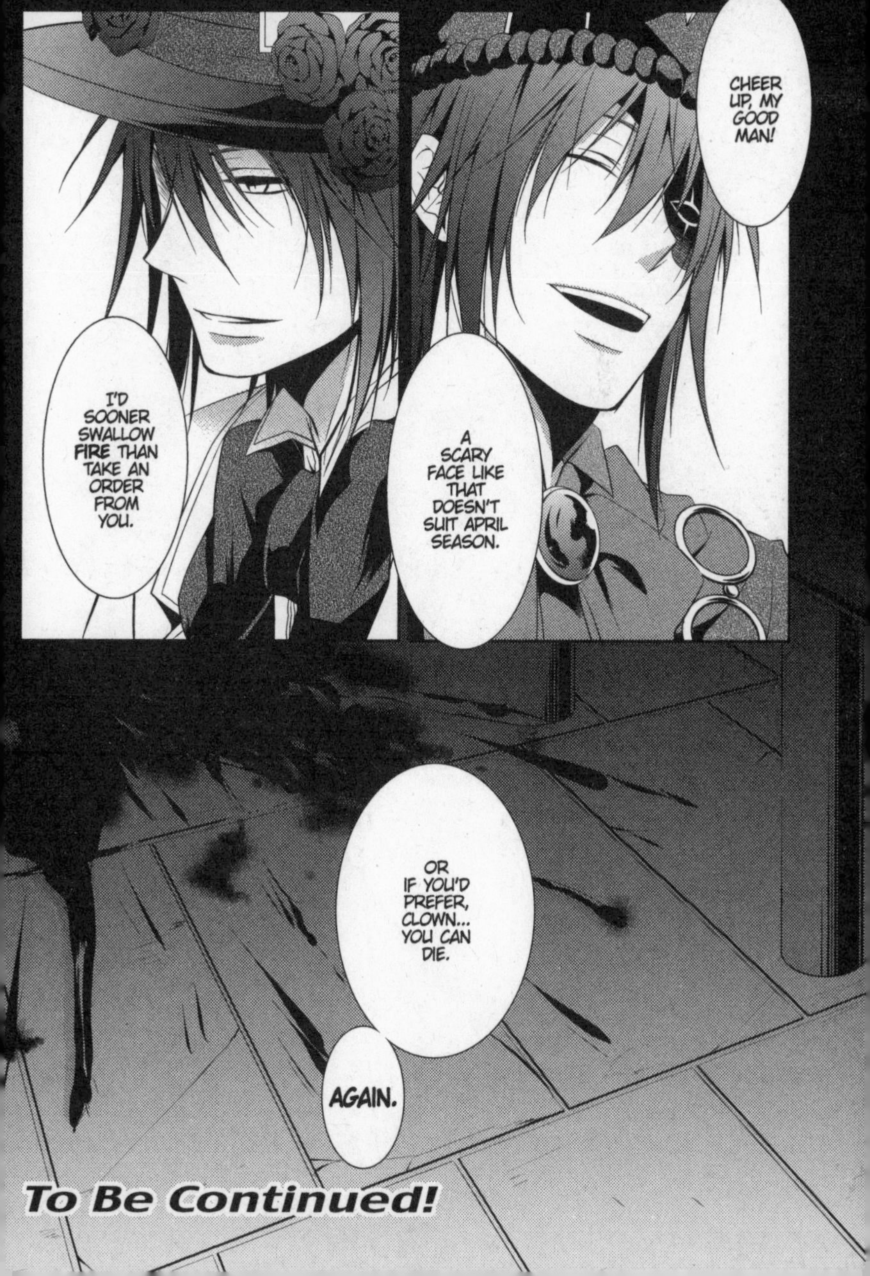
CHEER UP, MY GOOD MAN!
A SCARY FACE LIKE THAT DOESN'T SUIT APRIL SEASON.
I'D SOONER SWALLOW FIRE THAN TAKE AN ORDER FROM YOU.
OR IF YOU'D PREFER, CLOWN... YOU CAN DIE.
AGAIN.
To Be Continued!

MEET ME IN THE SECOND VOLUME, TOOTS.
WHO ARE YOU?

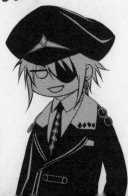

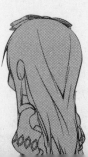

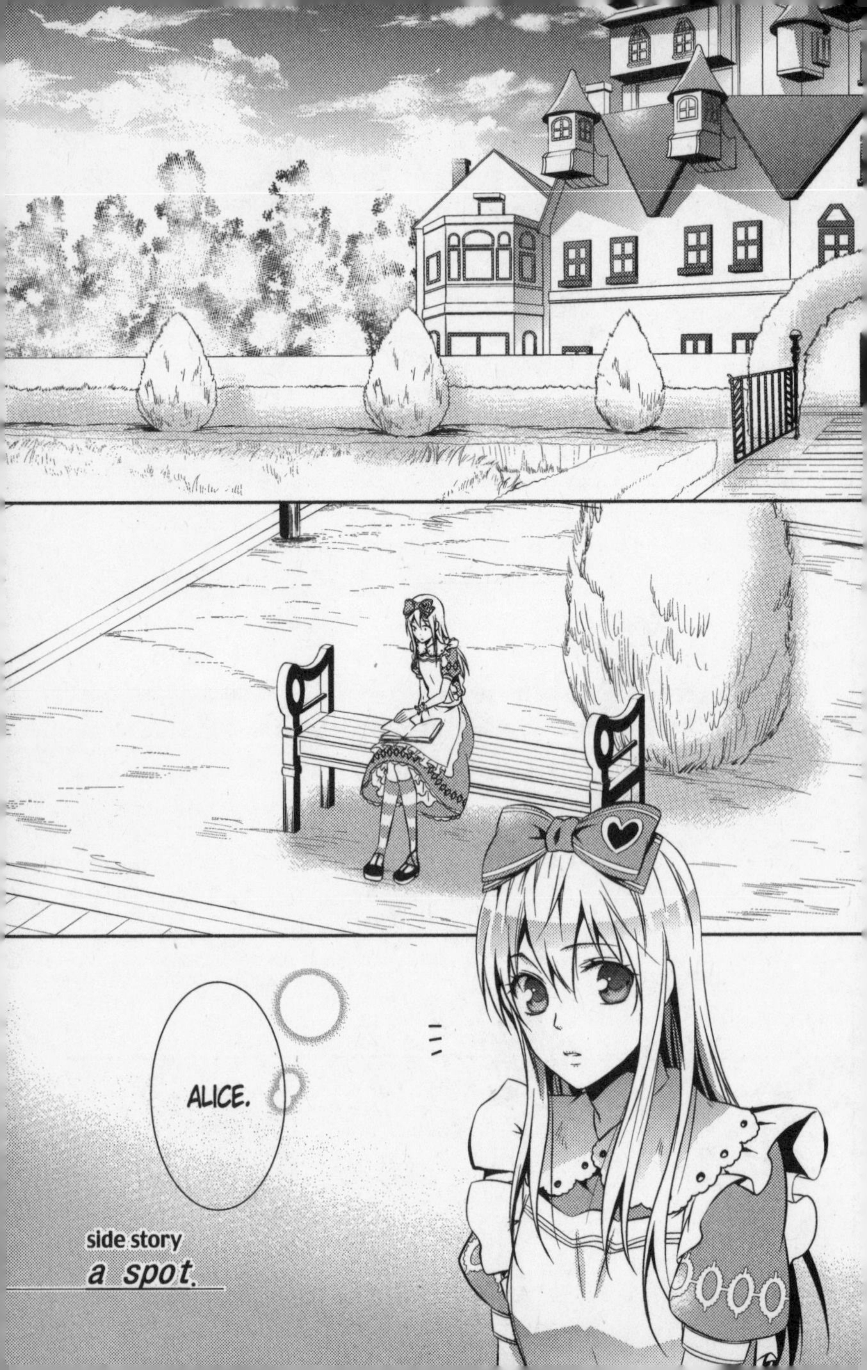
ALICE.
side story
a spot.

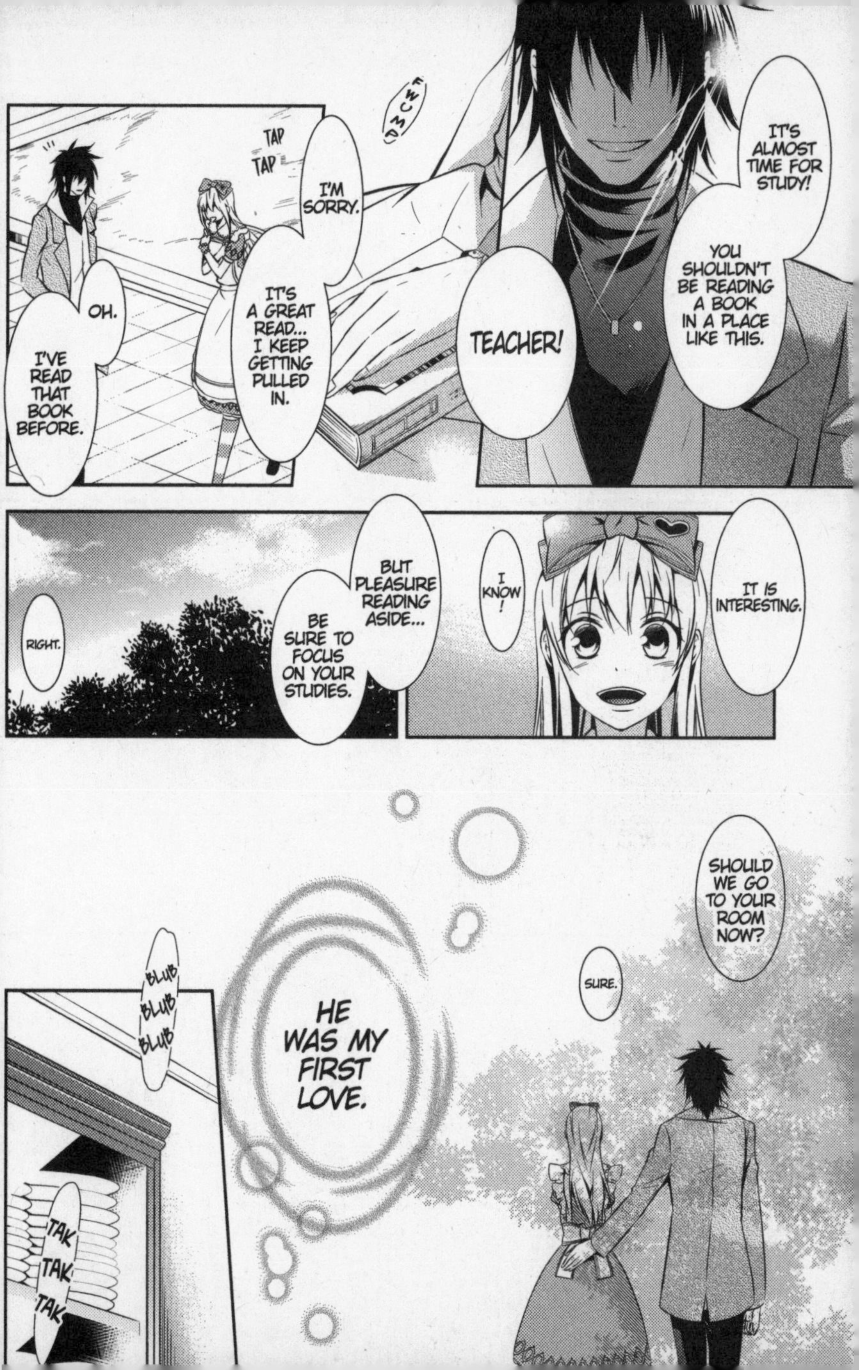
IT'S ALMOST TIME FOR STUDY!
YOU SHOULDN'T BE READING A BOOK IN A PLACE LIKE THIS.
TEACHER!
FWUMP
TAP TAP
I'M SORRY.
IT'S A GREAT READ... I KEEP GETTING PULLED IN.
OH.
I'VE READ THAT BOOK BEFORE.
IT IS INTERESTING.
I KNOW!
BUT PLEASURE READING ASIDE...
BE SURE TO FOCUS ON YOUR STUDIES.
RIGHT.
SHOULD WE GO TO YOUR ROOM NOW?
SURE.
HE WAS MY FIRST LOVE.
BLUB BLUB BLUB
TAK TAK TAK

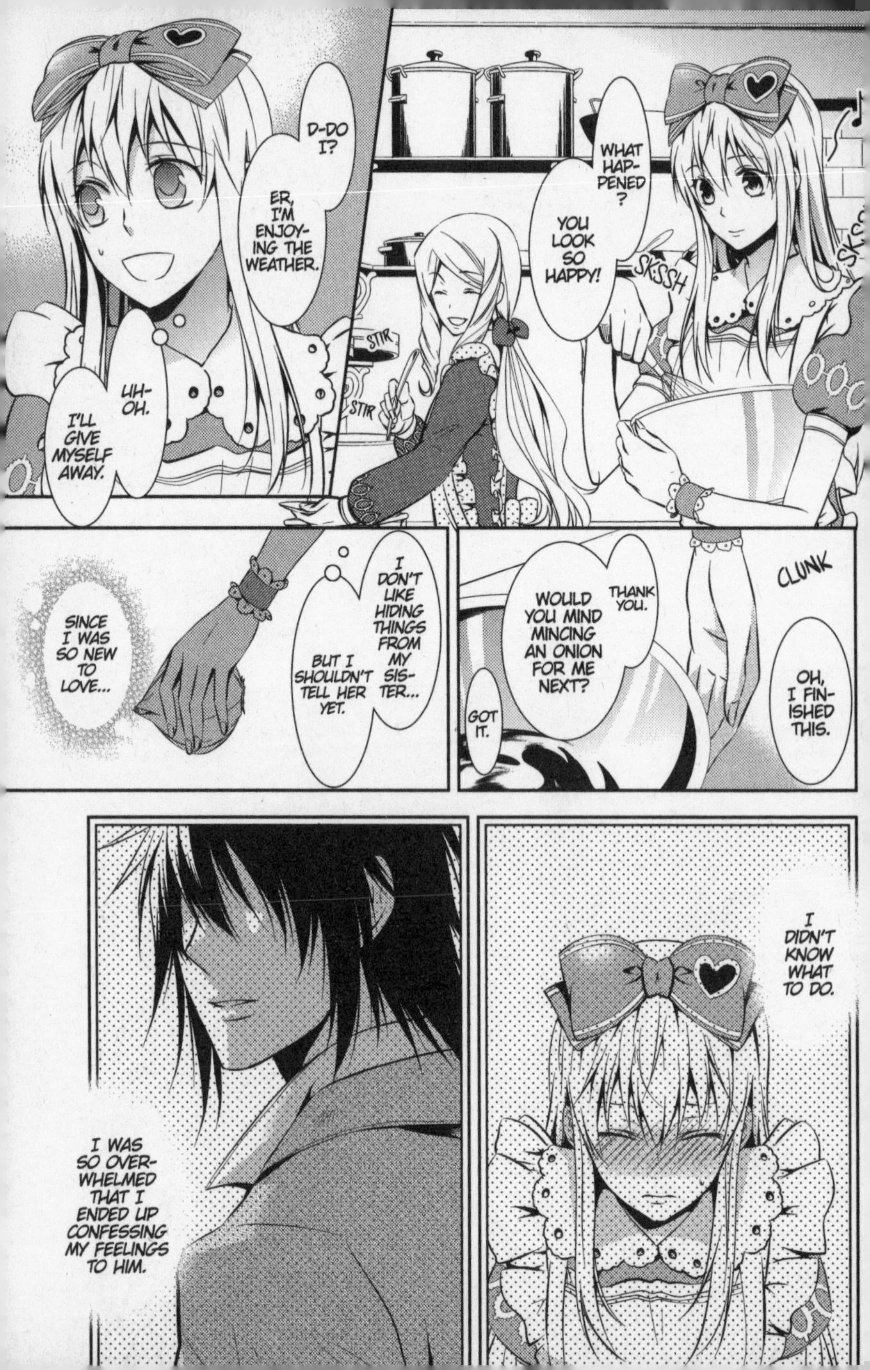
SKSS
WHAT HAPPENED?
YOU LOOK SO HAPPY!
SK-SSH
STIR
STIR
D-DO I?
ER, I'M ENJOYING THE WEATHER.
UH-OH.
I'LL GIVE MYSELF AWAY.
CLUNK
OH, I FINISHED THIS.
THANK YOU.
WOULD YOU MIND MINCING AN ONION FOR ME NEXT?
GOT IT.
I DON'T LIKE HIDING THINGS FROM MY SISTER...
BUT I SHOULDN'T TELL HER YET.
SINCE I WAS SO NEW TO LOVE...
I DIDN'T KNOW WHAT TO DO.
I WAS SO OVERWHELMED THAT I ENDED UP CONFESSING MY FEELINGS TO HIM.

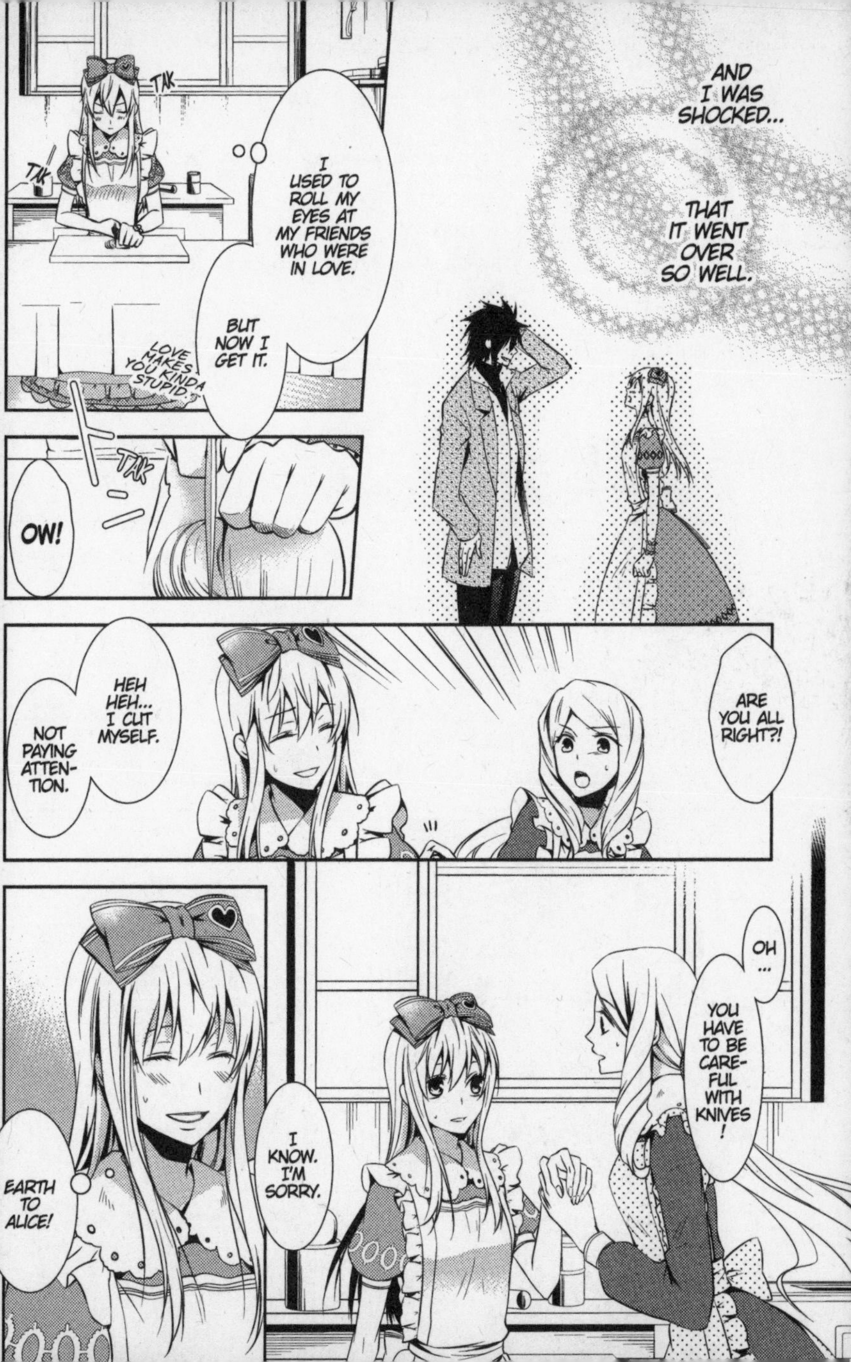
AND I WAS SHOCKED...
THAT IT WENT OVER SO WELL.
TAK
TAK
I USED TO ROLL MY EYES AT MY FRIENDS WHO WERE IN LOVE.
BUT NOW I GET IT.
LOVE MAKES YOU KINDA STUPID.
TAK
OW!
ARE YOU ALL RIGHT?!
HEH HEH... I CUT MYSELF.
NOT PAYING ATTEN-TION.
OH...
YOU HAVE TO BE CARE-FUL WITH KNIVES!
I KNOW. I'M SORRY.
EARTH TO ALICE!

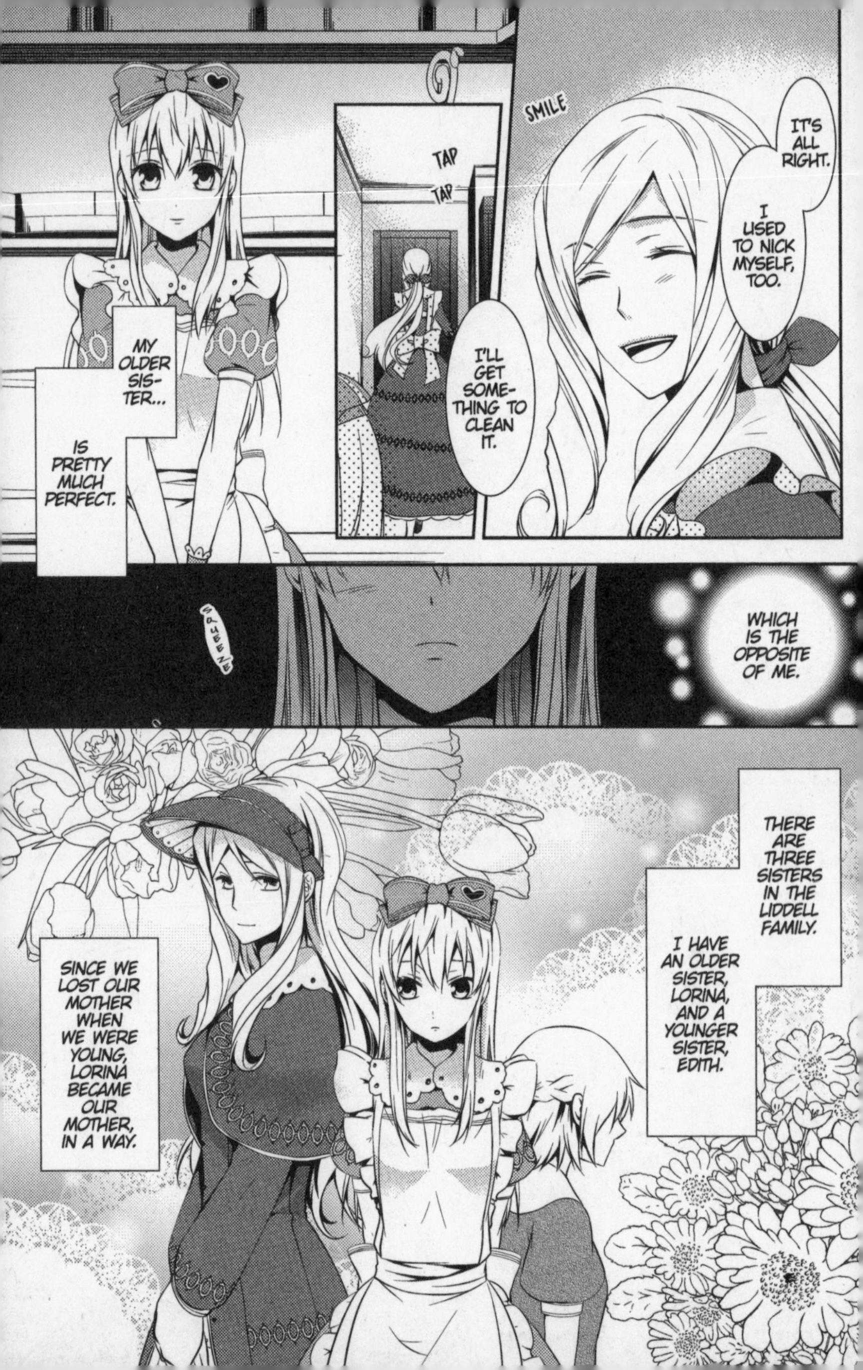
IT'S ALL RIGHT.
SMILE
I USED TO NICK MYSELF, TOO.
TAP
TAP
I'LL GET SOME-THING TO CLEAN IT.
MY OLDER SIS-TER...
IS PRETTY MUCH PERFECT.
WHICH IS THE OPPOSITE OF ME.
SQUEEZE
THERE ARE THREE SISTERS IN THE LIDDELL FAMILY.
I HAVE AN OLDER SISTER, LORINA, AND A YOUNGER SISTER, EDITH.
SINCE WE LOST OUR MOTHER WHEN WE WERE YOUNG, LORINA BECAME OUR MOTHER, IN A WAY.

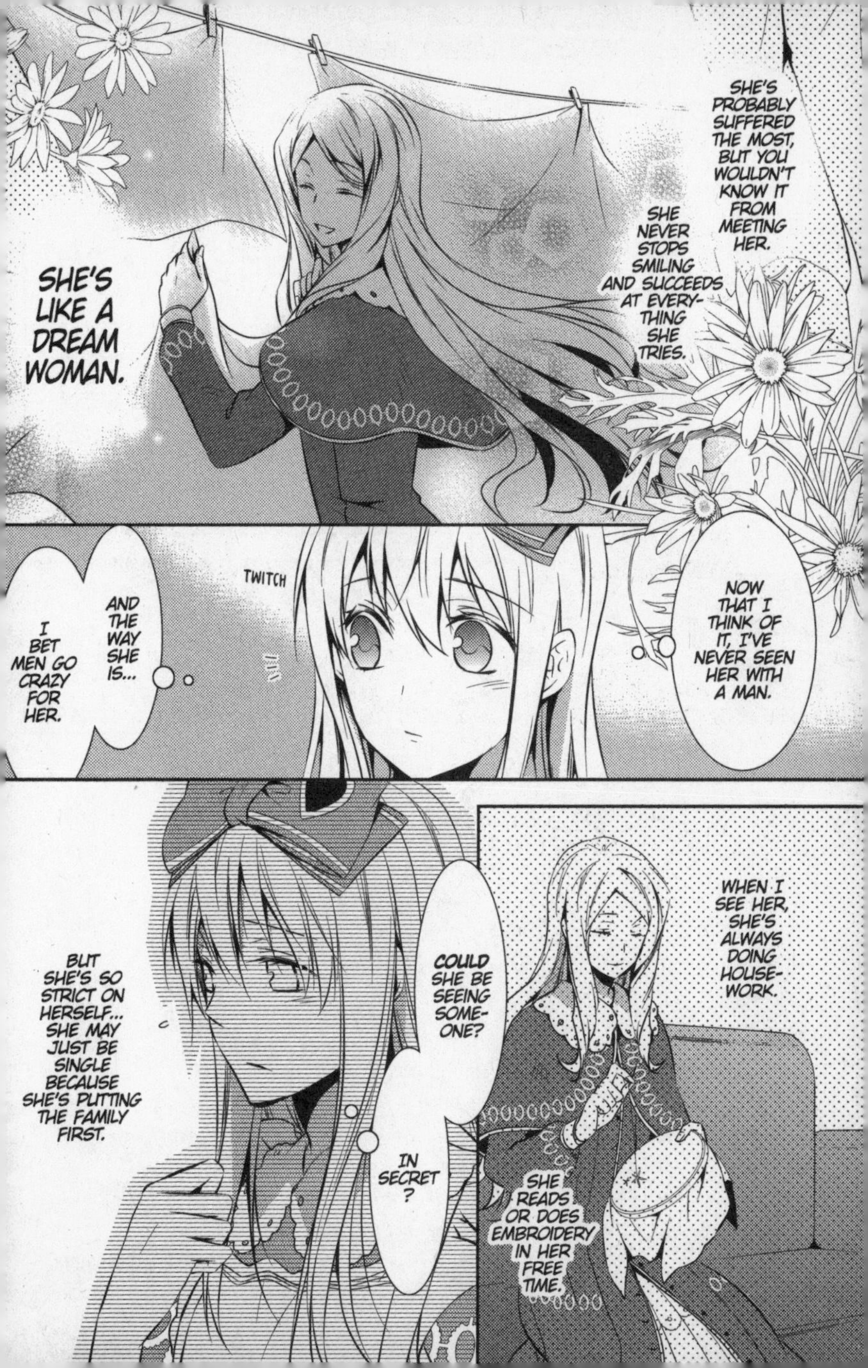
SHE'S PROBABLY SUFFERED THE MOST, BUT YOU WOULDN'T KNOW IT FROM MEETING HER.
SHE NEVER STOPS SMILING AND SUCCEEDS AT EVERY-THING SHE TRIES.
SHE'S LIKE A DREAM WOMAN.
NOW THAT I THINK OF IT, I'VE NEVER SEEN HER WITH A MAN.
TWITCH
AND THE WAY SHE IS...
I BET MEN GO CRAZY FOR HER.
WHEN I SEE HER, SHE'S ALWAYS DOING HOUSE-WORK.
SHE READS OR DOES EMBROIDERY IN HER FREE TIME.
COULD SHE BE SEEING SOME-ONE?
IN SECRET?
BUT SHE'S SO STRICT ON HERSELF... SHE MAY JUST BE SINGLE BECAUSE SHE'S PUTTING THE FAMILY FIRST.

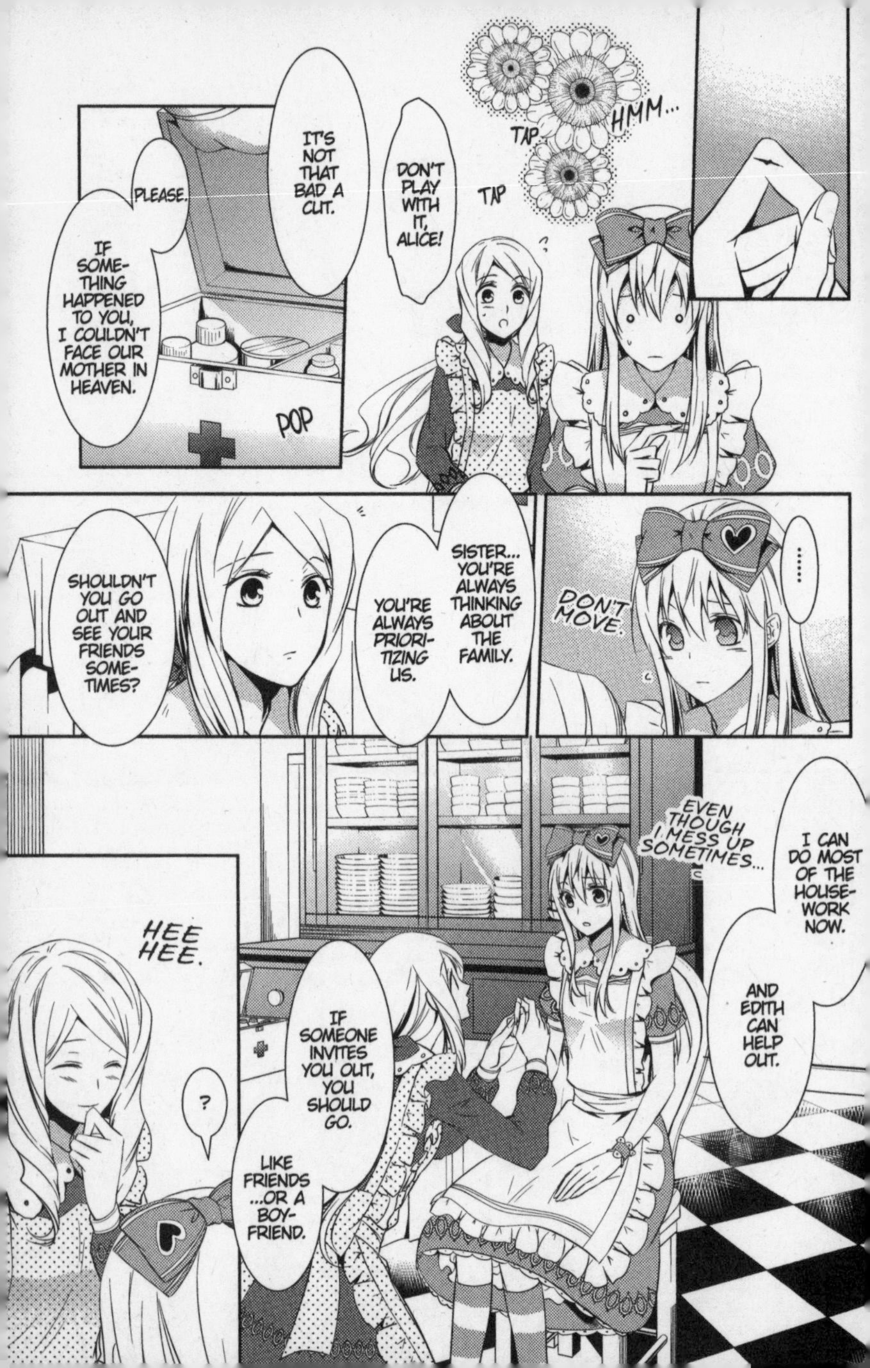
HMM...
TAP
TAP
DON'T PLAY WITH IT, ALICE!
IT'S NOT THAT BAD A CUT.
POP
PLEASE.
IF SOMETHING HAPPENED TO YOU, I COULDN'T FACE OUR MOTHER IN HEAVEN.
......
DON'T MOVE.
SISTER... YOU'RE ALWAYS THINKING ABOUT THE FAMILY.
YOU'RE ALWAYS PRIORITIZING US.
SHOULDN'T YOU GO OUT AND SEE YOUR FRIENDS SOMETIMES?
I CAN DO MOST OF THE HOUSEWORK NOW.
EVEN THOUGH I MESS UP SOMETIMES...
AND EDITH CAN HELP OUT.
IF SOMEONE INVITES YOU OUT, YOU SHOULD GO.
LIKE FRIENDS ...OR A BOYFRIEND.
HEE HEE.
?

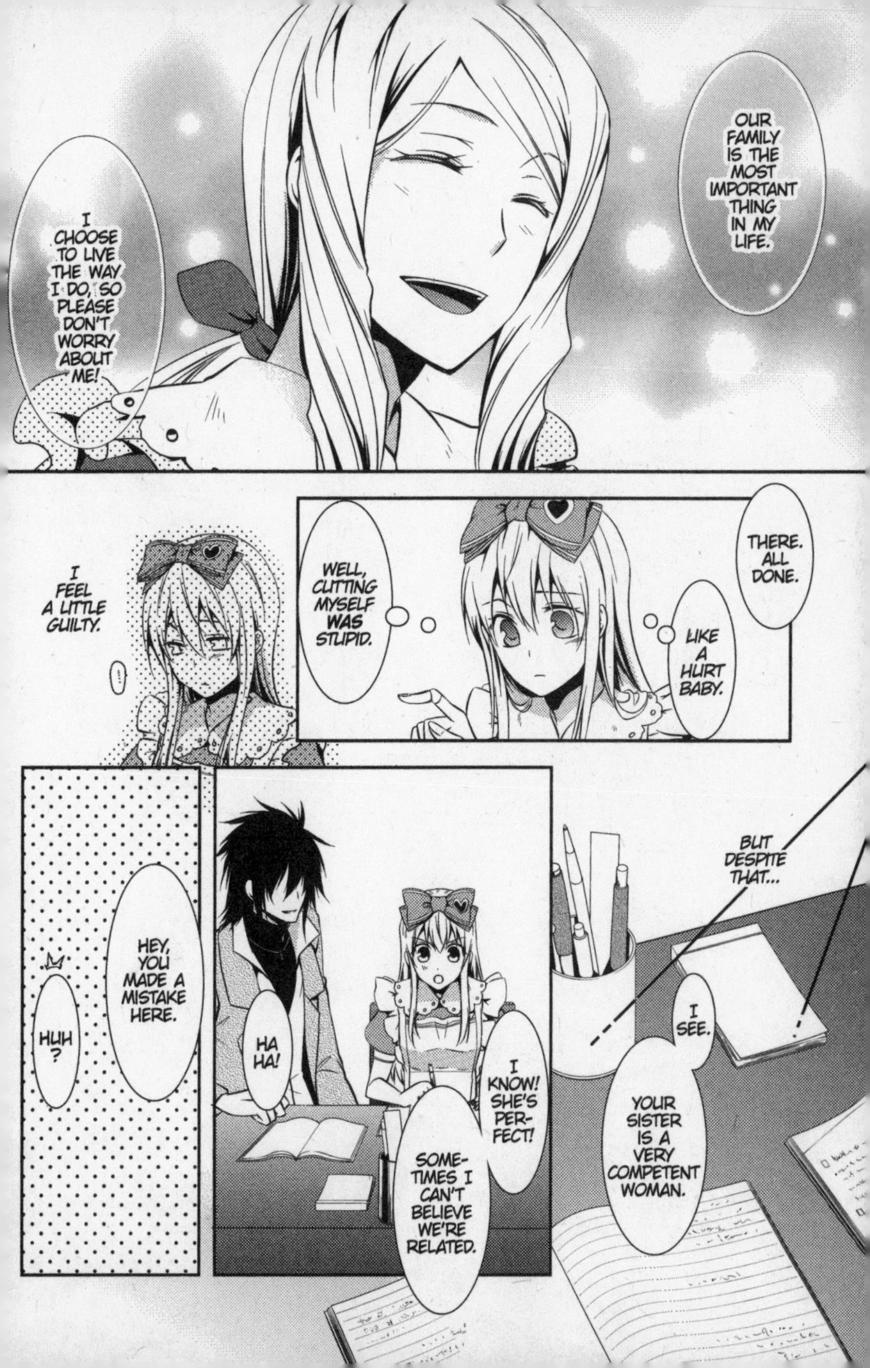
OUR FAMILY IS THE MOST IMPORTANT THING IN MY LIFE.
I CHOOSE TO LIVE THE WAY I DO, SO PLEASE DON'T WORRY ABOUT ME!
THERE. ALL DONE.
LIKE A HURT BABY.
WELL, CUTTING MYSELF WAS STUPID.
I FEEL A LITTLE GUILTY.
!
BUT DESPITE THAT...
I SEE.
YOUR SISTER IS A VERY COMPETENT WOMAN.
I KNOW! SHE'S PER-FECT!
SOME-TIMES I CAN'T BELIEVE WE'RE RELATED.
HA HA!
HEY, YOU MADE A MISTAKE HERE.
HUH?

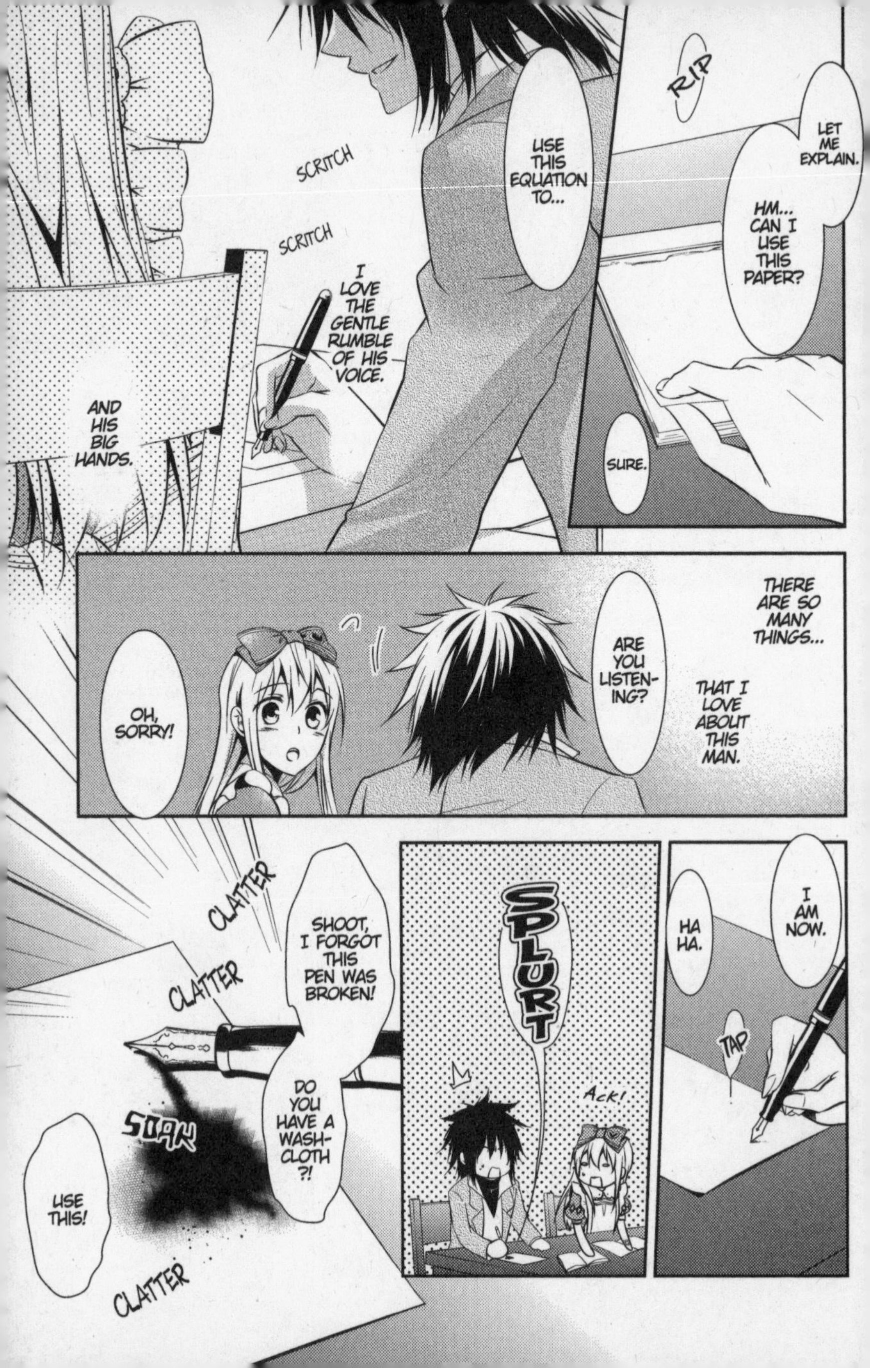
RIP
LET ME EXPLAIN.
HM... CAN I USE THIS PAPER?
SURE.
USE THIS EQUATION TO...
SCRITCH
SCRITCH
I LOVE THE GENTLE RUMBLE OF HIS VOICE.
AND HIS BIG HANDS.
THERE ARE SO MANY THINGS...
THAT I LOVE ABOUT THIS MAN.
ARE YOU LISTENING?
OH, SORRY!
I AM NOW.
HA HA.
TAP
SPLURT
ACK!
SHOOT, I FORGOT THIS PEN WAS BROKEN!
CLATTER
CLATTER
DO YOU HAVE A WASHCLOTH?!
SOAK
USE THIS!
CLATTER

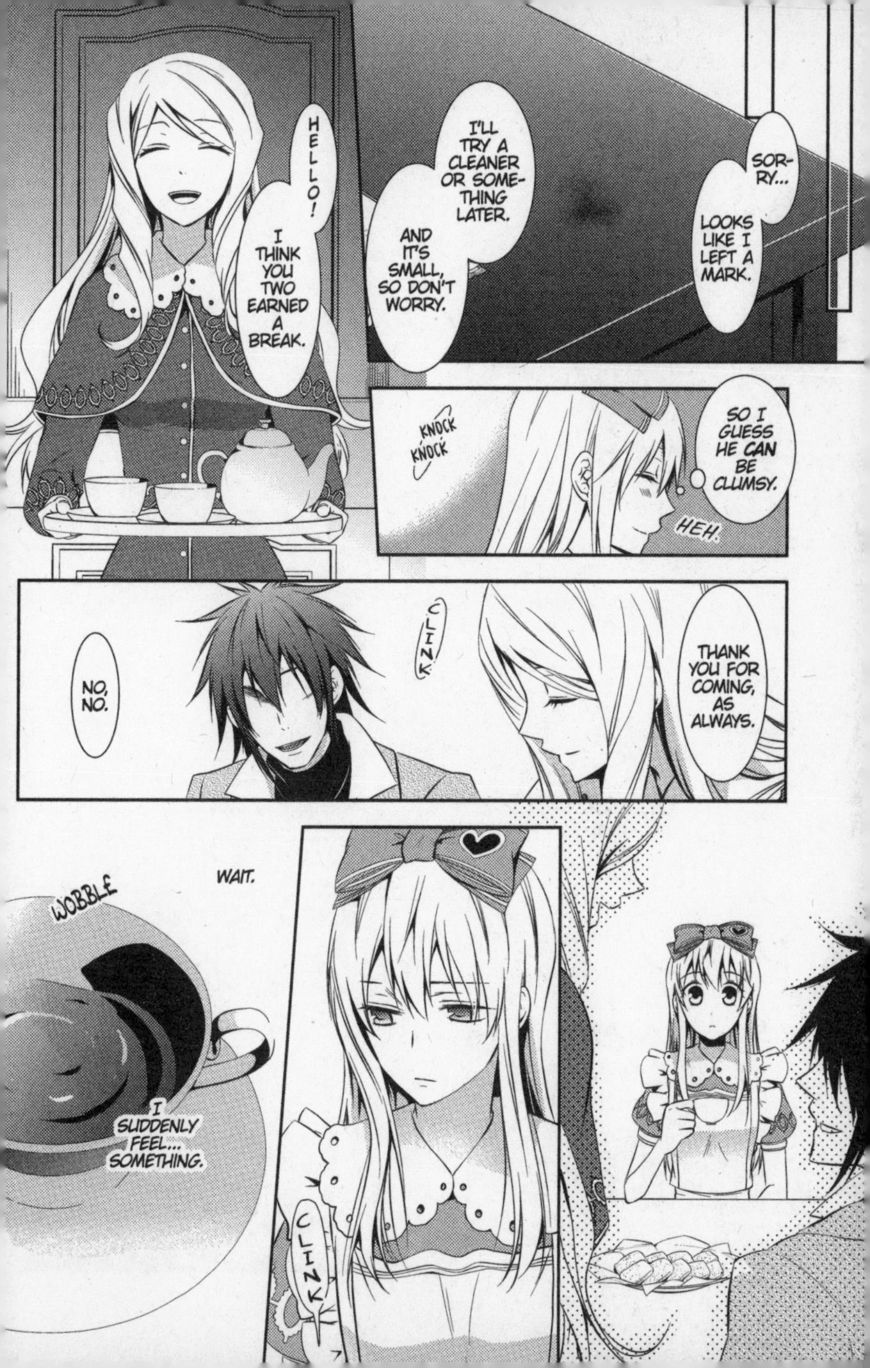
SORRY...
LOOKS LIKE I LEFT A MARK.
I'LL TRY A CLEANER OR SOMETHING LATER.
AND IT'S SMALL, SO DON'T WORRY.
SO I GUESS HE CAN BE CLUMSY.
HEH.
KNOCK KNOCK
HELLO!
I THINK YOU TWO EARNED A BREAK.
THANK YOU FOR COMING, AS ALWAYS.
CLINK
NO, NO.
CLINK
WAIT.
WOBBLE
I SUDDENLY FEEL... SOMETHING.

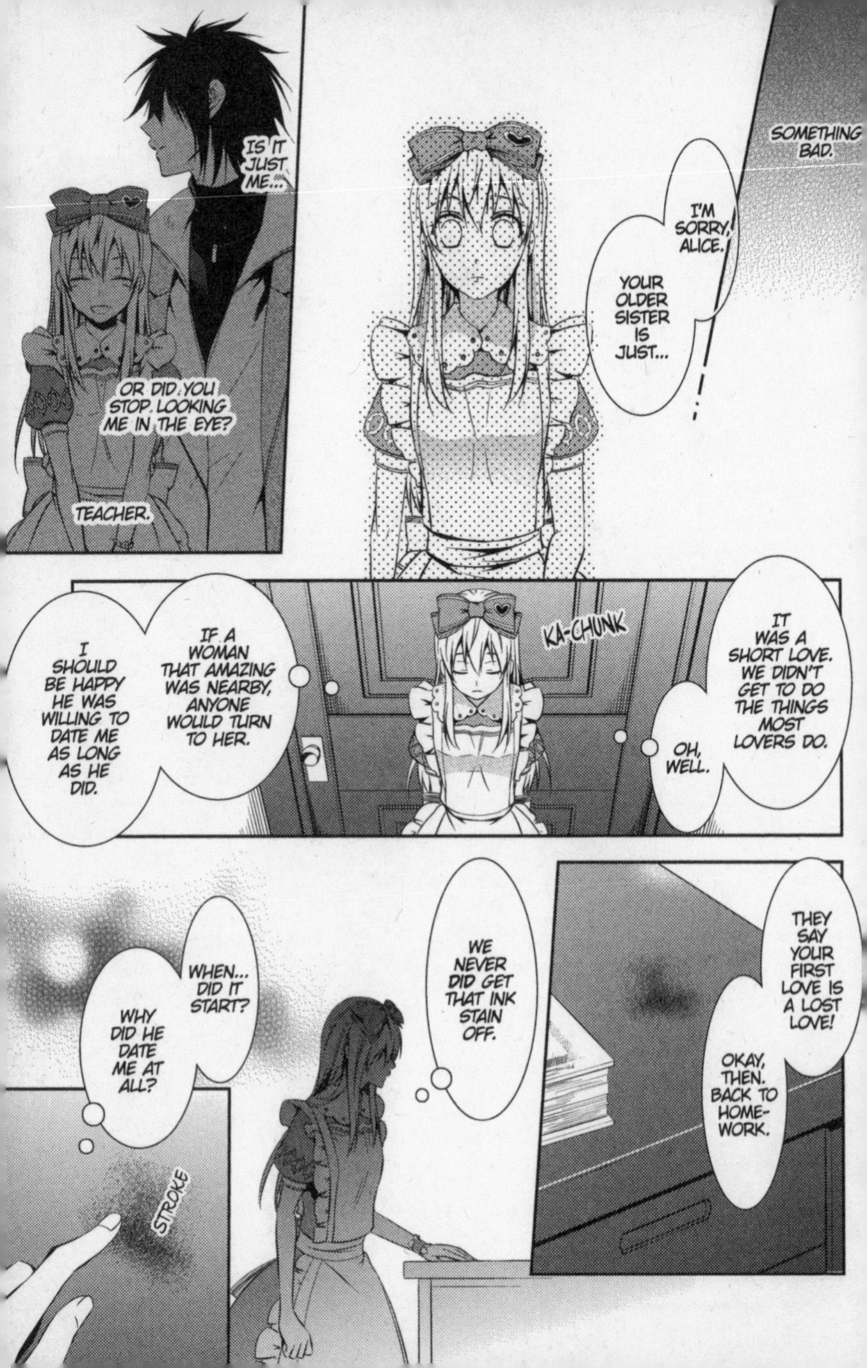
SOMETHING BAD.
I'M SORRY, ALICE.
YOUR OLDER SISTER IS JUST...
IS IT JUST ME...
OR DID YOU STOP LOOKING ME IN THE EYE?
TEACHER.
IT WAS A SHORT LOVE. WE DIDN'T GET TO DO THE THINGS MOST LOVERS DO.
OH, WELL.
KA-CHUNK
IF A WOMAN THAT AMAZING WAS NEARBY, ANYONE WOULD TURN TO HER.
I SHOULD BE HAPPY HE WAS WILLING TO DATE ME AS LONG AS HE DID.
THEY SAY YOUR FIRST LOVE IS A LOST LOVE!
OKAY, THEN. BACK TO HOME-WORK.
WE NEVER DID GET THAT INK STAIN OFF.
WHEN... DID IT START?
WHY DID HE DATE ME AT ALL?
STROKE

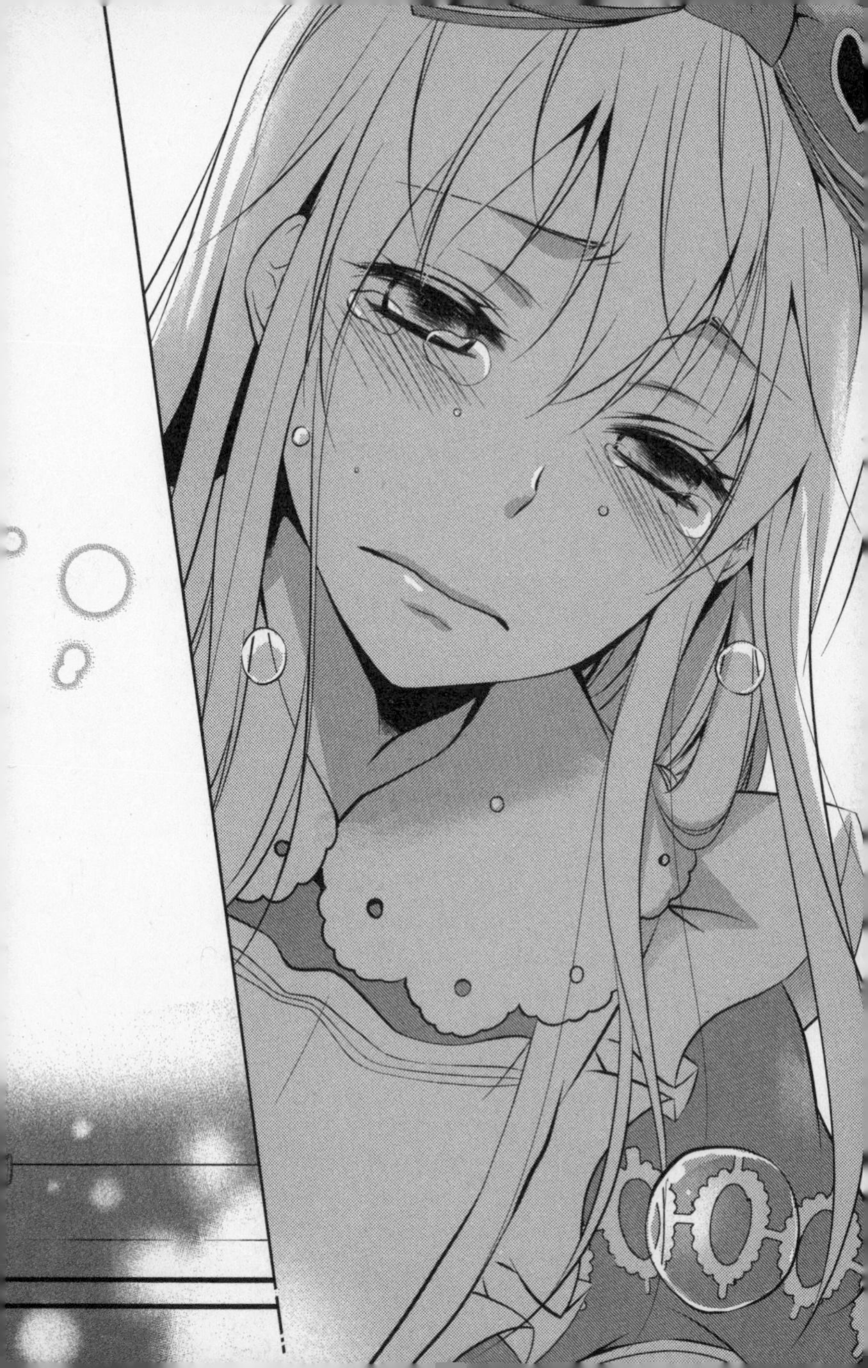

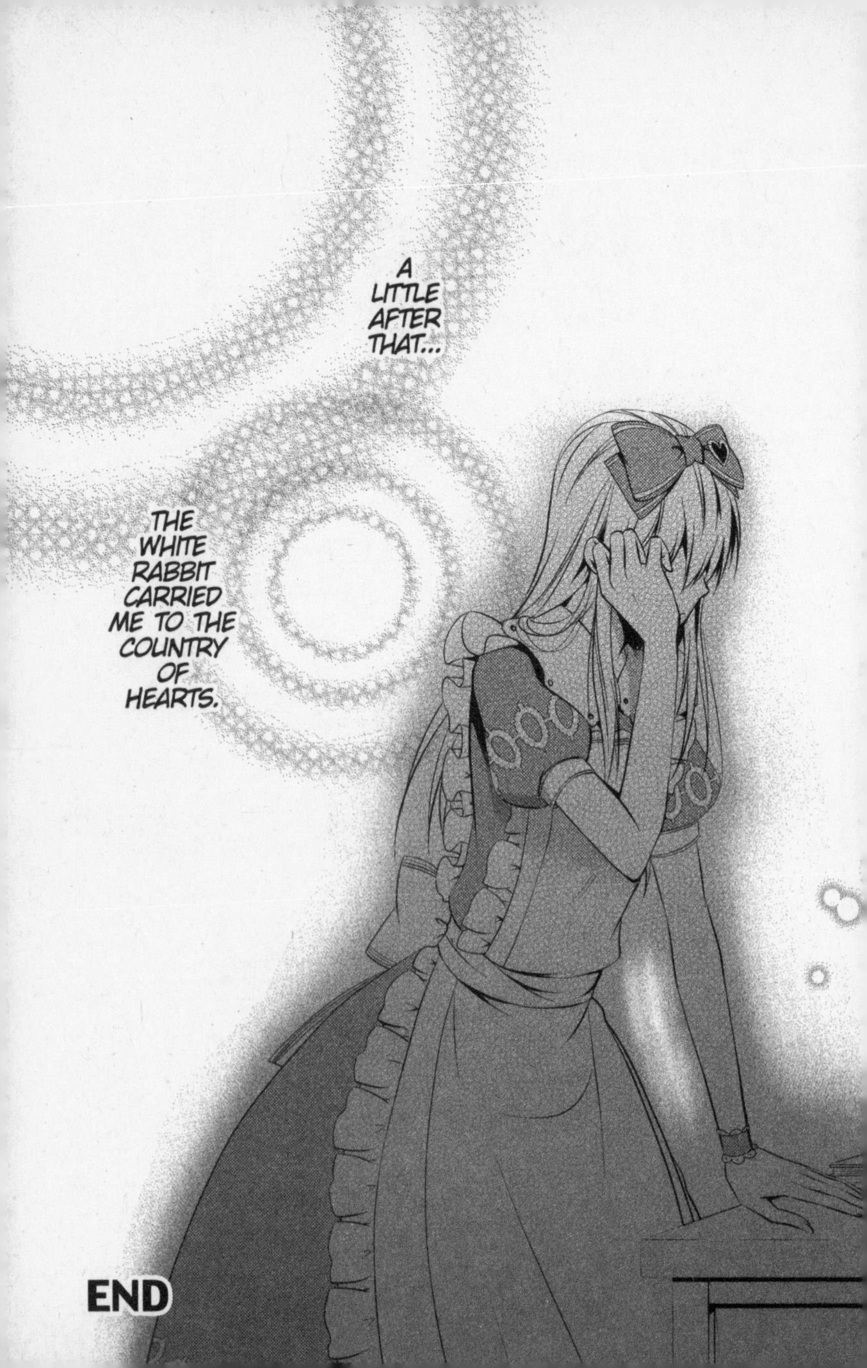
A LITTLE AFTER THAT...
THE WHITE RABBIT CARRIED ME TO THE COUNTRY OF HEARTS.
END

BONUS 4-PANEL COMICS!

WHAT IF... ALICE WAS SMALL?

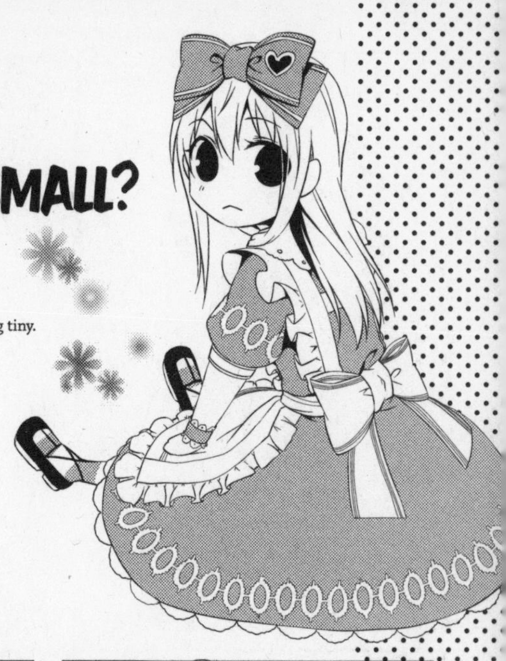

- This is a special 4-panel comic about Alice being tiny.
- It has nothing to do with the main story.
- Note: **Don't think too hard about it.**

↑ IMPORTANT!

For those who shut off their brains, enjoy!

↓

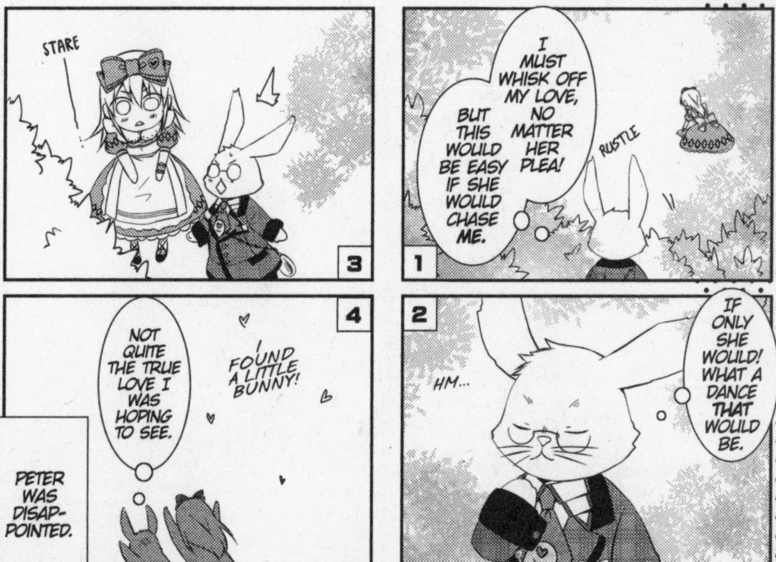
1
I MUST WHISK OFF MY LOVE, NO MATTER HER PLEA!
BUT THIS WOULD BE EASY IF SHE WOULD CHASE ME.
RUSTLE
2
IF ONLY SHE WOULD! WHAT A DANCE THAT WOULD BE.
HM...
3
STARE
4
NOT QUITE THE TRUE LOVE I WAS HOPING TO SEE.
I FOUND A LITTLE BUNNY!
PETER WAS DISAPPOINTED.

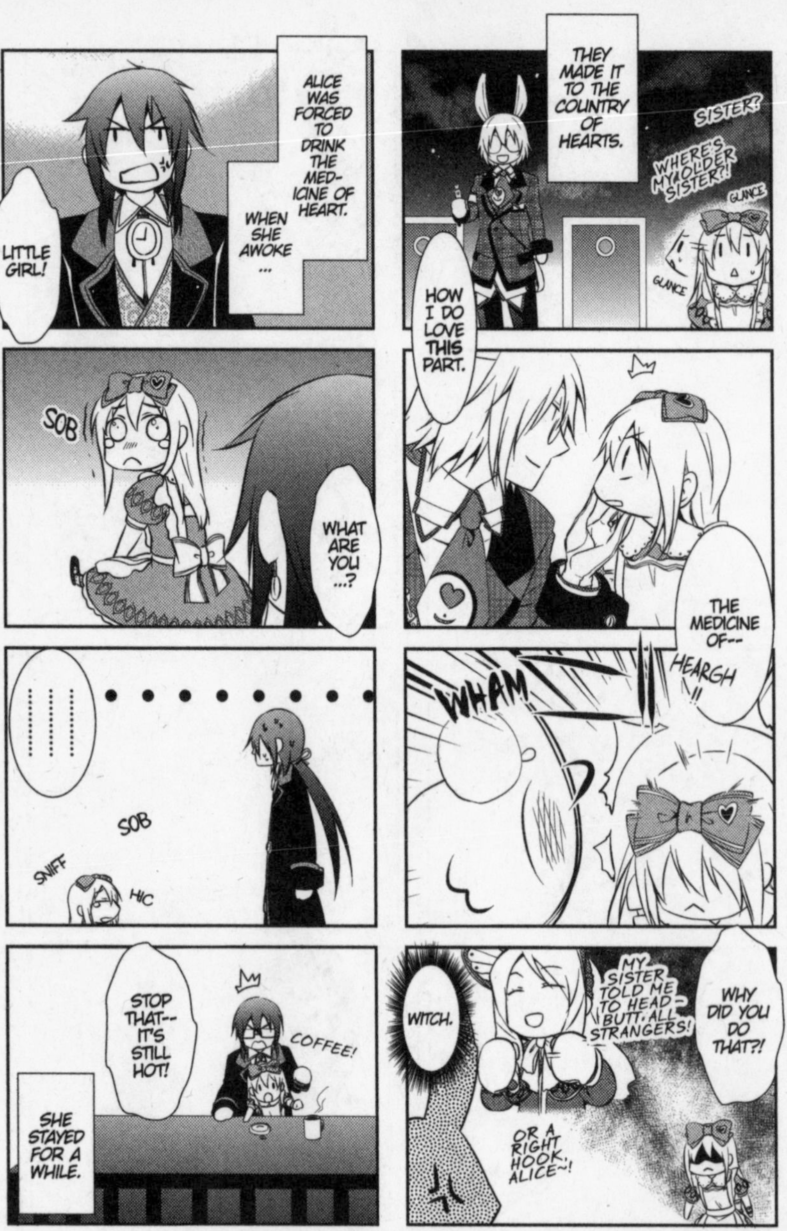
THEY MADE IT TO THE COUNTRY OF HEARTS.
SISTER?
WHERE'S MY OLDER SISTER?!
GLANCE
GLANCE
ALICE WAS FORCED TO DRINK THE MEDICINE OF HEART.
WHEN SHE AWOKE ...
LITTLE GIRL!
HOW I DO LOVE THIS PART.
THE MEDICINE OF--
SOB
WHAT ARE YOU ...?
WHAM
HEARGH !!
......
SOB
SNIFF
HIC
WHY DID YOU DO THAT?!
MY SISTER TOLD ME TO HEAD-BUTT ALL STRANGERS!
WITCH.
OR A RIGHT HOOK, ALICE~!
STOP THAT-- IT'S STILL HOT!
COFFEE!
SHE STAYED FOR A WHILE.

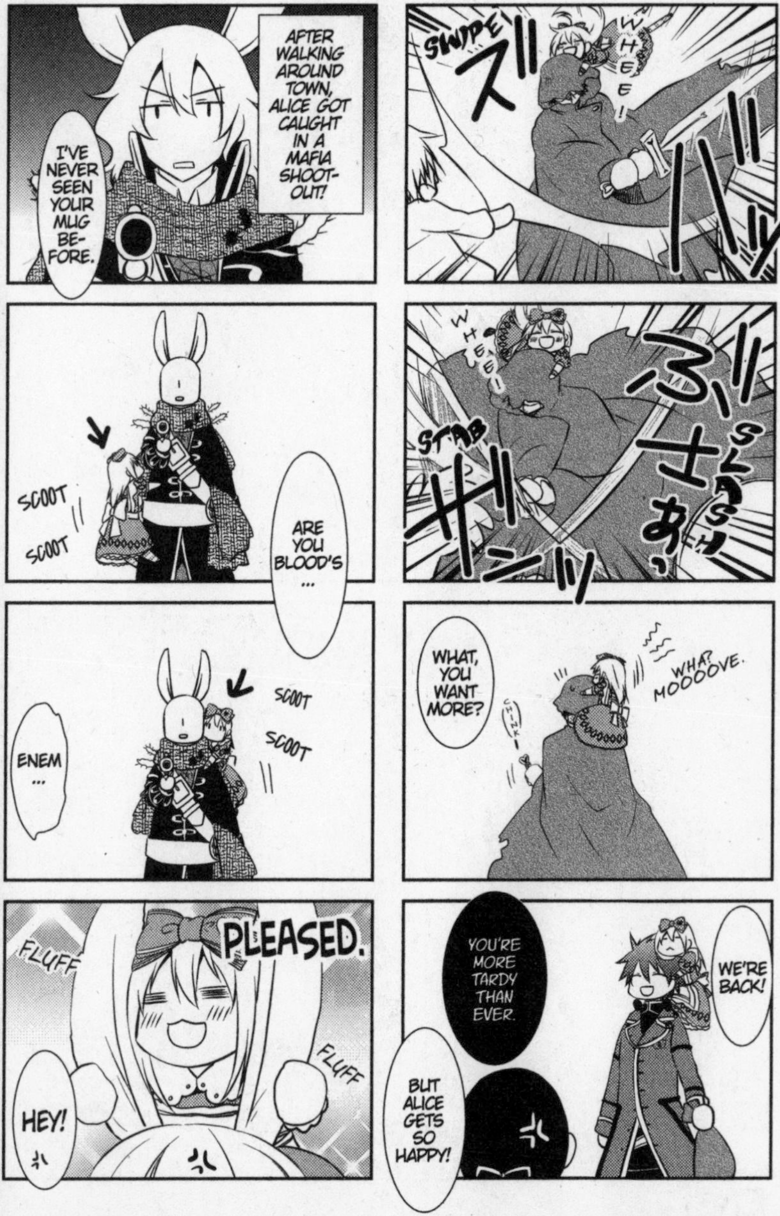
SWIPE
WHEE!
AFTER WALKING AROUND TOWN, ALICE GOT CAUGHT IN A MAFIA SHOOT-OUT!
I'VE NEVER SEEN YOUR MUG BE-FORE.
WHEE!
STAB
SLASH
ARE YOU BLOOD'S ...
SCOOT
SCOOT
WHAT, YOU WANT MORE?
WHA? MOOOOVE.
CHINK!
SCOOT
SCOOT
ENEM ...
WE'RE BACK!
YOU'RE MORE TARDY THAN EVER.
BUT ALICE GETS SO HAPPY!
PLEASED.
FLUFF
FLUFF
HEY!

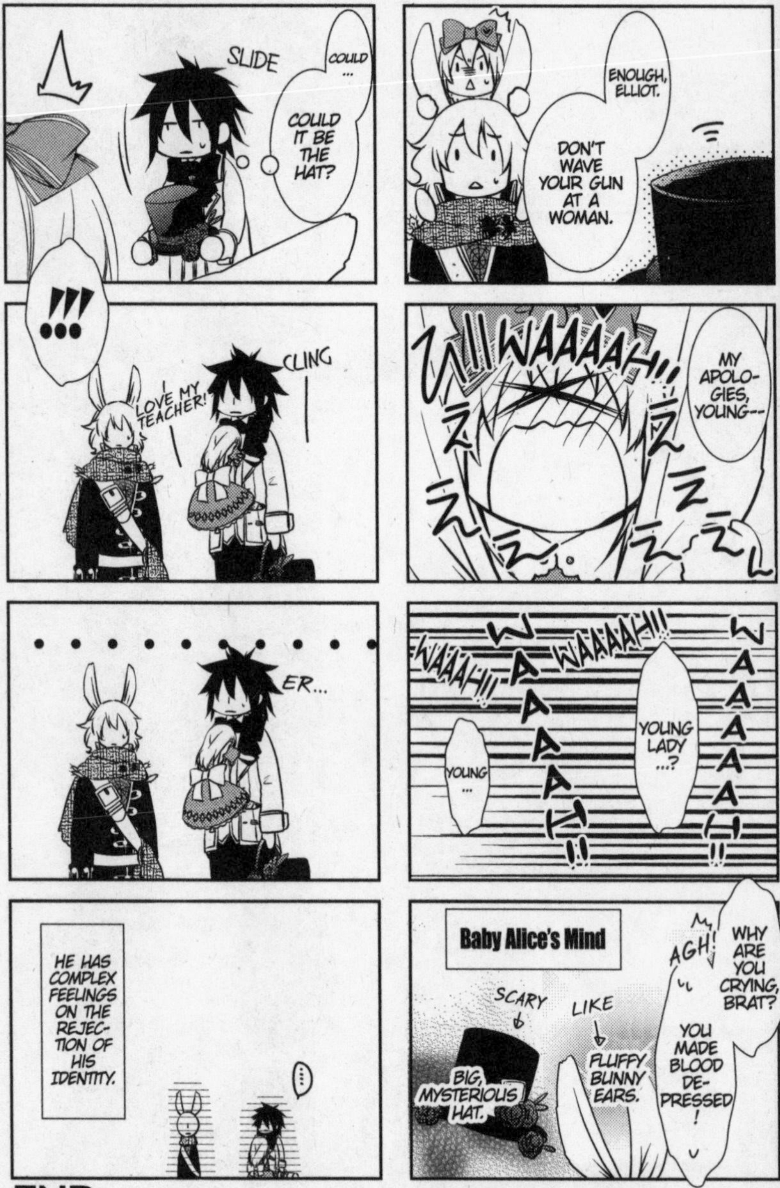
ENOUGH, ELLIOT.
DON'T WAVE YOUR GUN AT A WOMAN.
SLIDE
COULD ...
COULD IT BE THE HAT?
WAAAAAH!!
MY APOLOGIES, YOUNG--
!!!...
CLING
I LOVE MY TEACHER!
WAAAAH!!
WAAAAAAAH!!
YOUNG LADY ...?
WAAAAH!!
WAAAH!!
YOUNG ...
....
ER...
Baby Alice's Mind
WHY ARE YOU CRYING, BRAT?
AGH!
YOU MADE BLOOD DE-PRESSED!
LIKE
FLUFFY BUNNY EARS.
SCARY
BIG, MYSTERIOUS HAT.
HE HAS COMPLEX FEELINGS ON THE REJECTION OF HIS IDENTITY.
....

END

THANK YOU VERY MUCH!

To everyone who helped me in the creation of this book.

Friends & Family

Quinrose

The publisher

And most importantly, the readers!

EXCUSE ME... YOU LIKE ME? DOES THAT MEAN YOU DIDN'T RECOGNIZE ALL THE POSITIVE QUALITIES OF MY DEAR, SWEET ALICE? GOODNESS, YOU MUST BE A LOWER LIFE FORM WITH WEAK COMPREHENSION SKILLS. I'M SURE SHE'S HURT RIGHT NOW BECAUSE SHE FELL IN LOVE WITH SCUM LIKE YOU. OH, MY POOR ALICE. YOU'RE VERY STUPID. PLEASE SAY SOMETHING, **IMMORAL TEACHER.**

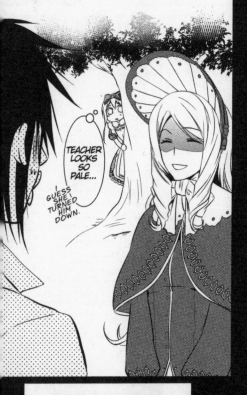

TEACHER LOOKS SO PALE...
I GUESS SHE TURNED HIM DOWN.

I THINK IT WOULD'VE BEEN NEAT IF LORINA HAD A RAZOR-SHARP TONGUE ALONG WITH HER MAJOR SISTER COMPLEX.

*AND ON TOP OF THAT, SHE KNEW SECRET INFORMATION!

[SUPPLEMENT]

PEOPLE WHO HAVE PLAYED THE FIRST GAME IN THE SERIES, *ALICE IN THE COUNTRY OF HEARTS* (INCLUDING THE ANNIVERSARY EDITION), MAY BE CONFUSED WITH THE BONUS STORY. PLEASE IMAGINE THE LAST MONOLOGUE WAS SET A LITTLE BEFORE ALICE WAS TAKEN TO THE COUNTRY OF HEARTS.

IT'S A PART THAT DEALS WITH THE "TRUTH" ROUTE, WHICH ISN'T RELEASED IN THE LOVE ROUTES. I THOUGHT THAT SINCE WE WERE HERE, I'D LIKE TO MIX IN THAT INFORMATION AS WELL. EVERY OTHER DAY I'VE BEEN STRUGGLING WITH THE COMPLEXITY OF THE THIRD GAME IN THE SERIES: *JOKER*.

I'M TRYING TO USE THIS MANGA TO MAKE THE STORY ENJOYABLE AND UNDERSTANDABLE FOR PEOPLE WHO HAVEN'T PLAYED THE GAME, BUT IF YOU'RE INTERESTED IN THE DIFFERENT CHARACTER ENDINGS OR WANT TO FOLLOW IT FROM THE BEGINNING...PLEASE PLAY THE GAMES.

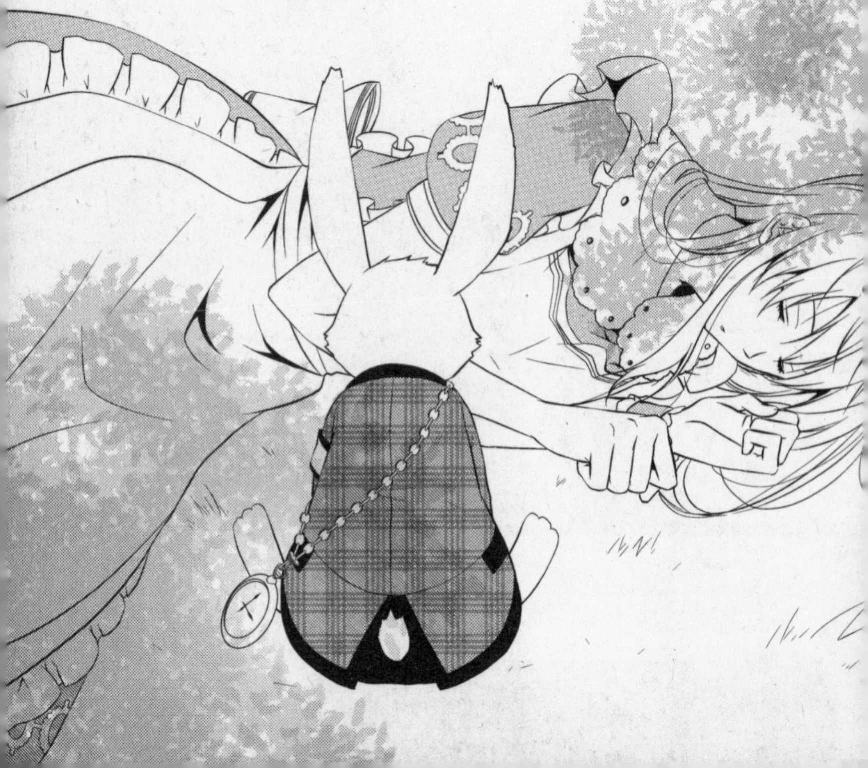

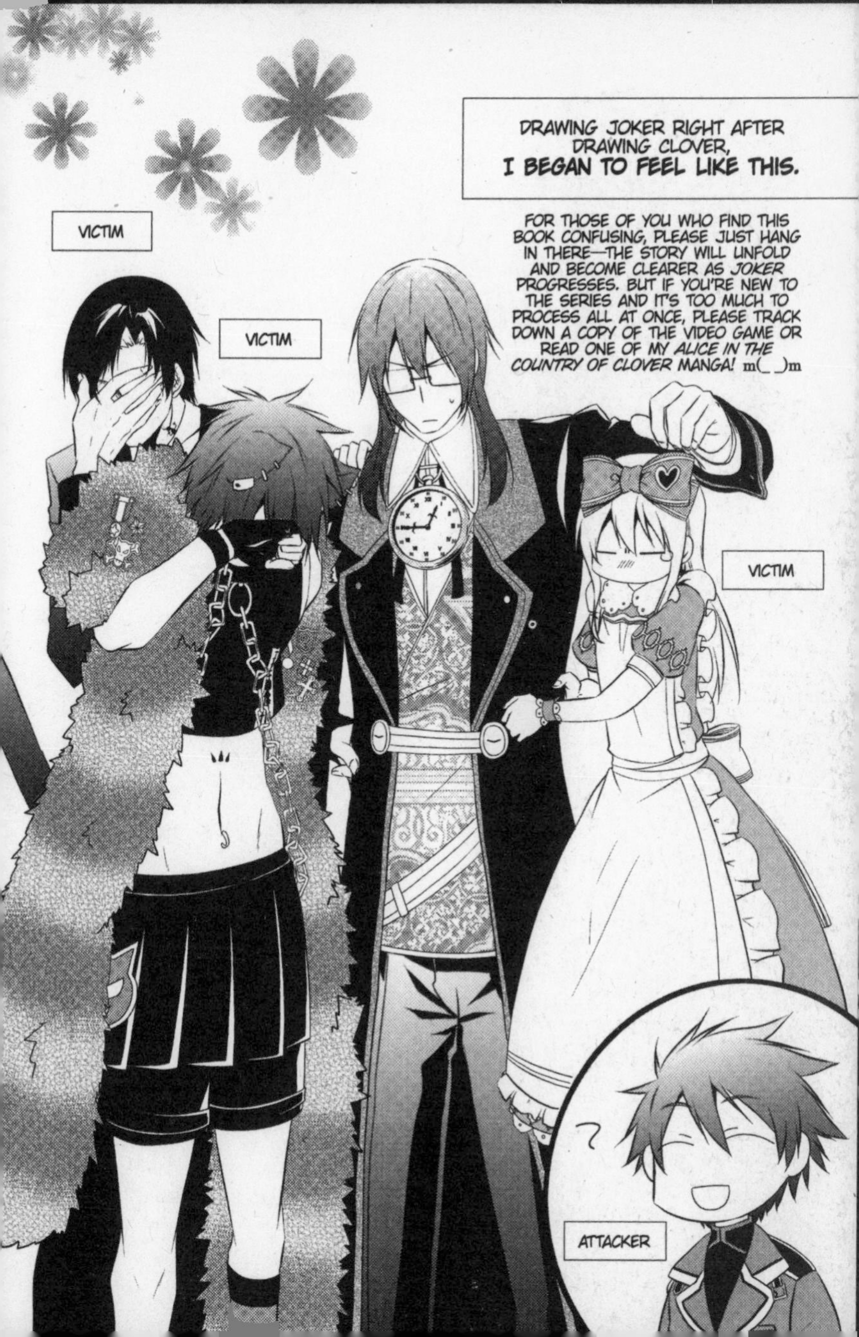
DRAWING JOKER RIGHT AFTER DRAWING CLOVER, **I BEGAN TO FEEL LIKE THIS.**
FOR THOSE OF YOU WHO FIND THIS BOOK CONFUSING, PLEASE JUST HANG IN THERE—THE STORY WILL UNFOLD AND BECOME CLEARER AS *JOKER* PROGRESSES. BUT IF YOU'RE NEW TO THE SERIES AND IT'S TOO MUCH TO PROCESS ALL AT ONCE, PLEASE TRACK DOWN A COPY OF THE VIDEO GAME OR READ ONE OF MY *ALICE IN THE COUNTRY OF CLOVER* MANGA! m(_ _)m
VICTIM
VICTIM
VICTIM
ATTACKER

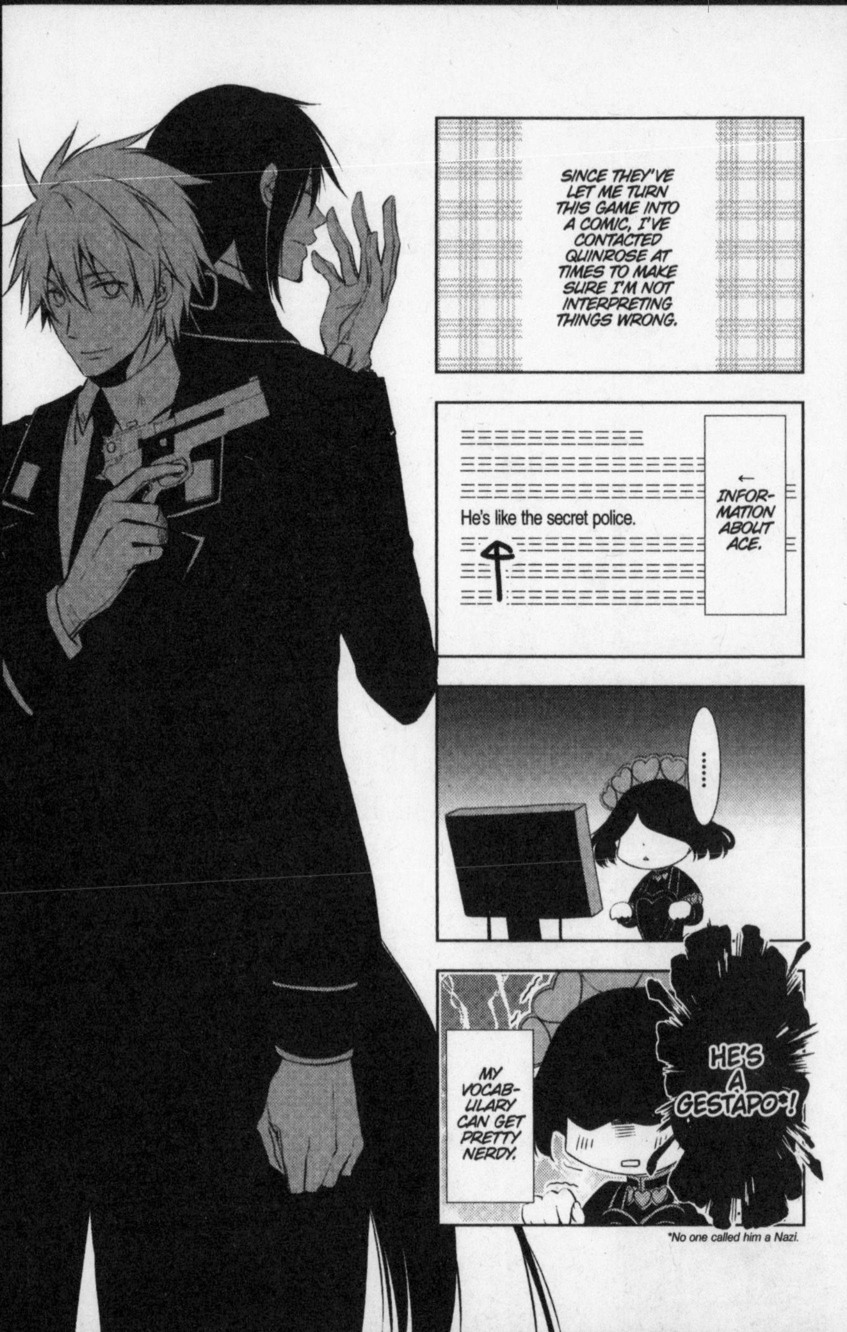
SINCE THEY'VE LET ME TURN THIS GAME INTO A COMIC, I'VE CONTACTED QUINROSE AT TIMES TO MAKE SURE I'M NOT INTERPRETING THINGS WRONG.
← INFOR-MATION ABOUT ACE.
He's like the secret police.
......
HE'S A GESTAPO*!
MY VOCAB-ULARY CAN GET PRETTY NERDY.
*No one called him a Nazi.

COMING SOON

MARCH 2013
Alice in the Country of Clover:
Cheshire Cat Waltz Vol. 4

APRIL 2013
Crimson Empire Vol. 1

MAY 2013
Alice in the Country of Joker:
Circus and Liar's Game Vol. 2

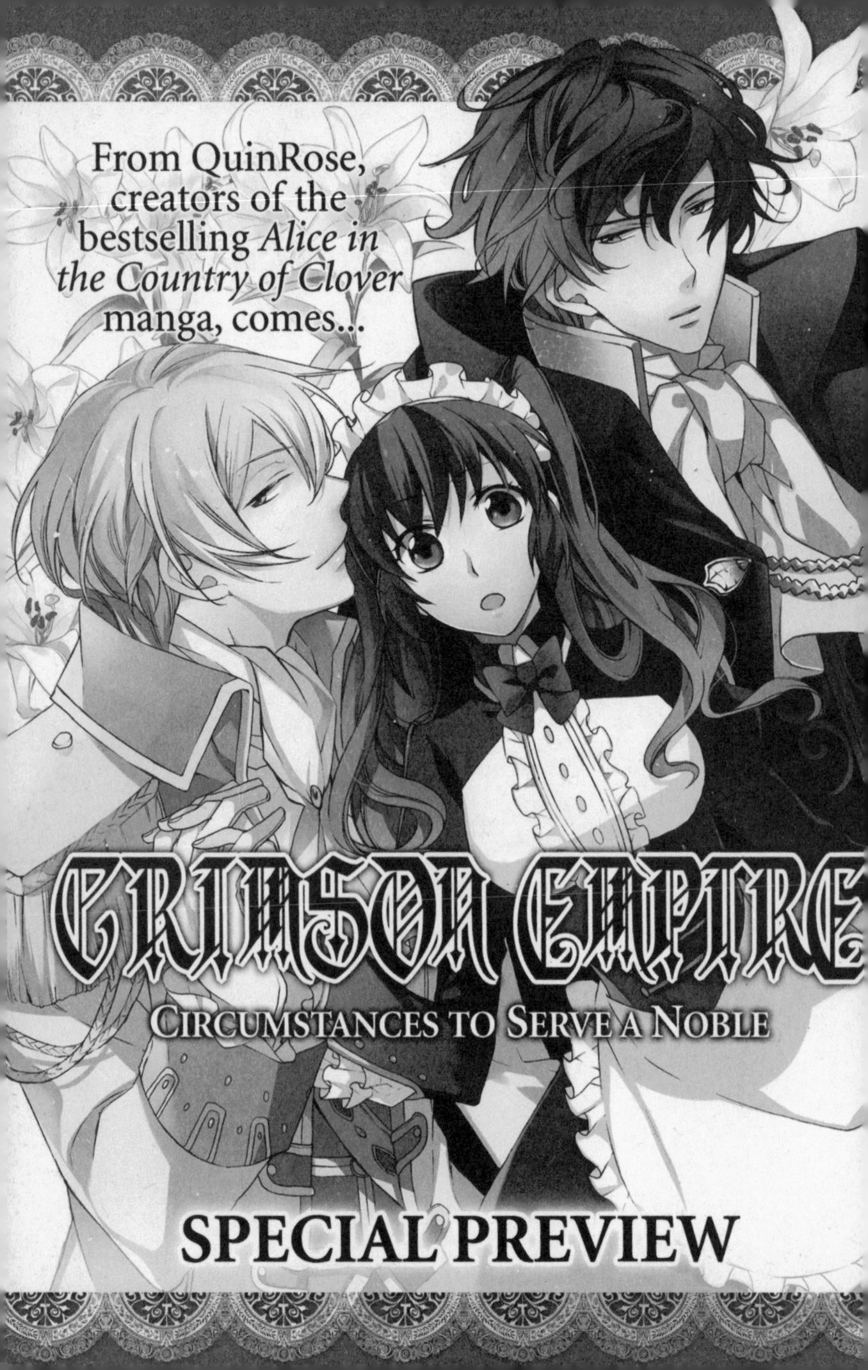
From QuinRose,
creators of the
bestselling *Alice in
the Country of Clover*
manga, comes...
CRIMSON EMPIRE
CIRCUMSTANCES TO SERVE A NOBLE
SPECIAL PREVIEW

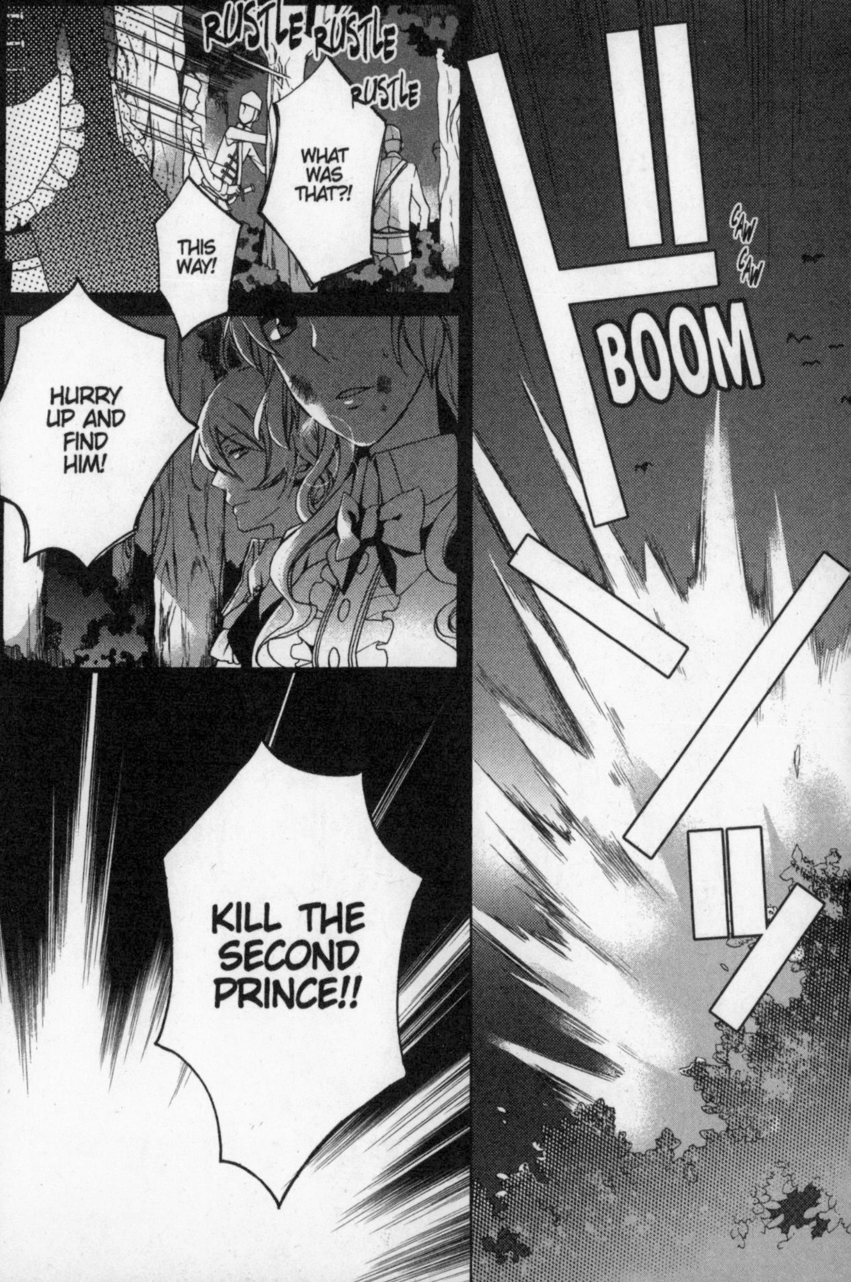
CAW CAW
BOOM
RUSTLE RUSTLE
RUSTLE
WHAT WAS THAT?!
THIS WAY!
HURRY UP AND FIND HIM!
KILL THE SECOND PRINCE!!

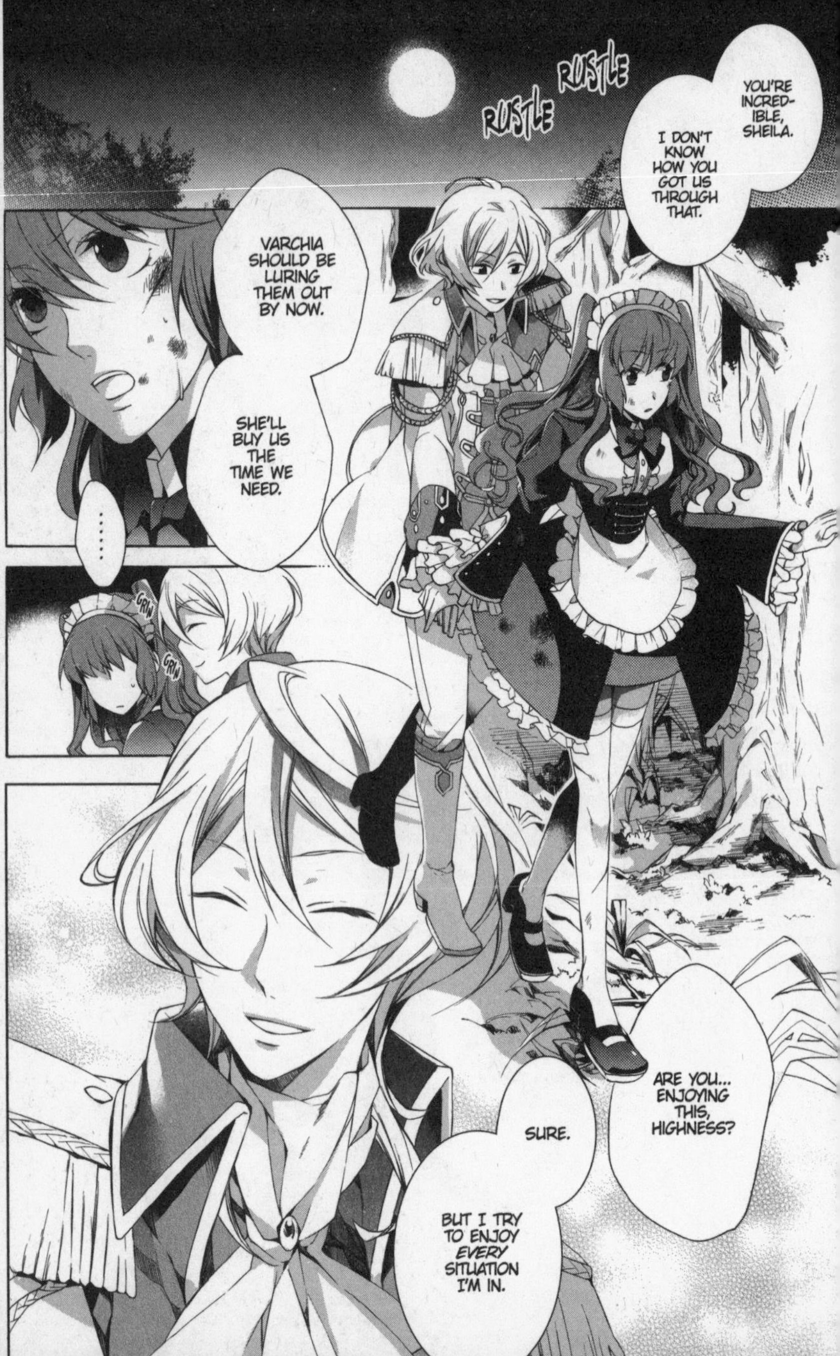
RUSTLE RUSTLE
YOU'RE INCRED-IBLE, SHEILA.
I DON'T KNOW HOW YOU GOT US THROUGH THAT.
VARCHIA SHOULD BE LURING THEM OUT BY NOW.
SHE'LL BUY US THE TIME WE NEED.
......
GRIN GRIN
ARE YOU... ENJOYING THIS, HIGHNESS?
SURE.
BUT I TRY TO ENJOY *EVERY* SITUATION I'M IN.

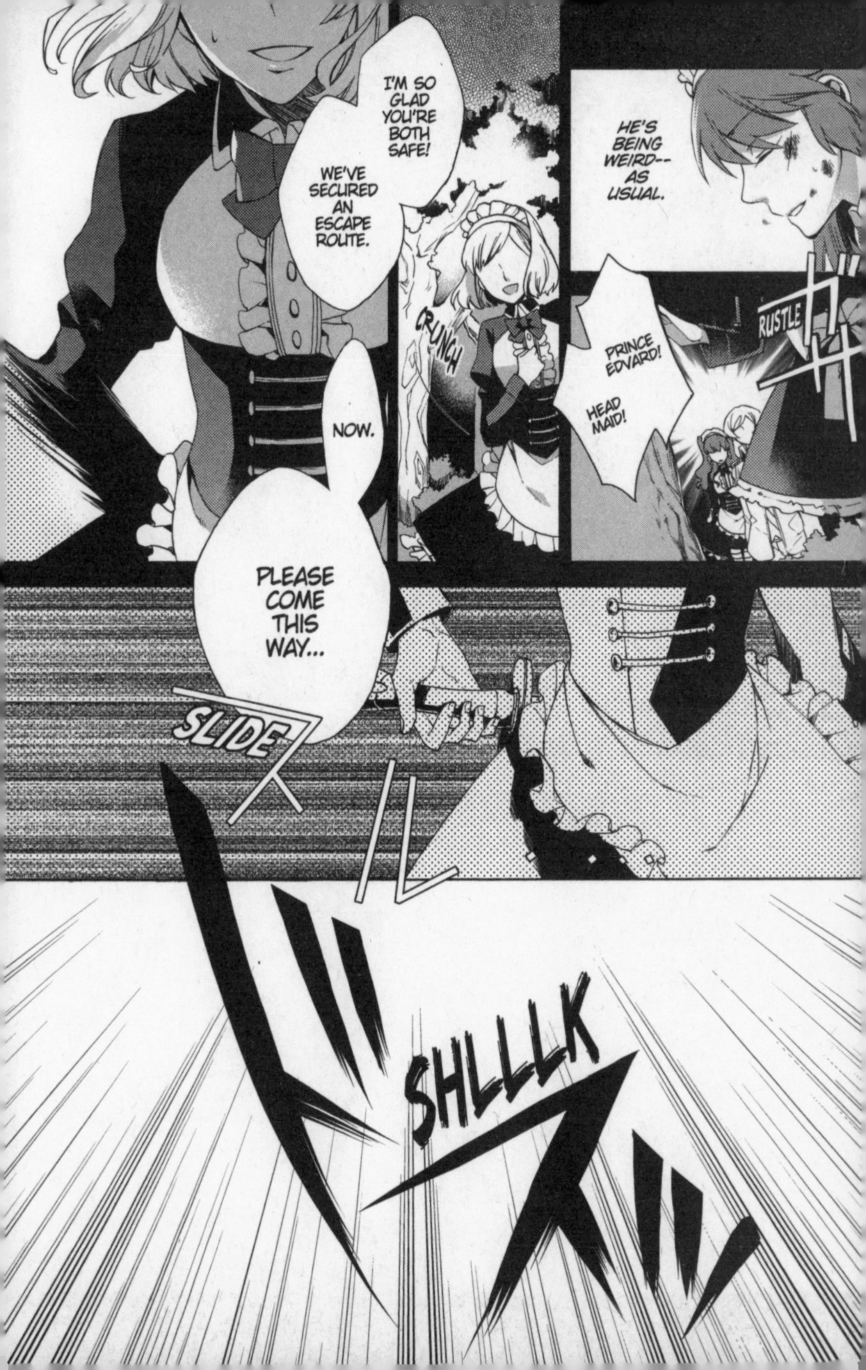
HE'S BEING WEIRD-- AS USUAL.
RUSTLE
PRINCE EDVARD!
HEAD MAID!
I'M SO GLAD YOU'RE BOTH SAFE!
WE'VE SECURED AN ESCAPE ROUTE.
CRUNCH
NOW.
PLEASE COME THIS WAY...
SLIDE
SHLLLK

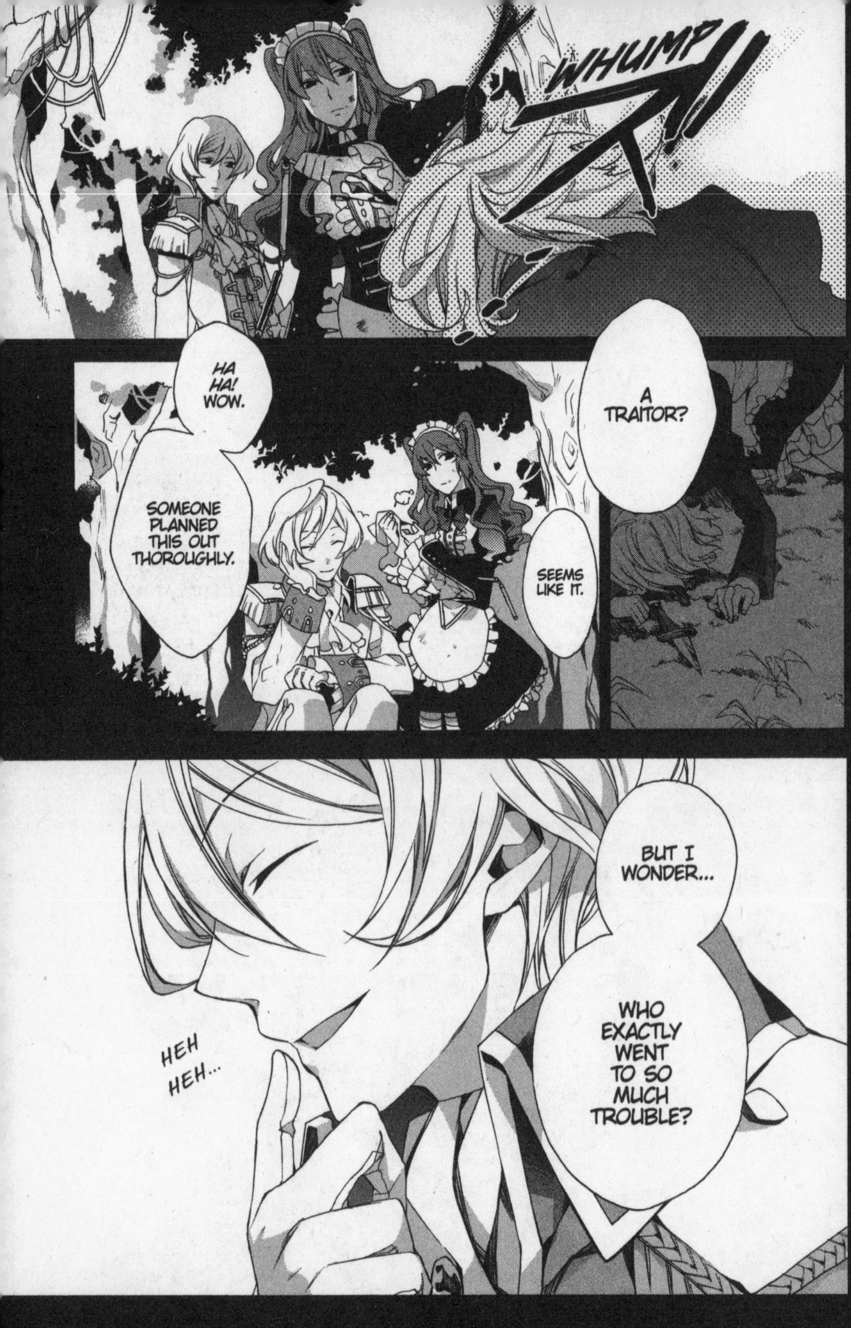
WHUMP!!
A TRAITOR?
SEEMS LIKE IT.
HA HA! WOW.
SOMEONE PLANNED THIS OUT THOROUGHLY.
BUT I WONDER...
WHO EXACTLY WENT TO SO MUCH TROUBLE?
HEH HEH...

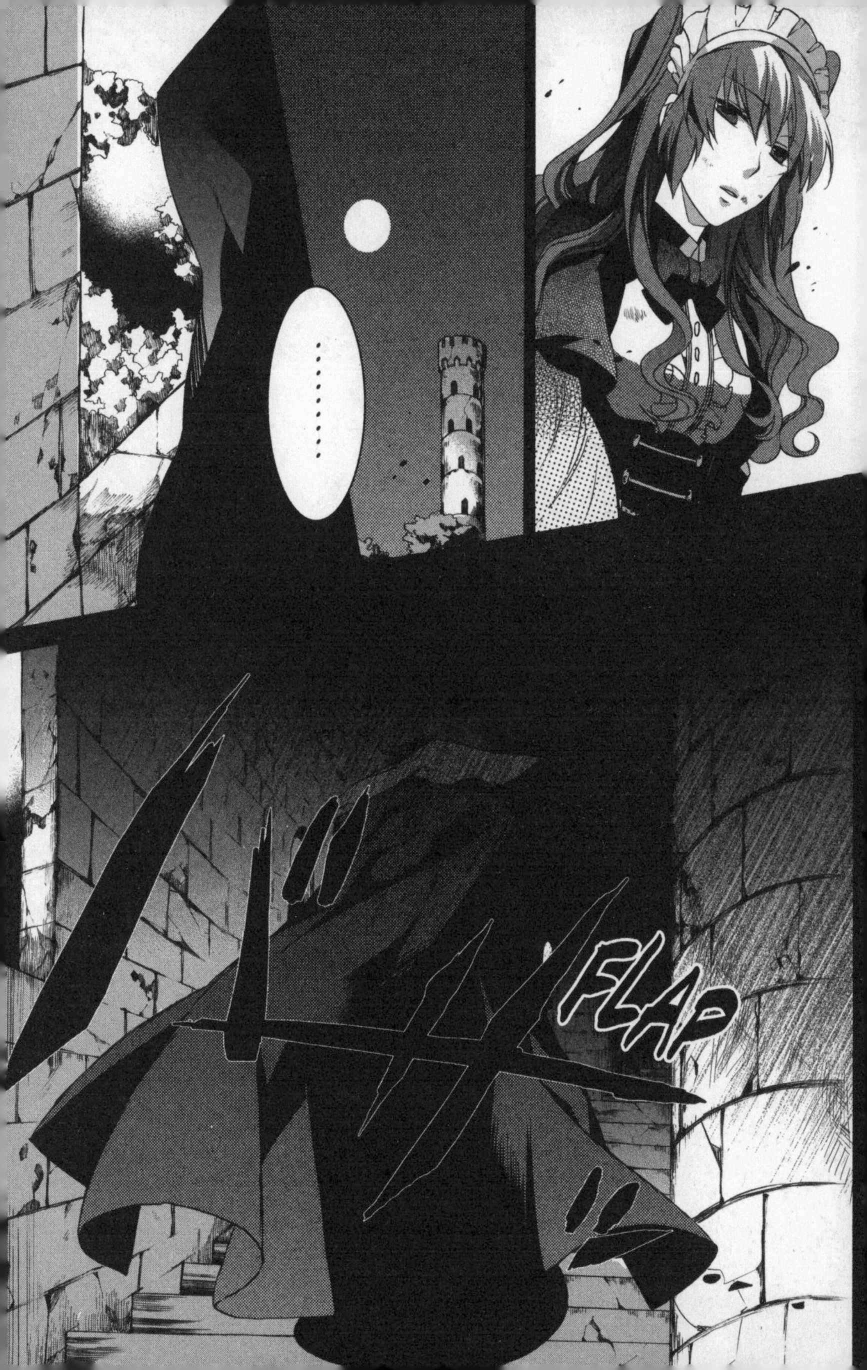
......
FLAP

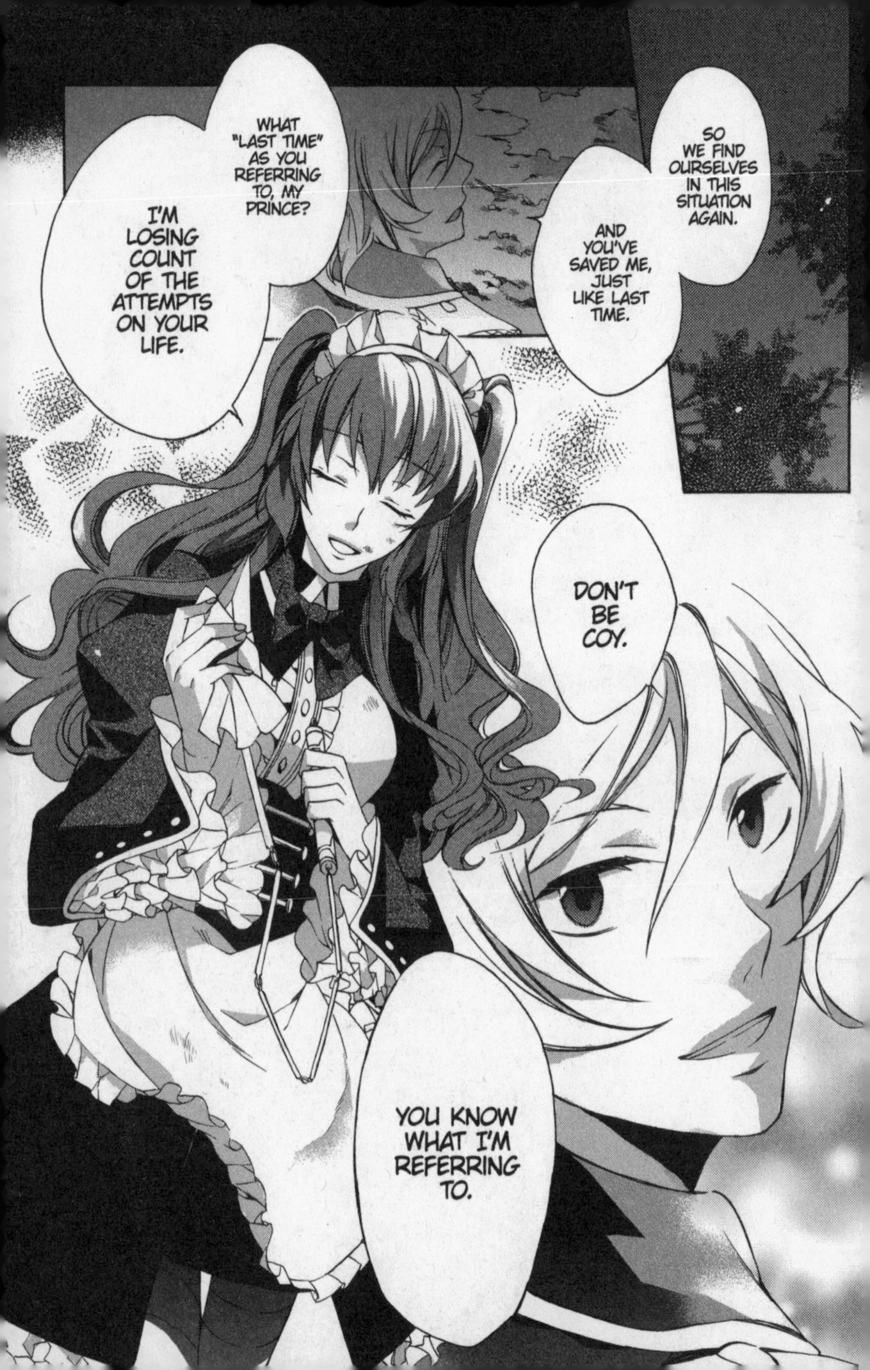
SO WE FIND OURSELVES IN THIS SITUATION AGAIN.
AND YOU'VE SAVED ME, JUST LIKE LAST TIME.
WHAT "LAST TIME" AS YOU REFERRING TO, MY PRINCE?
I'M LOSING COUNT OF THE ATTEMPTS ON YOUR LIFE.
DON'T BE COY.
YOU KNOW WHAT I'M REFERRING TO.

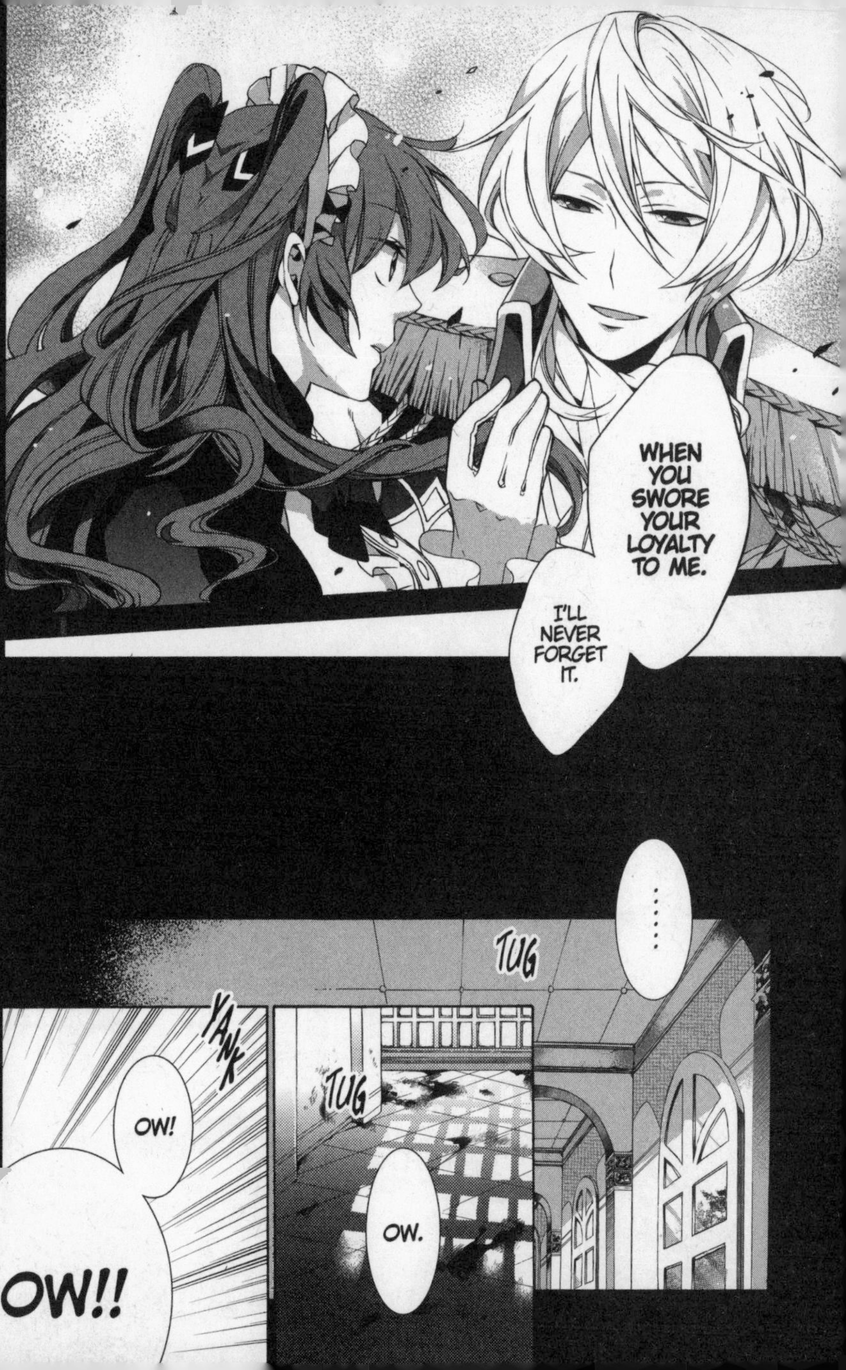
WHEN YOU SWORE YOUR LOYALTY TO ME.
I'LL NEVER FORGET IT.
......
TUG
TUG
OW.
YANK
OW!
OW!!

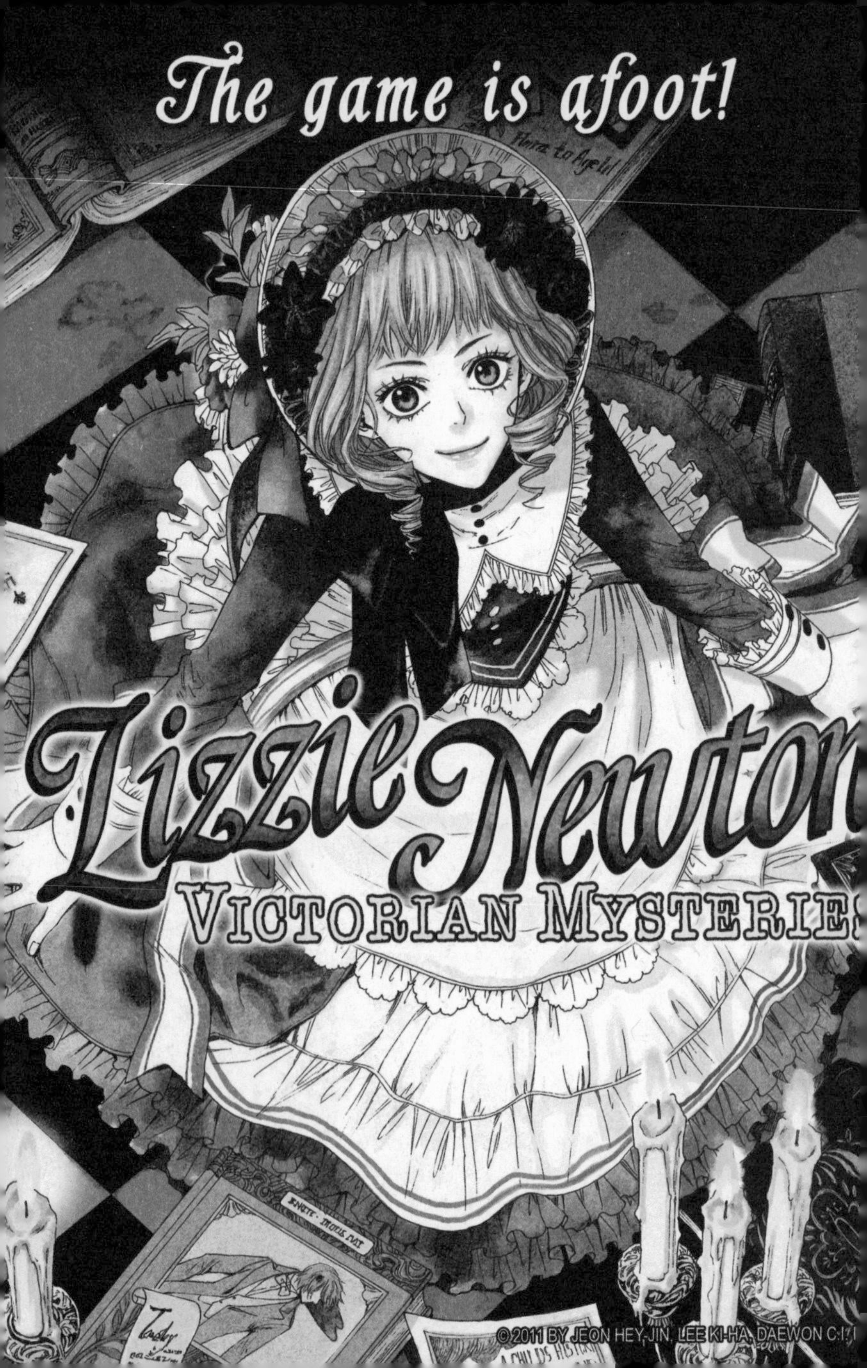
The game is afoot!
Lizzie Newton
VICTORIAN MYSTERIES
©2011 BY JEON HEY JIN, LEE KI-HA, DAEWON C.I. I

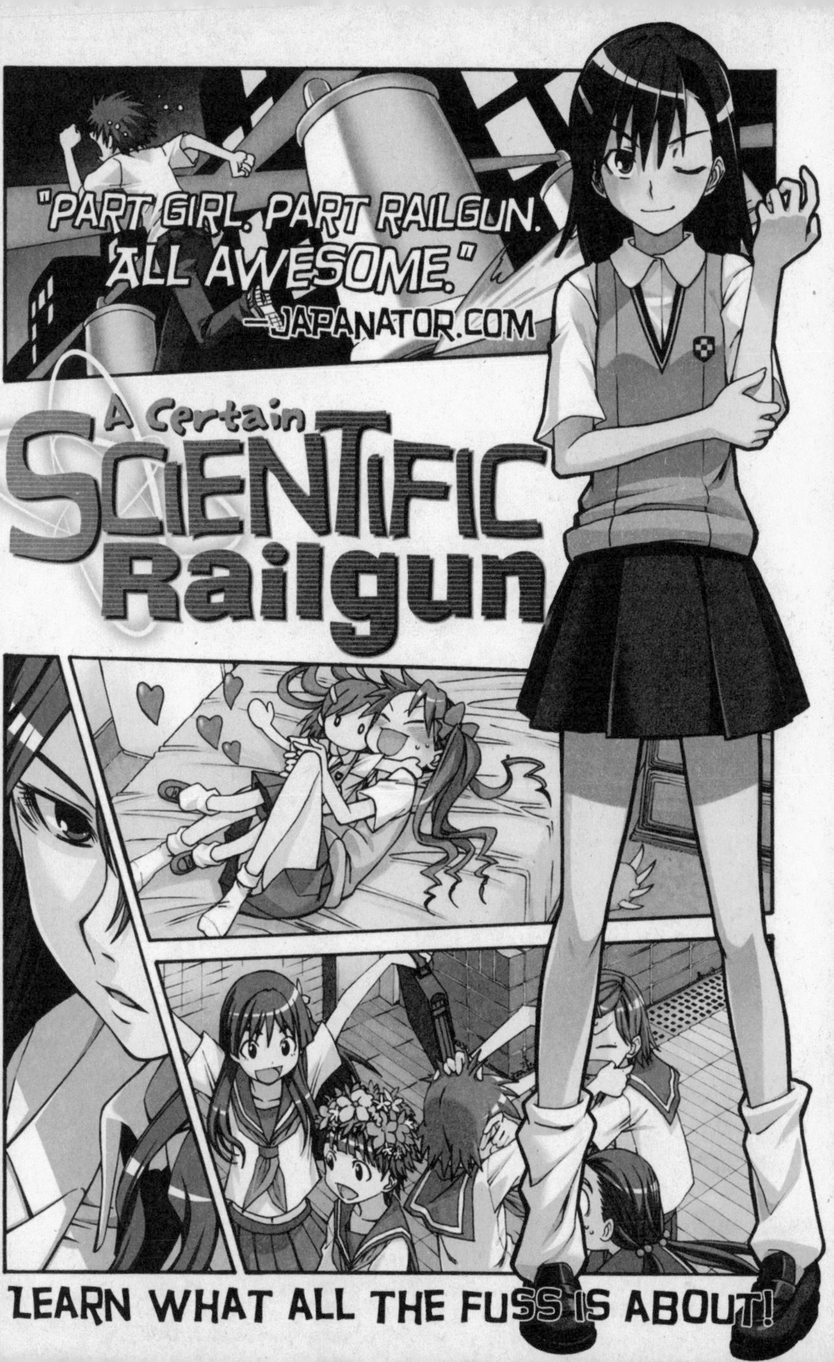
"PART GIRL. PART RAILGUN. ALL AWESOME."
—JAPANATOR.COM
A Certain SCIENTIFIC Railgun
LEARN WHAT ALL THE FUSS IS ABOUT!

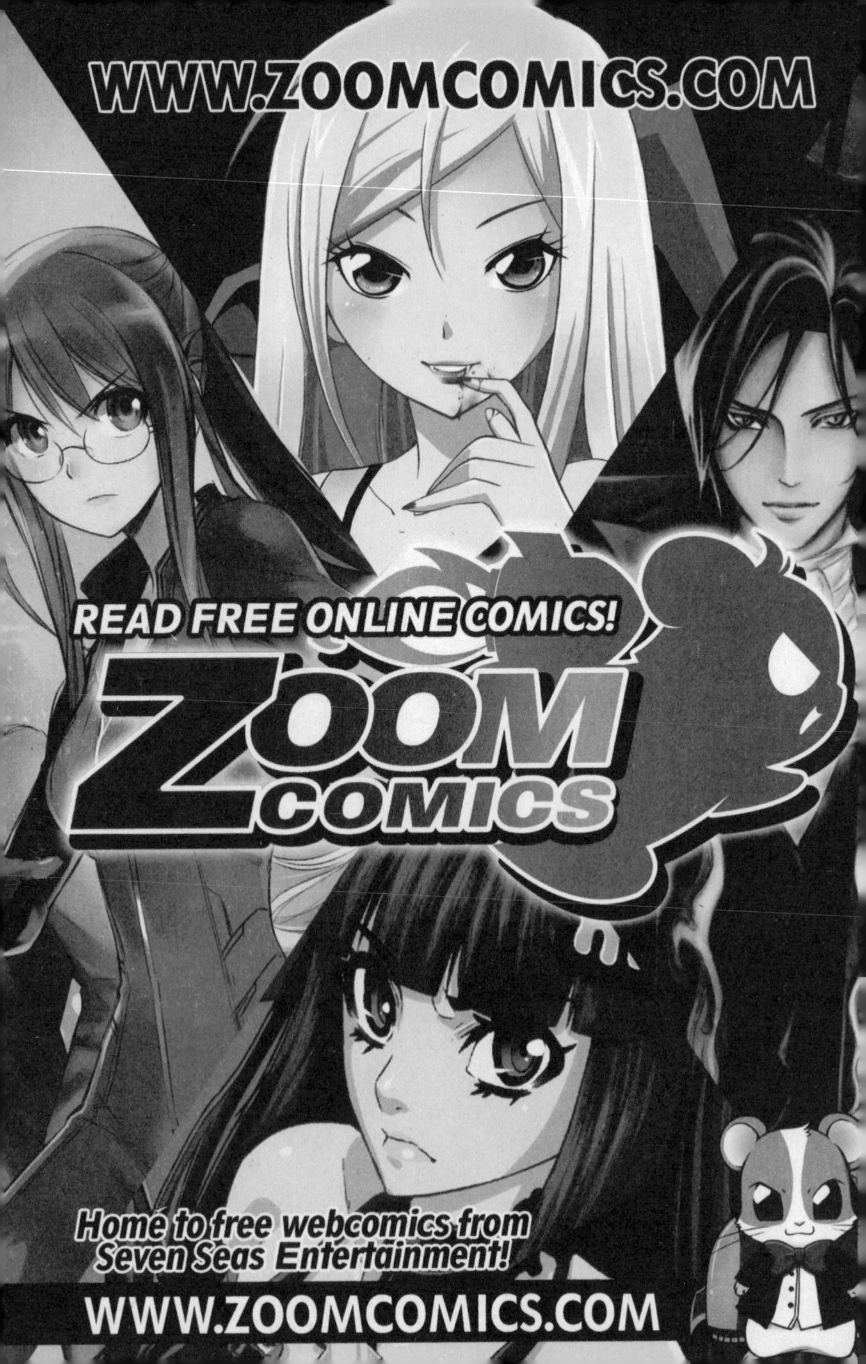

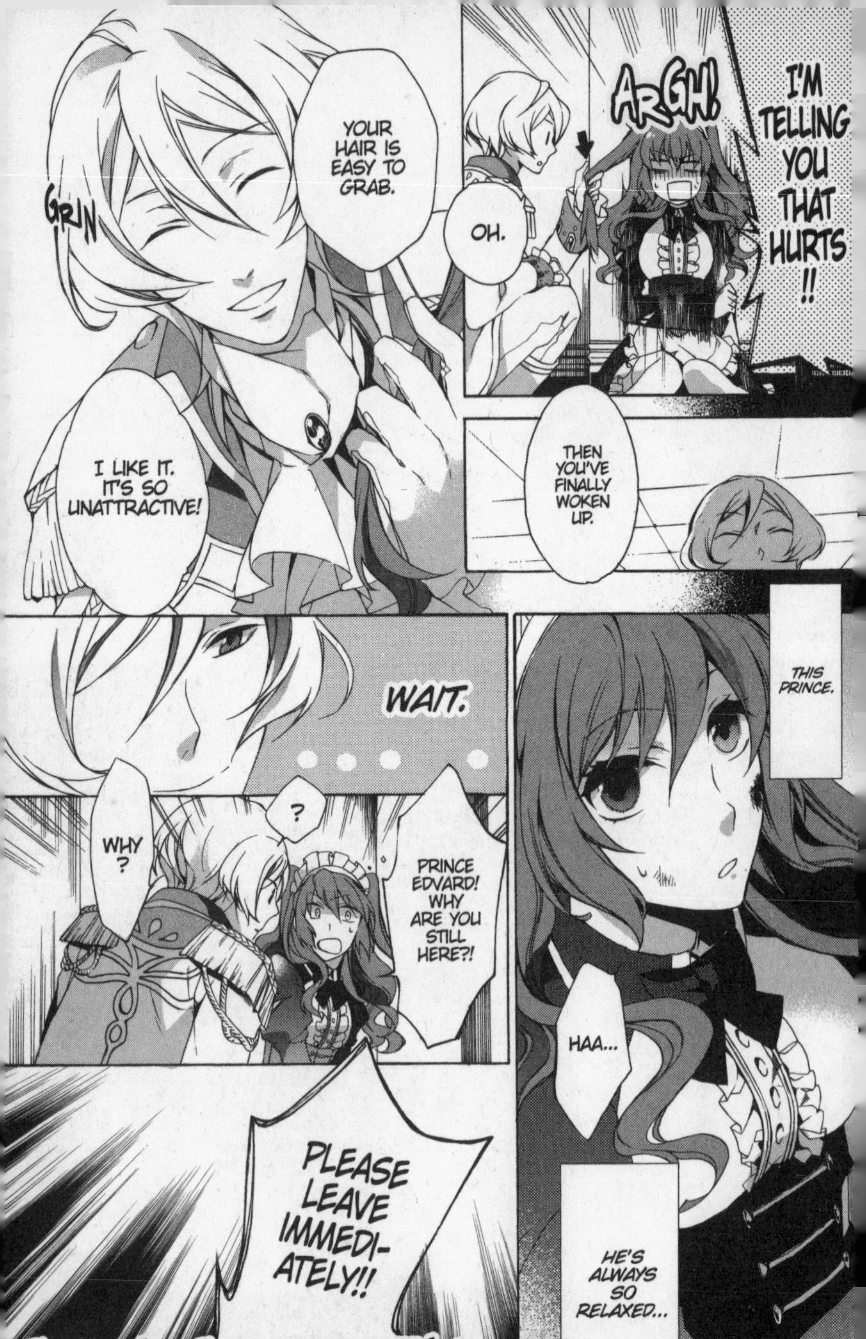
ARGH!
I'M TELLING YOU THAT HURTS!!
OH.
YOUR HAIR IS EASY TO GRAB.
GRIN
I LIKE IT. IT'S SO UNATTRACTIVE!
THEN YOU'VE FINALLY WOKEN UP.
THIS PRINCE.
HAA...
HE'S ALWAYS SO RELAXED...
WAIT.
....
?
PRINCE EDVARD! WHY ARE YOU STILL HERE?!
WHY?
PLEASE LEAVE IMMEDI-ATELY!!

Continued in Crimson Empire Vol. 1!

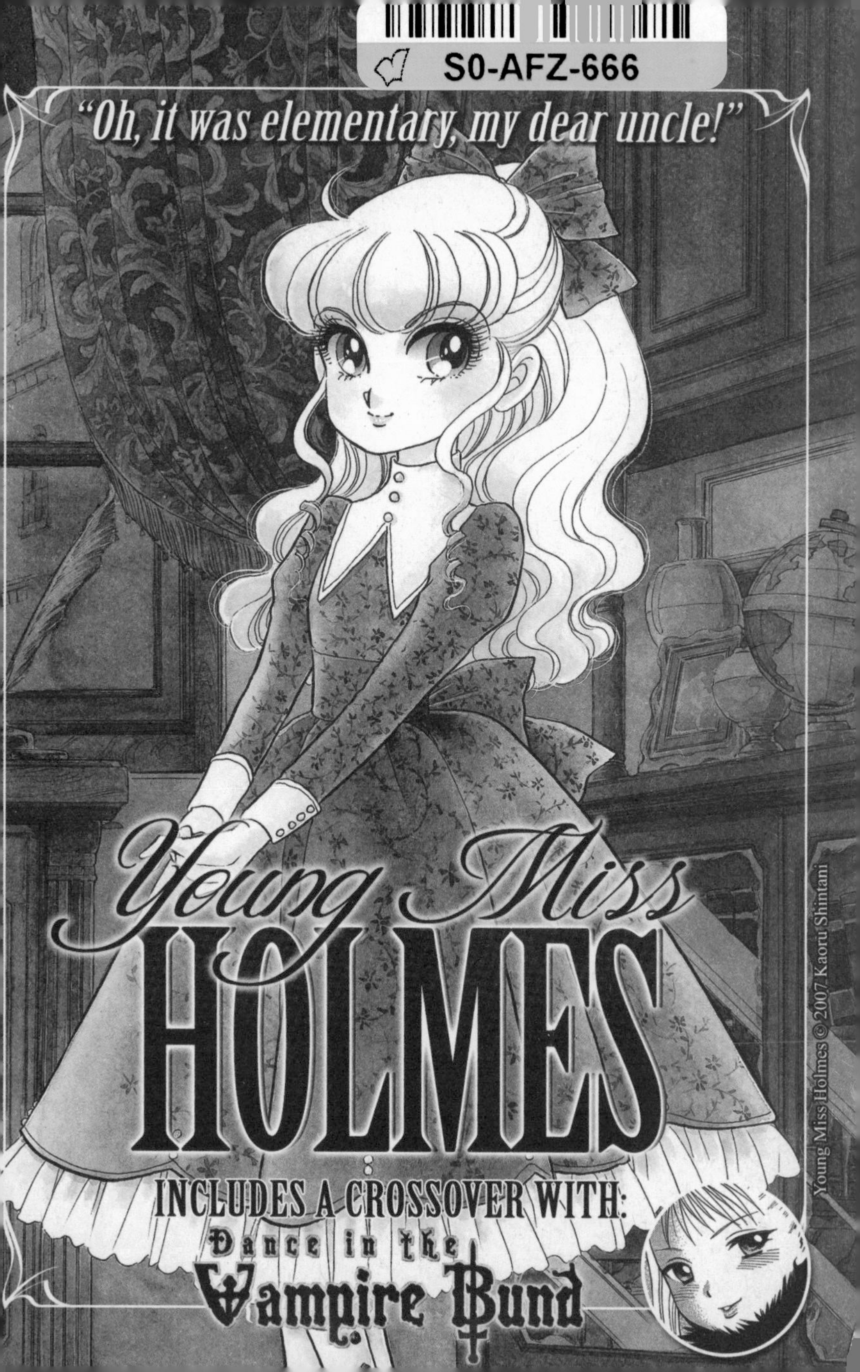
"Oh, it was elementary, my dear uncle!"
Young Miss
HOLMES
INCLUDES A CROSSOVER WITH:
Dance in the
Vampire Bund